Ken Foster

Frontiers in

Social Movement

Theory

Frontiers in Social Movement Theory

Edited by

Aldon D. Morris and Carol McClurg Mueller

YALE UNIVERSITY PRESS   New Haven and London

Published with assistance from the Louis Stern Memorial Fund.

Designed by Jill Breitbarth and set in New Baskerville and Gill Sans types by Tseng Information Systems, Inc., Durham, North Carolina. Printed in the United States of America by Vail-Ballou Press, Binghamton, New York.

Library of Congress Cataloging-in-Publication Data
Frontiers in social movement theory / edited by Aldon D. Morris and
   Carol McClurg Mueller.
      p. cm.
   Includes bibliographical references and index.
   ISBN 0-300-05485-8 (cl). — ISBN 0-300-05486-6 (pa)
   1. Social movements.   2. Social movements—United States.
  3. Social action.   4. Social action—United States.   I. Morris, Aldon D.
  II. Mueller, Carol McClurg.
  HN16.H765   1992
  303.48′4—dc20   92-3393
                 CIP

A catalogue record of this book is available from the British Library.

10 9 8 7 6 5 4 3 2

Contents

67

Preface

This volume grew out of a conference on social movements held at the University of Michigan in June 1988. By the time of the conference the resource mobilization (RM) approach to social movements had been dominant for nearly a decade. Indeed, RM had demonstrated that social movements could not be understood if their structural configurations and linkages to central political processes were not placed at the center of analysis.

Yet, from the very beginning, critics of the RM approach were quick to point out that social movements could not be reduced to business organizations or industries or to conventional political behavior. They argued that grievances, ideologies, manipulation of symbols through oratory and the written word, media portrayals, consciousness raising, and identities all had to be taken into account in studying a social movement. In short, the critics charged that RM was without a social psychology that could explain what real human beings do either inside movements or in reaction to them.

As a result, a significant number of RM scholars came to see the errors of their ways or at least the analytical cost of a one-sided theoretical approach to the social movement enterprise. The essays in this volume represent a first step toward the development of a social psychology that is appropriate for and complementary to the structural-political framework of RM. Here attention is focused on how social movements generate and are affected by the construction of meaning, consciousness raising, the manipulation of symbols, and collective identities. But structural, political, and theoretical issues find their way into this volume also. Intellectual puzzles regarding the mobilization process, the boundaries between movements and routine politics, and distinctions among various types of movements are addressed. The contributors are becoming increasingly aware that a viable conceptual framework of social movements must simultaneously explain both the structural and the symbolic side of movements.

We hope this volume illuminates some fundamental issues regarding an important topic, for, as Lewis Coser reminded us at the conference, "social movements are instrumentalities to abolish, or at least weaken, structures of political and social domination." He also made the point that many people who participate in social movements do so at great sacrifice because "they draw their sustenance not from the enhancement of present satisfaction but from a long-term time perspective sustained by the firm belief in the coming of a society embodying justice and democratic equality instead of the here and now of exploitation and denial of human dignity."

We appreciate the efforts of the contributors, who spent considerable time revising the papers they presented at the conference for publication in this volume. We thank the American Sociological Association for a Problems of the Discipline grant under the auspices of its Collective Behavior and Social Movement section. We also thank the University of Michigan for providing funds and the facilities for the original conference.

Contributors

ROBERT D. BENFORD is assistant professor of sociology at the University of Nebraska–Lincoln.

RICHARD A. CLOWARD is on the faculty of the Columbia University School of Social Work.

MYRA MARX FERREE is professor of sociology and women's studies at the University of Connecticut, Storrs.

DEBRA FRIEDMAN is assistant professor of sociology and visiting scholar at the Udall Center for Studies in Public Policy at the University of Arizona.

WILLIAM A. GAMSON is professor of sociology at Boston College and codirects the Media Research and Action Project (MRAP).

BERT KLANDERMANS is senior lecturer of social psychology at the Free University, Amsterdam, the Netherlands.

CLARENCE Y. H. LO is associate professor of sociology at the University of Missouri at Columbia.

GERALD MARWELL is Richard T. Ely Professor of Sociology at the University of Wisconsin–Madison and editor of the *American Sociological Review*.

DOUG MCADAM is professor of sociology at the University of Arizona.

JOHN D. MCCARTHY is professor of sociology and a member of the Life Cycle Institute at the Catholic University of America, Washington, D.C.

ALDON D. MORRIS is professor in the Department of Sociology and the Center for Urban Affairs and Policy Research at Northwestern University.

xi

CAROL MCCLURG MUELLER is associate professor of sociology in the Social and Behavioral Sciences Program of Arizona State University West.

PAMELA E. OLIVER is professor of sociology at the University of Wisconsin–Madison.

SHUVA PAUL is a graduate student in the Ph.D. program in sociology at the State University of New York at Stony Brook.

FRANCES FOX PIVEN is distinguished professor, Political Science Program, Graduate School and University Center, City University of New York.

MICHAEL SCHWARTZ is professor of sociology and director of the Institute for Social Analysis at the State University of New York at Stony Brook.

DAVID A. SNOW is professor and head of sociology at the University of Arizona in Tucson.

SIDNEY TARROW is Maxwell M. Upson Professor of Government at Cornell University.

VERTA TAYLOR is associate professor of sociology at Ohio State University, Columbus.

NANCY E. WHITTIER is assistant professor of sociology at Smith College.

MARK WOLFSON is assistant professor in the School of Public Health at the University of Minnesota.

MAYER N. ZALD is professor of sociology, social work, and business administration at the University of Michigan.

Part I

Introduction

Building Social Movement Theory

Carol McClurg Mueller

The resource mobilization paradigm brought new life to social movement research in the 1970s, when it was widely recognized that the work of McCarthy and Zald (1973, 1977), Gamson (1968, 1975), Oberschall (1973), and Tilly (1978) offered a viable alternative to previous traditions in scholarship concerning collective behavior, mass society, relative deprivation, and political sociology. Almost immediately the new paradigm dominated publications on social movements and collective action in the most prominent journals of sociology and political science (see Morris and Herring 1988, 182). For the decade of the seventies, over half (56 percent) of the social movement and collective action articles in the *American Sociological Review, the American Journal of Sociology, Social Forces,* and the *American Political Science Review* were based on the theoretical approach of resource mobilization, but by the early eighties it was almost three-quarters.

As Zald points out in an evaluation of the resource mobilization paradigm in this volume, the breakthrough was based on a set of simplifying assumptions that placed the study of social movements clearly within the instrumental, utilitarian natural science tradition. A major factor in the shift was the rational choice theory of economist Mancur Olson (1965), which placed the weighing of costs and benefits rather than deprivation and grievances at the center of a theory of public goods. Mobilization became the central problematic of the new research program. The new questions became: where are the resources available for the movement, how are they organized, how does the state facilitate or impede mobili-

The author acknowledges the wise, cogent, and incisive comments of Aldon Morris on earlier versions of this chapter.

3

zation, and what are the outcomes? Although the ratio of theorizing to research may still be less than ideal, Zald's chapter here, as well as a recent overview of research (McAdam, McCarthy, and Zald 1988), document a highly prolific research program.

As a program of research developed, the first generation of critics both tested and elaborated the model. Hypotheses were developed and tested on "the political opportunity structures" (Eisinger 1973; Jenkins and Perrow 1977; McAdam 1982), "grass roots mobilization" (Morris 1984), "co-optable networks" or "recruitment networks" (Freeman 1973; Snow, Zurcher, and Ekland-Olson 1980; McAdam 1986), "protest outcomes" (Gamson 1975; Piven and Cloward 1971, 1977), the "multiorganizational field" (Curtis and Zurcher 1973; Rosenthal et al. 1985), "counter movements" (Mottl 1980; Lo 1982; Zald and Useem 1987), external funding (Haines 1984; Jenkins and Eckert 1986), and the role of the state (Piven and Cloward 1977; Tilly, Tilly, and Tilly 1975; Jenkins 1983; Barkan 1985).

Yet even as the first round of commentary led to an elaboration of the original model, issues of meaning construction and of structural inequality that were considered peripheral or unproblematic in the resource mobilization paradigm gained increasing attention. It is these issues that inform most of the work in this volume. Within this second generation of commentary, the attempt to stay within the natural science framework of a utilitarian, instrumental model has become increasingly strained by the social constructionist perspective of many contributors, although proponents of this perspective have developed a variety of ingenious strategies for posing semiotic questions of meaning within the resource mobilization paradigm.

The questions of meaning discussed here reflect a heightened concern with the development of a comprehensive social psychology of social movements. The writers focus special attention on the definition of the actor, the social context within which meanings are developed and transformed, and the cultural content of social movements. A related, but theoretically separable, set of issues concerns the implications of structured inequalities in the distribution of resources that are mobilized by social movements, particularly the implications of differential reliance on constituent resources.

Do the new issues threaten the primacy of the resource mobilization paradigm, or do they represent simply a challenge of incorporation? One answer lies in resolving the more general debate within the social sciences on the possibility of compromise or synthesis between the worldviews of the mechanistic natural science framework and the semiotic, meaning-interpreting sciences. By taking grievances, goals, and preference structures as givens, resource mobilization neatly sidestepped the controversy over the explanation of "subjective experience and such 'things' as meanings, intentions, ideas, values, and emotions—non-things that Descartes long ago placed beyond the reach of the mechanistic sciences" (Shweder and Fiske 1986,7).

Judgments have been mixed on whether the natural science approach to social movements can be successfully merged with its more subjective counterpart. In an early review of resource mobilization theory, Jenkins (1983) argued that it would be less problematic to apply the organizational aspects of resource mobilization to the analysis of personal and cultural change than to extend meaning-constructing approaches like that of collective behavior to movements for institutional change. Cohen (1985) was equally pessimistic in her assessment of the possibility of synthesizing a neo-utilitarian model based in instrumental rationality like resource mobilization with the collective identity model of European new social movement theory. Zald in this volume, like many of the other contributors, is more optimistic in arguing that "semiotic, symbolic, and social constructionist approaches must supplement and articulate with our natural system analysis." Although the writers here have not resolved the issue, they offer a variety of strategies for bringing together the cultural and the structural, strategy and identity, the semiotic and the natural sciences of social movements, in the process addressing many issues that are central to a reformulation of social movement theory. The following discussion concerns one such set of issues.

THE SOCIAL PSYCHOLOGICAL BASE OF SOCIAL MOVEMENT THEORY

For more than a decade, critics have pointed to the absence of a plausible account of values, grievances, ideology, and collective identity in the resource mobilization (RM) paradigm (Zurcher and Snow 1981; Fireman and Gamson 1979; Jenkins 1983; Klandermans 1984; Cohen 1985; Ferree and Miller 1985). The first essays in this volume place these issues center stage, recasting the actor and the social context of meaning interpretation. If the key social psychological issue for the resource mobilization actor has centered on the problem of the free rider of rational choice theory, the new actor is conceptualized as socially embedded with loyalties, obligations, and identities that reframe issues of potential support for collective action. If the formal social movement organization has been the primary social unit of resource mobilization, the social network of face-to-face encounters is the more typical unit of social constructionists. If grievances, values, and ideology have been considered irrelevant to the process of mobilization, they emerge here prominently at the intersection of culture and collective identities.

A resurgent social psychology of social movements begins with three elements: a reconceptualization of the actor, the extension of the central role of micromobilization in face-to-face interaction within a variety of group contexts, and the specification of meaning generating oppositional elements within sociopolitical cultures at varying levels of temporal extensity, formality, and instrumental appropriation. Although total agreement on nomenclature does not exist, theorists increasingly concur on the centrality of these elements for the building of a viable social psychology of social movement theory.

The Actor

In his classic work on collective action and public goods, economist Mancur Olson challenged the common assumption that groups of individuals will act on behalf of their common interests just as single individuals can be expected to act on behalf of their personal interests (1965, 1). Instead, Olson argued, the rational, self-interested individual will ordinarily not act to achieve collective benefits because such public goods cannot be withheld from members of the group according to whether or not they contribute. The rational actor, then, is a "free rider"; but if everyone rides free, how does mobilization for collective action occur?

Although Olson's paradox was directed to the problems of large groups and interest group representation, it would be difficult to overestimate the importance of his rational choice model for the development of resource mobilization and collective action theory (see Oberschall 1973; Gamson 1975; McCarthy and Zald 1977; Tilly 1978). As Zald notes in this volume, the work of Olson and of Leites and Wolf (1970) on the implications of a rational choice model for collective action laid the groundwork for RM theory by highlighting the importance of mobilization and by challenging the received wisdom on the overriding importance of grievances. Micromobilization became one of the central problematics of social movement research based on the rational choice assumption that behavior entails costs, and therefore "grievances or deprivation does not automatically or easily translate into social movement activity, especially high-risk social movement activity" (Zald, this volume). Few social movement scholars would disagree with Zald's conclusion that it is in the area of micromobilization that the greatest progress has been made (for a summary of this literature, see McAdam, McCarthy, and Zald 1988). By taking Olson seriously, theorists have had to reexamine long-held assumptions regarding the centrality of grievances, solidarity, and ideology for mobilization.

The essays collected here, however, suggest that despite its advantages over earlier irrational models (see analysis in Morris and Herring 1988), a reconsideration of underlying assumptions based on a more sociological understanding of the actor is in order. The writers address three major points. They argue, first, that the actor is socially located or "embedded" in terms of group identities and is rooted in social networks, especially those based on nationality, race-ethnicity, class, gender, or religion; second, that social locations intersect and overlap in providing cultural materials that are drawn upon by a meaning-constructing actor who participates with others in interpreting a sense of grievances, resources, and opportunities; and third, that a new model based on shared fate replaces the free-rider paradox as the central problematic to be explained.

Echoing the words of Fireman and Gamson over ten years ago that sociologists should "beware of economists bearing gifts" (1979, 8), chapters by Ferree, Gamson, and Klandermans argue that the rational actor model has been a Trojan horse for social movement theory, bringing with it a radical individualism that presupposes a "pseudo-universal human actor without either a personal history or a gender, race, or class position within a societal history" (Ferree). They (as well as Morris in his chapter) call for more attention to the perceptions attached to social location and question the premise of a single objective reality at the core of rational choice models. Gamson, for instance, points out that individual utilitarian models such as Olson's assume the *absence* of collective identities as discussed by Melucci (1989) and new social movement theorists. Yet attention to issues of collective identity, Gamson and Klandermans argue, indicates that grievances, expectations, and the calculation of costs and benefits of action are socially constructed within a collective context.

Although Friedman and McAdam also find problematic the "atomistic view of the individual implicit in the rational choice model," their solution is to reframe rather than discard rational choice theory. In their synthesis of structural or network accounts of social movement activism and rational choice models of the individual, the propensity for social embeddedness emphasized by other authors becomes the basis for a new class of selective incentives available to social movement organizations.

The processes by which persons become active participants in the construction of meaning within a specific location is a second focus. Thus, Gamson, Klandermans, Taylor and Whittier, Lo, and Morris emphasize that "the social construction of protest . . . takes place within and between groups and social categories and within social networks" (Klandermans). These face-to-face exchanges occur within the "interpersonal life circles" of a society or sector of society. Although neither Klandermans's "interpersonal life circles" nor Gamson's "encounters" in micromobilization contexts connect directly with social structural locations, Morris provides such a link in his treatment of the sources of political consciousness conditioned by race, class, and gender. He argues that such consciousness and the grievances it identifies are constructed and shaped by the combination of specific group experiences of domination and inequality and of compromise with the more powerful hegemonic culture of the wider society.

With a socially embedded, meaning-constructing actor, Olson's (1965) free-rider problem is also recast. His classic paradox—that social movement participation is irrational if the rational actor can "free ride" on the efforts of others in achieving collective goods—has led to many ingenious solutions, particularly the recasting of social movement processes as selective incentives (Fireman and Gamson 1979). The contributions here by Ferree, Gamson, and Schwartz and Paul join a growing chorus in arguing that this preoccupation has been a misplaced emphasis for social movement theory.

Ferree, for instance, argues that the free rider can be considered a central problem only if self-interest is defined as the primary personal attribute of the actor. In contrast, she draws on feminist critics who contend that the pursuit of collective goals that imply underlying bonds of community do not seem as problematic "if mother-and-child, rather than the adult male, is seen as the basic human unit." Ferree also points to high levels of interdependence in preindustrial societies and in poor, working-class, and racial-ethnic communities within industrial societies. In these social locations, she argues, it is the self-interest of the solitary individual that is problematic. Although Friedman and McAdam share Ferree's assumption of initial network embeddedness, they argue that the seriousness of the free-rider problem varies across the life of a social movement in terms of the control the social movement organization (SMO) exerts over attaining the collective identity created by the movement.

Schwartz and Paul point to more specific conditions in which this sense of shared fate leads to a group logic that overrides the free-rider problem. In the course of distinguishing the mobilization potential of conflict and consensus movements, they point to evidence that the former has had far greater success in mobilizing members than the latter. Basing their argument on ethnographic strike data from Fantasia (1987), they assert that insofar as collective action is concerned, "individual logic is supplanted by group logic in a context of personal relationships in which individual ties among members activate obligations of each to the group." Given a sense of group fate, the two elements of group logic that overcome the free-rider problem in conflict movements are the "viability criterion"—the belief that nobody will benefit unless large numbers participate—and the "capacity to contribute criterion"—the inability of individuals to distinguish among themselves in terms of their capacity to contribute. Neither of these, they argue, is available to the consensus movement for which free riding is closer to the interest group model Olson originally addressed. Although the free-rider problem loses centrality with the assumption of a group-embedded actor, most of these authors concur that it will continue to be relevant for selected problems of mobilization, particularly in consensus movements that more closely resemble the interest groups that were Olson's immediate concern.

With the specification of the context in which free riding is problematic, a new set of issues emerges for socially embedded actors. They concern the context of social interaction and social structure, on the one hand, and the storehouse of meanings associated with a group or society's political culture, on the other. If, for instance, it is assumed that a sense of group fate and dense personal ties and obligations are typical rather than atypical for most movement participants, what are the conditions under which group logic not only supersedes individual logic but encourages collective action? Tarrow, for one, reminds us that the group *ressentiments* of highly embedded, traditional societies do not lead directly to collective action.

How do socially embedded actors perceive, evaluate, and construct political opportunities like those spelled out in Piven and Cloward's "breakdown theory" (1977), Tilly's "polity model" (1978), and McAdam's (1982) "political process model"? What are the intervening processes of social construction necessary for translating group obligations founded on survival needs into an assertive basis of collective identity linked to a sense of historic agency? Although the outcome of social construction may well assume the form of a "collective action frame" (Snow et al. 1986), a "collective identity" (Melucci 1989), or a "political consciousness" (Morris, this volume), the assumption of a socially embedded actor implies a group context for constructing grievances, opportunities, and resources. The writers in this volume point to a variety of contexts for the kind of face-to-face interaction in which new social constructions and group loyalties originate.

The Social Context of Interaction

Just as the rational actor model reoriented research in the early seventies to the analysis of mobilization, it also heightened interest in the role of formal social movement organizations as the "carriers" of a mature movement. Zald and Garner-Ash had earlier (1966) expanded on the tradition of work on social movement organizations to challenge the Weber-Michels theme of oligarchization and conservatism as inevitable organizational outcomes. With the elaboration of the resource mobilization paradigm, new interest focused on the formal SMO as the mediator between the larger sociopolitical environment and the ongoing mobilization of resources at the microlevel (see summary in McAdam, McCarthy, and Zald 1988). Although there has been considerable debate on the role of formal SMOs (Gamson 1975; Piven and Cloward 1977) and the optimal ratio of spontaneity to structure (Morris 1984; Killian 1984; Rosenthal and Schwartz 1989), the research agenda has expanded to encompass a variety of interorganizational relations.

Productive work on formal social movement organizations continues (see McCarthy and Wolfson, this volume; Zald, this volume, for an overview), and some scholars would suggest it has just begun (see Klandermans 1989), yet the emphasis here on social construction processes and the commitment of the individual to the collective identity of the movement and its organizational carriers focuses attention on what has been referred to as the "micromobilization context" (Gamson, Fireman, and Rytina 1982; McAdam, McCarthy, and Zald 1988) or on primary group interactions and their link with spontaneity and democracy (Rosenthal and Schwartz 1989). To the well-documented role of informal social networks in recruitment (Snow et al. 1980; Morris 1981, 1984; McAdam 1986, 1988) is added a conceptualization of the way in which informal, face-to-face interaction affects the micromobilization processes, especially in contexts in which actors construct meanings and make commitments.

The evolving micromobilization concept encompasses a variety of contexts in which face-to-face interaction is the social setting from which meanings critical to the interpretation of collective identities, grievances, and opportunities are created, interpreted, and transformed. It also focuses on the way group loyalties and commitments to the movement and its organizations are reinforced. Moreover, these processes of face-to-face interaction recur throughout the life of the movement.

The essays here address four points in expanding the concept of what might be termed *microconstruction*. First, the writers identify the centrality of face-to-face interaction for the processes of transforming hegemonic meanings and group loyalties. Second, they locate symbolic support for and resistance to enduring patterns of dominance and inequality in the interactional routines of everyday life. Third, they discern organizational linkages between microlevel interactions and larger structures of community and organizational networks. And finally, they identify conflict or struggle as a critical dynamic in the reconstruction of cultural meanings and group loyalties.

Klandermans, Gamson, and Schwartz and Paul place the process of social construction in the context of informal primary interactions. Each offers a broad array of movement-relevant contexts within which face-to-face interaction occurs. Klandermans's chapter invokes the individual's "interpersonal life circle," where protest meanings are constructed that define some social conditions as "grievances" and the probability of achieving collective goods (or bads) as "success expectations." The meanings associated with "public discourse," "persuasive communication," and "consciousness raising" are also constructed by specific actors at designated social locations. For Gamson, micromobilization is not only the context in which collective identities and action frames are constructed but also the locus where loyalties are created that contribute to the solidarity of the organizational carriers of the movement.

Primary groups based in relationships of face-to-face interaction are the key to social movement survival for Schwartz and Paul, especially in situations where tactical failure requires the creation of new programs and strategies to incorporate the lessons learned from past defeats. Interconnected, they contribute to the autonomy of conflict movements by serving as channels of communication that are independent of the mass media.

The chapters by Taylor and Whittier, Oliver and Marwell, and Lo place the processes of micromobilization explicitly within the society's system of culturally reinforced structured inequalities. Taylor and Whittier draw on a model for analyzing gender relations that links symbolic interaction perspectives with new social movement literature on collective identities. Arguing that gendered relations of dominance and subordination arise out of daily interactions, they postulate that resistance occurs in the politicization of symbolic presentations of everyday life.

For Lo also, the consciousness of inequality and class and its connection to goals and ideologies are shaped in locally based communities. He sees a basic distinction between interest groups tied to material resources and challengers who are dependent on constituency resources. Such polity challengers, he argues, will be locally based in communal protests arising out of physical proximity and high levels of personal, face-to-face interaction.

In the middle class also, the technologies of mobilization are adapted to and from community life. For Oliver and Marwell, the technologies for mobilizing either time or money in middle-class voluntarism are preserved informally among the activists who learn how to sustain collective causes during normal times "when most people are busy with their jobs, families, and ordinary routines." Middle-class civic action is geared to these constraints of everyday life in technologies designed to accommodate busy schedules.

The micromobilization experience is expanded outward from the social movement to support structures in the community as well as organizational carriers that compose what Klandermans calls its alliance and conflict systems. Taylor and Whittier isolate three micromobilization processes that contribute to the formation of political identity communities: (1) creation of cultural boundaries, (2) development of a shared consciousness, and (3) "valorization of a group's 'essential differences' through the politicization of everyday life." These conflictual processes tend to reinforce the community's solidarity, isolation, and collective identity, but other kinds of relationships are often supportive as well.

Gamson, for instance, points to the link between the individual and the social support system that sustains a social movement. He argues that preexisting social relationships contribute not only to recruitment but also to the continuing relationships among actors "that support and sustain the personal needs of participants and embody the movement's collective identity." These social support processes are found in the "free spaces," "prefigurative politics," and "affinity groups."

Both Klandermans and Lo connect the micromobilization context of the social movement to the larger environment and to the dynamics of social movement cycles. Klandermans explores the way that face-to-face exchanges within informal networks combine with formal organizations, including social movement organizations encompassed within a multiorganizational field of alliance systems and conflict systems. He argues that such systems expand and contract during processes of mobilization and countermobilization in a cycle of protest. Similarly, Lo points to connections between "challengers" that emerge in locally based communal protests and the more formal interest group organizations that link local groups, elicit outside funding, and create a professional staff to pursue the challengers' goals. This transformation also reflects a trajectory of change in the life cycle of the movement from that of challenger to polity member.

Conflict or struggle at the level of microconstruction emerges repeatedly in these chapters as a key dynamic leading to the reconstitution of beliefs and the recommitment of loyalties. Klandermans introduces the role of conflict both in consciousness raising and in the processes of confrontation and polarization through which beliefs and identities are modified and transformed. For Gamson, conflict centers on the encounters between challengers and authorities.

For Morris and for Taylor and Whittier, conflict plays a more central role. Morris's treatment of the intersection of race, class, and gender in the formation of political consciousness is likened to the processes by which class struggle generates class consciousness identified in Thompson's *Making of the English Working Class* (1963). The importance of an adversarial environment is also central to Taylor and Whittier's conception of the way in which oppositional communities transform their members into political actors. They define the oppositional community, or "political identity community," as "a network of individuals and groups loosely linked through an institutional base, multiple goals and actors, and a collective identity that offers members' common interests in opposition to dominant groups." For Lo and for Schwartz and Paul, conflict is the major characteristic distinguishing types of social movements.

The authors cited here continue the task of identifying key social locations in constructing meanings and securing loyalties that challenge dominant assumptions and create or transform communities. Yet the need to specify numerous other roles for microconstruction remains. Face-to-face interactions not only form the building blocks of larger aggregations and organizations but also serve as the social context in which hegemonic belief systems are broken down. Those theorizing from a macrolevel constructionist perspective in the tradition of Gramsci and Habermas have argued that hegemonic processes are so successful that the meanings necessary for collective action are only infrequently available. McAdam's political process model (1982) and Piven and Cloward's breakdown model (1977) incorporated a similar argument. Thus, a necessary context for redefining the cultural inheritance of the socially embedded actor is the face-to-face interaction of the informal group where grievances, resources, and opportunities as well as ideologies and symbolic representations of collective identities can be constructed and transmitted.

Sociopolitical Culture

Resource mobilization theory, as originally conceived, self-consciously minimized the role of ideas and beliefs and their elaboration. Like grievances, the cultural configurations that legitimate and make collective action meaningful were taken as givens. Recently, theorists have found a starting point for addressing cultural issues within the RM framework by examining the role of interpretive frameworks or "collective action frames," which focus on the meanings most proximate to collective action and most strategically constructed. Drawing on Goffman's ideas of signifying or framing, Snow and his associates (1986) have been most influential among American scholars in identifying strategies by which activists in social movement organizations link their "schemata of interpretation" to the existing cultural frames of potential supporters or targets of influence. Unlike formal ideologies, collective action frames share the emergent qualities of the social movement organizations that create them.

The chapters here extend the work on collective action frames and place them within a broader cultural context and a longer time frame. Also considered are less strategic configurations of meaning, such as collective identities, usually associated with the European tradition of "new social movement theory." First, collective action frames are situated within the relatively short life of the movement or cycle of protest and within the historic dimensions of political cultures such as societal mentalities and public discourse. Second, the multiple meanings and levels of analysis associated with collective identities are explored as they arise in both the strategic and the more spontaneous activities of the ongoing struggles of social movements.

Snow and Benford in this volume refer to collective action frames as "emergent action-oriented sets of beliefs and meanings that inspire and legitimate social movement activities and campaigns." Snow and his colleagues (1986) first identified four types of aligning work that social movement organizations engage in to create collective action frames: frame bridging, frame amplification, frame expansion, and frame transformation. The first three types range from simple to more complex forms of congruence between traditional ideas and those propounded by the movement. The last, frame transformation, involves the most far-reaching departures from traditional systems of meaning and the most innovative reconfigurations of symbolic elements.

Snow and Benford extend their framing work to encompass the master frames associated with the complex systems of ideas that inform entire cycles of protest. In expanding the framing conception, they draw particularly on Tarrow's (1983) work on protest cycles that are sequences of escalating collective action exhibiting greater frequency and intensity than normal. Master frames contribute to the emergence, sequencing, and tactical repertoires of various social movements within a cycle of protest.

Tarrow's chapter links collective action frames to "cultural choices" in which enterprising agents within social movements draw from existing mentalities and political culture to manipulate the symbols necessary for creating action-oriented frames of meaning that will mobilize others on behalf of movement goals. Tarrow sees collective action frames as less formal than ideologies but functioning similarly to link members of social movements to movement organizations and to one another. Like Klandermans, he points out that the most important of the characteristics identifying the frame's resonance are those that connect the collective action frame to cultural meanings and symbol systems of the movement's audience. Tarrow notes that "collective action is thus the stage on which new meanings are produced, as well as a text full of old meanings."

The work on framing is less explicit, however, in explaining how the purposive ideological symbols of social movements interact with the broader culture. In seeking to identify this link, Tarrow examines the oppositional potential in the theoretical traditions associated with concepts of societal mentalities and political culture. The oldest of these is the social historians' concept of *sociale mentalities* which identifies the sources of *ressentiment* that are endemic in traditional rural societies. Despite the identification of sociale mentalities with popular grievances, Tarrow points out that these beliefs lack a sense of agency that would connect grievances to action. More focused in terms of explicitly political meanings is Almond and Verba's (1964) conception of "political cultures," which is currently experiencing a revival in political science. Recent adaptations of the concept attempt to speak to its earlier deficits in conceptualizing oppositional components of culture. Tarrow argues, however, that theorists have yet to uncover a direct link between the work on oppositional elements of political culture and the more purposive collective action frames identified by Snow and his associates.

By moving from the more general level of societal mentalities and political culture to public discourse, however, Klandermans establishes a framework for connecting the "long-term processes of formation and transformation of collective beliefs . . . and the collective identities that determine the constraints of mobilization campaigns." Public discourse involves an interplay among media discourse, issue arenas, interpersonal interactions, and public opinion. Social movement actors attempt to anchor their collective action frames in the beliefs and identities that are developed out of public discourse. The social movement both draws from and attempts to influence public discourse by the way it frames issues, defines grievances, and stages collective actions to attract media attention. Its ideas are disseminated to individuals who identify with a particular group or category that is the target or the constituency of the movement. Thus, the work on collective identities attached to social locations, like that by Morris and Taylor and Whittier, serves as one of the key connecting links between the purposive communication of the social movement and the broader public discourse.

Collective identities serve in several other capacities, however. The chapters by Gamson, Taylor and Whittier, and Friedman and McAdam consider "collective identity" as a social construct linking the individual, the cultural system, and, in some cases, the organizational carrier of the movement. Friedman and McAdam define it as a "shorthand designation announcing a status as a set of attitudes, commitments, and rules for behavior," which is also "an individual announcement of affiliation, of connection with others." Social movement participation is examined as a potentially transformative experience in which subjective definitions of self become linked to a shared social construct, which is capable, under some circumstances, of exacting loyalty and commitment to the movement.

Gamson and Taylor and Whittier draw initially on the Italian new social movement theorist Alberto Melucci (1989), who argues that the construction of a collective identity is one of the most central tasks facing a movement. Like Melucci, they conceive of the construction of collective identities as a negotiated process. In contrast with him, however, they view most collective identities that are relevant to social movements as arising out of existing structured inequalities. Taylor and Whittier identify the process whereby collective identities are politicized. They view gender inequality as constantly re-created "through displays and interactions governed by gender-normative behavior that comes to be perceived as natural and normal." To contest the inequality, the symbolic representations must also be challenged. Thus, the collective identity of "radical feminism" or "radical lesbianism" arises out of both the structured inequality of homophobia and the opposition to its cultural as well as institutional manifestations. Whereas Morris and Taylor and Whittier emphasize the construction of social movement identities from existing structured inequalities, Klandermans and Friedman and McAdam locate social movement mobilization in existing collective identities associated with social roles that heighten a sense of grievance or offer a social basis for the mobilization.

Like Gamson, Friedman and McAdam reject Cohen's (1985) judgment that identity processes are incompatible with a strategically oriented paradigm. Instead, their argument suggests that agents of the social movement may construct a collective identity to maximize the strategic effectiveness of the SMO. Gamson's strategy for reconciliation of identity and resource mobilization paradigms is to give equal status to cultural change and institutional change as social movement goals. If cultural change is the goal, he argues, construction of a collective identity is one step in challenging cultural domination. Although a collective identity may bring individual fulfillment, its creation is also a "strategic step in achieving cultural changes that are mediated by the movement's external targets." Yet, even if creation of a collective identity is regarded as a goal in its own right, Gamson argues that "it has instrumental consequences for the rest of the process." Many of these are identified by Friedman and McAdam.

Master frames also differ from ideology in their emergent fluid qualities associated with the ongoing struggle of social movements. Unlike collective action frames, however, the question of agency is not so clearly addressed. Snow and his associates have indicated that the agents of social movement organizations create collective action frames as part of their strategic work. Although the attributes and the functions of a good master frame are spelled out, a mechanism for their development and dissemination such as the process of political struggle described by Morris and Taylor and Whittier has not yet been identified. Because master frames may be modified or transformed as they are appropriated by one social movement after another in a protest cycle, the dynamics of the process by which some frames are generalized and others are not remain an open question.

In addition to their ingenious efforts to elaborate the concepts of collective action frames and master frames, the authors here have focused considerable attention on developing the concept of "collective identity." Because of its location at the intersection of the individual, the culture, and the social movement group, collective identity has proved a useful if elusive concept in developing a social psychology of social movements.

VARIABLE DIMENSIONS OF SOCIAL MOVEMENTS

A distinguishing feature of recent social movement theory has been a narrowing of the phenomena under investigation. Reviews of resource mobilization theory by Jenkins (1983) and Cohen (1985) make the point: whereas the collective behavior tradition encompassed movements for institutional change as well as personal change, resource mobilization theorists have "restricted their focus to movements of institutional change" (Jenkins 1983, 529). Interest is limited to those movements that attempt to alter elements of the social structure or the reward distribution of society (McCarthy and Zald 1977) or to organize challenging groups or unrecognized interests that are excluded from the polity (Gamson 1975; Tilly 1978). Many of the chapters in this volume, particularly those written from a social psychological or social constructionist perspective, challenge this separation of institutional change and personal change, and the remaining chapters raise other issues related to the scope of social movement theory.

It is increasingly argued here and elsewhere that in simplifying the object of investigation, resource mobilization theory has also restricted the type of political movement to those that pursue middle-class reform goals and/or eschew violence and conflict as strategy and tactic (see, for instance, Kerbo 1982). It is also argued that much current theorizing fails to recognize this narrowed focus of attention and assumes a generic social movement as if all mobilizations were alike in terms of the nature of grievances and the degrees of change sought, of access to resources, and of political opportunities. There are exceptions, of course. Gamson (1975), Tilly, Tilly, and Tilly (1975), and Tilly (1978) explicitly consider the role of violence as a tactic. Case studies of specific movements, such as those of Piven and Cloward on ghetto rioting, McAdam and Morris on the civil rights movement, and Staggenborg and Taylor on the contemporary women's movement, describe the roles of violence and conflict. Yet, despite these prominent exceptions, the relationships among levels of violence and conflict, types of grievances, and the key variables of resource mobilization (resources, organization, opportunities) remain undeveloped. They do not receive systematic attention in the standard works on resource mobilization (Jenkins 1983; Cohen 1985; Morris and Herring 1988; McAdam, McCarthy, and Zald 1988).

Many of the writers here argue that further theorizing requires the reintroduction of those elements that will connect social movements more closely to social structure and to the associated disparities in resources and opportunities that lead differentially to the use of violence and conflict in the choice of tactics. That is, social location helps determine the nature of grievances, resources, and levels of organization. In addition, it plays a crucial role in whether movement tactics and strategies encompass violence and conflict and, thus, the level and type of mobilization that develops as well as the political opportunities that can be created or exploited. The distinctions introduced here between conflict and consensus movements (McCarthy and Wolfson, Schwartz and Paul), conventional and protest politics (Lo), normal and nonnormal collective action (Piven and Cloward), and ordinary times and periods of mass mobilization (Oliver and Marwell) suggest that further progress in theory building may require a more careful specification of the implications of structural locations as a source of grievances, resources, and type of mobilization. In some respects, these distinctions reflect recurring theoretical interest in designating typologies of collective behavior or social movements.

Themes from an earlier tradition of developing typologies in political sociology and collective behavior appear reframed in this book. First, it is argued that social movement theory of the last twenty years has neglected or minimized the more expressive, spontaneous, and disruptive role of conflict and violence by privileging the analysis of structure and organization. Second, it is argued that variation in tactics and strategies is linked to both the resources and the typical experiences of groups at different locations in the social structure as well as the degree to which the movement is accepted as legitimate throughout society. Third, the level of social change achieved is tied to the level of mass mobilization and institutional disruption.

The neglect of conflict, or the "normalization of protest," incurs a variety of costs to social movement theory that are examined in chapters by Lo, Schwartz and Paul, and Piven and Cloward. These authors trace the normalizing assumptions to a model of social movements that blurs the distinction between protest and conventional politics. The result, they argue, is to treat protest as more organized than it actually is and to minimize critical differences in social dynamics of rule-conforming and rule-violating behavior.

These writers claim that a social movement theory that fails to incorporate an adequate understanding of conflict and violence is weak in its inability to account for the following: (1) the origins and trajectories of political challengers in locally based communal protest dynamics (Lo); (2) the greater mobilization of participants by conflict movements than by consensus movements (Schwartz and Paul); and (3) the distinctive protest politics of lower-stratum groups and the continuities in the form of these politics from preindustrial to modern times (Piven and Cloward). The authors argue that all these issues are to some extent a consequence of differential access to conventional resources and to widespread legitimacy.

Social location influences not only the construction of meanings that define grievances, opportunities, and collective identities but the availability of specific types of resources as well. In addition, as Oliver and Marwell point out, the technologies for mobilizing these resources impose their own constraints on the forms of action that are possible. The issues raised here concern particularly the implications of dependence on constituencies compared to money and access to bureaucratic resources associated with the conventional channels of political influence. McCarthy and Wolfson distinguish types of movements and access to resources by the level of public support rather than by social location, arguing that movements with consensus levels of support among the public (80 to 90 percent) are much more likely to gain access to a full array of institutional (particularly state) resources than are conflict movements. This is especially true at the local level for "suddenly imposed grievances" (Walsch 1981) and at the national level if the goals of the movement coincide with those of government agencies. If the movement becomes involved in conflict, however, it stands to lose institutional resources.

Oliver and Marwell illustrate the underlying link between social location and knowledge about collective action tactics and strategies. In their analysis of the world of middle-class voluntary action, technologies for achieving goals (production technologies) as well as accumulating resources (mobilization technologies) are carefully designed to complement the stable, ordinary routines of family and community life during quiet times. They indicate, however, that even within the middle class important differences exist between the technologies for mobilizing money versus people. Technologies for mobilizing money lead to professional fund-raising and bureaucratic elaboration, whereas the mobilization of people's time is less specialized and depends on the activation of personal networks.

Yet consensus support or institutional resources are not an option for all social groups with collective grievances. The chapters by Lo, Schwartz and Paul, and Piven and Cloward concern the groups that lack one or both of these assets. These are the polity "challengers" engaged in conflict that disproportionately rely on either constituent resources (Lo, Schwartz and Paul) or violence (Piven and Cloward). Their dependence on constituent resources creates the dynamics of nonprofessionalized strategies and conflict that have important implications for social change.

The essays here are highly suggestive in arguing that heavy reliance on constituent resources sets in motion a dynamic that is more likely to create mass mobilization and greater social change than movements that depend on high levels of consensus, institutional resources and sponsorship, or professional staffs. Each author sees these dynamics somewhat differently. Lo, for instance, points to the creation of a new consensus based on system-challenging goals and ideologies and the consciousness of inequality and class developed through the social interactions of face-to-face communities. Schwartz and Paul emphasize both the massive size of mobilizations and tactical flexibility achieved by conflict movements in which a sense of efficacy, shared fate, and personal responsibility combine to create high levels of participation. Tactical flexibility is achieved by conflict movements because they are not constrained by the restrictions placed on movements endowed with institutional resources, official sponsorship, and media coverage. Piven and Cloward argue that, in the absence of bureaucratic resources, lower-stratum groups rely on rule-breaking behavior that has the powerful effect of disrupting major institutions and arousing the intervention of important third parties. It is this set of dynamics, they argue, that is likely to lead to structural dealignment and realignment by which political ends are gained that could never be achieved through conventional resources, tactics, and strategies.

Important directions for future research are suggested in these essays. First is that of distinguishing the level and type of likely resources available to prospective participants as a basic constraint on collective action. The failure to specify differential access to resources has been a major factor divorcing recent social movement theory from social structure and history. Second is the hypothesized link between constituency resources, mass mobilization, and major social change. Third is that of connecting the mechanisms of constituency mobilization leading to periods of mass participation with the carrying structures and oppositional subcultures that develop during periods of relative quiescence.

The causal link suggested between social location, available resources for collective action, and the selection of tactics deserves more careful consideration. Oliver and Marwell, for instance, have argued in regard to middle-class civic action that technologies are tightly linked to the type and extent of resources available. Although fund-raising drives, telephone canvassing, and nonviolent demonstrations may be hallmarks of middle-class civic action, it is not clear that violence is exclusively the tactic of the poor. Violence has been successfully utilized by protest groups throughout the social structure in U.S. history (Gamson 1975) and also appears to be the last recourse of middle-class activists marginalized in the declining stages of cycles of protest (della Porta and Tarrow 1986; Tarrow 1989).

Like the renewed focus on political culture and public discourse, the implications of these arguments draw attention to the temporal dimension of social movements, recognizing that very different dynamics distinguish periods of relative quiescence from those of mass participation. It may prove useful to couple McAdam's cycle of black insurgency (1982) and Tarrow's protest cycles (1983, 1989) with Morris's halfway houses and Taylor's abeyance structures (1989) to situate the current work in terms of concerns with the opening and closing of political opportunities and the differential availability of resources and legitimacy. Snow and Benford's work on master frames in cycles of protest; Klandermans's recognition of the expansion and contraction of alliance and conflict systems; Lo's trajectory from communal protest to interest group; Oliver and Marwell's distinction between technologies for ordinary times and those for times of turbulence point toward such theoretical developments. Piven and Cloward's distinction between normative and nonnormative collective action also anticipates the development of a theory that will link the rise and decline of mass mobilizations with political opportunity structures and the processes of socially constructing grievances and collective identities.

This collection of essays provides the foundation for a more comprehensive social movement theory built around those processes that lead to the social construction of the symbolic world of the individual actor, as well as social movement cultures and collective identities. In contrast with the economistic rational actor of early resource mobilization theory, the new social movement actor both actively constructs and is constrained by a world of social meanings rooted in specific historic contexts and based in the experiences and identities of race, gender, class, and nationality. Within these contexts, the new actor identifies and constructs the meanings that designate the relevance for mobilization of grievances, resources, and opportunities.

Consistent with Kuhnian analysis, critics of resource mobilization theory, such as Cohen (1985), have argued that a "strategy" paradigm based in the natural sciences cannot be reconciled with a semiotic, "identity" paradigm encompassing subjective concerns of ideology, consciousness, and collective identities. Yet the essays in this book suggest that one paradigm does not necessarily supersede the other, but rather affords a figure/ground shift in what is considered problematic. The building blocks of resource mobilization—resources, formal organization, tactics, and political opportunities—are not ignored, but rather reframed within a broader paradigm that is at once more sensitive to historical, cultural, and structural differences between groups seeking to mobilize on behalf of collective ends and more attuned to the micromobilization context in which social movement identities and grievances are forged out of specific experiences of constraint and opportunity. It is a paradigm that seeks to differentiate the social locations of movements based on constituent resources leading to mass mobilization from those that place heavier reliance on professional, bureaucratic resources and ties to institutional sponsors. It is a paradigm that looks for the organizational and cultural continuities between cycles of protest and periods of quiescence. Finally, it is a paradigm that raises the question of what combination and sequence of mobilizations initiate periods of major social change. The chapters that follow offer much to consider for the student of social movements.

REFERENCES

Almond, Gabriel, and Sidney Verba. 1964. *The Civic Culture*. Boston: Little, Brown.

Barkan, Steven E. 1985. *Protesters on Trial: Criminal Justice in the Southern Civil Rights and Vietnam Antiwar Movements*. New Brunswick, N.J.: Rutgers University Press.

Cohen, Jean L. 1985. "Strategy or Identity: New Theoretical Paradigms and Contemporary Social Movements." *Social Research* 52:663–716.

Curtis, Russell L., and Louis A. Zurcher, Jr. 1973. "Stable Resources of Protest Movements: The Multi-organizational Field." *Social Forces* 52:53–60.

Della Porta, Donatella, and Sidney Tarrow. 1986. "Unwanted Children: Political Violence and the Cycle of Protest in Italy, 1966–1973." *European Journal of Political Research* 14:607–32.

Eisinger, Peter K. 1973. "The Conditions of Protest Behavior in American Cities." *American Political Science Review* 67:11–28.

Fantasia, Rick. 1987. *Cultures of Solidarity: Studies in Consciousness and Action among Contemporary American Workers*. Berkeley: University of California Press.

Ferree, Myra Marx, and Frederick D. Miller. 1985. "Mobilization and Meaning: Toward an Integration of Social Psychological and Resource Perspectives on Social Movements." *Sociological Inquiry* 55:38–51.

Fireman, Bruce, and William H. Gamson. 1979. "Utilitarian Logic in the Resource Mobilization Perspective." In *The Dynamics of Social Movements*, ed. Mayer N. Zald and John D. McCarthy. Cambridge, Mass.: Winthrop.

Freeman, Jo. 1973. "The Origins of the Women's Liberation Movement." *American Journal of Sociology* 78:792–811.

Gamson, William A. 1968. *Power and Discontent*. Homewood, Ill.: Dorsey.

———. 1975. *The Strategy of Social Protest*. Homewood, Ill.: Dorsey.

Gamson, William A., Bruce Fireman, and Steven Rytina. 1982. *Encounters with Unjust Authority*. Homewood, Ill.: Dorsey.

Haines, Herbert H. 1984. "Black Radicalization and the Funding of Civil Rights, 1957–1970." *Social Problems* 32:31–43.

Jenkins, J. Craig. 1983. "Resource Mobilization Theory and the Study of Social Movements." *Annual Review of Sociology* 9:527–53.

Jenkins, J. Craig, and Craig M. Eckert. 1986. "Channeling Black Insurgency: Elite Patronage and Professional Social Movement Organizations in the Development of the Black Movement." *American Sociological Review* 51:812–29.

Jenkins, J. Craig, and Charles Perrow. 1977. "Insurgency of the Powerless: Farm Workers' Movements, 1946–1972." *American Sociological Review* 42:249–68.

Kerbo, Harold R. 1982. "Movements of Crisis and Movements of Affluence: A Critique of Deprivation and Resource Mobilization Theories." *Journal of Conflict Resolution* 26:645–63.

Killian, Lewis. 1984. "Organization, Rationality and Spontaneity in the Civil Rights Movement." *American Sociological Review* 49:770–83.

Klandermans, Bert. 1984. "Mobilization and Participation: Social-Psychological Expansions of Resource Mobilization Theory." *American Sociological Review* 49:583–600.

———, ed. 1989. *Organizing for Change: Social Movement Organizations in Europe and the United States*. International Social Movement Research, vol. 2. Greenwich, Conn.: JAI Press.

Leites, Nathan, and Charles Wolf, Jr. 1970. *Rebellion and Authority: An Analytic Essay on Insurgent Conflicts*. Chicago: Markham.

Lo, Clarence. 1982. "Counter-Movements and Conservative Movements in the Contemporary U.S." *Annual Review of Sociology* 8:107–34.

McAdam, Doug. 1982. *Political Process and the Development of Black Insurgency, 1930–1970*. Chicago: University of Chicago Press.

———. 1986. "Recruitment to High-Risk Activism: The Case of Freedom Summer." *American Journal of Sociology* 92:64–90.

———. 1988. *Freedom Summer*. New York: Oxford University Press.

McAdam, Doug, John D. McCarthy, and Mayer N. Zald. 1988. "Social Movements." In *Handbook of Sociology*, ed. Neil J. Smelser. Newbury Park, Calif.: Sage.

McCarthy, John D., and Mayer N. Zald. 1973. *The Trend of Social Movements in America: Professionalization and Resource Mobilization*. Morristown, N.J.: General Learning Press.

————. 1977. "Resource Mobilization and Social Movements: A Partial Theory." *American Journal of Sociology* 82:1212–41.

Melucci, Alberto. 1989. *Nomads of the Present: Social Movements and Individual Needs in Contemporary Society*. Philadelphia: Temple University Press.

Morris, Aldon D. 1981. "Black Southern Student Sit-In Movement: An Analysis of Internal Organization." *American Sociological Review* 46:744–67.

————. 1984. *The Origins of the Civil Rights Movement*. New York: Free Press.

Morris, Aldon D., and Cedric Herring. 1988. "Theory and Research in Social Movements: A Critical Review." In *Annual Review of Political Behavior*, vol. 2, ed. Samuel Long. Boulder, Colo.: Westview Press.

Mottl, Tahi. 1980. "The Analysis of Counter-Movements." *Social Problems* 27:620–35.

Oberschall, Anthony. 1973. *Social Conflict and Social Movements*. Englewood Cliffs, N.J.: Prentice-Hall.

Olson, Mancur. 1965. *The Logic of Collective Action*. Cambridge, Mass.: Harvard University Press.

Piven, Frances Fox, and Richard A. Cloward. 1971. *Regulating the Poor*. New York: Pantheon.

————. 1977. *Poor People's Movements*. New York: Pantheon.

Rosenthal, Naomi, Meryl Fingrutd, Michele Ethier, Roberta Karant, and David McDonald. 1985. "Social Movements and Network Analysis: A Case Study of Nineteenth-Century Women's Reform in New York State." *American Journal of Sociology* 90:1022–55.

Rosenthal, Naomi, and Michael Schwartz. 1989. "Spontaneity and Democracy in Social Movements." In *Organizing for Change: Social Movement Organizations in Europe and the United States*, ed. Bert Klandermans. International Social Movement Research, vol. 2. Greenwich, Conn.: JAI Press.

Shweder, Richard A., and Donald W. Fiske. 1986. "Introduction: Uneasy Social Science." In *Metatheory in Social Science: Pluralisms and Subjectivities*, ed. Donald W. Fiske and Richard A. Shweder. Chicago: University of Chicago Press.

Snow, David A., E. Burke Rochford, Jr., Steven K. Worden, and Robert D. Benford. 1986. "Frame Alignment Processes, Micromobilization, and Movement Participation." *American Sociological Review* 51:464–81.

Snow, David A., Louis A. Zurcher, Jr., and Sheldon Ekland-Olson. 1980. "Social Networks and Social Movements: A Microstructural Approach to Differential Recruitment." *American Sociological Review* 45:787–801.

Tarrow, Sidney. 1983. *Struggling to Reform: Social Movements and Policy Change during Cycles of Protest*. Ithaca, N.Y.: Western Societies Program, Cornell University.

————. 1989. *Democracy and Disorder: Protest and Politics in Italy, 1965–1975*. New York: Oxford University Press.

Taylor, Verta. 1989. "Social Movement Continuity: The Women's Movement in Abeyance." *American Sociological Review* 54:761–75.

Thompson, E. P. 1963. *The Making of the English Working Class*. New York: Random House.

Tilly, Charles. 1978. *From Mobilization to Revolution*. Reading, Mass.: Addison-Wesley.

Tilly, Charles, Louise Tilly, and Richard Tilly. 1975. *The Rebellious Century, 1830–1930*. Cambridge, Mass.: Harvard University Press.

Walsh, Edward J. 1981. "Resource Mobilization and Citizen Protest in Communities around Three Mile Island." *Social Problems* 29:1–21.

Zald, Mayer N., and Roberta Garner-Ash. 1966. "Social Movement Organizations: Growth, Decay and Change." *Social Forces* 44:327–41.

Zald, Mayer N., and Bert Useem. 1987. "Movement and Countermovement Interaction: Mobilization, Tactics and State Involvement." In *Social Movements in an Organizational Society*, ed. Mayer N. Zald and John D. McCarthy. New Brunswick, N.J.: Transaction Books.

Zurcher, Louis A., Jr., and David A. Snow. 1981. "Collective Behavior: Social Movements." In *Social Psychology: Sociological Perspectives*, ed. Morris Rosenberg and Ralph H. Turner. New York: Basic Books.

Part 2

The Social Psychology of Social Movements

The Political Context of Rationality

Rational Choice Theory

and Resource Mobilization

M y r a   M a r x   F e r r e e

Social movement theory was transformed in the United States in the 1970s by the emergence of what has come to be known as the resource mobilization (RM) approach. This change of direction in theory and research was a conscious and deliberate rebellion against the collective behavior studies of previous decades (Morris and Herring 1987). Two central assertions of the RM framework are (1) that social movement activities are not spontaneous and disorganized and (2) that social movement participants are not irrational. Both of these claims are seen as rebuttals of the classical collective behavior model.

The resource mobilization approach is thus readily characterized by its reliance on organizational studies and its resistance to traditional social psychological explanations for individuals' participation in social movements. In studying how movement organizations struggle to achieve particular goals and succeed or fail in these efforts, there are advantages to looking at the material resources they command rather than the social psychology of their participants. The absence of a plausible account of values, grievances, and ideology in the basic model, however, has increasingly been recognized as a problem, even by researchers who see themselves as working within that approach (e.g., Klandermans 1988a; Fireman and Gamson 1979; Snow et al. 1986; Ferree and Miller 1985).

The history of RM as a consciously propagated alternative to collective behavior research helps explain this limitation. The judgment that all earlier work was tainted by an unacceptable premise of participants' "irrationality"—and the derogatory view of movements this implied—inspired

My thanks to the many people who provided extensive and very helpful comments on the earlier version of this chapter, particularly Paula England, Bert Klandermans, Doug McAdam, Charles Perrow, and the editors of this volume.

researchers to look for models that would instead accord with Michael Schwartz's postulate that "social movement participants are at least as rational as those who study them" (Morris 1989). McCarthy and Zald (1977) and Oberschall (1973) suggested such a model could be found in Mancur Olson's microeconomic analysis of collective action (1965). Olson's now-familiar argument was that collective benefits alone would be insufficient to motivate a rational actor because free riding on the efforts of others would provide the same share of collective goods at less cost to the individual, and that (by definition) a rational actor would expect his or her efforts to contribute only imperceptibly to provision of the collective good at all. Olson therefore ignored variation in *perceived* efficacy, stressed the provision of selective benefits as the "rational" basis of collective action, and (in a section of his book selectively not quoted by RM researchers) explicitly denigrated many social movements as irrational (1965, 159–62).

The intent of this chapter is to argue that the model of rationality thus imported into the RM approach, the microeconomic theory of rational choice, is a Trojan horse. The superficial attractiveness of its empirically testable incentive formulations conceals theoretically dangerous assumptions, carried over uncritically from Olson, that threaten the ability of RM to explain what social movements are and do. Although other researchers are beginning to modify or drop certain of these assumptions in order to construct more realistic and workable models (e.g., Ennis and Scheuer 1987; Klandermans 1989), there has been little scrutiny given to the concept of rationality itself.

Conventional microeconomics defines rationality with reference to a simplifying but misleading postulate, namely, that individuals will always act to maximize their personal benefits and reduce their costs. This is not a testable proposition since the theory offers no rules for measuring preferences independent of the choices made (Taylor 1988). Whatever it is that people choose, they are said to do so because they "prefer" this alternative. This involves relabeling rather than explaining behavior: apparently irrational choices are said to reflect idiosyncratic "tastes" that are treated as exogenous and uninteresting—that is, in no need of explanation.

If its only problem were this well-known tendency toward tautology, rational choice theory, though not very useful, would present few dangers. There are, however, hidden assumptions in this model that pose serious problems for social movement theory. Perrow describes these economistic assumptions as echoing the theme of the movie *Invasion of the Body Snatchers*: in the rational choice account, "human forms are retained, but all that we value about human behavior—its spontaneity, unpredictability, selflessness, plurality of values, reciprocal influence, and resentment of domination—has disappeared" (1986, 41). Although rational choice theory gives a sociologically impoverished account of behavior in general, its dehumanizing assumptions are especially problematic in studies of social movements. In particular, it has led to first, a neglect of value differences and conflicts, second, a misplaced emphasis on the free-rider problem, and third, a presupposition of a pseudo-universal human actor without either a personal history or a gender, race, or class position within a societal history.

In the first part of this chapter, I review and critique rational choice theory, highlighting these three problems. Feminist theory provides one important vantage point for this critique. Then I offer some alternative suggestions for a broader but more realistic view of rationality. Within this expanded vision of rationality, both self- and other-regarding behaviors are seen as structurally situated. This, I argue, is more consistent with the macrolevel organizational emphasis of the resource mobilization approach, but does not reduce individuals to unthinking resources to be manipulated by a movement organization as it sees fit. Although this alternative treatment of rationality is sketchy, and a fully developed model still needs to be formulated, it may begin to suggest useful directions for integrating current empirical work and theory building into a new post-RM framework.

THE LIMITS OF RATIONAL CHOICE THEORY

The assumption of what neoclassical economists call "rationality"—individual profit-maximizing behavior—leads to numerous paradoxes and problems within the area of conventional economics. It is not within the scope of this chapter to review all these flaws (for critiques, see England 1989; Etzioni 1988; Hirschman 1986; Hartsock 1983; Perrow 1986; Taylor 1988). But suffice it here to note its widely recognized difficulties in dealing with interpersonal variation in what people value (e.g., avoiding "interpersonal comparison of utilities" leads to each person being tautologically assumed to have chosen his or her most rewarding alternative), with contextual differences in perception (all facts are objectively determinable and can be fully known), and with structural differences in power between individuals within organizations (e.g., coercion becomes defined as the less powerful person's "choice" of the less punishing alternative).

Neoclassical economists have often simply defined these intractable problems as out of their field of interest, leaving them for sociologists and social psychologists; at the same time they have often pursued the "imperialist" project of bringing microeconomic analysis of self-interest into all areas of human behavior (Hirschman 1986). The models thus developed exclude issues of power and stratification, as well as personality and attitudes, as the concerns of other disciplines, implicitly granting them little weight. The rational choice model, focusing as it does upon incentives and self-interest alone, imposes three dangerous limitations on RM: it offers only a one-dimensional view of rationality, insists on the theoretical significance of free riding, and presents a decontextualized view of individuals. As I will attempt to show below, ambivalence, altruism, and emotional experience are thereby made invisible and irrelevant.

One-Dimensional Rationality

The tautologies that arise from treating all forms of behavior as strategically rational by definition exclude a realistic explanation of when behavior may be more or less than an expression of self-interest, as some maverick economists have themselves noted (e.g., Frank 1987; Hirschman 1986; Sen 1977). Behavior that is not strategically rational (not maximizing individual profit as the individual sees it) can carry a variety of meanings for the individual actor. Effective analysis of action needs to take such motivational meanings into account.

On the one hand, some types of behavior fall short of standards of rationality in even the actor's own eyes. Frank (1987), for example, contrasts direct hedonic reward with perceived self-interest—he looks at the directly pleasurable activities of eating and the strategically rational efforts of many modern actors to control their diet in order to improve their health or appearance. His focus is on the conflict experienced in managing such demands for rationality; even as one succumbs to the tempting pastry, one knows this choice is not in one's self-interest and will be regretted later. Manipulating situations ("removing temptation") and mobilizing others to restrain oneself from behaviors perceived to be self-defeating ("don't let me . . .") are strategically rational ways of managing such conflict, but they are neither always attempted nor always successful. An excessively inclusive view of self-interest or rationality obscures the existence of the conflict and thus diverts attention from the methods adopted for managing it, most of which require anticipating the problem before it arises.

To recognize that all people do behave impulsively and irrationally at times *enriches* the account of rationality that can be given by including the individual and organizational problems of anticipating, managing, and reacting to such tendencies. Insisting on training in nonviolence is one obvious instance in which movement organizations attempt to anticipate and control noncalculated and self-defeating (but emotionally satisfying) responses to provocation. Although social movement participants are no more or less irrational than anyone else, achieving a measured and rational response is an *accomplishment*. This is not well understood by defining all behavior as rational.

On the other hand, some types of behavior may be meta-rational, in the sense of Weber's "value-rationality" as contrasted with merely instrumental rationality. These behaviors reflect considerations of ends or values rather than means. Socioeconomic models (e.g., Etzioni 1988; Hirschman 1986) define the motivations for such behavior as *moral commitments*—that is, as sources of value other than being better off, no matter how "better off" is defined. These moral commitments are explicitly distinguished from pleasure, both theoretically and experientially. Hirschman (1986) notes that such values act as "meta-preferences"—that is, a means of consciously reflecting on and deliberately changing one's preferences; they involve the choice of ends rather than the means of achieving a specified end. As Etzioni notes, such moral commitments are often "explicitly based on the denial of pleasure in the name of the principle(s) involved" (1988, 45).

Moral behavior as such distinctively expresses the *affirmation* of a value rather than its accomplishment or consumption. Efforts to express one's values Hirschman labels "striving" and suggests that this is what we experience as giving our lives purpose and meaning (1986, 149–55). In such behavior, effort expended is not a cost but rewarding in itself; striving to affirm a value is done "for its own sake." Hirschman distinguishes between collective goods that may be possessed or consumed and collective goods wherein the process of striving is itself the good; thus "democracy" as a given set of rules (i.e., universal suffrage or a multiparty system) may be achieved, but "democracy" as informed participation in public choice is a process of individual and collective striving. Many social movements are committed to such moral principles and attempt to realize them in the process of collective mobilization itself as much as in the stated outcome of such endeavors.

Etzioni (1988) describes both these non–instrumentally rational forms of behavior as indications of a multidimensional self: that is, people are not bundles of unambiguous and stable preferences that may simply be "followed"; rather they experience inner tension between conflicting desires and commitments. Any single "utility function," no matter how complex, obscures this dynamic interrelation among hedonic responses, instrumental goals, and moral commitments. Taylor (1988) distinguishes a "thin" view of rationality from a more substantial and useful one on the basis of the role it grants to "self-expressive" (or "identity-affirming") behaviors that may be directly in conflict with the satisfaction of individual self-interest. Classical rational choice theory, committed as it is to such a "thin" view of rationality, loses sight of the conflicts and tensions that are actually experienced in arriving at reasoned decisions, both in subordinating more irrational impulses and in affirming higher order values.

Recasting all decision making into the unidimensional language of rational choice and self-interest introduces three notable distortions in RM models. First, the idea of identity as such, a "self" that is significant, an inner life that distinctively enters into but is not identical with observed behavior, tends to disappear (see Cohen 1985). For example, Hechter's rational choice account of "group solidarity" is strictly behaviorist—it is not a moral commitment but an individual behavior (turning over individual resources to group control) and is not surprisingly seen as "most reliably produced" by coercive social control (1987, 59). Hirschman, in contrast to Hechter, defines group solidarity ("loyalty") as a group member continuing "to care about the activity and output of the organization even after he has left it" (1970, 99). Although "irrational" from the vantage point of rational choice theory, such collective commitment is an obviously more realistic description of both the subjective choice and its objective outcome, as political exiles and those who risk their lives for social change constantly demonstrate (Calhoun 1989; McAdam 1986).

Second, all motivations become reduced to incentives, or extrinsic rewards (see Ferree and Miller 1985). These biases produce an incapacity in the theory to recognize individual conflict, ambivalence, and conscious change. When values enter rational choice models of social movements, they do so not as the "metapreferences" that frame choices but as "nonmaterial incentives." Thus perceptions of legitimacy become relabeled incentives (e.g., Muller and Opp 1986) as do beliefs about what is going to happen as a result of the action (e.g., Ennis and Scheuer 1987). All such "incentives" are then modeled as if they were interchangeable, or at least additive, and logically prior to the actions that "follow" from them. But much research demonstrates that two "incentives" are not necessarily better than one. Extrinsic motivators, such as financial rewards or the threat of punishment, tend to be more salient as causes of behavior; when they are present, they tend to reduce the extent to which intrinsic motivators (perceived interest, value, or commitment) are seen as producing behavior both in oneself and in others (Bem 1970). Thus adding external incentives to an intrinsically motivated task can actually *decrease* the amount of effort devoted to it oneself and discredit the motives of others as "merely" self-interested (see Hirschman 1986).

Third, the role that movements play in actively changing individual values is distorted by incentive terminology, when not ignored entirely.

Individual preferences are not a single set of stable values attached to "objective" outcomes but rather the result of contextual frames by which the outcomes are interpreted (see Snow and Bensford 1988). Kahneman and Tversky (1984) used a creative series of social psychological experiments to demonstrate the ubiquity and significance of such framing effects. Confronted with very simple sets of objectively equivalent decisions, subjects expressed notably different preferences depending on the contextual framing of the choice. Thus they were more willing, for example, to "bet $5" to have a chance to "win $100" than they were to "lose $5" or "gain $95" with exactly the same probability as the "bet." Similarly, decisions to act or not were quite different when the result was phrased as "saving 90%" or "losing 10%" of the lives at risk, even though the outcomes are obviously identical. Although these subjects reasoned in consistent and predictable ways, the linguistic context played a much larger role in giving the outcomes meaning, and thus changing their value, than any model of stable preference structures allows.

The rational choice model has encouraged RM researchers to see attitudes or preferences as preexisting and stable structures, logically prior to and predictive of behavior, rather than considering movement organizations as contesting the frames in which choices are perceived (see Ferree and Miller 1985). For example, Klandermans (1988b) emphasizes "consensus mobilization" as a *precondition* for "action mobilization" rather than as a possible outcome of action itself. Hirsch (1986) argues, however, that action mobilization is frequently used to create consensus mobilization rather than the reverse (Bookman and Morgen 1988; Krauss 1989). Social movement organizers themselves have long known that getting people to act can, under some conditions, literally change what and how they see (see Fantasia 1988). For example, Ella Baker distinguished between "organizing" and "mobilizing" on the basis of the extent to which a change in perception in movement actors themselves was the goal (Payne 1989). Feminist organizing in particular has tended to emphasize consciousness-raising experiences, but all movements rely on such processes to some degree (Hirsch 1986).

In sum, the thin view of individual rationality that erases conflict, ambivalence, and other forms of subjective experience in favor of a behaviorist account of incentive-driven action hampers the RM approach in dealing with actual mobilization experiences. The organizational problems of creating structures that will encourage self-restraint of impulse and/or the affirmation of moral commitments are not addressed. Individual identity, expressed in striving to express one's values, and subjective experiences of perceiving, explaining, and evaluating one's own behavior as well as that of others disappear from a rational choice account. External and internal motivators are collapsed and preferences are taken out of their social context and placed inside unchanging individual actors. From this vantage point, RM ends up treating people as empty resources to be mobilized by a strategically rational organization that appears out of the blue and acts as if it were indifferent to the hearts and minds of its members.

Free Riding as a Problem

The only organizational problem people seem to pose for rational choice accounts of mobilization is the need to overcome their supposed tendency to free ride on the efforts of others. The centrality of free riding as a problem for microeconomic models of collective action arises from the premise of individual self-interest as the only meaningful attribute of persons. The economic definition of rationality defines people as essentially asocial; they are assumed to be, by "nature," independent individuals for whom community is problematic. Both from a feminist and from a social constructionist perspective, this model is highly debatable.

As Nancy Hartsock (1983) and other feminist theorists have pointed out, giving theoretical primacy to contract relationships and the choices made by independent individuals is possible only by imagining a "state of nature" made up of unrelated adults (see England 1989; Folbre and Hartmann 1988). But no one is born that way. Our first and most fundamental human relationships are those of trust and dependence as infants, and any society that will reproduce itself has to create the conditions under which such diffuse obligations will be satisfied. If mother-and-child, rather than adult male, is seen as the basic human unit, creating community does not seem so fraught with difficulty, nor does competition seem the archetypal human emotion. Hartsock and others (e.g., Gilligan 1982; England 1989; Elshtain 1982) identify a fundamental androcentric bias in the assumption of independent adults as the basic social actors, rather than acknowledging infant dependency and the human community as our universal history.

Infants are hardly the only people without sufficient resources to survive on their own; individualism has not only a gender but also a class bias, expressing the perspective of the modern bourgeoisie (Calhoun 1988). Evidence about preindustrial societies suggests that most forms of social organization are based in group needs to manage given interdependencies to ensure collective survival rather than in some perception of individual advantage. For example, suicide by individuals who perceive themselves to be a burden to the community is well documented (Briggs 1970). As Folbre and Hartmann (1988) show, even such stalwart proponents of rational choice as Adam Smith and Gary Becker assume the continued necessity

of benevolence and solidarity for the survival of society, but they con-
sign such relations only to the supposedly natural, private, and apolitical
sphere of the family. Kinship societies (pejoratively called primitive) are
understood to operate by similar rules.

Communities such as these come under pressure when confronted with
alternative value systems, such as individual self-interest, but there is no
reason to believe that the values of the market necessarily triumph in all
such confrontations, as Zelizer (1988) points out. But communities based
in diffuse interdependency, and the collective action that sustains them,
may be easier to maintain if unpredictable and potentially unbounded
need is anticipated rather than economic and emotional independence
(Curtis 1986; Calhoun 1988). Even in modern American cities, poor and
working-class households rely on extended networks of diffuse obligation
that rapidly absorb individual windfalls and block individual mobility (see
a review by Rapp 1982). Women, working-class people, and disadvantaged
racial-ethnic groups may be especially likely to reject competitive individualism as a feasible value and put considerable emphasis instead on
maintaining viable networks of relationships. Gilligan (1982) suggests that
a choice between self-interest and altruism as opposite poles of a single
scale makes sense only within the individualist value system; she argues
for the existence of other standards of evaluation in which the good of self
is not separate from the network of care for others. Decision making based
on sustaining relationships as a value, which Gilligan found in the judgments of some women and girls (1982), is also expressed in some African-
American people's affirmation that their participation in the struggle for
survival of the community as such is what gives purpose and meaning to
their lives (see Stack 1986).

For rational choice theory, and RM models based on it, the ability to
come to any sense of the collective good at all is made problematic by beginning with individuals out for themselves and searching for reasons they
should "enter" a community rather than with people who from infancy are
already part of a number of communities of greater and lesser salience.
Even the definition of a collective good is biased by this assumption. Since
in Olson's conventional rational choice account collective goods are defined as those that cannot be limited to persons who contribute (1965), the
rational actor is reluctant to act collectively without additional "selective"
incentives. Hirschman, in contrast, defines collective goods thus: "there
is no escape from consuming them without leaving the community." The
significance of this latter definition is made clear as he goes on to note,
"thus he who says public goods says public evils. . . . what is a public good
for some—say a plentiful supply of police dogs and atomic bombs—may

well be judged a public evil by others in the same community" (1970, 101).

Thus when the definition of collective goods begins from the premise of persons socially located within given communities, public goods automatically involve issues of power and legitimacy—the ability and the right to determine outcomes not only for oneself but for other people. The actor who does *not* act collectively, in this model, abandons to others the right to determine even his or her own individual outcomes, as well as any claim to be acting responsibly or altruistically toward others. Social location implies social construction not only of grievances but of goods, both individual and collective. Within such a social constructionist model, *perceptions* take on a significance that the premise of a single objective reality in rational choice accounts seeks to deny (Klandermans, 1989).

Insofar as definitions of collective goods are other people's definitions of collective bads, the free-rider dilemma that has gripped the imagination of RM theorists appears to be largely chimerical. As is already well documented, mobilization begets countermobilization not by providing selective incentives but by highlighting the threat of collective bads that it would be difficult, if not impossible, to escape (Conover and Gray 1983). Since few, if any, collective outcomes are unambiguously good or bad for everyone in the same way, movements (and their opponents) expend considerable resources in framing the issues and defining the affected community in ways that they perceive will give them a strategic advantage (see Bork 1988; Snow and Bensford 1988; Ennis and Scheuer 1987). Paradoxically, perceived dissensus—not the consensus Olson assumes—may have mobilizing effects (see Gamson, this volume).

Besides the feminist and social constructionist arguments against the theoretical significance of free riding, there is also considerable empirical evidence that selective incentives are unnecessary or even irrelevant in many instances (see the review in Knoke 1988). In practice, when action has a collective purpose (such as influencing federal policy), people participate and contribute to the extent that they value that goal, not because they get anything out of it as individuals (Knoke 1988). When people are pessimistic about the odds of others contributing to a collective goal they value highly, they increase their own contributions (Oliver 1983). Activists may sometimes be annoyed that others fail to contribute as they "should," but this does not seem to be the deterrent to collective action that rational choice theory would predict (see Hirsch, 1986).

Moreover, the free-rider problem presents a radically individualized view of both costs and rewards. Well-socialized actors are not likely to be insensitive to the costs their actions impose on others. For example, some parents are embarrassed when their children are arrested and most

are distraught if they are beaten or killed; fear of such indirect consequences can restrain people who would be willing to take risks on their own
account. But how can the individualistic view of strategic rationality deal
with the fact that some people would apparently prefer to be tortured or
killed themselves than to contribute to the suffering or death of family or
friends (Calhoun 1989)? Only a tautological view of self-interest that gives
other people's lives more utility than one's own in the individual's preference structure will rescue the theory, but at the expense of its empirical
usefulness.

The effects of social ties as restraints on collective action (recognized
but exaggerated by mass-society theories) are apparently more than bal-
anced by their positive contributions. Social networks may have their
well-documented effects on mobilization not only because they provide
an opportunity structure for action but also because collective goods have
positive collective implications. The fact that nonparticipants will also
enjoy a share of the benefit at no additional cost to the participant would
then be seen as enhancing (rather than detracting from) the value of the
collective good. Identity-affirming motives make people enjoy giving gifts
to people they value, thus, people who are well-integrated socially should
tend to get more enjoyment from benefiting other members of the group,
including those who have not contributed or even been able to contribute,
such as future offspring. This contrasts with the rational choice view of
the individual as seeking selfish advantage alone and hence experiencing
nonparticipants' share in the collective good as something negative. Most
social movement participants appear to be what Hirschman (1970) calls
"loyal"—that is, they care about the outcomes enjoyed by the group as a
whole, whether or not they personally share in all of them.

The rational choice premise that "individuals will join in collective action
only when they expect the private benefits to exceed the costs" (Friedman
and McAdam, this volume) appears to be empirically unrealistic, but the
weight of evidence against the free-rider hypothesis has not yet led RM to
abandon it as a theoretical dead end. Instead, there have been attempts
to recast group properties (solidarity, collective identity) as individual incentives, as quasi-material objects that can be controlled, possessed, and
consumed by individuals (e.g., Hechter 1987; Friedman and McAdam,
this volume). But as Knoke has pointed out, "neither affective-bonding
nor normative-conformity motivations can be reduced to utilitarian cost
benefits, except by a tortuous logic that renders the latter concept universal
and, therefore, useless for empirical work" (1988, 315). Whereas collective behavior theories erred by overemphasizing the importance of social
ties as restraining forces on potentially risky social protests (by seeing the

collective costs without noticing the collective rewards), the rational choice model errs by erasing meaningful social ties and thus undervaluing the significance of collective goods for collective action.

Simply adding a "collective incentive" term to the model (e.g., Muller and Opp 1986) does not remedy the basic problem, which is the inability of rational choice theory to explain the variation in the extent to which people share and value a collective identity that fosters a sense of commitment to the good of the group (see Whittier and Taylor, this volume). The radical transformation of consciousness that feminism brought in defining a "group called women" (Cassell 1977) that could gain or lose collectively is dramatic evidence for the significance of such a collective identity (see Mueller 1987). The feminist experience in this regard is somewhat different from that of African-Americans in the civil rights movement. In the latter case, there was less need to develop an awareness that the group itself, rather than individuals within it, was disadvantaged, but both movements struggled to create a sense of positive identity and empowerment (see Morris 1984).

The variable strength of perceived dissensus and of group identity ought to make free riding arise as a significant deterrent to collective action only (1) where consensus is perceived to be great enough that others can be trusted to act reliably on one's behalf or (2) at the individualistic extreme where the group among whom the good (or bad) will be distributed is of little salience or value. Because rational choice theory assumes that this level of consensus and social isolation is typical, it overgeneralizes the ubiquity of the free-rider problem and thus especially distorts the experience of groups that have a history of both conflict and solidarity, such as African-Americans in the United States or ethnic minorities in Eastern Europe. Selective incentive models also make the process of identity transformation and the community building that goes along with it theoretically invisible, which gives a particularly false view of the women's movement (see Buechler 1989; Whittier and Taylor, this volume). Whenever collective identity is important, collective incentives will be important too, and vice versa: when collective goods and bads are disputed, collective identity must be made salient, no matter how difficult that task.

The Pseudo-Universal Individual

When and how is group membership important? Rational choice theory does not typically even attempt to come to terms with this question because it thinks of all individuals as essentially interchangeable units; insofar as they vary, such differences are thought to be idiosyncratic and hence essentially random (e.g., Hechter 1987). Although differences in tastes may be invoked to legitimate different outcomes, the reasons for these differences, whether between groups or individuals, are treated as exogenous and uninteresting (see England 1989). Structural conflicts, when recognized at all, are seen as generating oppositional interests, but not distinctive experiences or perspectives.

In theory, the potential participant in collective action is seen as a pseudo-universal human actor: a person for whom race, class, gender, and historical circumstances do not determine perceptions in any systematic or socially significant way. In practice, this means that the values and perspectives attributed to everyone are those of white middle-class men in Western capitalist systems (see Hartsock 1983; Hess 1989; Jaggar 1989). The supposedly universal attributes of human nature that form the basis of reasoning and choosing are those that are understood simultaneously to best describe relatively affluent white men. Thus the self-interest claimed as universal is also historically grounded in a system that prescribed that women should be "selfless," that nonwhites and women should be "protected" rather than self-determining, and that other cultures were "primitive" and "backward" because they did not operate by these rules (see Folbre and Hartmann 1988).

Offering this particular perspective as a universal rationality erases the possibility of other ways of seeing the world or discredits them as less rational or less fully human (see Gilligan 1982). The issue here is not the distribution of individual motivation but the theoretical validity of alternative ways of seeing the world, shaped in alternative experiences of reality. Rational choice theory fails to recognize its own premises as being socially determined and group specific. In contrast, feminist and social constructionist perspectives argue that *all* values, including those that appear to be "natural" and "objective," rest in social experience of some sort. As Farganis puts it, "individuals are not divorced from time and place, housed in some conflict-free world populated only by themselves. Instead, individuals, men and women, are historically embodied concrete persons whose perspective is a consequence of who they are. . . . thought bears the marks of a thinker's social characteristics and how these are socially regarded" (1988, 208). Feminist theory emphasizes that the values that appear most "natural" and "objective" today are those derived from the experiences of nineteenth-century, white, Western, middle-class men (e.g., Hartsock 1983). Rational choice theory itself embodies such values.

One historically constructed value central to the rational choice perspective and especially significant for social movement theory is the false dichotomy imposed on reason and emotion (see Jaggar 1989; Hess 1989). Hirschman (1977) documents in detail how the accounts of behavior that arose after capitalism employed this division uniquely to exempt self-interest from being a value or expressing an emotion. Once a "passion" like others, by the nineteenth century self-interest had become the sole value accepted as "rational" and "dispassionate." The separation of reason from emotion is not value-neutral; emotionality is denigrated, along with the persons of whom it is thought to be characteristic: women and the "lower orders" of men (see the review in Jaggar 1989). The split between reason and emotion mapped onto gender is also tied to other cultural dichotomies: strong/weak; cold/warm; separate/connected; public/private.

Rational choice theory affirms this division as natural and shows a decided preference for one side. It defines cold, dispassionate calculation as the preferred mode of accurate decision making and emotion as something that interferes with good decisions (for contrary evidence, see Taylor 1981). It typically contrasts "sentimental attachments" against "rational interests" and thus not only devalues the former but obscures the ways in which community relations and rootedness are, for many people, inseparable from their self-interest (Calhoun 1988).

The implicit devaluation of emotion in social movements as an indication of irrationality could thus be carried over unchallenged from the collective behavior school (which thought it typical) to resource mobilization (which thinks it rare). The historically constructed cultural prejudice that to describe behavior as emotional is to discredit it remained unexamined and thus can continue to be directed against women and other marginal groups. For example, the language and imagery of "defense" planners are rich in feeling about the beauty of the weapons and competitive advantage in the size of the stockpile, but this is defined as "rational," whereas those who express concern about casualties are dismissed as "merely" emotional (Cohn 1987). The critique of instrumental reason characteristic of many "new" social movements (e.g., Jasper and Poulsen 1989; Cohen 1985) thus fails to be incorporated in RM's own theoretical perspective and a particular point of view becomes universalized as the objective description of the situation.

In contrast, Jaggar argues that oppressed people particularly need and value emotions as a means of affirming the values and people that the rational standards of the culture demean. When rationality is defined to include the reasoned choice of values as well as the selection of means, emotion may be an indispensable aid rather than a hindrance to reliable judgment (Taylor 1981; Fiske 1981). Jaggar argues that "emotions provide the experiential basis for values. If we had no emotional responses to the world, it is inconceivable that we should ever come to value one state of affairs more highly than another" (1989, 153). From direct emotional experiences, such as anger or joy, people acquire their own perspectives and learn either to challenge or to respect the definition of value provided by the hegemonic (patriarchal, racist) order.

Contemporary feminism has been particularly concerned with consciously and deliberately constructing perspectives on social life grounded in women's own experiences. "Culture" as a term expresses this integration of experience, knowledge, and emotion that many groups in society feel they enjoy, and the study of groups as cultureless aggregates of pseudo-universal individuals systematically prevents RM from dealing with the practical decision-making constraints that culture imposes (Oberschall 1989; Ennis 1987). Resource mobilization theory appears to have particular difficulty in dealing with the women's movement, perhaps because the attempt to integrate reason and emotion, both in theory and in the practices of organizing, plays such a central role (e.g., Warnock 1982; Fisher 1984). As social movement theory increasingly attempts to deal with issues such as the formation of "oppositional consciousness" (Morris, this volume), it may find the feminist perspective offers useful models of the relations among values, knowledge, and social position (see Rose 1983; Jaggar 1989; Farganis 1988). Such approaches could dissolve the rigid dichotomy imposed between "instrumental" and "expressive" behavior and begin to account for some of the frames issues acquire in the historical experience of contending groups.

ALTERNATIVES TO RATIONAL CHOICE THEORY

In view of the significant limitations of rational choice theory in its conception of human nature, the collective good, and reason itself, one might wonder why RM researchers persist in attempting to apply it to social movements. Hirschman (1986) describes the seductiveness of rational choice as its illusion of parsimony: the persistent failure of its simple models to fit empirically can be disguised by relabeling everything as some form of self-interest or incentive. But attempts to develop more realistic accounts of even narrowly economic behavior currently abound (see reviews in Etzioni 1988; Taylor 1988; Zelizer 1988), suggesting that the limits of this strategy are increasingly evident. These current, more complex views of the market suggest that all human behavior involves complex overlays of moral commitment and the pursuit of pleasure, and of self-interest and reciprocal regard (Folbre and Hartmann 1988).

Efforts to develop less reductionist and more empirically useful models have begun to move in the direction of including more structural and contextual variables (e.g., Lawler, Ridgeway, and Markovsky 1989; Kelley 1983). Rather than beginning from the premise of asocial individuals for whom any form of collective action is problematic, they presume that people are structurally located (e.g., Calhoun 1989). Their given position in organizations and in relation to macro-social conflicts is seen to affect their perceptions and values, as well as their ability to act on them (e.g., Perrow 1986). Moreover, rather than beginning from a static and essentialist view of an objectively perceived reality, context is essential to perception (e.g., Kahneman and Tversky 1984), perception is grounded in relationship and change (e.g., Lappin 1981), and emotional responsiveness is an integral part of the process of perception (e.g., Fiske 1981).

The postulate that individuals are self-interested, which rational choice theory makes a primary and universal attribute of human nature, can be reexamined more fruitfully in the form of testable hypotheses about the structural conditions under which material self-interest will emerge as a characteristic or dominant value. Such structures may be the societal context in which the movement as a whole operates, or they may reflect the internal group processes of specific movement organizations. A "post-RM" view of rationality as historically and structurally constituted will have to consider both of these levels. This, of course, demands considering structures that systematically foster other-regarding and/or identity-affirming behaviors instead.

Society as Structure

At the level of social context, Curtis reminds us, "social scientists have long thought that contractual social relationships based on economic exchange were not the only kind and that contractual relationships have only come to dominate in relatively recent history" (1986, 175). He extends the familiar model of Gemeinschaft and Gesellschaft by drawing out the implications of the persistence of social rules of generalized obligation and long-term trust in a society now dominated by economic definitions of rationality. For example, women can be charged with the moral obligation to maintain noncalculating behavior as a "haven in a heartless world" for men and yet also be penalized for doing so. Under each set of rules certain behaviors are "unthinkable" and certain uses of resources illegitimate, but neither economic nor social exchange rules apply universally.

Curtis (1986) emphasizes that social and economic exchange are both legitimate normative systems, but that they inherently contradict each other. What is expected in one is disallowed in the other (as women routinely learn in divorce court). Control over *resources* leads to power in

economic systems, but uncollected *debts* (or favors) are the sources of leverage in social exchange. In economic exchange, "relationships come to be
defined as if they were commodities" (1986, 176); in social exchange commodities are valued because of the relationship within which they were
transferred ("sentimental value"). Economic exchange is specific and en-
forceable; social exchange is based in generalized goodwill and trust in a
person and a relationship.

Because noneconomic exchange has an open-ended quality, Curtis sees
it as especially relevant for "people whose resources are variable and uncertain" (1986, 176). He argues that poor and working-class communities
often find sharing whatever one has today in the expectation that one
may need unlimited help at some future time to be their most reasonable
principle of exchange (see Stack 1974; Calhoun 1988). African-American
and other racial-ethnic and poor communities seem especially likely to
be found to follow these rules, even at the cost of individual advantage
(see review in Rapp 1982). This may be a reflection both of structure (the
current uncertainty of resources) and of culture (the group's history of
reliance on communal networks).

Rather than emphasizing Gemeinschaft as the distinguishing characteristic of families and traditional societies per se, Curtis notes that "social
exchange is not unusual in the marketplace and economic exchange is
not unusual in families" (1986, 177). Trading favors and creating debts
are also frequently important in political parties and movement organizations. People engaged in a collective enterprise "must lay plans about
unknown events far in the future. They cannot, therefore, rely on current
economic exchanges, but must try to establish some basis for trust in one
another" (Curtis 1986, 175). Structurally, the longer the time horizon and
the riskier the situation, the more actors should rely on social rules and
encourage the development of trust. For example, when members of the
Student Non-Violent Coordinating Committee reflect that "we would have
died for each other," they are expressing a diffuse but intense social obligation of long-term trust in a situation of high risk (McAdam 1986). Debts
and relationships, in addition to resources and commodities, are crucial to
understanding these mobilization processes.

Organizational Form as Structure

These different forms of relationship may also be grounded
in the organizational structure of the movement itself. Rothschild-Whitt
(1979) highlights the organizational forms and basis of authority associated
with formal (or instrumental) rationality and substantive (or value) rationality. She contrasts the group processes of collectivist organizations with

those of bureaucracies: bureaucracies tend toward role-based, segmented, instrumental relationships between people, whereas value-rational organizations attempt to create community, that is, relationships that are holistic, affective, and ends in themselves. This means that the values and priorities of instrumental rationality conflict, normatively and organizationally, with value-rationality.

Many, but not all, social movement organizations struggle to maintain a value-rational structure in which people are treated holistically, division of labor is minimized, and authority is vested in the group as a whole (e.g., Downey 1986; Ryan 1989; Newman 1980). Downey, for example, describes how an identity as "persons opposed to relations of domination" led members of the Clamshell Alliance to insist on certain organizational principles; many members preferred to see Clamshell fail to achieve particular instrumental objectives than to sacrifice the goal of achieving a nonoppressive internal structure (1986). Similar values are central to the collective identity of many radical feminists, who believe that "as women" they cannot participate in structures that are hierarchical and strive for alternative forms of organization that are more compatible with this identity (Martin 1990; Ryan 1989; Baker 1982). Ryan (1989), for example, points out that the feminists with a history of involvement in the New Left had a self-definition as "radicals" that led them to differentiate themselves from "mainstream" feminists more on this dimension of organizational structure than on specific programmatic points.

Perrow (1986) takes a different tack in connecting structure to principles of rationality. Rather than focusing on how principles lead to the selection of organizational forms, he emphasizes how organizational structure shapes the relative value of self- and other-regarding behavior and offers specific testable propositions about the characteristics of organizations, rather than of individuals, that should be expected to produce more or less altruistic decisions. Many of the characteristics of capitalist firms are those that Perrow predicts will encourage self-interest: continuing interaction is minimized, rewards can be stored over time, individual contributions are measured, interdependent efforts are limited, authority relations are stable and generalized across situations, and tall hierarchies of authority and reward are favored (1986, 16–17). Analogies between such firms and social movements suggest, incorrectly, that there are not characteristic differences in structure between them; in practice social movements show a great variety of organizational types (see Martin 1990) and the type of structure itself influences organizational goals and activities (Staggenborg 1988).

In sum, this analysis suggests that ideologies and identities that affirm principles other than self-interest encourage value-rational participants to develop organizations consistent with their beliefs. Such organizations will tend not to measure individual contribution, not allow accumulation of advantages, and not generalize authority relations in stable, tall structures; they should therefore be characterized by a higher proportion of other-regarding actions. The prevalence of bureaucratically structured organizations and the individual utilitarian calculus in our society, these movements remind us, can make being structured like a profit-making company appear natural. Analysts of social movements, however, need to challenge both these hegemonic social constructions if they are to be "at least as rational" as the social movement participants they study.

CONCLUSIONS

This chapter has attempted to move social movement theory beyond the current limitations of RM to a more multidimensional and empirically useful view of rationality. Rational choice theory has been specifically critiqued for introducing a model of human nature that treats people as abstract individuals, thus universalizing the experience and perspective of white, Western, middle-class men. Rational choice theory thus introduces a significant but largely invisible political bias to the resource mobilization framework. The narrow definition of what is rational excludes the principles, goals, and means of expression that have been historically favored by subordinated groups.

The thin, implausible, and politically biased version of rationality discussed here is a Trojan horse, not a straw person. Although specific departures from some of the assumptions of the rational choice model are frequently made, the underlying premises of rational choice are evident in the language and overall research agenda of RM, its focus on incentives, obsession with free riding, distrust of emotionality, and excessively bureaucratic view of social movement organizations. From this perspective, one sees social movements as ad hoc groups of self-interested, pseudo-universal individuals calculating their short-term gains and losses.

In contrast, I have argued that a "post-RM" view could recognize that there are different types of rationality associated with different forms of social organization. The formal organizations and calculating economic exchange relationships that are so prominent in current RM literature exist, of course, but as an expression of only one of several types of rational behavior for both men and women. An expanded view of rationality considers impulsive and identity-affirming acts to be expressing different principles than self-interest, but to be equally significant for the development of movement structures and strategies.

This approach to rationality would certainly lead the RM research agenda in a new direction, without sacrificing its significant emphasis on social structure. The dictum that "social movement participants are as rational as those who study them" can be especially revealing if it is taken literally, that is, not as a claim to absolute or universal rationality on either side of the equation but as a challenge to consider the advantages and limitations of commitment to certain values and assumptions on the part of scholars and activists alike.

REFERENCES

Baker, Andrea. 1982. "The Problem of Authority in Radical Movement Groups: A Case Study in Lesbian Feminist Organization." *Journal of Applied Behavioral Science* 18:323–41.

Bem, Darryl. 1970. *Beliefs, Attitudes and Human Affairs*. Belmont, Calif.: Brooks/Cole.

Bookman, Ann, and Sandra Morgen. 1988. *Women and the Politics of Empowerment*. Philadelphia: Temple University Press.

Bork, Kathy. 1988. "The Selling of the Gender Gap: The Role of Organized Feminism." In Carol Mueller, ed., *The Politics of the Gender Gap*. Beverly Hills, Calif.: Sage.

Breines, Wini. 1982. *Community and Organization in the New Left*. New York: Praeger.

Brickman, P., R. Folger, E. Goode, and Y. Schul. 1981. "Microjustice and Macrojustice." In M. Lerner and S. Lerner, eds., *The Justice Motive in Social Behavior*. New York: Plenum.

Briggs, Jean. 1970. *Never in Anger*. Cambridge, Mass.: Harvard University Press.

Buechler, Steven. 1989. "Organization and Community in Women's Movements: An Historical Overview." Paper presented at the meeting of the American Sociological Association.

Calhoun, Craig. 1988. "The Radicalism of Tradition and the Question of Class Struggle." In Michael Taylor, ed., *Rationality and Revolution*. New York: Cambridge University Press.

———. 1989. "The Problem of Identity in Collective Action." Paper presented at the meeting of the American Sociological Association.

Cassell, Joan. 1977. *A Group Called Women: Sisterhood and Symbolism in the Feminist Movement*. New York: David McKay.

Cohen, Jean. 1985. "Strategy or Identity: New Theoretical Paradigms and Contemporary Social Movements." *Social Research* 52:663–716.

Cohn, Carol. 1987. "Sex and Death in the Rational World of Defense Intellectuals." *Signs* 12, no. 4:687–718.

Conover, Pamela, and Virginia Gray. 1983. *Feminism and the New Right*. New York: Praeger.

Curtis, Richard. 1986. "Household and Family in Theory on Inequality." *American Sociological Review* 51:168–83.

Downey, Gary L. 1986. "Ideology and the Clamshell Identity: Organizational Dilemmas in the Anti-Nuclear Power Movement." *Social Problems* 33, no. 5:357–73.

Elshtain, Jean Bethke, 1982. "Thank Heaven for Little Girls: The Dialectics of Female Development." In Jean Bethke Elshtain, ed., *The Family in Political Thought*. Amherst: University of Massachusetts Press.

England, Paula. 1989. "A Feminist Critique of Rational Choice: Implications for Sociology." *American Sociologist* 20, no. 1:14–28.

Ennis, James. 1987. "Fields of Action: Structure in Movements' Tactical Repertoires." *Sociological Forum* 2, no. 3:520–33.

Ennis, James, and Richard Scheuer. 1987. "Mobilizing Weak Support for Social Movements: The Role of Grievance, Efficacy and Cost." *Social Forces* 62, no. 2: 390–409.

Etzioni, Amitai. 1988. *The Moral Dimension: Toward a New Economics*. New York: Free Press.

Fantasia, Richard. 1988. *Cultures of Solidarity*. Berkeley: University of California Press.

Farganis, Sondra. 1988. "Feminism and the Reconstruction of Social Science." In Alison Jaggar and Susan Bordo, eds., *Gender/Body/Knowledge: Feminist Reconstrutions of Being and Knowing*. New Brunswick, N.J.: Rutgers University Press.

Ferguson, Kathy. 1984. *The Feminist Case against Bureaucracy*. Philadelphia: Temple University Press.

Ferree, Myra Marx, and Frederick Miller. 1985. "Mobilization and Meaning: Toward an Integration of Social Psychological and Resource Perspectives on Social Movements." *Sociological Inquiry* 55, no. 1:38–61.

Fireman, Bruce, and William Gamson. 1979. "Utilitarian Logic in the Resource Mobilization Perspective." In Mayer Zald and John McCarthy, eds., *The Dynamics of Social Movements*. Cambridge, Mass.: Winthrop.

Fisher, Berenice. 1984. "Guilt and Shame in the Women's Movement: The Radical Ideal of Action and Its Meaning for Feminist Intellectuals." *Feminist Studies* 10:185–212.

Fiske, Susan. 1981. "Social Cognition and Affect." In John Harvey, ed., *Cognition, Social Behavior and the Environment*. Hillsdale, N.J.: Erlbaum, 227–64.

Folbre, Nancy, and Heidi Hartmann. 1988. "The Rhetoric of Self-Interest: Selfishness, Altruism and Gender in Economic Theory." In Arjo Klamer, Donald McCloskey, and Robert Solow, eds., *The Consequences of Economic Rhetoric*. New York: Cambridge University Press.

Frank, Robert. 1987. "Shrewdly Irrational." *Sociological Forum* 2, no. 1:21–41.

Gilligan, Carol. 1982. *In a Different Voice*. Cambridge, Mass.: Harvard University Press.

Hartsock, Nancy. 1983. *Money, Sex and Power*. New York: Longman.

Hechter, Michael. 1987. *Principles of Group Solidarity*. Berkeley: University of California Press.

Hess, Beth. 1989. "Beyond Dichotomy: Making Distinctions and Recognizing Differences." Presidential address at the meeting of the Eastern Sociological Society.

Hirsch, Eric. 1986. "The Creation of Political Solidarity in Social Movement Organizations." *Sociological Quarterly* 27:373–87.

Hirschman, A. O. 1970. *Exit, Voice and Loyalty*. Cambridge, Mass.: Harvard University Press.

———. 1977. *The Passions and the Interests: Political Arguments for Capitalism before Its Triumph*. Princeton: Princeton University Press.

———. 1986. *Rival Views of Market Society and Other Essays*. New York: Viking.

Jaggar, Alison. 1989. "Love and Knowledge: Emotion in Feminist Epistemology."

In Alison Jaggar and Susan Bordo, eds., *Gender/Body/Knowledge: Feminist Reconstructions of Being and Knowing*. New Brunswick, N.J.: Rutgers University Press, 145–71.

Jasper, James, and Jane Poulsen. 1989. "Animal Rights and Anti-Nuclear Protest: Condensing Symbols and the Critique of Instrumental Reason." Photocopy.

Kahneman, Daniel, and Amos Tversky. 1984. "Choices, Values and Frames." *American Psychologist* 39, no. 4:341–50.

Kelley, H. H. 1983. "The Situational Origins of Human Tendencies: A Further Reason for the Formal Analysis of Structures." *Personality and Social Psychology Bulletin* 9, no. 1:8–30.

Klandermans, Bert. 1988a. "Mobilization into Social Movements: Synthesizing European and American Approaches." In Bert Klandermans, Hanspeter Kriesi, and Sidney Tarrow, eds., *From Structure to Action: Comparing Social Movement Research across Cultures*. International Social Movement Research, vol. 1. Greenwich, Conn.: JAI Press.

———. 1988b. "The Formation and Mobilization of Consensus." In Bert Klandermans, Hanspeter Kriesi, and Sidney Tarrow, eds., *From Structure to Action: Comparing Social Movement Research across Cultures*. International Social Movement Research, vol. 1. Greenwich, Conn.: JAI Press.

———. 1989. "Grievance Interpretation and Success Expectations: The Social Construction of Protest." *Social Behavior* 4:113–25.

Knoke, David. 1988. "Incentives in Collective Action Organizations." *American Sociological Review* 53, no. 3:311–29.

Krauss, Celene. 1989. "Community Struggles and the Shaping of Democratic Consciousness." *Sociological Forum* 4, no. 2:227–39.

Lappin, Joseph. 1981. "The Relativity of Perception, Choice and Social Knowledge." In John Harvey, ed., *Cognition, Social Behavior and the Environment*. Hillsdale, N.J.: Erlbaum, 341–72.

Lawler, Edward, Cecelia Ridgeway, and Barry Markovsky. 1989. "Structural Social Psychology: An Approach to the Micro-Macro Problem." Paper presented at the meeting of the American Sociological Association.

Martin, Patricia Yancey. 1990. "Rethinking Feminist Organizations." *Gender & Society* 4, no. 2:182–206.

McAdam, Doug. 1986. "Recruitment to High-Risk Activism: The Case of Freedom Summer." *American Journal of Sociology* 92, no. 1:64–90.

McCarthy, John, and Mayer Zald. 1977. "Resource Mobilization and Social Movements." *American Journal of Sociology* 82:1212–41.

McNall, Scott. 1987. "Thinking about Social Class: Structure, Organization and Consciousness." In Rhonda Levine and Jerry Lembcke, eds., *Recapturing Marxism: An Appraisal of Recent Trends in Sociological Theory*. New York: Praeger, 223–45.

Morris, Aldon D.. 1984. *The Origins of the Civil Rights Movement*. New York: Free Press.

———. 1989. "Reflections on Social Movement Scholarship." Paper presented at the meeting of the Eastern Sociological Society.

Morris, Aldon D., and Cedric Herring. 1987. "Theory and Research in Social Movements: A Critical Review." In Samuel Long, ed., *Annual Review of Political Science*. Vol. 2. Norwood, N.J.: Ablex.

Mueller, Carol. 1987. "Collective Consciousness, Identity Transformation and the

Rise of Women in Public Office in the U.S." In Mary Katzenstein and Carol Mueller, eds., *The Women's Movements of the United States and Western Europe*. Philadelphia: Temple University Press, 89–108.

Muller, E., and Karl-Dieter Opp. 1986. "Rational Choice and Rebellious Collective Action." *American Political Science Review* 80:471–86.

Newman, Katherine. 1980. "Incipient Bureaucracy: The Development of Hierarchy in Egalitarian Organizations." In Gerald Britan and R. Cohen, eds., *Hierarchy and Society: Anthropological Perspectives on Bureaucracy*. Philadelphia: Institute for the Study of Human Issues.

Oberschall, Anthony. 1973. *Social Conflict and Social Movements*. Englewood Cliffs, N.J.: Prentice-Hall.

———. 1989. "Culture Change and Social Movements." Paper presented at the meeting of the American Sociological Association.

Oliver, Pamela. 1983. "The Mobilization of Paid and Volunteer Activists in the Neighborhood Movement." *Research in Social Movements: Conflict and Change* 5: 133–70.

Olson, Mancur. 1965. *The Logic of Collective Action*. Cambridge, Mass.: Harvard University Press.

Payne, Charles. 1989. "Ella Baker and Models of Social Change." *Signs* 14, no. 4: 885–89.

Perrow, Charles. 1986. "Economic Theories of Organization." *Theory and Society* 15:11–45.

Rapp, Rayna. 1982. "Family and Class in Contemporary America: Notes toward an Understanding of Ideology." In Barrie Thorne with Marilyn Yalom, eds., *Rethinking the Family*. New York: Longman.

Rose, Hilary. 1983. "Hand, Brain and Heart: A Feminist Epistemology for the Natural Sciences." *Signs* 9, no. 1:73–90.

Rothschild-Whitt, Joyce. 1979. "The Collectivist Organization: An Alternative to Rational-Bureaucratic Models." *American Sociological Review* 44:509–27.

Ryan, Barbara. 1989. "Ideological Purity and Feminism: The U.S. Women's Movement from 1966 to 1975." *Gender & Society* 3, no. 2:239–57.

Sen, Amartya. 1977. "Rational Fools." *Philosophy and Public Affairs* 6, no. 4:317–44.

Snow, David, and Robert Benford. 1988. "Ideology, Frame Resonance and Participant Mobilization." In Bert Klandermans, Hanspeter Kriesi, and Sidney Tarrow, eds., *From Structure to Action: Comparing Social Movement Research across Cultures*. International Social Movement Research, vol. 1. Greenwich, Conn.: JAI Press.

Snow, David, Burke Rochford, Steven Worden, and Robert Benford. 1986. "Frame Alignment Processes, Micro-Mobilization and Movement Participation." *American Sociological Review* 51:464–81.

Stack, Carol. 1974. *All Our Kin*. New York: Harper and Row.

———. 1986. "The Culture of Gender: Women and Men of Color." *Signs* 11, no. 2:321–24.

Staggenborg, Suzanne. 1988. "The Consequences of Professionalization and Formalization in the Pro-Choice Movement." *American Sociological Review* 53, no. 4: 585–605.

Taylor, Michael. 1988. "Rationality and Revolutionary Collective Action." In Michael Taylor, ed., *Rationality and Revolution*. New York: Cambridge University Press, 63–97.

Taylor, Shelley. 1981. "The Interface of Cognitive and Social Psychology." In

John Harvey, ed., *Cognition, Social Behavior and the Environment*. Hillsdale, N.J.: Erlbaum, 341–72.

Warnock, Donna. 1982. "Mobilizing Emotions: Organizing the Women's Pentagon Action." *Socialist Review* 12, nos. 3–4:37–47.

Whittier, Nancy, and Verta Taylor. 1989. "Social Movement Culture and Identity Transformation: Collective Identity in Lesbian Feminist Communities." Paper presented at the meeting of the American Sociological Association.

Zelizer, Viviana. 1988. "Beyond the Polemics on the Market: Establishing a Theoretical and Empirical Agenda." *Sociological Forum* 3, no. 4:614–34.

3

The Social Psychology of
Collective Action

W i l l i a m   A .   G a m s o n

Social psychology bashing among students of social movements is over. It had its day, and with good reason. Movement participants saw social psychology used to disparage their motives and their good sense. In some hands it seemed naive and reductionist, diverting attention from underlying structural conditions of conflict and oppression. Many American social scientists, reacting especially to that part of the collective behavior tradition flowing from Gustave Le Bon and other antidemocratic theorists of the nineteenth and early twentieth centuries, seemed ready to reject the entire social psychological project. One writer, for example, called the collective behavior tradition "stultifying" and a "straightjacket" for the study of social protest.[1]

In the United States, the 1970s were the decade of organizational theory and utilitarian economic models in the study of social movements. Problems of ideology and the emergence of shared beliefs of injustice were given short shrift. "Ideas and beliefs that have a revolutionary potential are usually present and are available for use by a protest leadership. Sentiments of opposition, of being wronged, are also frequently present in the lower orders and can be easily linked with the more elaborate ideologies and world views," wrote Oberschall (1973, 133–34). Similarly, McCarthy and Zald argued that a focus on discontent is misplaced since there is

I am indebted to David Croteau, Josh Gamson, Hanna Herzog, William Hoynes, Bert Klandermans, Sharon Kurtz, Aldon Morris, Mary Murphy, Charlotte Ryan, Ted Sasson, Cassie Schwerner, David Stuart, and Ralph Turner for helpful comments and criticisms on earlier drafts of this chapter.
    1. See Gamson (1990, 130), the first edition of which appeared in 1975.

always enough "to supply the grass roots support for a movement," and "grievances and discontent may be defined, created, and manipulated by issue entrepreneurs and organizations" (1977, 1215).

But as social movement theory continued to encounter the movements of the 1970s and 1980s, social psychology emerged again with such vigor that it has now become a major frontier. By the mid-1980s, Klandermans was asserting that "resource mobilization theory went too far in nearly abandoning the social-psychological analysis of social movements" (1984, 583–84), and Cohen was asking "Hasn't the critique of the collective behavior tradition thrown out the baby with the bathwater by excluding the analysis of values, norms, ideologies, projects, culture, and identity in other than instrumental terms?" (1985, 688).

This distrust of social psychology was largely limited to the emerging resource mobilization approach in the United States. New social movement theorists in Europe had no need to exorcise the long-departed ghost of Le Bon and his ilk. Their dialectic was not with heavily social psychological mass society and collective behavior theory but with various strains of Marxist theory whose social psychology was primitive and undeveloped. Nor did theorists of third world liberation movements need to escape from any social psychological straightjackets.

The resurgent social psychology has jettisoned the old baggage of irrationality and social pathology. Even the American collective behavior tradition has been cleansed of the idea that social movements are the destructive outbursts of "people going crazy together" (Martin 1920). In the "emergent norm" approach of Turner and Killian (1987), the process by which mobilization for collective action occurs becomes the central problem. The authors repudiate the idea that such action is more emotional or irrational than institutionalized forms. Emotion and reason are not irreconcilables, they argue. "To attempt to divide the actions of individuals into 'rational' versus 'emotional' or 'irrational' types is to deny the complexity of human behavior" (14).

None of this social psychology denies the importance of organization, social location, and the calculation of costs and benefits by movement actors. But there is an increasing recognition that an exclusive focus on such components leaves some of the most critical and difficult questions unanswered. As Ferree and Miller write, "Costs and benefits play a role in generating movement support, but the translation of objective social relationships into subjectively experienced group interests is also critical in building movements, as in political activity generally" (1985, 39).

Many of the major questions animating contemporary work on social movements are intrinsically social psychological. Cohen (1985) has suggested three central problematics—collective identity, solidarity, and consciousness—to which we can add a fourth that cross-cuts all of them: micromobilization. This chapter will attempt to show, for each of these topics, its roots in a more generic social psychological literature that is not focused on social movements, how the ideas have manifested themselves in recent social movement writings, and the unresolved questions and major puzzles that need our attention.

Of course, there is not one social psychological tradition but several. In addressing questions on social movements, both psychological and sociological traditions have something to say at different points and we need awareness of both. My own tradition is an interdisciplinary one that is concerned with the interaction between different levels of analysis. This tradition begins with the distinctions among personality, social, and cultural systems: social psychological questions are those involving the mesh between self and society.

Each of the central problematics—collective identity, solidarity, consciousness, and micromobilization—concerns this mesh. In practice, the processes are thoroughly interwoven, but the distinction is useful analytically. Collective identity concerns the mesh between the individual and cultural systems. More specifically, the question is how individuals' sense of who they are becomes engaged with a definition shared by coparticipants in some effort at social change—that is, with who "we" are.

Solidarity, as defined here, concerns the mesh between individual and social system. More specifically, the question is how individuals develop and maintain loyalty and commitment to collective actors—that is, to groups or organizations who act as carriers of social movements. Consciousness also involves a mesh between individual and cultural levels. The question here is how the meaning that individuals give to a social situation becomes a shared definition implying collective action.

Micromobilization examines the microevents that operate in linking individual and sociocultural levels in the operation of identity, solidarity, and consciousness processes. It is social psychological in its attempt to understand the social interaction and group processes involved in collective action.

Much of the social movement work discussed below is by those who have no disciplinary identification with social psychology, but this is irrelevant to my argument. The questions, not the answers, are social psychological, and one must look to many different disciplines and traditions to understand how individual and social processes mesh.

COLLECTIVE IDENTITY

Social psychologists have always emphasized the centrality of social relationships and social location in the development of personal identity. Indeed, in the old pathological tradition in the study of social movements, identity theory provided the crucial link between social system breakdown and collective action. It is expressed most clearly in such classics as Fromm's *Escape from Freedom* (1941).

In cruder hands, such as Hoffer's *The True Believer* (1951), movements were seen in general as providing a substitute for a spoiled identity. "The frustrated follow a leader," Hoffer writes, "less because of their faith that he is leading them to a promised land than because of the immediate feeling that he is leading them away from their unwanted selves. Surrender to a leader is not a means to an end but a fulfillment" (116).

Cleansed of its assumptions about a spoiled or ersatz identity, there is a central insight that remains. Participation in social movements frequently involves an enlargment of personal identity for participants and offers fulfillment and realization of self. Participation in the civil rights movement, women's movement, and New Left, for example, was frequently a transformative experience, central to the self-definition of many participants in their later lives.

Work in the American resource mobilization tradition has been slow to recognize and address issues of personal and collective identity. But the opposite has been true for European writers who emphasize the centrality of identity issues in such "new" social movements as the environmental, antinuclear, and peace movements.[2] Their central message is only a paraphrase away from the Hoffer quotation above: "Participation in a social movement is not only a means to an end but a fulfillment."

For my purposes here, Melucci (1989) is the best exemplar of those writing in this tradition. He not only has an especially rich discussion of identity issues but also is most explicit in his social psychological orientation. He describes his arguments as deliberately cutting "a circuitous path between collective social and political processes and the subjective personal experiences of everyday life." Furthermore, Melucci's arguments are the most successful in combining elements of what Cohen (1985) calls "identity-oriented" and "strategically-oriented" paradigms.

Melucci suggests that the construction of a collective identity is the most central task of "new" social movements. This is a negotiated process in

2. For good reviews of the new social movement literature, see especially Cohen (1985) and Klandermans and Tarrow (1988)

which the "we" involved in collective action is elaborated and given meaning. New social movement theorists emphasize the reflexivity of these movements—that is, their tendency to ask themselves explicit questions about "who we are." They argue that, since the participants do not define themselves in terms of their common social location in a class or ethnic group, the question is intrinsically problematic.

Some nascent movement groups will fail to produce any collective identity that engages the participants' self-definition, but others are quite successful. "This on-going process of construction of a sense of 'we' can succeed for various reasons," Melucci writes, "for instance, because of effective leadership, workable organizational forms or strong reserves of expressive action. But it can also fail, in which case collective action disintegrates" (1989, 218).

Melucci's central point is not simply the strategic one that a strong sense of collective identity is instrumental to the success of collective action but that it is a goal in its own right requiring us to rethink the concept of success. He argues against "an exclusively political view centered on the 'instrumental' dimension of action" because it treats "as 'expressive' or residual the self-reflective investments of the movements" (1989, 73–74). The creation of an ongoing collective identity that maintains the loyalty and commitment of participants is a cultural achievement in its own right, regardless of its contribution to the achievement of political and organizational goals.

The "we" that these movements construct is adversarial but not necessarily "political" because they "challenge the logic of complex systems on cultural grounds. . . . Linking personal change with external action, collective action functions as a new medium which illuminates the silent and arbitrary elements of the dominant codes as well as publicizes new alternatives" (Melucci, 1989, 23 and 63).

Nothing in this argument denies that social movement actors make strategic judgments based on their expectations about costs and benefits. The point is, rather, that any strategic paradigm necessarily presupposes a theory of identity. Assumptions about social identity are implicit. In individual utilitarian models such as Olson's (1965), the absence of a collective identity is assumed. This assumption ignores much of what we know about the social definition of identity and its impact on individual preference structures. When people bind their fate to the fate of a group, they feel personally threatened when the group is threatened. Solidarity and collective identity operate to blur the distinction between individual and group interest, undermining the premises on which such utilitarian models operate.

But even in more sophisticated rational actor models that postulate a *collective* actor making strategic judgments of cost and benefit about collective action, the existence of an *established* collective identity is assumed. As Melucci observes, "Only if individual actors can recognize their coherence and continuity as actors will they be able to write their own script of social reality and compare expectations and outcomes." Expectations are socially constructed and outcomes can be evaluated only by actors "who are capable of defining themselves and the field of their action. The process of constructing, maintaining, and altering a collective identity provides the basis for actors to shape their expectations and calculate the costs and benefits of their action" (1989, 32 and 34).

Blind Spots in New Social Movement Theory

Having granted the helpfulness of this paradigm in highlighting important issues of meshing personal and collective identities, let me turn to its own blind spots, crystallized in the term *new social movements.* The term is objectionable on several fundamental grounds.

First, it privileges one particular, albeit interesting, subset of social movements that happen to be predominantly white, middle class, and located in Western Europe and North America. These movements are well worth studying. But when they become a reified category of analysis—*the* new social movements—many of the most important social movements of the past two decades are rendered invisible. In a world larger than Western Europe and North America, one might notice such "new" social movements as Solidarity in Poland, the movement against the apartheid regime in South Africa, the *communidades de base* movement in Latin America, and the intifada in the Middle East, for starters.

I do not claim that the meshing of personal and collective identity is any less important for these movements than for the subset privileged by new social movement theorists. On the contrary, I accept it as a fundamental issue for all movements, past and present, in Western industrialized countries and elsewhere. But as the context changes, so does the status of such claims as: collective identity is especially problematic because participants do not define themselves in terms of their social location in a class or ethnic group. It seems reasonable to suppose that the problem of meshing individual and collective identity will take a different form in different types of movements.

Changing language from "new" social movements to "contemporary" social movements, as Cohen (1985) does, is clearly inadequate in overcoming the ethnocentrism of privileging a particular type. If recency is the relevant criterion, the Eastern European and third world movements referred to above are every bit as contemporary as the Greens in West Germany.

Reifying newness as a category of analysis also diverts attention from the collective identity processes involved in past movements and blurs what may be instructive continuities. Simultaneously, it obscures important differences in the collective identity problems of movements that are only superficially similar. In his study of ACT UP, an AIDS activist group, J. Gamson shows the insufficiency of lumping together movements "simply because of a shared cultural and identity focus. . . . Identity assertions in ACT UP point up boundaries, using the fear of the abnormal against the fearful" (1989, 364). The specific operations involved may be shared by movements that are subject to stigmatization and, hence, are in a similar position to "shock." But these operations may be inappropriate and irrelevant for other, equally culturally oriented movements. Hence, the category of "newness" can serve as a substitute for a concrete analysis of how collective identity processes operate in movements facing quite different sets of problems.

Expanding the Strategic Paradigm

Can such lessons about the centrality of identity processes be incorporated in strategically oriented paradigms such as resource mobilization? Cohen thinks not. "One cannot simply add a consideration of solidarity, collective identity, consciousness, or ideology to the resource mobilization perspective without bursting its framework," she argues (1985, 687).

She is right, of course, in the sense that a strategic focus will not highlight all aspects of the process of constructing a collective identity. But it does not even strain the paradigm let alone burst it to integrate many of the central insights. Strategy does not apply only to political or economic change as objectives. The first step is to recognize that people may mobilize resources and pursue various forms of collective action in the pursuit of cultural change. Change in the cultural definition of the "normal" serves as an excellent example.

Once one gives changes at the cultural level the same status as institutional changes, a further broadening of the resource mobilization paradigm is required. Political and economic changes involve more easily defined targets of influence—some set of authorities whose decisions affect the goals of challengers. But in the pursuit of cultural change, the target is often diffused through the whole civil society. State institutions continue to play a role, but in the twentieth century they have increasingly withdrawn from becoming directly involved in what Foucault (1979) calls the "normalization" process. The mass media frequently become a central target as the most visible purveyor of the broader cultural definitions they both reproduce and reflect.

Construction of a collective identity is one step in challenging cultural domination. The content must necessarily be adversarial in some way to smoke out the invisible and arbitrary elements of the dominant cultural codes. No matter how personally important it becomes for participants, it is never merely a fulfillment but a strategic step in achieving cultural changes that are mediated by the movement's external targets.

If the concept of collective identity sometimes seems excessively vague and difficult to operationalize, this may be in part because of the tendency to blur individual and cultural levels in some discussions of the concept. The locus of collective identity is cultural; it is manifested through the language and symbols by which it is publicly expressed. We know a collective identity through the cultural icons and artifacts displayed by those who embrace it. It is manifested in styles of dress, language, and demeanor. Collective identity need not be treated as some mysterious intangible but can be as empirically observable as a T-shirt or haircut. To measure it, one would ask people about the meaning of labels and other cultural symbols, not about their own personal identity.

Social psychology helps us recognize that it is a task of all social movements to bridge individual and cultural levels. One does this by enlarging the personal identities of a constituency to include the relevant collective identity as part of their definition of self. New social movement theory suggests that this bridging process is especially critical in movements that (1) emphasize changes at the cultural level, (2) have the civil society rather than state or economic institutions as a primary target of influence, and (3) have a constituency that chooses whether or not to make visible their connection with the relevant group. But it is not particularly helpful when the construction of a collective identity is made *the* task of social movements at the inevitable expense of slighting other, equally critical components.

Resource mobilization theory suggests that the bridging of personal and collective identity can be viewed strategically, as one part of the mobilization process. Even when we regard the construction of a collective identity as an achievement in its own right, it has instrumental consequences for the rest of the process. It is central in understanding people's willingness to invest emotionally in the fate of some emergent collective entity and to take personal risks on its behalf. It has consequences for how people understand the sociocultural system they are attempting to change and which strategies and organizational forms they will see as appropriate. Groups that have achieved a successful integration of personal and collective identity will have an easier time doing what it takes to launch many kinds of collective actions.

But this depends in part on the type of collective action and its target. Many of the unanswered questions about identity processes concern the strategic consequences emphasized by resource mobilization theory. We still need to ask how and under what conditions the strength of a collective identity and its specific content make a difference for achieving movement goals.

SOLIDARITY

There is both a social and a cultural level involved in loyalty and commitment to a social movement. Solidarity processes focus on how people relate to social movement carriers—that is, to the various collective actors who claim to represent the movement. These carriers need not be formal organizations but can include entities as varied as an advocacy network grouped around a journal or a grass-roots Christian community in El Salvador.

In practice, of course, collective identity and solidarity are closely intertwined, but it is possible to have one aspect of commitment without the other. A person may embrace the collective identity offered by a movement and feel alienated from its major organizational carriers. Conversely, there may be organizational loyalists whose personal lives are thoroughly intertwined with the fate of the carrier but feel little identification with any broader "we" that includes movement constituents.

What characteristics of movement carriers promote solidarity? Recent social movement literature has attempted to answer this in two ways: one focusing on the use of preexisting social relationships, the other on organizational forms that support and sustain the personal needs of participants and embody the movement's collective identity.

The argument that recruitment to a movement follows lines of preexisting social relationships and that recruitment networks are a critical part of the mobilization process has become part of our shared knowledge.[3] Strong, preexisting friendship ties seem especially important where the risk is high. McAdam (1986) examined the high-risk activism involved in participating in the 1964 Mississippi Freedom Summer project, comparing those who signed up and later withdrew with those who actually went to Mississippi. Those with strong ties to other participants had a drop-out rate of only 12 percent (compared to a 25 percent rate for the group as a whole).

Certainly any social psychologist reviewing the extensive literature on

3. For evidence and elaboration of this point, see Bolton (1972), Orum (1974), Wilson and Orum (1976), Snow, Zurcher, and Eckland-Olson (1980), Klandermans (1986), McAdam (1986), and Klandermans and Oegama (1987).

social support networks would have predicted this. Study after study has emphasized their importance in sustaining people through life's existential crises of illness, death, and separation.[4] High-risk activism is high-stress activity. Preexisting friendships are helpful in recruitment, no doubt, but unless the *continuing* relationships among activists have some of the qualities of a primary social support network, it seems hard to imagine that participants will develop organizational solidarity.

Insights about the centrality of social support processes have entered the social movement literature through discussions of cultural "free spaces," "prefigurative politics," and "affinity groups." Movements that practice high-risk activism operate in an adversarial environment and have a special need to create a protected subenvironment. As Evans and Boyte develop their concept of free spaces, "they are defined by their roots in community, the dense, rich networks of daily life; by their autonomy; and by their public or quasi-public character as participatory environments which nurture values associated with citizenship and a vision of the common good" (1986, 20).

Rather than creating such spaces de novo, movements try, when possible, to transform existing communal institutions into such protected environments. Morris (1984) shows the multifaceted role of the black church in providing such space for the civil rights movement as well as "movement halfway houses" such as the Highlander Folk School. He quotes its director, Myles Horton: "We never spent any time stating what we believed, and how we felt, or anything like that. . . . We just went ahead and ran our program and everybody was accepted as an equal and treated as an equal and they got the message" (148).

Highlander embodied in its practice Breines's concept of "prefigurative politics." The central task of such politics, she argues, is "to create and sustain within the lived practice of the movement relationships and political forms that 'prefigured' and embodied the desired society" (1982, 6). In the New Left movement she studied, it was intimately connected with the vision of a community that united public and private spheres. "By community," she writes, "I mean a network of relationships more direct, more total and more personal than the formal, abstract and instrumental relationships characterizing state and society"(6).

The organizational form that seems most clearly to reflect the needs for a sustaining social support system is that of "affinity groups." The movements against the Vietnam War, nuclear power, and intervention in Cen-

---

4. For good reviews of the centrality of a social support network in health and its buffering effects in coping with stress, see House, Umberson, and Landis (1988) and House, Landis, and Umberson (1988).

tral America all spawned challengers that made use of this form of organization. Ideally, an affinity group, which is small (perhaps ten to twenty people), takes responsibility for activating its own members and participates as a unit in collective action. In addition to providing members with emotional support, these groups are typically expected to provide many of their instrumental needs for transportation, food, and shelter.

Affinity groups may employ an internal division of labor. The Pledge of Resistance, a challenger in the Central American anti-intervention movement, sometimes used site occupations as a tactic. Members of its affinity groups would decide in advance which ones would risk arrest and jail and which ones would act as partners for those detained, helping them meet the continuing demands of everyday life, of family and work.

All movements, of course, have informal friendship networks that help sustain the members. Affinity groups are innovative in formalizing the system of social support, making explicit who is affiliated with which subgroups and endowing them with decision-making and governance functions. Unlike the cells in more hierarchical organizations, affinity groups reflect a commitment to decentralization.

Free spaces, prefigurative politics, and affinity groups reflect sound social psychological insights on building commitment and solidarity, but they frequently exist in tension with the strategic imperatives of social movement organizations. The reconciliation or trade-offs involved remains one of the unsolved problems on the frontiers of social movement theory.

Breines's (1982) interpretation of the New Left movement highlights the conflict between prefigurative and strategic politics. The practice suggested by prefigurative politics has many implications for organization: direct participation rather than representation, decentralization rather than centralization, and holistic personal relationships rather than bureaucratic and segmented role relationships.

All well and good for building commitment, solidarity, and a collective identity, but social movement organizations frequently face the challenge of responding rapidly and skillfully to unexpected events or the actions of their adversaries. In the fall of 1965, for example, Students for a Democratic Society (SDS) was in the media spotlight and under attack for "sabotaging the war effort." Sale (1973) and Gitlin (1980) describe how SDS officers, in an effort "to take the heat off," held a press conference and issued a statement offering "to build, not to burn; to teach, not to torture; to help, not to kill."

The statement received widespread coverage and apparently achieved its immediate tactical purpose in reframing the discourse to center on the immorality of the war rather than on draft resistance. It proved helpful in recruiting on a number of campuses. In addition, it temporarily reduced the pressure on SDS while bolstering its allies and supporters.

This apparent success, however, produced mostly harsh internal criticism from SDS chapters around the country. It was not only the content that dismayed some members; as Gitlin (1980) puts it, "There was much feeling that [SDS officers] had usurped the right to make any policy statement at all." The national secretary was not entitled to set policy in SDS. One critic suggested that reporters "should have simply been referred to local chapters which would tell them what was going on in any particular area" (Sale 1973).

Similarly, Barkan (1979) describes some of the problems that the Clamshell Alliance experienced in using affinity groups in the attempted occupation of the Seabrook, New Hampshire, nuclear site. The Clam had a coordinating committee of affinity group representatives, but this body had no established legitimacy among the rank and file, and representatives were required to return to their affinity groups for consent for proposed actions. When decisions were inevitably made by the coordinating committee under time pressure, members challenged the results and charged that the Clam was "controlled by a few 'heavyweights'" (Barkan, 1979).

The trick, of course, is to find a way to combine prefigurative and strategic politics, to reconcile organizational forms that sustain commitment with those that can meet situational demands for rapid and skillful action. Can one mix decentralization for social support with more centralized decision making? Or does this reduction of participation in decision making inevitably undermine the importance of affinity groups and render them ineffective in building solidarity and commitment? Does formalizing and making explicit the social support system really add anything to what can be achieved through warm and supportive informal social relationships? The social support tradition in social psychology helps us understand the dilemma, but it doesn't provide the solution.

Finally, there is another tradition in social psychology that suggests that, notwithstanding the virtues described above, social support can have a distinctly negative side. An extensive literature on conformity, going back to the classical experimental studies by Sherif (1936) and Asch (1952), emphasizes the potential tyranny of groups. Participants in some social movements find an oppressive and stifling side to close-knit personal relationships.

So-called cultural free spaces sometimes become prisons from which some participants would like to escape but cannot because they lack the courage to defy the group censure and ostracism that would follow. At some point, social support can become social pressure. Students of social movements need to understand the conditions under which this occurs and how challengers can keep their social relationships liberating rather than having them become a new and more subtle form of oppression.

CONSCIOUSNESS

Consciousness concerns the mesh between cognition and culture—between individual beliefs about the social world and cultural belief systems and ideologies. We can learn something of value from work that focuses on a single level, but neither is adequate by itself if we want to understand the kind of political consciousness that affects people's willingness to be quiescent or to engage in collective action.

At the cognitive level, the most useful literature concerns the operation of "schemata" and "scripts."[5] These ideas are especially relevant for students of social movements because they assume an active processor who is constructing meaning rather than a passive recipient. They imply agency, providing a natural fit with strategically oriented social movement paradigms.

Schema theory does little to call our attention to the nature of the world that people encounter with their cognitive structures. It is simply there, a received world whose process of social construction is not itself treated as problematic. It is helpful to start with the assumption that people are active processors of meaning but not if this leads us to forget that, in the political world we encounter, meaning is already organized. Information and facts are always ordered into interpretive frames, and we must understand this process as well.

The cultural side of political consciousness is represented by traditions that focus on ideology and discourse. Most of this work is critical, emphasizing the shaping of political consciousness as part of a process of class or elite domination. Any change in consciousness involves an uphill symbolic struggle since every regime has some legitimating frame that provides the citizenry with a reason to be quiescent—except in the pursuit of their civic duty. It is a formidable task to cut what Freire (1970) calls the "umbilical cord of magic and myth which binds [the oppressed] to the world of oppression."

It is not through force or coercion that a regime maintains itself but through its ability to shape our worldview. As Edelman puts it, "Government affects behavior chiefly by shaping the cognitions of large numbers

5. For especially useful discussions, see Neisser (1976) and Abelson (1981).

of people in ambiguous situations. It helps create the beliefs about what is proper; their perceptions of what is fact; and their expectations of what is to be done" (1971, 7).

At the center of this process of "manufacturing consent," to use Herman and Chomsky's (1988) phrase, are the mass media. Edelman (1988) calls the social construction constituted by news reporting a "political spectacle." It is an apt term for his argument since he emphasizes the institutionalized power at the root of the production process and the passivity and helplessness of the spectators. It is a great circus for the minority of news junkies who follow it, providing them with "weekly, daily, sometimes hourly triumphs and defeats" (6). Meanwhile, the masses go on with their daily lives, largely oblivious to the spectacle except intermittently.

Edelman is enormously impressed with the powerful social control that is exercised, largely unconsciously, through the manipulation of symbolism used in constructing the spectacle. The actors themselves get caught up in it and are avidly taken in by it even as they have a hand in its creation. The fetishes they create—for example, "world communism"—end up dominating and mystifying their creators. Problems, enemies, crises, and leaders are constantly being constructed and reconstructed to create a series of threats and reassurances. In Edelman's gloomy world, obliviousness may be the only faint protection from this pervasive form of social control; to take it in is to be taken in by it.

Work rooted in Gramsci's concept of ideological hegemony has a similar thrust. Gramsci recognized that there is no automatic passage from economic to political dominance. Consent must be created and actively maintained. He calls our attention not only to explicit beliefs but also to how the routine, taken-for-granted structures of everyday thinking contribute to a structure of dominance. Gramsci urges us to expand our notion of ideology to include the world of common sense. Creating alternative consciousness requires a struggle to forge a "new common sense and with it a new culture and new philosophy which will be rooted in the popular consciousness with the same solidity and imperative quality as traditional beliefs" (1971, 424).

The unraveling of such processes is an intellectual agenda, not an answer. As long as the mechanisms are left vague and unspecified, the analysis remains excessively abstract. Hegemony becomes a label that substitutes for explanation rather than providing it. In many discussions, as Gitlin puts it, hegemony appears as "a sort of immutable fog that has settled over the whole public life of capitalist societies to confound the truth of the proletarian telos. Thus to the question, 'Why are radical ideas suppressed in the schools?' 'Why do workers oppose socialism?' and so on, comes the single Delphic answer: hegemony. 'Hegemony' becomes the magical explanation of last resort. And as such it is useful neither as explanation nor as guide to action. If 'hegemony' explains everything in the sphere of culture, it explains nothing" (1979, 252).

There are undeniable truths and insights in the critical literature that attempts to explain how such institutions as the state and mass media collaborate to produce a quiescent political consciousness. But the active agent of schema theory seems to disappear. In the face of such deep-rooted institutional and cultural power, the possibilities of changing political consciousness seem remote.

Taken alone, both psychological and sociocultural approaches seem incomplete. Students of social movements need a social psychology that treats consciousness as the interplay between two levels—between individuals who operate actively in the construction of meaning and sociocultural processes that offer meanings that are frequently contested. The concept of "framing" offers the most useful way of bridging these levels of analysis. As Goffman (1974) uses the term, it contains what Crook and Taylor call a fundamental "ambiguity": "between the passive and structured on the one hand, and the active and structuring on the other. Experiences are framed, but I frame my experiences" (1980, 246). Goffman warns us that "organizational premises are involved, and those are something cognition somehow arrives at, not something cognition creates or generates" (1974, 247). At the same time, he calls attention to the fragility of frames in use and their vulnerability to tampering.

This is no ambiguity but a necessary and desirable antinomy. It underlines the usefulness of framing as a bridging concept between cognition and culture. A cultural-level analysis tells us that our political world is framed, that reported events are preorganized and do not come to us in raw form. But we are active processors and however encoded our received reality, we may decode it in different ways. The very vulnerability of the framing process makes it a locus of potential struggle, not a leaden reality to which we all inevitably must yield. On most political issues, there are competing interpretations, ways of framing information and facts in alternative ways. Indeed, one can view social movement actors as engaged in a symbolic contest over which meaning will prevail. Particular frames ebb and flow in prominence and require constant updating to accommodate new events.

Students of social movements have applied this social psychological analysis through the concept of what Snow and Benford, in this volume, call "collective action frames." They define them as "emergent action-oriented sets of beliefs and meanings that inspire and legitimate social

movement activities and campaigns." *Emergent* calls attention to their for-
mative character and the importance of understanding the process of what
Turner and Killian (1987) call "emergent norms." *Action-oriented* calls attention to the mobilizing character of collective action frames—that is,
their call that those who share the frame can and should do something
about the situation.

There is a striking amount of convergence on another aspect of the
content: collective action frames are *injustice* frames (e.g., see Turner and
Killian 1987, 242; Piven and Cloward 1977, 12; Moore 1978, 88; McAdam
1982, 51). They face a field of combat that is already occupied by a competing legitimating frame that is established and quiescent rather than
emergent and action-oriented. When truly hegemonic, the legitimating
frame is taken for granted. Would-be challengers face the problem of
overcoming a definition of the situation that they themselves may take as
part of the natural order.

It is an achievement, then, for a challenger to force the sponsors of a
legitimating frame to defend its underlying assumptions. The sheer existence of a symbolic contest is evidence of the breakdown of hegemony and
a major accomplishment for a challenger.

To claim that collective action frames are emergent, action-oriented, injustice frames still leaves a number of ambiguities and questions. What is
it about them that is emergent? Quiescence should not be confused with
acceptance of a legitimating frame. For many groups, the injustice component may be of long standing and can hardly be said to be "emergent"
at the time of collective action. Quiescence can be produced, even when
injustice is taken for granted by a dominated group, through the belief
that resistance is hopeless and fraught with peril.

For many social movements, the important emergent component may
have much less to do with legitimacy than it does with mutability. Splits
among authorities and the successes of the movement itself may make a
social order that once seemed unassailable look increasingly vulnerable.
The idea of "emergence" is useful in focusing attention on a reframing
process, but the specific component that is changing may be different for
different movements.

There are also unresolved issues concerning the "collective" component
in mobilizing frames. Various authors have suggested that the content
must define a collective cause and solution for the problem being addressed and specify antagonists—an "us" and a "them" (e.g., see Donati
1988; Ryan 1991). The collective identity defined by the frame must necessarily be oppositional or adversarial. But this is precisely what some social
movements—McCarthy and Wolfson (this volume) call them "consensus
movements"—seem to lack.

Some environmental groups, for example, emphasize the thoughtless actions of individuals and see the solution to be large numbers of us changing our life-styles. This frame suggests neither a collective solution nor an us and them. Donati (1988), in his study of the Italian ecology movement, shows how the advertising industry used many symbolic elements from the movement's frame to suggest solutions through individual consumer behavior.

Can one mobilize for *collective* action on the basis of a frame that suggests no clear antagonist or target and, although action-oriented, sees change occurring through the aggregation of individual behaviors? Do some social movement actors challenge the legitimating frame without offering a collective action frame? And, if so, how does one characterize the alternative they offer? Do such alternatives help collective action frames by weakening the dominance of the legitimating frame or hurt them by undercutting the call for collective solutions?

The model of political consciousness offered here also raises difficult epistemological questions. The dilemma is especially well illustrated by Snow and his colleagues who have made the most sustained attempt to integrate into social movement theory a well-specified model of signifying work or framing (see Snow and Benford 1988 and this volume; Snow et al. 1986). In trying to explain the mobilizing potency of different frames, they suggest that one major factor is the "empirical credibility" of a frame. "By 'empirical credibility,' " they write, "we refer to the evidential basis for a master frame's diagnostic claims." Following this, they speak of its claims being "empirically verified" and conclude that "to the extent that there are events or occurrences that can be pointed to as documentary evidence, . . . then a master frame has empirical credibility" (Snow and Benford, this volume).

The authors have their feet planted solidly in a conventional positivist epistemology while their heads are in the clouds of a post-positivist, constructionist world. The very term "empirical credibility" suggests the unresolved conflict. They might have called it "empirical validity," making clear their commitment to positivist assumptions about frame-free methods of determining this. But the "credibility" term contains a subtle hedge; it is not that some frames can be proven true but that they have the *appearance* of truth. And they acknowledge, "Of course, what is constitutive of evidence for any particular claim is itself subject to debate" (1988, 208). This at least hints at the idea that whether a master frame seems plausible to the observer is itself an accomplishment of successful signifying work.

A successful theory of framing must be based on an epistemology that recognizes facts as social constructions and evidence as taking on its meaning from the master frames in which it is embedded. The essence of frame contests is competition about what evidence is seen as relevant and what gets ignored. Bootlegging in assumptions that some master frames are more empirically verifiable than others by an objective, frame-free observer simply blurs this essential point.

The same problem arises when Snow and Benford discuss master frames being overwhelmed by events, likening it to a scientific theory being disproven. Kuhn's (1962) point about scientific "paradigms"—a close relative if not a synonym for frames—is that they are overthrown not by negative evidence but by rival paradigms that win the allegiance of a new generation. To extend the point here, it is not events that overcome frames but rival frames that do better at getting their interpretations to stick.

Does such a position lead us, as some would have it, to an "epistemological chasm" (Charles Tilly, private conversation, March 1989)? Are we inevitably led to what Goodman (1978) calls a "flabby relativism" in which all frames have an equal claim in interpreting the world and it is all a matter of whose marketing techniques are the most effective? Does the social construction model force us to abandon all attempts to evaluate the implications of empirical evidence for the claims of competing interpretations?

Clearly, there is an important and complicated relationship between the characteristics of events and the success of certain frames. To take an example from the nuclear power issue, the accidents at Three Mile Island and Chernobyl have not made life easy for those who frame nuclear power development as technological progress. But neither did they provide empirical refutation of this frame. As its advocates will point out, Three Mile Island "proved" that the "defense in depth" safety system works; even in this most serious of nuclear accidents, no one was killed and no significant amounts of radiation were released. And Chernobyl "proved" the wisdom of the American nuclear industry in building reactors with the reinforced concrete containment structures the Chernobyl plant lacked.

If "empirical credibility" illustrates the wrong epistemology, Snow and Benford's concept of "narrative fidelity" (or what other authors have called "narrative fit") has no such untenable assumptions. They define narrative fidelity as "the degree to which proffered framings resonate with cultural narrations, that is, with the stories, myths, and folk tales that are part and parcel of one's cultural heritage and thus function to inform events and experiences in the immediate present" (1988, 210). Like empirical credibility, this concept also deals with the relationship between frames and events, but here it is recognized that events take on their meaning from the story line contained in a master frame. Some events fit the scenario well, but others do not, even when they can be worked in by a creative rendering.

Frames, like metaphors, are ways of organizing thinking about political issues. One should ask not whether they are true or false—that is, their empirical validity—but about their usefulness in increasing understanding and their economy and inclusiveness in providing a coherent explanation of a diverse set of facts. But there is no need to abandon empirical claims about the relative success of a given frame in political discourse and in what accounts for its rise and fall.

Finally, there are unresolved issues concerning the role of public discourse in general, and mass media discourse in particular, in shaping people's willingness to adopt collective action frames. Much of what adherents of a movement see, hear, and read is beyond the control of any movement organization and is likely to overwhelm in sheer volume anything that movement sources try to communicate. Because media discourse is so central in framing issues for the attentive public, it becomes, to quote Gurevitch and Levy, "a site on which various social groups, institutions, and ideologies struggle over the definition and construction of social reality" (1985, 19).

Acknowledging the importance of media discourse doesn't tell us how and in what ways it operates on the consciousness of different parts of the audience. Notwithstanding the powerful arguments showing the tendency of media discourse to produce quiescence, social movements do occur. Media practices both help and hurt social movement efforts in complex ways that differ from issue to issue.[6]

It is a reasonable working hypothesis that the importance of media discourse in shaping political consciousness is heavily dependent on the type of issue involved. The precise nature of this dependence has yet to be adequately developed. I suspect that we will understand consciousness more fully when we can explain how media discourse interacts with what Giddens (1984) calls "practical consciousness"—the complex tacit knowledge that people develop about the conditions and consequences of what they do in their daily lives.

MICROMOBILIZATION

Micromobilization concerns the interaction mechanisms by which individual and sociocultural levels are brought together. It draws

---

6. For insightful discussions of the complex relationship between movements and media in the United States, see Ryan (1991) and Gitlin (1980), and, for Israel, Wolfsfeld (1988).

especially on those long-standing social psychological traditions that illuminate the operation of face-to-face encounters and group dynamics. The key concept is the *mobilizing act*: words or deeds that further the mobilization process among some set of potential challengers.

There has been only one attempt to develop a full-fledged theory of micromobilization—presented in a book that I co-authored: *Encounters with Unjust Authority* (Gamson, Fireman, and Rytina 1982). Norms against self-promotion make it a bit awkward, but I will cast them aside here and argue unabashedly that the theory presented in *Encounters* offers a large part of what we need for the systematic study of micromobilization.

Different micromobilization processes are highlighted by different kinds of encounters: recruitment meetings, internal meetings, mass media encounters, encounters with allies, encounters with countermovement groups, and encounters with authorities. In the course of these encounters, potential challengers say or do things that help (or hinder) the development of a collective identity, solidarity, and a collective action frame. If one defines a successful mobilization career as one that culminates in collective action, then a mobilizing act is one that increases the probability of such action occurring.

Encounters unpacks the overall process into three simultaneous subprocesses: working together, breaking out, and adopting an injustice frame. Each process is advanced by different types of mobilizing acts, called respectively organizing, divesting, and reframing acts.

An *organizing act* is one that increases the capacity of the potential challengers to act as a unit. Encounters with authorities are not the best venue for studying the process since the bulk of such development takes place in encounters and informal interactions among members and sympathizers, away from the public arena of confrontations with authorities. Encounters with authorities, however, are frequently proving grounds, testing the degree to which various organizational problems have been solved.

Divesting acts, another type of mobilizing act, are necessary to break the bonds of authority that keep people quiescent. In addition to reification and other processes that make the legitimating frame seem part of the natural order, there are considerations of face-work in social interaction that help keep people in line. Goffman (1959) reminds us that every social interaction is built upon a working consensus among the participants, and its disruption has the character of moral transgression. Open conflict about the definition of the situation is incompatible with polite exchange.

Agents of authority, projecting a legitimating frame, benefit from these face-work considerations. Since the norms of polite interaction prohibit discrediting the claims of others, potential challengers run the risk of making asses of themselves in challenging the compliance demands of authorities. Apart from any consideration of sanctions, they may appear boorish and rude.

Finally, the process of adopting an injustice frame involves specific *reframing acts*. It is insufficient if individuals privately adopt a different interpretation of what is happening. For collective adoption of an injustice frame, it must be shared by the potential challengers in a public way. This allows the participants to realize not only that they share the injustice frame but that everyone is aware that it is shared. This process takes time and is rarely compressed into a single encounter.

Heirich (1971) suggests a useful distinction between two types of reframing acts. *Attention-calling* acts are words or deeds that point to something questionable in what the authority is doing or about to do. They say to other participants: "Look at what is happening here. Something that is not normal and unexceptionable is occurring." *Context-setting* acts identify or define what is wrong by applying an injustice frame to the encounter in an explicit and public way.

This theory offers a beginning but leaves many issues unresolved. As the context, type of encounter, and stage of the process change, different mobilizing acts may become appropriate. Those that work in one context may be inappropriate or counterproductive in another. Take humor, for example. In some contexts, one can see how it might help in the formation of a collective identity, but it is not hard to imagine circumstances under which joking seems to defuse or deflect collective action. Humor can be a substitute for action, expressing a fatalism or resignation that countermands a collective action frame. Even when it expresses hostility toward an antagonist, the subtext may be "grin and bear it." We are still a long way from specifying the conditions under which any alleged mobilizing act furthers the process.

The theory developed in *Encounters* is inevitably influenced by its focus on encounters with authority. For example, it differentiates the closely related processes of divesting and reframing but includes quite different kinds of acts under the general rubric of organizing. Hence, acts such as "speaking for the group" that contribute to the construction of a collective identity are thrown together with "apparatus-building" acts that work on the logistics and infrastructure of collective action. A theory focused on a broader range of internal movement encounters is likely to differentiate the varied processes of producing collective identity, managing internal conflicts, and building an infrastructure for supporting collective action.

CONCLUSION

To explain how identity, solidarity, and consciousness operate in mobilization for collective action, we must link individual and sociocultural levels of analysis. Collective identity is a concept at the cultural level, but to operate in mobilization, individuals must make it part of their personal identity. Solidarity centers on the ways in which individuals commit themselves and the resources they control to some kind of collective actor—an organization or advocacy network. Adopting a collective action frame involves incorporating a product of the cultural system—a particular shared understanding of the world—into the political consciousness of individuals. Individual and sociocultural levels are linked through mobilizing acts in face-to-face encounters.

These frontiers of social movement theory are in social psychological territory. The processes that European new social movement theorists, American resource mobilization theorists, and some third world theorists are attempting to unravel require an analysis that brings together individual and sociocultural levels. All four of the processes discussed here —collective identity, solidarity, consciousness, and micromobilization— have roots in long-standing social psychological traditions that are much broader than the study of social movements.

The authors who illuminate these processes vary in the explicitness of their identification with the social psychological project, but, regardless, their work reflects a renewal of this focus. If it is necessary to call attention to it, as this essay does, it is only because of a past in which social psychology seemed wedded to the disparagement of social movements and their participants. But this, it turns out, was mere historical accident, not the immutable character of the field.

REFERENCES

Abelson, Robert A. 1981. "Psychological Status of the Script Concept." *American Psychologist* 36 (July):715–29.
Asch, Solomon E. 1952. *Social Psychology*. Englewood Cliffs, N.J.: Prentice-Hall.
Barkan, Steven E. 1979. "Strategic, Tactical, and Organizational Dilemmas of the Protest Movements against Nuclear Power." *Social Problems* 27:19–37.
Bolton, Charles D. 1972. "Alienation and Action: A Study of Peace Group Members." *American Journal of Sociology* 78:537–61.
Breines, Wini. 1982. *Community and Organization in the New Left, 1962–1968: The Great Refusal*. New York: Praeger.
Cohen, Jean L. 1985. "Strategy or Identity: New Theoretical Paradigms and Contemporary Social Movements." *Social Research* 52, no. 4:663–716.

Crook, Steve, and Laurie Taylor. 1980. "Goffman's Version of Reality." In Jason Ditton, ed., *The View from Goffman*. New York: St. Martin's Press.

Donati, Paulo. 1988. "Citizens and Consumers: The Ecology Issue and the 1970s Movements in Italy." Master's thesis, Sociology Department, Boston College.

Edelman, Murray. 1971. *Politics as Symbolic Action*. Chicago: Markham.

———. 1988. *Constructing the Political Spectacle*. Chicago: University of Chicago Press.

Evans, Sara M., and Harry C. Boyte. 1986. *Free Spaces*. New York: Harper and Row.

Ferree, Myra Marx, and Frederick D. Miller. 1985. "Mobilization and Meaning: Toward an Integration of Social Psychological and Resource Perspectives on Social Movements." *Sociological Inquiry* 55, no. 1:38–61.

Foucault, Michel. 1979. *Discipline and Punish*. New York: Vintage.

Freire, Paulo. 1970. *Pedagogy of the Oppressed*. New York: Herder and Herder.

Fromm, Erich. 1941. *Escape from Freedom*. New York: Farrar and Rinehart.

Gamson, Josh. 1989. "Silence, Death, and the Invisible Enemy: AIDS Activism and Social Movement 'Newness.'" *Social Problems* 36:351–67.

Gamson, William A. 1990. *The Strategy of Social Protest*. 2d ed. Belmont, Calif.: Wadsworth.

Gamson, William A., Bruce Fireman, and Steven Rytina. 1982. *Encounters with Unjust Authority*. Homewood, Ill.: Dorsey.

Giddens, Anthony. 1984. *The Constitution of Society*. Berkeley: University of California Press.

Gitlin, Todd. 1979. "Prime Time Ideology: The Hegemonic Process in Television Entertainment." *Social Problems* 26 (February):251–66.

———. 1980. *The Whole World Is Watching*. Berkeley: University of California Press.

Goffman, Erving. 1959. *The Presentation of Self in Everyday Life*. New York: Doubleday Anchor.

———. 1974. *Frame Analysis*. Cambridge, Mass.: Harvard University Press.

Goodman, Nelson. 1978. *Ways of Worldmaking*. Indianapolis: Hackett.

Gramsci, Antonio. 1971. *Selections from the Prison Notebooks*, ed. Quintin Hoare and Geoffrey Nowell Smith. New York: International Publishers.

Gurevitch, Michael, and Mark R. Levy. 1985. *Mass Communication Review Yearbook*, no. 5. Beverly Hills, Calif.: Sage.

Heirich, Max. 1971. *The Spiral of Conflict: Berkeley, 1964*. New York: Columbia University Press.

Herman, Edward S., and Noam Chomsky. 1988. *Manufacturing Consent*. New York: Pantheon.

Hoffer, Eric. 1951. *The True Believer*. New York: Harper and Row.

House, James S., Karl R. Landis, and Debra Umberson. 1988. "Social Relationships and Health." *Science* 241:540–45.

House, James S., Debra Umberson, and Karl R. Landis. 1988. "Structures and Processes of Social Support." *Annual Review of Sociology* 14:293–318.

Klandermans, Bert. 1984. "Social Psychological Expansions of Resource Mobilization Theory." *American Sociological Review* 49 (October):583–600.

———. 1986. "New Social Movements and Resource Mobilization: The European and the American Approach." *International Journal of Mass Emergencies and Disasters* 4:13–37.

Klandermans, Bert, and Dirk Oegama. 1987. "Potentials, Networks, Motivations and Barriers." *American Sociological Review* 52:519–31.

Klandermans, Bert, and Sidney Tarrow. 1988. "Mobilization into Social Movements: Synthesizing European and American Approaches." In Bert Klandermans, Hanspeter Kriesi, and Sidney Tarrow, eds. *From Structure to Action: Comparing Social Movement Research across Cultures.* International Social Movement Research, vol. 1. Greenwich, Conn.: JAI Press.

Kuhn, Thomas S. 1962. *The Structure of Scientific Revolutions.* Chicago: University of Chicago Press.

Martin, Everett D. 1920. *The Behavior of Crowds.* New York: Harper.

McAdam, Doug. 1982. *Political Process and the Development of Black Insurgency.* Chicago: University of Chicago Press.

———. 1986. "Recruitment to High-Risk Activism: The Case of Freedom Summer." *American Journal of Sociology* 82 (May):64–90.

McCarthy, John D., and Mayer N. Zald. 1977. "Resource Mobilization in Social Movements: A Partial Theory." *American Journal of Sociology* 82 (May):1212–34.

Melucci, Alberto. 1989. *Nomads of the Present: Social Movements and Individual Needs in Contemporary Society.* Philadelphia: Temple University Press.

Moore, Barrington, Jr. 1978. *Injustice: The Social Bases of Obedience and Revolt.* White Plains, N.Y.: M. E. Sharpe.

Morris, Aldon D. 1984. *The Origins of the Civil Rights Movement.* New York: Free Press.

Neisser, Ulric. 1976. *Cognition and Reality.* San Francisco: W. H. Freeman.

Oberschall, Anthony. 1973. *Social Conflict and Social Movements.* Englewood Cliffs, N.J.: Prentice-Hall.

Olson, Mancur, Jr. 1965. *The Logic of Collective Action.* Cambridge, Mass.: Harvard University Press.

Orum, Anthony M. 1974. "On Participation in Political Protest Movements." *Journal of Applied Behavioral Science* 10:181–207.

Piven, Frances Fox, and Richard A. Cloward. 1977. *Poor People's Movements.* New York: Vintage.

Ryan, Charlotte. 1991. *Prime Time Activism.* Boston: South End Press.

Sale, Kirkpatrick. 1973. *SDS.* New York: Random House.

Sherif, Muzafer. 1936. *The Psychology of Social Norms.* New York: Harper.

Snow, David A., and Robert D. Benford. 1988. "Ideology, Frame Resonance, and Participant Mobilization." In Bert Klandermans, Hanspeter Kriesi, and Sidney Tarrow, eds., *From Structure to Action: Comparing Social Movement Research across Cultures.* International Social Movement Research, vol. 1. Greenwich, Conn.: JAI Press.

Snow, David A., E. Burke Rochford, Jr., Steven K. Worden, and Robert D. Benford. 1986. "Frame Alignment Processes, Micromobilization, and Movement Participation." *American Sociological Review* 51 (August):464–81.

Snow, David A., Louis A. Zurcher, Jr., and Sheldon Eckland-Olson. 1980. "Social Networks and Social Movements." *American Sociological Review* 45:787–801.

Turner, Ralph H., and Lewis M. Killian. 1987. *Collective Behavior.* 3d ed. Englewood Cliffs, N.J.: Prentice-Hall.

Wilson, K., and Anthony M. Orum. 1976. "Mobilizing People for Collective Political Action." *Journal of Political and Military Sociology* 4:187–202.

Wolfsfeld, Gadi. 1988. *The Politics of Provocation.* Albany, N.Y.: SUNY Press.

4

The Social Construction of Protest and Multiorganizational Fields

Bert Klandermans

Several years ago, in reviewing resource mobilization and new social movement literature, I concluded that the two approaches together could complement one another neatly if they did not share an important weakness (Klandermans 1986). Neither explains what makes people define their situation in such a way that participation in a social movement seems appropriate. The new social movement approach, indeed, did try to discover the origins of the "demand" for the social movements that arose during the previous two decades, but it failed to see that structural change—however unpleasant—does not automatically generate social movements. Resource mobilization theory, in the meantime, investigated the "supply" of social movement organizations but overlooked the fact that the presence of movement organizations does not by itself produce grievances and convince people that movement participation is effective.

Social problems are not objective phenomena. After all, many situations that could be considered a social problem never become an issue, even though they may be no less troublesome than situations that do become a rallying point. Further, a social problem does not *inevitably* generate a social movement. Resource mobilization theory recognized this fact insofar as it postulated that resources play a significant role in the generation of social movements. Nevertheless, the resource mobilization approach did not take into account mediating processes through which people attribute meaning to events and interpret situations. Scholars of social movements have become increasingly aware that individuals behave according to a *perceived* reality. This principle holds true not only in the case of grievances but also in relation to resources, political opportunities, and the outcomes of collective action.

In the five years since I first compared resource mobilization theory

and the new social movement approach, cumulative criticism has stimulated a growing interest in the themes these approaches neglected. Now
new concepts and theories elaborating a social constructionist approach to
social movements are proliferating. As yet, however, it is difficult to discern much of a system in this literature. But now that the first flood of
ideas has found its outlet, perhaps this is a good time to try to establish
some order in this innovating industry. In the first part of this chapter I
will try to do just that.

This endeavor will highlight a crucial characteristic of these processes of
signifying, interpreting, and constructing meaning: that is, they are *social*,
they take place in interaction among individuals, and thus they are conceptualized as the social construction of protest. The bonds and networks
that are the vehicles of these processes of social construction have received
much less attention in the literature than have the cognitive constructions
generated by these processes. As a consequence, the literature sometimes
gives the impression that it is a study of ideas. But the concept of protest as
a social construction becomes meaningful only if we anchor it in the actual
operation of specific social structures. To this end, I elaborate the concept
of multiorganizational fields in the second part of the chapter.

SOCIAL CONSTRUCTIONIST APPROACHES
TO SOCIAL MOVEMENTS

The idea that social problems are not objective and identifiable conditions but the outcome of processes of collective definition of
the situation is not new. For many years now, students of social problems
have argued that social problems are situations that are *labeled* as problems (e.g., Spector and Kitsuse 1973). Nevertheless, this line of thought
never really caught on in social movement literature, presumably because,
once resource mobilization captured the field, the idea that grievances
could explain political protest became obsolete. And even recent work
on social construction within the social movement field shows surprisingly
little awareness of these predecessors. Yet we can learn much from scholars in the field of social problems, both in terms of grievance interpretation and in terms of the politicization of grievances (e.g., Hilgartner and
Bosk 1988).

During the past ten years students of social movements have developed various frameworks for the analysis of the social construction of
protest. These frameworks are theoretical exercises that have in common
the understanding that collective action proceeds from a significant transformation in the collective consciousness of the actors involved. The cen-

tral question that arises time and again is, how does this transformation come about? The search for an answer has taken scholars in several directions. Following is an overview of five frameworks that social movement scholars have developed in the past few years.

Cognitive Liberation.   McAdam (1982) proposed this term to signify the transformation of consciousness among potential participants in collective action. He describes cognitive liberation as a change in consciousness in three ways: (1) the system loses legitimacy, (2) people who are ordinarily fatalistic begin to demand change, and (3) they develop a new sense of political efficacy. McAdam sees shifting political conditions as a crucial impetus to the process of cognitive liberation, for they force a change in the symbolic content of member-challenger relations. When the members of a political system alter their response to a particular challenger, insurgents recognize that the political system is becoming increasingly vulnerable to challenges.

Public Discourse and Sponsorship of Ideological Packages. Gamson (1989), more emphatically than any other scholar, stressed how important the mass media are for the mobilization of social movements. Because the mass media play such a central role in modern societies, social movements are increasingly involved in a symbolic struggle over meaning and interpretations. Gamson believes that unless we examine media discourse and investigate how it changes over time, we will not be able to understand the formation and activation of the mobilization potential of social movements.

At any particular moment in a given society, one political theme will be represented by several ideological packages (Gamson and Modigliani 1989). In addition, each political theme generates a set of packages and counterpackages. The mass media in particular are responsible for disseminating ideological packages throughout a society.

Social movement organizations themselves contribute to the public discourse. As sponsors of ideological packages and as organizers of collective action in support of those packages, they influence the discussion in the media. Of course, they do not have the media all to themselves. They must compete with sponsors of other packages: representatives of the "official" position, opponents, and competitive organizations, all of whom want a voice in the public debate.

The Formation and Mobilization of Consensus.   Klandermans (1984) introduced the distinction between consensus mobilization and action mobilization. In a more recent publication (1988) he distinguishes consensus *mobilization* from consensus *formation*: the former is defined as a deliberate attempt by a social actor to create consensus among a subset of the population; the latter concerns the unplanned convergence of meaning in social networks and subcultures. To further refine the concept of consensus mobilization, he identifies two aspects: consensus mobilization in the context of the formation of mobilization potential in a society and consensus mobilization in the context of action mobilization. The first refers to the generation of a set of individuals predisposed to participate in a social movement—and so implies that movement organizations win attitudinal and ideological support; the second refers to the activation of participants in collective action—hence to the legitimation of concrete goals and means of action.

Frame Alignment.   Snow and his colleagues (1986) try to describe how the cognitive frame of individual participants becomes aligned with the ideological frame of a movement organization. Social movements frame—that is, assign meaning to and interpret—relevant events and conditions in ways that are intended to mobilize potential adherents and constituents, garner bystander support, and demobilize antagonists. In mobilization campaigns, movement organizations try to connect the interpretations of individuals with their own so that they are congruent or complementary. Snow et al. break down the process of frame alignment into four distinct activities: frame bridging, frame amplification, frame extension, and frame transformation. They suggest that frame bridging is the primary form of alignment used most often by social movement organizations today.

In elaborating the notion of frame alignment, Snow and Benford (1988) have tried to identify the key factors that determine the success of a movement's framing efforts. They suggest that two determinants of effective framing are the nature of the belief system held by potential participants and the extent to which the framing effort resonates within the "life world" of potential participants.

Collective Identity.   In Melucci's eyes social movements are themselves social constructions (1989). He conceives of a social movement—or more precisely collective action—as a process through which actors produce meanings, communicate, negotiate, and make decisions. Present-day social movements are formed in "networks submerged" in daily life. Within these invisible settings movements question and challenge the dominant codes of everyday life. These submerged networks surface whenever collective actors confront or come into conflict with public life. Melucci, then, localizes the process of the construction of meaning completely within the groups of participants that constitute a social movement. A central task for these groups is the formation of a collective identity. To form a collective identity, a group must define itself as a group, and its members must develop shared views of the social environment, shared goals, and shared opinions about the possibilities and limits of collective action. Groups can be more or less successful in developing a collective identity. If a group fails in this, it cannot accomplish any collective action.

These five frameworks share a concern with the symbolic aspects of mobilization. It is clear, however, that each elaborates a different part of the process, focusing on either collective or individual behavior. Gamson and Modigliani highlight changes in public discourse and public opinion rather than changes in the attitude of individuals; Snow et al. and Klandermans theorize about persuasive communication by movement organizations. Their vantage point is the interface of movement organizations and individual citizens. McAdam and Melucci share an interest in the changing collective consciousness of social actors. None of the approaches, however, combines analyses of behavior at both the collective and the individual level. Yet any theoretical framework designed to study the formation and transformation of collective beliefs must recognize that a comprehensive explanation of these phenomena requires analyses of behavior at both levels. After all, without individuals there is nobody to share with, and without collective beliefs there is nothing to share. Any analysis of how collective beliefs change must also take into account these two levels. Unless we can assume that some individuals are able to deviate from a shared definition of the situation or perceive discrepancies between their own definition and that shared collectively or even rebel against dominating frames, we will find it difficult to imagine that collective beliefs can change other than as a result of enforcement or domination.

One more conclusion is suggested by this review of the various frameworks. It strikes me that none of the authors has given much attention to the social construction of meaning in action situations. What I have in mind here is not consensus mobilization in the context of action mobilization or the cognitive liberation necessary for collective action to occur or the collective identity that must develop before groups can accomplish collective action. Rather, I am referring to the processes of interpreting, defining, and consciousness raising that occur among participants who interact during episodes of collective action.[1] Empirical evidence shows

1. "Consciousness raising" here is a generic term rather than a reference to the particular meaning this phrase has within the context of the women's movement. That is, it

not only that people change their minds radically during such episodes (Fantasia 1988; Heirich 1968; Hirsch 1990; Reicher 1984) but that these changes are remarkably stable (McAdam 1989).

A social constructionist approach to protest and social movements should, therefore, include collective action as both a dependent and an independent variable in its analyses. On the one hand, the social construction of meaning precedes collective action and determines its direction; on the other, collective action in its turn determines the process of meaning construction. This relationship suggests that processes of meaning construction take place at three levels: (1) the level of public discourse and the formation and transformation of collective identities; (2) the level of persuasive communication during mobilization campaigns by movement organizations, their opponents, and countermovement organizations; and (3) the level of consciousness raising during episodes of collective action.

The first level has been analyzed by Gamson and Modigliani, and Melucci and McAdam; the second by Snow et al. and Klandermans; the third somehow vanished from social movement literature after Heirich published his account of the Berkeley free speech movement (1968), and it has reappeared only recently in the work of Fantasia (1988) and Hirsch (1990).

At each of the three levels the beliefs that are formed and transformed in the process of meaning construction are collective beliefs. Accordingly, a discussion of such beliefs will provide a context for an examination of the more specific issue of the social construction of protest.

COLLECTIVE BELIEFS

The literature signifying collective beliefs contains several terms, each in some way related to Durkheim's concept of collective representations. Moscovici (1984) suggests the concept of "social representations." Although he never really defines this term, we can deduce from his work that social representations should be seen as a socially determined universe of opinions or beliefs about the material or social environment. Wildemeersch and Leirman adopt Habermas's notion of "life world," describing it as "a frame of reference which gives meaning to the aspirations and actions of people. [It is a set of] taken-for-granted perspectives, which are culturally transmitted and organized in a communicative way" (1988, 19). Oberschall uses the expression "thought-world." A thought-world consists of "a structure of classifications and distinctions by

---

denotes the restructuring of beliefs that occurs as a result of participation in collective action.

means of which information gets framed, stored, and retrieved in organized meaning-bundles for thought and action. . . . A thought-world creates a common framework in which communication among fellow humans
becomes possible" (1989, 13).

Whether they are called social representations, life worlds, or thought-
worlds, collective beliefs are clearly social in origin, they are shared, and
consequently they become part of a social reality itself. Precisely because
they are shared, collective beliefs acquire an existence independent of the
individual. Every person is born or received into a community that has a
well-established set of beliefs. And Oberschall, for example, argues that
these beliefs, or thought-worlds, endure a long time, "longer than the life
span of much social organization, . . . and far, far longer than the even
briefer life-experiences of individuals, and the rise and decline of social
movements" (1989, 14). The number of individuals who share a particular
belief does not affect the "degree" to which the belief is collective. Beliefs
held by two individuals are collective, as are those shared by the members
of a group, an organization, a society, or an entire culture.

The way collective beliefs are transformed depends to a great extent on
the fact that they are, by definition, shared. Obviously, collective beliefs are
created by individuals not in isolation but in the course of communication
and cooperation: in routine social exchanges, in conversations in pubs, at
parties, in meeting rooms, in railway compartments, and, in today's world,
over the telephone or via fax or E-mail. Within these interpersonal life
circles, populated with relatives, friends, and acquaintances, events and
new information are discussed, interpreted, and commented on. The cate-
gorizing and labeling that take place in discussions and interpretations
transform the unfamiliar and uncertain into the familiar (Moscovici 1984;
Oberschall 1989).

Even information and events that are inconsistent with the collective beliefs a group adheres to can be categorized and labeled so that they fit
into the collective belief system. One interesting illustration of the way this
psychological mechanism works appears in Willoughby's study of the impact of the Korean airliner incident on attitudes toward a nuclear freeze
(1986). Both supporters and opponents of a freeze selected and interpreted various cues from the incident in a way that reinforced their own
positions. Gamson (1988) obtained similar results in his study of the impact of nuclear accidents on public discourse. We can conclude, then, that
collective beliefs tend to be stable and durable.

Accordingly, anyone who wants to persuade other individuals to change
their minds must take these characteristics into account. As long as the
speaker and listeners share the same body of collective beliefs, chances

are that the speaker will succeed in persuading the audience. If speakers and audiences do not share the same beliefs, persuasion can become a rather hopeless undertaking, as, for example, supporters and opponents of cruise missiles in Europe discovered in the beginning of the 1980s. While opponents argued that deployment would threaten peace, supporters argued, conversely, that refraining from deployment would threaten peace. Five years later the same camps were debating whether the INF treaty was achieved because or in spite of the peace movements' campaigns against cruise missiles. In other words, unless an audience identifies with the speaker's perception of the world, audience and speaker will attach different meanings to the speaker's arguments.

This argument implies that a public can be persuaded if one of the three following conditions prevails: the public adheres to the collective belief system of the persuading agent; the persuading agent can, in one way or another, anchor its arguments in the collective beliefs of the public; or the persuading agent succeeds in transforming the collective beliefs of the public. This reasoning, of course, is akin to Snow et al.'s approach to frame alignment (1986), except for the fundamental argument that *neither anchoring nor transformation takes place among individuals in isolation.* Just as interpersonal interactions form collective beliefs, so do they amplify, extend, or transform them.

Although collective beliefs tend to be stable, I do not imply that they cannot change. Two fundamental aspects of social life can produce changes. First, any group or society itself embraces rival systems of collective beliefs that may compete for dominance or adapt to the others. As Gamson and Modigliani argue, we should conceive of collective beliefs dialectically: "there is no theme without a countertheme" (1989, 6). In a similar vein, Oberschall mentions "thought-worlds and meaning systems at variance with the dominant culture and ruling groups that survive in viable social and ecological enclaves and subcultures" (1989, 18). Second, as Billig (1987) observed, individuals are capable of counterarguing. Every coin has two sides; every argument has its opposite argument. Inevitably, then, some members of a community will always deviate from its collective beliefs. And although every community has mechanisms for neutralizing dissent (Oberschall 1989), the seeds of transformation that these dissenting members bear cannot be entirely obliterated.

Thus, beliefs are contested, refuted, reformulated, and defended within as well as between groups. Attitudes and opinions are justifications that emerge in debates over controversial issues, as Litton and Potter (1985) demonstrated in their study of newspaper editorials and opinion articles commenting on the St. Paul's riot in Bristol, England: they observed that the commentators gradually constructed their explanations of the riot to negate competing explanations. Typically, they defended their own explanatory schemata by contrasting them with alternative "mistaken" schemata.

Events can change the relative importance of different collective belief systems over time, as we can see from Gamson and Modigliani's (1989) discussion of the fate of the different ideological packages concerning nuclear energy. Hard facts do have an impact on collective beliefs, but, if we analyze the effect of such an event as the downing of the Korean airliner or the Chernobyl accident, we realize that this impact is always filtered through social interaction. It takes time for people to assimilate new events and information through the routine, daily processes of labeling and categorization. Thus, the transformation of collective beliefs is necessarily a gradual process, comparable to the development of scientific knowledge. Changing circumstances and external events make some beliefs less tenable and their protagonists less credible. Subjective definitions of reality and collective beliefs are then no longer complementary. The contradictions that are manifested necessitate a search for solutions. This search, again, does not take place in isolation. Dialogical communication is the way to tackle threatening events or opinions, and widening the circle of communication in order to find new partners who may help redefine the situation is often necessary (Wildemeersch and Leirman 1988).

The preceding discussion makes it clear that the transformations of collective beliefs requisite for social protest are difficult to achieve. Therefore, it is perhaps not so surprising that social protest is an exception rather than a rule. Nevertheless, protest does occur and collective beliefs do change both as a prelude to and a consequence of protest activity.

THE SOCIAL CONSTRUCTION OF PROTEST

In approaching a more detailed discussion of the social construction of protest, we can look first at two examples of collective beliefs that are transformed in the process of meaning construction: grievances and success expectations.

An important aspect of the social construction of protest is the construction of an injustice frame: situations are defined as unjust and grievances are transformed into demands. Defining the roots of the problem, suggesting collective rather than individual solutions, and identifying an antagonist are crucial elements in the process of grievance interpretation. The emergence of the problem of battered wives exemplifies this process. Tierney has described how, in less than ten years, the problem of battered wives was transformed "from a subject of private shame and misery to an object of public concern" (1982, 209).

A rather extensive literature affirms that protest takes place in the belief that the challengers' collective action can eliminate their grievances. Elsewhere (Klandermans 1984) I have demonstrated that the general category "success expectations" can be broken down into three particular types: expectations about (1) the effectiveness of collective action, (2) the effectiveness of the individual's contribution, and (3) the behavior of other individuals. Organizers of protest movements cannot take it for granted that any of these expectations will arise spontaneously; each must be constructed socially—that is, in interactions among potential participants. Hence, these expectations are in a sense self-fulfilling: the greater the number of individuals who believe that collective action will be successful, the more likely it is that mass action will materialize and that authorities will respond. The other side of the coin, of course, is pluralistic ignorance: in the absence of any person who acts overtly on an issue, collective action seems inconceivable. Rule (1989) takes this reasoning further, arguing that "seeing others take seriously a cause that might previously have seemed a strictly hypothetical possibility for action may revamp participants' perceived options for behavior" (1989, 154).

How are transformations like those described above brought about? Or more generally, how does the social construction of protest take place? The answer to this question depends on which level of meaning construction we are considering: (1) the level of public discourse, at which collective identities are formed and transformed; (2) the level of persuasive communication conducted by movement organizations, their opponents, and countermovement organizations; or (3) the level of consciousness raising during episodes of collective action. At each level the process of meaning construction has its own dynamics, as we can infer simply from the different sets of individuals involved. Public discourse and the formation and transformation of collective identities in principle involve everyone in a society or a particular sector within a society. Persuasive communication affects only those individuals who are targets of persuasion attempts, and consciousness raising during episodes of collective action concerns primarily participants in the action, although sympathetic spectators can be affected as well. Thus at each level the processes forming and transforming collective beliefs take place in different ways: at the first level, through the diffuse networks of meaning construction, at the second level, through deliberate attempts by social actors to persuade, and at the third level, through discussions among participants in and spectators of the collective action. Although a smaller or larger number of people will be involved at each level, the number of individuals affected is irrelevant, since, as noted earlier, the distinguishing feature of a collective belief is simply that it is shared.

The three levels of meaning construction are interdependent. The social construction of protest can be seen as a value-added process in which each level sets the terms for the next level. At the first, the most encompassing level, the long-term processes of formation and transformation of collective beliefs take place, and the collective identities that determine the constraints of mobilization campaigns are formed. At the second level, competing and opposing actors attempt to mobilize consensus by anchoring their definitions of the situation in the collective beliefs of various social groups. The degree of discrepancy between an actor's definition of the situation and a group's collective beliefs (formed in the public discourse) makes it more or less difficult to align these groups. And at the third level, which involves only those individuals who participate in or observe an episode of collective action, collective beliefs are formed and transformed under the impact of direct confrontations with opponents and competitors.

Until now the literature on social movements did not distinguish systematically between these three levels of social construction. Snow and his colleagues, for instance, discuss the complete range of framing processes—from frame bridging to frame transformation—within the same context. Other scholars, in exploring one level of the social construction process, claim the superiority of their own approach and criticize those who have been studying another level for neglecting crucial variables (e.g., Fantasia 1988; Hirsch 1990; Melucci 1989). There is no reason, however, to consider one level more important than the others, let alone to define investigations into one of the three as more or less fundamental than examinations of the others.

The Impact of Public Discourse on Collective Identities

Social issues are debated in arenas of public discourse and action (Gamson and Modigliani 1989; Hilgartner and Bosk 1988; Rucht 1988). Jenson (1987) argued that an issue can spark protest only if it gains access to arenas of public discourse, as—in her view—the feminist movement was able to do. The same issue can be on the agenda in different arenas, and within these arenas, several issues compete with one another for attention. The safety of nuclear power plants, for example, was debated among nuclear physicists long before it became an issue among politicians; and in Europe in the 1980s the nuclear power issue lost out in competition with the nuclear arms issue.

In public discourse, arguments evolve in response to counterarguments, new information, and new events. Media discourse has now become a crucial element in this evolutionary process. In describing the career of the nuclear power issue, Mazur (1981) demonstrated that it was the public's generally heightened awareness of environmental issues that spurred newspapers to publish the experts' initial debates. The media attention created a climate favorable to the anti–nuclear power movement. As a result, anti–nuclear power activists were able to mobilize more massive opposition, which in turn produced more media coverage, and so on. Over time, such processes can generate substantial changes in public opinion, as both Gamson and Modigliani's (1989) and Mazur's (1988) studies have shown. Events such as the accidents at Three Mile Island and Chernobyl also accelerate the process of change, but both these studies make it clear that such events can have this effect only when they occur in a climate of opinion that is already sympathetic to change. The development of the nuclear arms issue presents a similar story (Rochon 1988; Schennink 1988).

Social movement organizations themselves can have a profound impact on media discourse: they frame the issues, define the grievances, and stage collective actions that attract the attention of the mass media. The movement's message is not transmitted without bias, however, and the media's biases do not always favor the movement (Gitlin 1980). Media attention influences not only grievance interpretations but success expectations. Knowledge of one group's success can instill hope in other groups and so motivate other collective actions. According to Tarrow (1989b) the perception of other groups' successes is the major mechanism behind the upswing in a cycle of protest.

The way in which individuals process the information the media transmit has as great an influence on public discourse as do the media themselves. As I mentioned in the discussion of collective beliefs, information is processed not by individuals in isolation but by people interacting with other people in informal circles, primary groups, and friendship networks. Much of what goes on within these networks concerns the formation of consensus (Klandermans 1988). People tend to validate information by comparing and discussing their interpretations with significant others (Festinger 1954), especially when the information involved is complex. People prefer to compare their opinions with those of like-minded individuals. As a rule, the set of individuals interacting in one's social networks—especially one's friendship networks—is relatively homogeneous and composed of people not too different from oneself. These processes of social comparison produce collective definitions of a situation.

This kind of interaction depends on the existence of a social or collective identity—the way an individual defines him- or herself as a member of a group or category (Hewstone, Jaspars, and Lalljee 1982). Because they identify with a particular group or category, individuals willingly adopt the beliefs and norms that define the category, as the diffusion of feminist consciousness in the United States and Europe in the sixties and seventies illustrates (Klein 1987). Klein describes how the dramatic changes in the division of labor between the sexes provided women with a new social identity: the self-image of "women as workers" replaced that of "women as mothers." This new identity did not automatically lead to political activism, but it created new standards for social comparison; comparison generated the belief that the category "women" was treated unjustly; and this belief was an impetus to political activism. A similar process of identification took place in the early stages of the Dutch peace movement, as Schennink (1988) describes. In the seventies there emerged a network of church-related groups composed of church members who increasingly began to define themselves as members of the peace movement. This network was crucial to the success of mass mobilizations in the eighties.

Public discourse, then, implies an interplay of media discourse and interpersonal interactions governed in many ways by existing collective beliefs and identities. Although the mass media play a crucial role in framing the themes and counterthemes of public discourse, the actual formation and transformation of collective beliefs take place in exchange within the groups and categories with which individuals identify. Such groups may be small, composed of people whom one encounters in daily life (colleagues, friends, carpoolers), or large generic categories (e.g., whites, workers, farmers, Europeans, union members). The themes and counterthemes that arise in media discourse may, to a greater or lesser degree, harmonize with the collective beliefs of these groups or categories. (Occasionally, too, public discourse will bring one group or category into special prominence: a debate about tollways, for instance, may reinforce the collective identity of car drivers.) To the degree that an individual's beliefs coincide with an element in the public discourse, the individual will identify with that element and adopt beliefs that in their turn become part of the collective beliefs of a group or category.

Persuasive Communication

The social construction of protest proceeds in the context of mobilization and countermobilization campaigns, as different actors in a social conflict try to persuade individual citizens to take their side. Unlike public discourse and the process through which collective identities are formed and transformed, the construction of meaning at this level involves deliberate attempts to influence beliefs. Movement organizations, opponents, and countermovement organizations alike try to convince the individual that they are right. Organizers are "social reconstructionists," to quote Delgado (1986, 76); they construct an alternative view of social reality. In many ways this aspect of the social construction of protest is very visible: it is publicized in statements by officials, in printed material, in encounters with representatives of the movement, and in debates with competing organizations, opponents, and countermovement organizations.

Persuasive communication, however, also has a much less visible side. Like public discourse, persuasive communication involves interpersonal exchanges. The individuals who are targeted by a movement campaign discuss the persuasive messages with people in their environment. Accordingly, the individual evaluates these messages in relation to the collective beliefs of the groups or categories with which he or she identifies. From our previous discussions we can deduce that the success of an actor's attempts to persuade depends on the extent to which he or she can appeal to the collective beliefs of target groups. Of course, though the actor may feel that his or her arguments can be anchored in the collective beliefs of a group, it is not the actor but members of the group who, by their interactions, decide how closely the actor's and their own beliefs coincide. Thus this part of consensus mobilization is not only difficult for an outsider to perceive, it is also much less controllable by the actor. Most likely, a persuasive campaign will end up swaying only those individuals who already share at least some of the actor's beliefs, as Di Giacomo's study of student protest at a Flemish university illustrates (1980).

Frame alignment (Snow et al. 1986) and consensus mobilization (Klandermans 1984, 1988) are the two concepts that have been proposed to analyze persuasive communication by movement organizations. Although these concepts were introduced for the analysis of movement campaigns, they apply as well to campaigns waged by opponents and countermovement organizations. As we have already noted, and as Snow et al. (1986) in fact suggest, frame bridging is the principal route to alignment. We may wonder whether at this level any other approach works at all. Indeed, movement organizations find it difficult enough to keep their original sympathizers from being carried away by the stream of counterarguments. Although the polarization of actors has a homogenizing effect on an actor's beliefs, it also increases the cognitive dissonance of those individuals who are caught in between parties. In a paper on the erosion of support during mobilization campaigns, for example, Klandermans and Oegema (1990) demonstrated that supporters of the peace movement who identified with political parties opposed to the movement came under the cross fire of the actors opposed to each other, and in many cases they withdrew their support from the peace movement. Not infrequently, the movement's campaign itself evokes the counterarguments that cause some of the initial sympathizers to change their minds: both Mansbridge's discussion (1986) of the drives for and against the Equal Rights Amendment (ERA) and Chafetz and Dworkin's analysis (1987) of feminist and antifeminist movements illustrate this phenomenon.

Because goals and means are essential elements of consensus mobilization, the way a campaign frames its protest goals and means determines its appearance. Individual reactions to a protest goal depend not only on the content of the demands it represents but also on how those demands are symbolized or packaged for the public (Conover and Gray 1983). Hence, a campaign will frame its goal in terms of preventing a collective bad rather than producing a collective good (Mitchell 1984); it will invoke past successes (Waddington 1986); and it will use condensation symbols rather than referential symbols to define the issue (Edelman 1964). But even if an individual does come to identify with a cause, he or she will not necessarily engage in protest. For protest activities have concrete goals, and campaign organizers cannot take it for granted that potential participants will feel that these goals are related to their own particular dissatisfactions and aspirations. Nor can campaigners assume that other people will believe that participation in the movement's activities can be effective. Protest goals and means must be legitimated, and to gain that legitimacy is the challenge a movement organization faces in mobilizing consensus in the context of action mobilization. A campaign gains legitimacy in confrontations with competing organizations, opponents, and countermovements (Chafetz and Dworkin 1987; Conover and Gray 1983; Mansbridge 1986). The impact that various sources of information will have on potential participants differs according to the perceived credibility of those sources. Naturally, people find the groups and organizations with which they identify more credible than those with which they do not identify. Consequently, consensus mobilization often consists of preaching to the converted.

In sum, consensus mobilization is a matter of symbolic politics—it entails a struggle to determine which group's symbolic definition of the situation will prevail (Edelman 1964). As this struggle continues, the social construction of meaning proceeds: issues are redefined, and means of action and outcomes are reevaluated; movement organizations, opponents, and countermovement organizations may be discredited; beliefs and ideologies are challenged or refuted; and competing organizations are deemed unreliable.

Consciousness Raising during Episodes of Collective Action

The process of social construction does not come to an end once individuals, for whatever reason, decide to join in collective action. In his study of the Berkeley free speech movement, for example, Heirich

(1968) convincingly demonstrated how a true reconstruction of social reality took place during the "spiral of conflict" that developed at the time. Organizers know that during episodes of collective action the participant's consciousness is raised considerably, and some grass-roots organizations use action mobilization to create consensus. The ACORN model, for instance, capitalizes on the impact of successful collective action "to affirm from the beginning the ability of people to change their social reality through collective action" (Delgado 1986, 85). But even when organizers do not exploit collective action to raise individuals' consciousness, such action can have a tremendous influence on the participant's beliefs. In the case of the Three Mile Island accident, for example, Walsh (1988) reported that attendance at a public meeting, hearing, or rally shortly after the accident was a key variable in determining who eventually became an activist. Collective action, of course, does not necessarily affect only the participants. Consciousness raising may also occur among sympathetic spectators. For many Irish people, for example, the perception that the state represses collective action is reason enough to support the provisional Irish Republican Army (White 1989). Clearly, such a response among nonparticipants indicates their sympathy with the collective actor, as Reicher (1984) demonstrated in his account of the St. Paul's riot, in which consciousness raising took place only among those spectators who identified with the ethnic groups involved in the riots.

Hirsch (1990) and Fantasia (1988) have made consciousness raising during action episodes the core of their approaches to collective action. Not accidentally, solidarity is a central concept in the work of these authors— a concept they apply to the collective identity that developed in the course of the collective actions they were describing. It is clear from the work of both authors that many participants were initially unwilling to join or were passers-by, as Hirsch found in his study of the divestment protest at Columbia University. Both authors stress, however, that collective action can strengthen solidarity only if it is founded on existing collective beliefs. At Columbia University, several years of consensus mobilization by a group called Coalition for a Free South Africa laid the groundwork for the successful divestment protest (Hirsch 1990). Within the companies Fantasia investigated, the workers' identification with existing work groups and social groups provided the basis for the "cultures of solidarity" that developed during the collective actions he describes (1988).

Both Hirsch and Fantasia demonstrate that during an action episode the collective action dilemma is resolved by generating positive success expectations. At an actual protest site all the participants see how many other people are willing to protest. If large numbers are protesting, success seems possible. This appearance of collective strength encourages individuals who are less committed, an effect that confirms Rule's assertion that "witnessing previously inconceivable forms of action, or perceiving others taking the possibility of such action seriously, itself creates a new-found readiness to act" (1989, 157).

Episodes of collective action have an enduring impact on the participants; their collective identities are formed and transformed. The successful wildcat strike in one of the companies Fantasia (1988) studied created a new collective identity incorporating the workers' recently demonstrated militancy. Attending a demonstration in Washington made inhabitants of the area around Three Mile Island aware that they were part of a larger protest movement and also made them more militant (Walsh 1988). Participants in the first mass demonstration of the Dutch peace movement—many of whom were demonstrating for the first time in their lives—acquired a new collective identity as supporters of the peace movement, and an overwhelming number took part in the second demonstration and the People's Petition (Schennink 1988). The little research conducted on the biographical consequences of activism suggests that these newly formed identities endure for many years (McAdam 1989) and thus in turn influence public discourse.

To summarize: the social construction of protest occurs at different levels and in different stages. First, individuals are born into social environments in which specific collective beliefs that describe and interpret the world prevail; people are socialized into groups and organizations whose members share a certain set of beliefs; they enter groups with specific collective identities. Collective beliefs and identities alike are formed and transformed through public discourse. Second, movement organizations, opponents, and countermovement organizations try to persuade individuals to see the world as they do, and attempts to persuade will be more or less successful depending on the degree to which movements can anchor their views in existing beliefs or identities. Because these beliefs are by definition collective—shared by individuals who identify with a particular group or category—the critical question of anchoring is sorted out as individuals within these groups or categories interact. Third, once individuals become involved in an episode of collective action their view of the world may change dramatically. They acquire new collective identities as participants in collective action. These new identities, however, do not necessarily represent a disjunction with the past, since they evolve from beliefs an individual already shared with the collective.

The social construction of protest, then, takes place within and betweeen groups and social categories and within social networks. To study the structural vehicles of the social construction of protest we can, as I have proposed elsewhere (Klandermans 1990), use the concept of a multi-organizational field.

MULTIORGANIZATIONAL FIELDS

As we examine the subject of multiorganizational fields, we should keep in mind a point I emphasized earlier: beliefs and identities can be shared by any number and by any group of individuals. At the most general level, individuals can be classified in terms of structural categories such as class, gender, race, religion, ethnicity, nationality, and so on, and to the extent they identify with these categories, they come to share the beliefs of others within the same category. Individuals who transfer from one category to another—converts or immigrants, for example—experience the full force of this collective identity because they must become familiar with a new set of beliefs. As powerful as such macrostructural categories are, however, it is not these categories per se that determine the beliefs individuals adhere to. If we consider that individuals can be classified according to each of these categories and that there is no inherent reason an individual should identify with one rather than another, we will see that we need to find more specific factors to explain social identification.

At a more specific level, individuals belong to associations and organizations (churches, unions, leisure clubs, neighborhood or student organizations, etc.) and groups (friends, colleagues, neighbors, sports teams, roommates, etc.). The constituency of these organizations and groups often follows the lines of social categorization (race, gender, religion, ethnicity); accordingly, participation in these groups reinforces the individual's identification with these categories. I suggest that these groups—especially primary groups—and organizations play a crucial role in the social construction of protest. By proposing the term *catnet* (an amalgam of *cat*egory and *net*work) to signify a social category with a collective identity, Tilly (1978) similarly referred to social networks as the structural foundation a social category requires in order to generate a collective identity. As noted earlier, these networks—whether subcultural (Oberschall 1989) or countercultural (Kriesi 1988)—usually remain submerged in everyday life; they become visible only when employed by mobilization and counter-mobilization campaigns, which educe otherwise latent structures.

The critical question, of course, is, why do these submerged structures become involved in a political struggle? The answer seems to be that they are co-opted by one of the parties in a conflict or that they themselves come into conflict with a public policy. We can perceive these processes more clearly if we observe them within the context of the multiorganizational field.

According to Curtis and Zurcher, "The concept of 'multiorganizational field' suggests that organizations in a community setting approximate an ordered, coordinated system. Interorganizational processes within the field can be identified on two levels, which conceptually overlap: the *organizational* level, where networks are established by joint activities, staff, boards of directors, target clientele, resources, etc.; and the *individual* level, where networks are established by multiple affiliations of members" (1973, 56).

Movement organizations, like any other, are embedded in a multiorganizational field, which we can define as the total possible number of organizations with which the movement organization might establish specific links. Until recently the literature focused primarily on the *support* a social movement organization receives from sectors of the multiorganizational field and contained surprisingly little about the fact that multiorganizational fields need not necessarily be supportive. Opponents, in fact, always constitute some part of the multiorganizational field of a movement organization.

In other words, its multiorganizational field contains both supportive and antagonistic sectors. The first we can describe as a social movement organization's alliance system, consisting of groups and organizations that support it; the second, as the organization's conflict system, consisting of representatives and allies of the challenged political systems, including countermovement organizations (Kriesi 1985). Alliance systems provide resources and create political opportunities; conflict systems drain resources and restrict opportunities. The boundaries between the two systems remain fluid and may change in the course of events. Specific organizations that try to keep aloof from the controversy may be forced to take sides. Parts of the political system (parties, elites, governmental institutions) can coalesce with social movement organizations and join the alliance system. Coalitions can fall apart, and former allies can become part of the conflict system.

Different social movement organizations have different but overlapping conflict and alliance systems. The greatest overlap will exist among organizations from the same social movement industry (e.g., the women's movement, the environmental movement). But movement organizations from different industries will also have overlapping conflict and alliance systems. Many activists from the peace movement, for example, were also involved in the women's movement or the environmental movement (Klandermans

1990). And the cleavage between an organization's alliance and conflict systems may coincide with other cleavages, such as those created by social class, ethnic divisions, or Left-Right affiliation.

The specific makeup of the multiorganizational field will vary over time and with the particular movement and situation. The proportion of the multiorganizational field engaged in one of the two systems expands or contracts according to cycles of protest. At the peaks of protest, almost every organization will be enmeshed in one system or the other; in the valleys most organizations will not belong to either.

Although other movement organizations constitute a major part of the *alliance system* of a social movement organization, almost any kind of organization can become engaged in it: those representing recreational interests, youth, students, women, conservationists, business people, consumers, and community advocates, as well as political parties, unions, churches, and sometimes even governmental institutions. The alliance system of the Dutch peace movement, for example, comprised (apart from other movement organizations) political parties, unions, churches, and a variety of local social welfare, neighborhood, and specialized organizations (Klandermans 1990). Further, like the composition of the multiorganizational field as a whole, the composition of alliance systems changes in the course of the cycle, as Tarrow's research on the Italian protest cycle in the sixties and seventies shows (1989a). Although traditional and institutional actors did not take part in the initial phases of this cycle, they became involved in and indeed took over events at the peak of the cycle, either to channel protest into more moderate directions or to use the accumulated political pressure to advance their own interests. At the downturn of the cycle, the alliance system rapidly disintegrated and eventually contracted to a network of political radicals (della Porta and Tarrow 1986).

The principal components of a social movement organization's *conflict system* are its targets: governmental institutions, employers' or business organizations, elites, political parties, and so on. But just as an alliance system will accept any kind of organizational ally, so a conflict system will admit any opponent. Occasionally the actions of the social movement organization itself push others into the conflict system. Protests inevitably have spill-over effects that penalize people other than those who are the target, and these people may ally themselves with the organization's opponents.

MULTIORGANIZATIONAL FIELDS AND THE SOCIAL CONSTRUCTION OF PROTEST

Long before a controversy develops into an open conflict and challengers enter the scene, *public discourse* has created various sectors within a society, each with its own opinions and position. Opinions about social issues develop within subcultures of groups of individuals who already share many attitudes and agree on certain principles. The direction in which these opinions develop suggests the initial contours of the multi-organizational field of a would-be challenger. Individuals, organizations, and groups may be antipathetic, sympathetic, or indifferent toward the issues at hand; these attitudes are influenced by the leaders of one's own groups, by the media, or by spokespersons. When new facts and information appear, they are diffused and processed along the preexisting lines of opinion and within the circles these opinions have created.

In this situation, *persuasive communication* by a challenger resonates first among individuals from those sectors who have some sympathy or affinity for the challenger's viewpoints. Many a persuasive campaign never goes beyond these sectors. Oliver and Marwell (1988) hypothesize that the average organizer will at first try to mobilize people whom he or she knows and who already sympathize with the cause. And, these authors argue, if such mobilization attempts are sufficient to achieve the movement's goals, why should it try to reach beyond that circle? In fact, messages often find their own way within the networks of a subculture without much active persuasion on the part of the movement campaign. Kriesi (1988), for instance, suggested that the countercultural networks in some parts of the Netherlands were so dense and so sympathetic to the message of the peace movement that this message spread throughout the networks with little assistance from the movement organization itself.

We should emphasize that movement campaigns direct their messages not only to potential supporters but to opponents as well. Indeed, a large number of a challenger's arguments emerge in interactions with its opponents. As a result, an us-them dynamic tends to develop. Mansbridge describes this process, frequently discussed in the literature on intergroup relations, in relation to the proponents and opponents of the ERA: "Building an organization on belief in a principle, when the world refuses to go along with that principle, produces a deep sense of us against them; when two movements are pitted against each other reality will provide plenty of temptations to see the opposition as evil incarnate" (1986, 179). Organizations such as social movement organizations, which rely on volunteers, are especially susceptible to such polarization because it "requires an exaggerated, black or white vision of events to justify spending time and money on the cause" (Mansbridge 1986, 6).

Such intergroup dynamics easily end up dominating the conflict system, particularly if a countermovement develops. As the controversy escalates, justifications of the rival viewpoints multiply and the sector of indifference shrinks. Individuals, groups, and organizations take sides, usually in response to persuasive campaigns of the contending parties. Persuasive campaigns largely reinforce existing lines of division within the multiorganizational field of a challenger. When those individuals and organizations that were initially indifferent to the controversy eventually choose sides (at the insistence of the rival parties), they will choose the side whose position seems most congenial to their own. Furthermore, simply because social distances between sectors are greater than those within sectors, it is much more likely that a person or organization will be approached by an actor from its own sector than by one from an opposing sector. The persuasive campaigns conducted by movement organizations, opponents, and countermovement organizations also accentuate the difference among the collective beliefs of the opposing sectors of a multiorganizational field.

Consciousness raising during episodes of collective action affects primarily people engaged in a collective action, although outsiders who sympathize with an actor can become affected as well. These individuals process information, discuss their experiences and the moves of the opponent, and learn about their situation. Networks, groups, and organizations that are part of the alliance system of an actor facilitate these activities and thus play an extremely important role in consciousness raising. Morris (1984), for example, describes the significance of what he called local movement centers in the southern civil rights movement—which are akin to what I have called the alliance system of the multiorganizational field—and he makes it clear that these centers played a crucial role in defining and interpreting the situation during collective action episodes. Fantasia (1988) similarly describes how existing links among the workers within the companies he studied determined interaction patterns within the work force during episodes of action and how these interactions helped shape the culture of solidarity. Hirsch's (1990) account of the divestment protest at Columbia University shows that preexisting ties and affinities were the key factors that determined which passers-by joined the demonstration. The collective experience of withstanding the administration and the related discussions on the stairs of Columbia created a new sense of solidarity and developed new collective beliefs among the participants.

Consciousness raising during collective action takes place simultaneously within the alliance and conflict systems of the multiorganizational field. As groups of supporters and opponents discuss ongoing events and incoming information, they become more aware of the issues and of their positions. As a result, they become more aware of each other and their mutual relationships become more polarized. Consciousness raising thus reinforces the us-them dynamic, and so, usually, individuals become radicalized—as the studies by Morris, Fantasia, and Hirsch demonstrate.

By situating social movement organizations within multiorganizational fields, we see the movements as something much more dynamic than the self-contained phenomenon that appears in earlier studies. In this new context, the career of a social movement organization is determined by the dynamics of its field. Such factors as the relationship between an organization and its opponents, the presence of countermovements, the formation of coalitions, the movement's relationship with sympathetic and opposition political parties, and its relationship with the mass media all shape the field of tension in which social movement organizations develop, change, and decline.

The concept of a multiorganizational field also provides us with a new way of looking at the mobilization of individual citizens. We can no longer analyze mobilization and participation within the simple frame of an organization that appeals to separate individuals. We have seen that individuals (like organizations) occupy positions within multiorganizational fields, and depending on their place in these complex fields, they become more or less involved in events. The social construction of protest takes place within the context of a community's multiorganizational field. It is there that grievances are interpreted, means and opportunities are defined, opponents are appointed, strategies are chosen and justified, and outcomes are evaluated. Interpretations and evaluations are as a rule controversial; each of the various actors may challenge the interpretations of the others. As a social movement organization competes to influence public opinion or the opinion of its constituency, its multiorganizational field determines its relative significance as an individual actor.

CONCLUSION

Collective beliefs and the way they are formed and transformed are the core of the social construction of protest; interpersonal networks submerged in multiorganizational fields are the conduits of this process of meaning construction. Collective beliefs are constructed and reconstructed over and over: in public discourse, during the mobilization of consensus, and in the process of consciousness raising during episodes of collective action. Because collective beliefs are formed and transformed in interpersonal interactions, attempts to change the mind of a single individual would not be very effective in changing collective beliefs unless that individual is influential in his or her interpersonal circle. Incoming information is processed and anchored in existing collective beliefs through interpersonal interaction. Only when actors are able to direct this interaction so that their message becomes anchored in existing beliefs can they transform collective beliefs. Thus every actor will be able to mobilize consensus more easily in some groups or categories than in others.

Since beliefs can and will be disputed, the social construction of protest is a struggle among various actors to determine whose definition of the situation will prevail. In the clashes and confrontations between competing or opposing schemes, meaning is constructed. The various meanings that emerge represent the multiple sectors in a multiorganizational field: those that support a movement organization, those that oppose it, and those that are indifferent to the issue in question. Because of the complex makeup of the multiorganizational field, individuals are objects of persuasive communications emanating not only from movement organization A but also from competing organization B, opponent C, countermovement organization D, and so on.

This line of thought leads students of social movements into territory they have yet to explore. Social psychologists have hardly begun to study the complex phenomenon of the formation and transformation of collective beliefs, and the social construction of reality is a process we are only now beginning to understand. To grapple with the complexities of the social construction of protest, social movement research must pursue new methods and investigate new topics. Discourse analysis and the study of collective beliefs and interpersonal interaction are approaches that bring social psychology back into play. For too long scholars of social movements have equated social psychology with the study of relative deprivation; it is time to discard this stereotype.

REFERENCES

Billig, Michael. 1987. *Arguing and Thinking: A Rhetorical Approach to Social Psychology*. Cambridge: Cambridge University Press.

Conover, Pamela Johnston, and Virginia Gray. 1983. *Feminism and the New Right: The Conflict over the American Family*. New York: Praeger.

Chafetz, Janet Saltzman, and Anthony Dworkin. 1987. "Action and Reaction: An Integrated, Comparative Perspective on Feminist and Antifeminist Movements." Paper presented at the annual meetings of the American Sociological Association, Chicago, Ill., August.

Curtis, Russell L., and Louis A. Zurcher. 1973. "Stable Resources of Protest Movements: The Multi-organizational Field." *Social Forces* 52:53–61.

Delgado, Gary. 1986. *Organizing the Poor: The Roots and Growth of ACORN*. Philadelphia: Temple University Press.

Della Porta, Donatella, and Sidney Tarrow. 1986. "Unwanted Children: Political Violence and the Cycle of Protest in Italy, 1966–1973." *European Journal of Political Research* 14:607–32.

Di Giacomo, J. P. 1980. "Intergroup Alliances and Rejections with a Protest Movement: Analysis of Social Representations." *European Journal of Social Psychology* 10:309–22.

Edelman, Murray. 1964. *The Symbolic Uses of Politics*. New York: Longman.

Fantasia, Rick. 1988. *Cultures of Solidarity: Consciousness, Action, and Contemporary American Workers*. Berkeley: University of California Press.

Festinger, Leon. 1954. "A Theory of Social Comparison Processes." *Human Relations* 7:117–40.

Gamson, William A. 1988. "Political Discourse and Collective Action." In *From Structure to Action: Comparing Movement Participation across Cultures*. International Social Movement Research, vol. 1, ed. Bert Klandermans, Hanspeter Kriesi, and Sidney Tarrow. Greenwich, Conn.: JAI Press, 219–47.

———. 1989. *The Strategy of Social Protest*. 2d ed. Belmont: Wadsworth.

Gamson, William A., and Andre Modigliani. 1989. "Media Discourse and Public Opinion on Nuclear Power." *American Journal of Sociology* 95:1–38.

Gitlin, Todd. 1980. *The Whole World Is Watching: The Media in the Making and Unmaking of the New Left*. Berkeley: University of California Press.

Heirich, Max. 1968. *The Spiral of Conflict: Berkeley, 1964*. New York: Columbia University Press.

Hewstone, M., J. Jaspars, and M. Lalljee. 1982. "Social Representations, Social Attribution and Social Identity: The Intergroup Image of 'Public' and 'Comprehensive' Schoolboys." *European Journal of Social Psychology* 12:241–69.

Hilgartner, Stephen, and Charles L. Bosk. 1988. "The Rise and Fall of Social Problems: A Public Arenas Model." *American Journal of Sociology* 94:53–79.

Hirsch, Eric L. 1990. "Sacrifice for the Cause: The Impact of Group Processes on Recruitment and Commitment in Protest Movements." *American Sociological Review* 55:243–54.

Jenson, Jane. 1987. "Changing Discourse, Changing Agendas: Political Rights and Reproductive Policies in France." In *The Women's Movements of the United States and Western Europe: Consciousness, Political Opportunity, and Public Opinion*, ed. Mary Fainsod Katzenstein and Carol McClurg Mueller. Philadelphia: Temple University Press.

Klandermans, Bert. 1984. "Mobilization and Participation: Social-Psychological Expansions of Resource Mobilization Theory." *American Sociological Review* 49:583–600.

———. 1986. "New Social Movements and Resource Mobilization: The European and the American Approach." *International Journal of Mass Emergencies and Disasters* 4, no. 2:13–39.

———. 1988. "The Formation and Mobilization of Consensus." In *From Structure to Action: Comparing Movement Participation across Cultures*. International Social Movement Research, vol. 1, ed. Bert Klandermans, Hanspeter Kriesi, and Sidney Tarrow. Greenwich, Conn.: JAI Press, 173–97.

———. 1989. "Grievance Interpretation and Success Expectations: The Social Construction of Protest." *Social Behaviour* 4:113–25.

———. 1990. "Linking the 'Old' and the 'New': Movement Networks in the Netherlands." In *Challenging the Political Order*, ed. Russell J. Dalton and Manfred Kuechler. Cambridge: Polity Press.

Klandermans, Bert, and Dirk Oegema. 1990. "Erosion of a Movement's Support: The Unwanted Effects of Action Mobilization." Submitted for publication.

Klein, Ethel. 1987. "The Diffusion of Consciousness in the United States and Western Europe." In *The Women's Movements of the United States and Western Europe: Consciousness, Political Opportunity, and Public Opinion*, ed. Mary Fainsod Katzenstein and Carol McClurg Mueller. Philadelphia: Temple University Press, 23–43.

Kriesi, Hanspeter. 1985. *Bewegung in der Schweizer Politik: Fallstudien zu politischen Mobilierungsprozessen in der Schweiz*. Frankfurt and New York: Campus Verlag.

———. 1988. "Local Mobilization for the People's Petition of the Dutch Peace Movement." In *From Structure to Action: Comparing Movement Participation across Cultures*. International Social Movement Research, vol. 1, ed. Bert Klandermans, Hanspeter Kriesi, and Sidney Tarrow. Greenwich, Conn.: JAI Press, 41–83.

Litton, I., and J. Potter. 1985. "Social Representations in the Ordinary Explanation of a 'Riot.'" *European Journal of Social Psychology* 15:371–88.

Mansbridge, Jane L. 1986. *Why We Lost the ERA*. Chicago: University of Chicago Press.

Mazur, Allan. 1981. *The Dynamics of Technical Controversy*. Washington, D.C.: Communication Press.

———. 1988. "Mass Media Effects on Public Opinion about Nuclear Power Plants." Manuscript, Syracuse University, Department of Sociology.

McAdam, Doug. 1982. *Political Process and the Development of Black Insurgency*. Chicago: University of Chicago Press.

———. 1989. "The Biographical Consequences of Activism." *American Sociological Review* 54:744–60.

McAdam, Doug, John D. McCarthy, and Mayer N. Zald. 1988. "Social Movements." In *Handbook of Sociology*, ed. Neil J. Smelser. Beverly Hills, Calif.: Sage, 695–739.

Melucci, Alberto. 1989. *Nomads of the Present: Social Movements and Individual Needs in Contemporary Society*. London: Hutchinson Radius.

Mitchell, Robert C. 1984. "Moving Forward vs. Moving Backwards: Motivation for Collective Action." Paper presented at the annual meeting of the American Sociological Association, San Antonio.

Morris, Aldon D. 1984. *The Origins of the Civil Rights Movement*. New York: Free Press.

Moscovici, S. 1984. "The Phenomenon of Social Representations." In *Social Representations*, ed. R. M. Farr and S. Moscovici. Cambridge: Cambridge University Press, 3–71.

Oberschall, Anthony. 1989. "Culture Change and Social Movements." Paper presented at the annual meeting of the American Sociological Association, San Francisco, August 9–13.

Oliver, Pamela E., and Gerald Marwell. 1988. "Mobilizing Technologies and the Micro-Meso Link." Paper presented at the workshop on Frontiers in Social Movement Theory, June 8–11, University of Michigan, Ann Arbor.

Reicher, S. D. 1984. "The St. Paul's Riot: An Explanation of the Limits of Crowd Action in Terms of a Social Identity Model." *European Journal of Social Psychology* 14:1–21.

Rochon, Thomas R. 1988. *Mobilizing for Peace: The Antinuclear Movements in Western Europe*. Princeton: Princeton University Press.

Rucht, Dieter. 1988. "Themes, Logics, and Arenas of Social Movements: A Structural Approach." In *From Structure to Action: Comparing Movement Participation across Cultures*. International Social Movement Research, vol. 1, ed. Bert Klandermans, Hanspeter Kriesi, and Sidney Tarrow. Greenwich, Conn.: JAI Press, 305–29.

Rule, James B. 1989. "Rationality and Non-rationality in Militant Collective Action." *Sociological Theory* 7:145–60.

Schennink, Ben. 1988. "From Peace Week to Peace Work: Dynamics of the Peace Movement in the Netherlands." In *From Structure to Action: Comparing Movement Participation across Cultures.* International Social Movement Research, vol. 1, ed. Bert Klandermans, Hanspeter Kriesi, and Sidney Tarrow. Greenwich, Conn.: JAI Press, 247–81.

Snow, David A., E. Burke Rochford, Jr., Steve K. Worden, and Robert D. Benford. 1986. "Frame Alignment Processes, Micro-Mobilization and Movement Participation." *American Sociological Review* 51:464–81.

Spector, Malcolm, and John I. Kitsuse. 1973. "Social Problems: A Re-formulation." *Social Problems* 21:145–59.

Tarrow, Sidney. 1989a. *Democracy and Disorder: Protest and Politics in Italy, 1965–1975.* Oxford: Oxford University Press.

———. 1989b. "Struggle, Politics, and Reform: Collective Action, Social Movements, and Cycles of Protest." Western Societies Paper no. 21, Cornell University.

Tierney, Kathleen J. 1982. "The Battered Women Movement and the Creation of the Wife Beating Problem." *Social Problems* 29:207–20.

Tilly, Charles. 1978. *From Mobilization to Revolution.* Reading, Mass.: Addison-Wesley.

Waddington, David P. 1986. "The Ansell Brewery Dispute: A Social-Cognitive Approach to the Study of Strikes." *Journal of Occupational Psychology* 59:231–46.

Walsh, Edward J. 1988. *Democracy in the Shadows: Citizen Mobilization in the Wake of the Accident at Three Mile Island.* Westport, Conn.: Greenwood.

White, Robert W. 1989. "From Peaceful Protest to Guerrilla War: Micromobilization of the Provisional Irish Republican Army." *American Journal of Sociology* 94:1277–1303.

Wildemeersch, Danny, and Walter Leirman. 1988. "The Facilitation of the Lifeworld Transformation." *Adult Education Quarterly* 39:19–30.

Willoughby, M. J. 1986. "Nuclear Freeze Attitude Structures: A Pre- and Post-test of the Impact of the Korean Airliner Incident." *Social Science Quarterly* 67:534–44.

5

Collective Identity in Social Movement Communities

Lesbian Feminist Mobilization

Verta Taylor and

Nancy E. Whittier

Understanding the relationship between group consciousness and collective action has been a major focus of social science research (Morris 1990). The resource mobilization and political process perspectives, in contrast to earlier microlevel analyses, have shifted attention to the macrolevel, deemphasizing group grievances and focusing instead on the external political processes and internal organizational dynamics that influence the rise and course of movements (Rule and Tilly 1972; Oberschall 1973; McCarthy and Zald 1973, 1977; Gamson 1975; Jenkins and Perrow 1977; Schwartz 1976; Tilly 1978; McAdam 1982; Jenkins 1983; Morris 1984). But the resource mobilization and political process theories cannot explain how structural inequality gets translated into subjectively experienced discontent (Fireman and Gamson 1979; Ferree and Miller 1985; Snow et al. 1986; Klandermans 1984; Klandermans and Tarrow 1988; Ferree, this volume). In a recent review of the field, McAdam, McCarthy, and Zald (1988) respond by offering the concept of the micromobilization context to characterize the link between the macrolevel and microlevel processes that generate collective action. Drawing from a wide range of research documenting the importance of preexisting group ties for movement formation, they view informal networks held together by strong bonds as the "basic building blocks" of social movements. Still missing, however, is an understanding of the way these networks transform their members into political actors.

European analyses of recent social movements, loosely grouped under the rubric "new social movement theory," suggest that a key concept that

We thank Myra Marx Ferree, Susan Hartmann, Joan Huber, Craig Jenkins, Laurel Richardson, Leila J. Rupp, Beth Schneider, Kate Weigand, and the editors of this volume for helpful comments on earlier drafts.

allows us to understand this process is collective identity (Pizzorno 1978; Boggs 1986; Cohen 1985; Melucci 1985, 1989; Touraine 1985; B. Epstein 1990). Collective identity is the shared definition of a group that derives from members' common interests, experiences, and solidarity. For new social movement theorists, political organizing around a common identity is what distinguishes recent social movements in Europe and the United States from the more class-based movements of the past (Kauffman 1990). It is our view, based on existing scholarship (Friedman and McAdam, this volume; Fantasia 1988; Mueller 1990; Rupp and Taylor 1990; Whittier 1991), that identity construction processes are crucial to grievance interpretation in all forms of collective action, not just in the so-called new movements. Despite the centrality of collective identity to new social movement theory, no one has dissected the way that constituencies involved in defending their rights develop politicized group identities.

In this chapter, we present a framework for analyzing the construction of collective identity in social movements. The framework is grounded in exploratory research on the contemporary lesbian feminist movement in the United States. Drawing from Gerson and Peiss's (1985) model for analyzing gender relations, we offer a conceptual bridge linking theoretical approaches in the symbolic interactionist tradition with existing theory in social movements. Our aim is to provide a definition of collective identity that is broad enough to encompass mobilizations ranging from those based on race, gender, ethnicity, and sexuality to constituencies organized around more focused visions.

After discussing the data sources, we trace the evolution of lesbian feminism in the early 1970s out of the radical branch of the modern women's movement and analyze lesbian feminism as a social movement community. Substantively, our aim is to demonstrate that lesbian feminist communities sustain a collective identity that encourages women to engage in a wide range of social and political actions that challenge the dominant system. Theoretically, we use this case to present an analytical definition of the concept of collective identity. Finally, we conclude by arguing that the existence of lesbian feminist communities challenges the popular perception that feminists have withdrawn from the battle and the scholarly view that organizing around identity directs attention away from challenges to institutionalized power structures (B. Epstein 1990).

We have used two main sources of data: published primary materials and interviews with participants in lesbian feminist communities. The written sources include books, periodicals, and narratives by community members (Johnston 1973; Koedt et al. 1973; Daly 1978; Baetz 1980; Cruikshank 1980; Stanley and Wolfe 1980; Moraga and Anzaldua 1981; Beck 1980; Smith 1983; Daly and Caputi 1987; Frye 1983; Grahn 1984; Johnson 1987) and newsletters, position papers, and other documents from lesbian feminist organizations. We have also incorporated secondary data from histories of the women's movement and ethnographies of lesbian communities (Hole and Levine 1971; Barnhart 1975; Ponse 1978; Lewis 1979; Wolf 1979; Krieger 1983; Davis and Kennedy 1986; Lockard 1986; Lord, unpublished; Echols 1989).

In addition, we have conducted twenty-one interviews with lesbian feminists who served as informants about their communities, which included Boston, Provincetown, and the rural Berkshire region of Massachusetts; Portland, Maine; Washington, D.C.; New York City; Key West and St. Petersburg, Florida; Columbus, Yellow Springs, Cleveland, and Cincinnati, Ohio; Minneapolis; Chicago; Denver; Atlanta; and Charlotte, North Carolina. The informants range in age from twenty-one to sixty-eight; sixteen are white, four are black, and one is Hispanic; the majority are from middle-class backgrounds. They are employed as professionals or semi-professionals, small-business owners, students, and blue-collar workers. Interviewees were recruited through snowballing procedures and announcements and notices posted at lesbian events. The in-depth interviews were open-ended and semistructured, lasting from one to three hours, and were tape-recorded and transcribed. The analysis also draws on our experiences as members of the larger community.

Since this work focuses primarily on lesbian feminist activism in the midwestern and eastern regions of the United States, we regard our conclusions as exploratory and generalizable primarily to this sector of the larger lesbian community. It is important to keep in mind that not all lesbians are associated with the communities described here.

THE LESBIAN FEMINIST SOCIAL MOVEMENT COMMUNITY

Analyzing the historical evolution of organizational forms in the American women's movement, Buechler (1990) proposes the concept of a social movement community to expand our understanding of the variety of forms of collective action. Buechler's concept underscores the importance to mobilization of informal networks, decentralized structures, and alternative institutions. But, like most work in the resource mobilization tradition, it overlooks the values and symbolic understandings created by discontented groups in the course of struggling to achieve change (Lofland 1985).

Here it is useful to turn to recent literature on lesbian communities that emphasizes the cultural components of lesbian activism, specifically the development of counterinstitutions, a politicized group identity, shared norms, values, and symbolic forms of resistance (Wolf 1979; Krieger 1983; Lockard 1986; Davis and Kennedy 1986; Phelan 1989; Esterberg 1990). From this perspective, we expand on Buechler's model by defining a social movement community as a network of individuals and groups loosely linked through an institutional base, multiple goals and actions, and a collective identity that affirms members' common interests in opposition to dominant groups.

We describe lesbian feminism as a social movement community that operates at the national level through connections among local communities in the decentralized, segmented, and reticulated structure described by Gerlach and Hine (1970). Like other new social movements, the lesbian feminist movement does not mobilize through formal social movement organizations. Rather, structurally the movement is composed of what Melucci (1989) terms "submerged networks" propelled by constantly shifting forms of resistance that include alternative symbolic systems as well as new forms of political struggle and participation (Emberley and Landry 1989). Although participants use different labels to describe the movement, we are interested here in the segment of the contemporary women's movement characterized as "cultural feminism" (Ferree and Hess 1985; Echols 1989) or "lesbian feminism" (Adam 1987; Phelan 1989). We prefer "lesbian feminism" for three reasons. It is the label most often used in movement writings, although participants also refer to the "women's community," "feminist community," and "lesbian community." Second, it locates the origins of this community in the contemporary women's movement. Finally, the term makes explicit the vital role of lesbians in the women's movement. The term "cultural feminism" erases the participation of lesbians and obscures the fact that a great deal of the current criticism leveled at cultural feminism is, in reality, directed at lesbian feminism.

Scholars have depicted the women's movement that blossomed in the 1960s and 1970s as having two segments, a women's rights or liberal branch and a women's liberation or radical branch (Freeman 1975). The liberal branch consisted primarily of national-level, hierarchically organized, formal organizations like the National Organization for Women (NOW) that used institutionalized legal tactics to pursue equal rights (Gelb and Palley 1982). The radical branch emerged in the late 1960s out of the civil rights and New Left movements and formed a decentralized network of primarily local, autonomous groups lacking formal organization and using flamboyant and disruptive tactics to pursue fundamental transformation of patriarchal structures and values (Hole and Levine 1971; Evans

1979). It is impossible to comprehend contemporary lesbian feminism without locating it in the radical feminist tradition.

Ideologically and strategically, radical feminism opposed liberalism, pursued social transformation through the creation of alternative nonhierarchical institutions and forms of organization intended to prefigure a utopian feminist society, held gender oppression to be primary and the model of all other forms of oppression, and emphasized women's commonality as a sex-class through consciousness raising. Although it coalesced around common issues such as rape, battering, and abortion, radical feminism was never monolithic (Jaggar and Struhl 1978; Ferree and Hess 1985). By the mid-1970s, radical feminism confronted an increasingly conservative and inhospitable social climate and was fraught with conflict over differences of sexuality, race, and class (Taylor 1989a). Recent scholarship argues that the most important disputes focused on the question of lesbianism (Echols 1989; Ryan 1989).

Conflict between lesbian and heterosexual feminists originated in the early 1970s. Although women who love other women have always been among those who participated in the feminist struggle, it was not until the emergence of the gay liberation movement that lesbians demanded recognition and support from the women's movement. Instead they encountered overt hostility in both the liberal and radical branches. The founder of NOW, Betty Friedan, for example, dismissed lesbianism as the "lavendar herring" of the movement. Since charges of lesbianism have often been used to discredit women who challenge traditional roles (Rupp 1989; Schneider 1986), feminists sought to avoid public admission that there were, in fact, lesbians in their ranks.

Echols (1989) traces the beginning of lesbian feminism to 1971 with the founding of the Furies in Washington, D.C. This was the first separate lesbian feminist group, and others formed shortly after in New York, Boston, Chicago, San Francisco, and other urban localities around the country. The Furies is significant because it included women such as Charlotte Bunch, Rita Mae Brown, and Colletta Reid who, along with Ti-Grace Atkinson, ex-president of the New York Chapter of NOW and founder of the Feminists, articulated the position that would lay the foundation for lesbian feminism (Hole and Levine 1971; Atkinson 1974; Bunch 1986). They advocated lesbian separatism and recast lesbianism as a political strategy that was the logical outcome of feminism, the quintessential expression of the "personal as political." As a result, heterosexual feminists found themselves increasingly on the defensive.

If early radical feminism was driven by the belief that women are more alike than different, then the fissures that beset radical feminism in the mid-1970s were about clarifying the differences—on the basis of race, class, and ethnicity as well as sexual identity—among the "group called women" (Cassell 1977). Recent scholarship argues that such conflict ultimately led to the demise of radical feminism and the rise of what its critics have called "cultural feminism," leaving liberal feminism in control of the women's movement (Echols 1989; Ryan 1989).

We agree with the dominant view that disputes over sexuality, class, and race contributed to the decline of the radical feminist branch of the movement. We do not, however, agree that radical feminism was replaced by a cultural haven for women who have withdrawn from the battle (Snitow, Stansell, and Thompson 1983; Vance 1984; Echols 1989). Rather, we hold that radical feminism gave way to a new cycle of feminist activism sustained by lesbian feminist communities. These communities socialize members into a collective oppositional consciousness that channels women into a variety of actions geared toward personal, social, and political change.

Although no research has been undertaken to document the extent of lesbian communities across the nation, existing work has focused on a number of different localities (e.g., Barnhart's [1975] ethnography of Portland, Wolf's [1979] study of San Francisco, Krieger's [1983] ethnography of a midwestern community, Lockard's [1986] description of a southwestern community). White (1980) describes the major trend-setting centers of the gay and lesbian movement as Boston, Washington, San Francisco, and New York. Although our analysis is exploratory and based on only seventeen communities, our data suggest that developments in the major cities are reflected throughout the United States in urban areas as well as in smaller communities with major colleges and universities.

COLLECTIVE IDENTITY: BOUNDARIES, CONSCIOUSNESS, AND NEGOTIATION

The study of identity in sociology has been approached at the individual and systemic levels as well as in both structural and more dynamic social constructionist terms (Weigert et al. 1986). New social movement theorists, in particular Pizzorno (1978), Boggs (1986), Melucci (1985, 1989), Offe (1985), and Touraine (1985), take the politics of personal transformation as one of their central theoretical problematics, which is why these approaches are sometimes referred to as "identity-oriented paradigms" (Cohen 1985). Sometimes labeled postmodernist, new social movement perspectives are social constructionist paradigms (B. Epstein 1990). From this standpoint, collective political actors do not exist de facto by virtue of individuals sharing a common structural location; they are created in the course of social movement activity. To understand any politicized identity community, it is necessary to analyze the social and political struggle that created the identity.

In some ways, the most apparent feature of the new movements has been a vision of power as operating at different levels so that collective self-transformation is itself a major strategy of political change. Reviewing work in the new social movement tradition suggests three elements of collective identity. First, individuals see themselves as part of a group when some shared characteristic becomes salient and is defined as important. For Touraine (1985) and Melucci (1989), this sense of "we" is evidence of an increasingly fragmented and pluralistic social reality that is, in part, a result of the new movements. A crucial characteristic of the movements of the seventies and eighties has been the advocacy of new group understandings, self-conceptions, ways of thinking, and cultural categories. In Touraine's model, it is an awareness of how the group's interests conflict with the interests of its adversaries, the adoption of a critical picture of the culture as a whole, and the recognition of the broad stakes of the conflict that differentiate contemporary movements from classical ones. Thus, the second component of collective identity is what Cohen (1985) terms "consciousness." Consistent with the vision of the movements themselves, Melucci defines a movement's "cognitive frameworks" broadly to include not only political consciousness and relational networks but its "goals, means, and environment of action" (1989, 35). Finally, for new social movement theorists, the concept of collective identity implies direct opposition to the dominant order. Melucci holds that social movements build "submerged networks" of political culture that are interwoven with everyday life and provide new expressions of identity that challenge dominant representations (1989, 35). In essence, as Pizzorno (1978) suggests, the purposeful and expressive disclosure to others of one's subjective feelings, desires, and experiences—or social identity—for the purpose of gaining recognition and influence is collective action.

Our framework draws from feminist theoretical approaches in the symbolic interactionist tradition (Gerson and Peiss 1985; Margolis 1985; West and Zimmerman 1987; Chafetz 1988). These formulations differ from structural and other social psychological approaches that tend to reify gender as a role category or trait of individuals. Instead, they view gender hierarchy as constantly created through displays and interactions governed by gender-normative behavior that comes to be perceived as natural and normal. Gerson and Peiss (1985) offer a model for understanding how gender inequality is reproduced and maintained through social interaction. Although they recognize the social change potential of the model, they do not address this aspect systematically.

Building on their work, we propose three factors as analytical tools for understanding the construction of collective identity in social movements. The concept of *boundaries* refers to the social, psychological, and physical structures that establish differences between a challenging group and dominant groups. *Consciousness* consists of the interpretive frameworks that emerge out of a challenging group's struggle to define and realize its interests. *Negotiation* encompasses the symbols and everyday actions subordinate groups use to resist and restructure existing systems of domination. We offer this scheme as a way of analyzing the creation of collective identity as an ongoing process in all social movements struggling to overturn existing systems of domination.

Boundaries

Boundaries mark the social territories of group relations by highlighting differences between activists and the web of others in the contested social world. Of course, it is usually the dominant group that erects social, political, economic, and cultural boundaries to accentuate the differences between itself and minority populations. Paradoxically, however, for groups organizing to pursue collective ends, the process of asserting "who we are" often involves a kind of reverse affirmation of the characteristics attributed to it by the larger society. Boundary markers are, therefore, central to the formation of collective identity because they promote a heightened awareness of a group's commonalities and frame interaction between members of the in-group and the out-group.

For any subordinate group, the construction of positive identity requires both a withdrawal from the values and structures of the dominant, oppressive society and the creation of new self-affirming values and structures. Newer approaches to the study of ethnic mobilization define ethnicity not in essentialist terms but in relation to socially and politically constructed boundaries that differentiate ethnic populations (Barth 1969; Olzak 1983). This is a useful way of understanding the commonalities that develop among members of any socially recognized group or category organized around a shared characteristic. It underscores the extent to which differentiation and devaluation is a fundamental process in all hierarchical systems and has two advantages over other approaches (Reskin 1988).

First, the concept of boundaries avoids the reification of ascriptive and other differentiating characteristics that are the basis for dominance systems (Reskin 1988); second, it transcends the assumption of group sameness implied by single-factor stratification systems because it allows us to analyze the impact of multiple systems of domination based on race, sex, class, ethnicity, age, sexuality, and other factors (Morris 1990). These distinct hierarchies not only produce differentiation within subordinate groups but affect the permeability of boundaries between the subordinate and dominant groups (Collins 1989; Morris 1990; Zinn 1990).

Boundary markers can vary from geographical, racial, and religious characteristics to more symbolically constructed differences such as social institutions and cultural systems. Our analysis focuses on two types of boundary strategies adopted by lesbian feminists as a means of countering male domination: the creation of separate institutions and the development of a distinct women's culture guided by "female" values.

Alternative institutions were originally conceived by radical feminists both as islands of resistance against patriarchy and as a means to gain power by improving women's lives and enhancing their resources (Taylor 1989a; Echols 1989). Beginning in the early 1970s, radical feminists established separate health centers, rape crisis centers, battered women's shelters, bookstores, publishing and record companies, newspapers, credit unions, and poetry and writing groups. Through the 1980s, feminist institutions proliferated to include recovery groups, business guilds, martial arts groups, restaurants, AIDS projects, spirituality groups, artists' colonies, and groups for women of color, Jewish feminists, disabled women, lesbian mothers, and older women. Some lesbian feminist groups were not entirely autonomous but functioned as separate units or caucuses in existing organizations, such as women's centers and women's studies programs in universities.

As the mass women's movement receded in the 1980s, the liberal branch abandoned protest and unruly tactics in favor of actions geared toward gaining access in the political arena (Rupp and Taylor 1986; Mueller 1987; Echols 1989). An elaborate network of feminist counterinstitutions remained, however, and increasingly were driven by the commitment of lesbian feminists. This is not to say that they were the sole preserve of lesbians. Rather, it is our view that what is described generally as "women's culture" to emphasize its availability to all women has become a predominantly lesbian feminist culture.

A number of national events link local lesbian feminist communities, including the annual five-day Michigan Womyn's Music Festival attended by four thousand to ten thousand women, the National Women's Writers' Conference, and the National Women's Studies Association Conference. In addition, local and regional events and conferences on the arts, literature, and, in the academic professions, feminist issues proliferated through the 1980s. National newspapers such as *Off Our Backs*, national magazines such as *Outlook*, publishing companies such as Naiad, Persephone, and Kitchen Table Women of Color presses, and a variety of journals and newsletters continue to publicize feminist ideas and activities.

In short, throughout the 1980s, as neoconservatism was winning political and intellectual victories, lesbian feminists struggled to build a world apart from male domination.

The second boundary that is central to lesbian feminist identity is the creation of a symbolic system that affirms the culture's idealization of the female and, as a challenge to the misogyny of the dominant society, vilifies the male. Perhaps the strongest thread running through the tapestry of lesbian feminist culture is the belief that women's nature and modes of relating differ fundamentally from men's. For those who hold this position, the set of traits generally perceived as female are egalitarianism, collectivism, an ethic of care, a respect for knowledge derived from experience, pacifism, and cooperation. In contrast, male characteristics are thought to include an emphasis on hierarchy, oppressive individualism, an ethic of individual rights, abstraction, violence, and competition. These gender boundaries are confirmed by a formal body of feminist scholarship (see, e.g., Rich 1976, 1980; Chodorow 1978; Gilligan 1982; Rubin 1984; Collins 1989) as well as in popular writings (see, e.g., Walker 1974; Daly 1978, 1984; Cavin 1985; Dworkin 1981; Johnson 1987). Johnson, for example, characterizes the differences between women and men as based on the contrast between "masculine life-hating values" and "women's life-loving culture" (1987, 226).

Our interviews suggest that the belief that there are fundamental differences between women and men is widely held by individual activists. One lesbian feminist explains that "we've been acculturated into two cultures, the male culture and the female culture. And luckily we've been able to preserve the ways of nurturing by being in this alternative culture."

Because women's standards are deemed superior, it is not surprising that men, including older male children, are often excluded from community events and business establishments. At the Michigan Womyn's Music Festival, for example, male children over the age of three are not permitted in the festival area, but must stay at a separate camp. Reversing the common cultural practice of referring to adult women as "girls," it is not unusual for lesbian feminists to refer to men, including gay men, as "boys."

Maintaining an oppositional identity depends upon creating a world apart from the dominant society. The boundaries that are drawn around a group are not entirely a matter of choice. The process of reshaping one's collective world, however, involves the investiture of meaning that goes beyond the objective conditions out of which a group is created. Seen in this way, it is easy to understand how identity politics promotes a kind of cultural endogamy that, paradoxically, erects boundaries within the challenging group, dividing it on the basis of race, class, age, religion, ethnicity, and other factors. When asked to define the lesbian feminist community, one participant highlights this process by stating that "if there is such a thing as a lesboworld, then there are just as many diversities of communities in that world as there are in the heteroworld."

Consciousness

Boundaries locate persons as members of a group, but it is group consciousness that imparts a larger significance to a collectivity. We use the concept of consciousness to refer to the interpretive frameworks that emerge from a group's struggle to define and realize members' common interests in opposition to the dominant order. Although sociologists have focused primarily on class consciousness, Morris (1990) argues that the term *political consciousness* is more useful because it emphasizes that all systems of human domination create opposing interests capable of generating oppositional consciousness. Whatever the term, the important point is that collective actors must attribute their discontent to structural, cultural, or systemic causes rather than to personal failings or individual deviance (Ferree and Miller 1985; Touraine 1985).

Our notion of consciousness builds on the idea of cognitive liberation (McAdam 1982), frames (Snow et al. 1986), cognitive frameworks (Melucci 1989), and collective consciousness (Mueller 1987). We see the development of consciousness as an ongoing process in which groups reevaluate themselves, their subjective experiences, their opportunities, and their shared interests. Consciousness is imparted through a formal body of writings, speeches, and documents. More important, when a movement is successful at creating a collective identity, its interpretive orientations are interwoven with the fabric of everyday life. Consciousness not only provides socially and politically marginalized groups with an understanding of their structural position but establishes new expectations regarding treatment appropriate to their category. Of course, groups can mobilize around a collective consciousness that supports the status quo. Thus, it is only when a group develops an account that challenges dominant understandings that we can use the term *oppositional consciousness* (Morris 1990).

Contemporary lesbian feminist consciousness is not monolithic. But its mainspring is the view that heterosexuality is an institution of patriarchal control and that lesbian relationships are a means of subverting male domination. The relationship between feminism and lesbianism is well summarized by the classic slogan "feminism is the theory and lesbianism is the practice," mentioned by a number of our informants. Arguing that sexism and heterosexism are inextricably intertwined, lesbian feminists in the early 1970s characterized lesbianism as "the rage of all women condensed to the point of explosion" (Radicalesbians 1973, 240) and held that women who choose lesbianism are the vanguard of the women's movement (Birkby et al. 1973; Myron and Bunch 1975; Daly 1978, 1984; Frye 1983; Hoagland 1988). The classic rationale for this position, frequently reprinted in newsletters and other lesbian publications, is Ti-Grace Atkinson's analogy: "Can you imagine a Frenchman, serving in the French army from 9 A.M. to 5 P.M., then trotting 'home' to Germany for supper overnight?" (1974, 11).

Despite the common thread running through lesbian feminist consciousness that sexual relationships between women are to be understood in reference to the political structure of male supremacy and male domination, there are two distinct strands of thought about lesbian identity. One position holds that lesbianism is not an essential or biological characteristic but is socially constructed. In a recent analysis of the history of lesbian political consciousness, Phelan (1989) argues that lesbian feminist consciousness emerged and has been driven by a rejection of the liberal view that sexuality is a private or individual matter. A classic exposition of the social constructionist position can be found in Rich's "Compulsory Heterosexuality and Lesbian Existence" (1980), which defines lesbian identity not as sexual but as political. Rich introduces the concept of the "lesbian continuum" to include all women who are woman-identified and who resist patriarchy. By locating lesbianism squarely within the new scholarship on the female world, Rich, like other social constructionists, suggests that sexuality is a matter of choice.

If it is not sexual experience but an emotional and political orientation toward women that defines one as lesbian, then, as the song by Alix Dobkin puts it, "any woman can be a lesbian." Lesbian feminist communities in fact contain women who are oriented toward women emotionally and politically but not sexually. These women are sometimes referred to as "political dykes" or "heterodykes" (Clausen 1990; Smeller, unpublished), and community members think of them as women who "haven't come out yet." Some women who have had both male and female lovers resist being labeled bisexual and cling to a lesbian identity. For example, well-known singer and songwriter Holly Near explains: "I am too closely linked to the political perspective of lesbian feminism. . . . it is part of my world view, part of my passion for women and central in my objection to male domination" (1990). The significance of lesbian identity for feminist activists is well summarized by the name of a feminist support group at a major university, Lesbians Who Just Happen to Be Dating Politically-Correct Men.

The second strand of lesbian feminist thought aims to bring sex back into the definition of lesbianism (Treblecot 1979; Califia 1982; Ferguson 1982; Zita 1982; Hollibaugh and Moraga 1983; Rubin 1984; Nestle 1987;

Penelope 1990). Criticizing the asexuality of lesbian feminism, Echols suggests that, in contemporary women's communities, "women's sexuality is assumed to be more spiritual than sexual, and considerably less central to their lives than is sexuality to men's" (1984, 60). Putting it more bluntly, sadomasochism advocate Pat Califia characterizes contemporary lesbian feminism as "anti-sex," using the term "vanilla feminism" to dismiss what she charges is a traditionally feminine passive attitude toward sex (1980). These "pro-sex" or "sex radical" writers tend to view sexuality less as a matter of choice and more as an essential characteristic. So, too, do some lesbian separatists, who have little else in common with the sex radicals. Arguing against social constructionism, Penelope (1990) places lesbianism squarely in the sexual arena. She points to the historical presence of women who loved other women sexually and emotionally prior to the nineteenth-century invention of the term *lesbian* and emphasizes that currently there are a variety of ways that women come to call themselves lesbian. In our interviews with lesbian activists, it was not uncommon for women who embraced essentialist notions to engage in biographical reconstruction, reinterpreting all of their prelesbian experiences as evidence of lesbian sexuality.

The emphasis on sexuality calls attention to the unknown numbers of women engaged in same-sex behavior who do not designate themselves lesbian and the enclaves of women who identify as lesbian but have not adopted lesbian feminist ideology and practice. These include lesbians who organize their social lives around gay bars (Nestle 1987), women who remain in the closet, pretending to be heterosexual but having sexual relationships with other women, and women who marry men and have relationships with women on the side. Describing the variousness of the contemporary lesbian experience and the multiple ways women come to call themselves lesbian, one of our interviewees discussed "pc [politically correct] dykes," "heterodykes," "maybelline dykes," "earth crunchy lesbians," "bar dykes," "phys ed dykes," "professional dykes," and "fluffy dykes."

For a large number of women, locating lesbianism in the feminist arena precludes forming meaningful political alliances with gay men. In part, this is because issues of sexual freedom that many feminists have viewed as exploiting women, including pornography, sexual contact between the young and old, and consensual sadomasochism, have been central to the predominantly male gay liberation movement (Adam 1987). Adam, however, suggests that, despite some conflicting interests, the latter part of the 1980s saw growing coalitions between lesbian feminists and gay liberationists surrounding the issue of AIDS. Our data confirm this hypothesis.

Yet it is perhaps not coincidental that at a time when lesbian feminist communities serve increasingly as mobilization contexts for the larger lesbian and gay movement, lesbian activists describe a resurgence of lesbian separatism. Calls for more "women only space" pervaded gay and lesbian newsletters by the end of the 1980s (Japenga 1990).

Thus, our analysis suggests that an important element of lesbian feminist consciousness is the reevaluation of lesbianism as feminism. A number of recent studies, though admittedly based on small samples, confirm that the majority of women who openly embrace a lesbian identity interpret lesbianism within the framework of radical feminist ideology (Kitzinger 1987; Devor 1989; Phelan 1989). Removing lesbian behavior from the deviant clinical realm and placing it in the somewhat more acceptable feminist arena establishes lesbian identity as distinct from gay identity. Yet an increasingly vocal segment of lesbian feminists endorses a more essentialist, or what Steven Epstein (1987) terms "modified social constructionist," explanation of lesbianism. They have undoubtedly been influenced by the identity politics of the liberal branch of the gay liberation movement that has, in recent years, advocated that sexuality is less a matter of choice and more a matter of biology and early socialization.

Highlighting the significance of a dominated group's own explanation of its position for political action, Kitzinger (1987) uses the term *identity accounts* to distinguish the range of group understandings that emerge among oppressed groups to make sense of themselves and their situation. Our findings confirm that these self-understandings not only influence mobilization possibilities and directions but determine the types of individual and collective actions groups pursue to challenge dominant arrangements. In the next section, we examine lesbian feminist practice, emphasizing that it is comprehensible only because it presupposes the existence of a theory of lesbian identity.

Negotiation

Viewing collective identity as the result of repeatedly activated shared definitions, as new social movement theorists do, makes it difficult to distinguish between "doing" and "being," or between social movement organizations and their strategies. Although recent social movement analyses tend to emphasize primarily the political and structural aims of challenging groups, personal transformation and expressive action have been central to most movements (Morris 1984; Fantasia 1988; McNall 1988). The insistence that the construction and expression of a collective vision is politics, or the politicization of the self and daily life, is nevertheless the core of what is "new" about the new social movements (Breines

1982; Melucci 1988; Kauffman 1990). Thus, we propose a framework that recognizes that identity can be a fundamental focus of political work.

Margolis (1985) suggests the concept of negotiation, drawn from the symbolic interactionist tradition, as a way of analyzing the process by which social movements work to change symbolic meanings. Most interactions between dominant and opposing groups reinforce established definitions. Individuals differentiated on the basis of devalued characteristics are continuously responded to in ways that perpetuate their disadvantaged status (Reskin 1988). West and Zimmerman (1987) use the term *identificatory displays* to emphasize, for example, that gender inequality is embedded and reproduced in even the most routine interactions. Similar analyses might be undertaken with regard to class, ethnicity, sexuality, and other sources of stratification. From a social movement standpoint, the concept of negotiations points to the myriad of ways that activists work to resist negative social definitions and demand that others value and treat oppositional groups differently (Goffman 1959).

The analysis of social movement negotiations forces us to recognize that, if not sociologically, then in reality, "doing" and "being" overlap (West and Zimmerman 1987). Yet we need a way to distinguish analytically between the politics of the public sphere, or world transformation directed primarily at the traditional political arena of the state, and the politics of identity, or self-transformation aimed primarily at the individual. We think that the concept of negotiations calls attention to forms of political activism embedded in everyday life that are distinct from those generally analyzed as tactics and strategies in the literature on social movements.

Building on Margolis's (1985) work on gender identity, we suggest two types of negotiation central to the construction of politicized collective identities. First, groups negotiate new ways of thinking and acting in *private* settings with other members of the collectivity, as well as in *public* settings before a larger audience. Second, identity negotiations can be *explicit*, involving open and direct attempts to free the group from dominant representations, or *implicit*, consisting of what Margolis terms a "condensed symbol or display" that undermines the status quo (1985, 340). In this section, we identify actions that lesbian feminist communities engage in to renegotiate the meaning of "woman." Opposition to male domination and the societal devaluation of women is directed both at the rules of daily life and at the institutions that perpetuate them.

In many respects, the phrase "the personal is political," coined by radical feminist Carol Hanisch and elaborated in Kate Millett's *Sexual Politics* (1969), is the hallmark of radical feminism (Echols 1989). Influenced by the civil rights and New Left movements, feminists began in the late 1960s

to form consciousness-raising groups designed to reinterpret personal experiences in political terms. Analyzing virtually every aspect of individual
and social experience as male-dominated, the groups encouraged participants to challenge prevailing representations of women in every sphere of
life as a means of transforming the institutions that produced and disseminated them (Cassell 1977). The politicization of everyday life extended
beyond the black power and feminist movements into other movements of
the 1960s. In contemporary lesbian feminist communities the valorization
of personal experience continues to have a profound impact.

Community members see lesbianism as a strategy for feminist social
change that represents what one respondent describes as "an attempt
. . . to stop doing what you were taught—hating women." Other women
speak of the importance of learning to "value women," becoming "woman-
centered," and "giving women energy." Being woman-centered is viewed
as challenging conventional expectations that women orient themselves
psychologically and socially toward men, compete with other women for
male attention, and devalue other women. To make a more complete break
with patriarchal identities and ways of life, some women exchange their
male-given surnames for woman-centered ones, such as "Sarachild" or
"Blackwomyn." Loving and valuing women becomes a means to resist a
culture that hates and belittles women. Invoking Alice Walker's (1974)
concept of "womanist," one black woman that we interviewed explained,
"My lesbianism has nothing to do with men. It's not about not choosing
men, but about choosing women."

At the group level, lesbian feminists structure organizations collectively
(Rothschild-Whitt 1979) and attempt to eliminate hierarchy, make decisions by consensus, and form coalitions only with groups that are not, as
one activist said, "giving energy to the patriarchy." Demands for societal
change seek to replace existing organizational forms and values with ones
similar to those implemented in the community (Breines 1982). A worker
at a women's festival illustrated the importance of community structure as
a model for social change by commenting to women as they left the festival, "You've seen the way the real world can be, and now it's up to you to
go out there and change it."

Because a traditionally feminine appearance, demeanor, self-concept,
and style of personal relations are thought to be among the mainsprings of
women's oppression, lesbian feminist communities have adopted different
standards of gender behavior. For example, one of the visions of feminism
has been to reconstitute the experience of victimization. Thus, women
who have been battered or raped or have experienced incest and other
forms of abuse are termed "survivors" to redefine their experiences as re-

sistance to male violence. New recruits to the community are resocialized through participating in a variety of organizations—women's twelve-step programs, battered women's shelters, martial arts groups, incest survivors' groups—that provide not only self-help but also a means for women to renegotiate a lesbian feminist identity. The very name of one such organization in New York City, Identity House, is illustrative. Lesbian mothers organize support groups called "momazonians" or "dykes with tykes" to emphasize that motherhood is a crucial locus of contestation. "Take Back the Night" marches against violence, prochoice demonstrations, participation in spontaneous protests, and feminist music, theater, and dramatic presentations are other examples of public arenas for negotiating new standards of gender behavior.

Essential to contemporary lesbian feminist identity is a distinction between the lesbian who is a staunch feminist activist and the lesbian who is not of the vanguard. Thus, commitment to the politics of direct action distinguishes members of the lesbian feminist community from the larger population of lesbians. One participant illustrates the importance of this distinction, stating that women "who say that they are lesbians and maybe have sexual relationships with women, but don't have the feminist politics" compose a category who "could have been in the community, but they've opted out." Women even choose partners based on political commitment, noting that "sleeping with a woman who is not a feminist just doesn't work for me; there's too much political conflict." The tendency to choose life partners and form other close personal relationships based on shared political assumptions is not, however, unique to lesbian feminism but has been reported in relation to other movements as well (Rupp and Taylor 1987; McAdam 1988). In short, negotiating new gender definitions is central to lesbian feminist collective identity.

Challenging further the notion of femininity as frailty, passivity, and preoccupation with reigning standards of beauty, many women wear clothing that enables freedom of movement, adopt short or simple haircuts, walk with firm self-assured strides, and choose not to shave their legs or wear heavy makeup. Devor (1989) terms this mode of self-presentation "gender blending," arguing that it represents an explicit rejection of the norms of femininity and, by extension, of women's subjugation. By reversing reigning cultural standards of femininity, beauty, and respectability, lesbian feminists strike a blow against female objectification. How central this is to lesbian feminist identity is illustrated by a lesbian support group at a major university with the name Women in Comfortable Shoes.

Because appearance and demeanor are also implicit means of expressing one's opposition, community members' presentation of self is subject to close scrutiny or, to use the vernacular of the activists themselves, is monitored by the "pc police." Women who dress in stereotypically "feminine" ways are often criticized and admit to feeling "politically incorrect." As one respondent commented, "I've always had a lot of guilt feelings about, why don't I just buckle down and put on some blue jeans, and clip my hair short, and not wear makeup, and go aggressively through the world." Some of our interviewees report a return to gendered fashion in contemporary lesbian communities. Women who identify as sex radicals, in particular, have adopted styles of dress traditionally associated with the "sex trade," or prostitution, such as miniskirts, low-cut tops, and fishnet stockings, sometimes combined with more traditionally masculine styles in what is known as a "gender fuck" style of dressing. Suggesting that "the most profound and potentially the most radical politics come directly out of our own identity" (Combahee River Collective 1982), African-American feminists criticize the tendency of many white lesbian feminists to dictate a politics based on hegemonic cultural standards. Some women who are identifiably butch and dress in studded leather clothing and punk and neon haircuts offer class-based motivations for their demeanor, and African-American, Asian-American, and Latina lesbians embrace different cultural styles. In short, the changes in appearance and behavior women undergo as they come out cannot be fully understood as individually chosen but are often the ultimatum of identity communities (Krieger 1982).

We have presented three dimensions for analyzing collective identity in social movements: the concepts of boundaries, consciousness, and negotiation. Although we have treated each as if it were independent, in reality the three interact. Using these factors to analyze lesbian feminist identity suggests three elements that shape the social construction of lesbian feminism. First, lesbian feminist communities draw boundaries that affirm femaleness and separate them from a larger world perceived as hostile. Second, to undermine the dominant view of lesbianism as perversion, lesbian feminists offer identity accounts that politicize sexuality. Finally, by defining lesbians as the vanguard of the women's movement, lesbian feminists valorize personal experience, which, paradoxically, further reifies the boundaries between lesbians and nonlesbians and creates the impression that the differences between women and men and between lesbian and heterosexual feminists are essential.

CONCLUSION

In this chapter, we argue that lesbian feminist consciousness is rooted in a social movement community with ties to but distinguishable from both the gay liberation and the liberal feminist movements. In effect, we are suggesting that with the absorption of the liberal feminist agenda into the liberal mainstream, the legacy of radical feminism continues in the lesbian feminist community. It is difficult to imagine an argument that would be more controversial in feminist circles, for it confirms the premise that, at least in the contemporary context, lesbianism and feminism are intertwined. This leads to the question posed in a recent speech by feminist philosopher Marilyn Frye (1990), "Do you have to be a lesbian to be a feminist?" It is our view that lesbian communities are a type of social movement abeyance structure that absorbs highly committed feminists whose radical politics have grown increasingly marginal since the mass women's movement has receded (Taylor and Whittier 1992). However insulated, they function to sustain the feminist challenge in a less receptive political climate (Taylor 1989b). Our findings are controversial in another respect. By calling attention to the centrality of feminism for lesbian activism, our study paints a picture of the tenuousness of the coalition between gay men and lesbians in the larger gay and lesbian movement.

Drawing from new data and recent scholarship on lesbian communities, we use this case to illustrate the significance of collective identity for mobilization and to present a framework for analyzing identity processes in social movements. Adapting Gerson and Peiss's (1985) framework, we identify as factors that contribute to the formation of collective identity: (1) the creation of boundaries that insulate and differentiate a category of persons from the dominant society; (2) the development of consciousness that presumes the existence of socially constituted criteria that account for a group's structural position; and (3) the valorization of a group's "essential differences" through the politicization of everyday life.

The concept of collective identity is associated primarily with the social movements of the 1970s and 1980s because of their distinctive cultural appearance. It is our hypothesis, however, that collective identity is a significant variable in all social movements, even among the so-called traditional nineteenth-century movements. Thus, we frame our approach broadly to apply to oppositional identities based on class, race, ethnicity, gender, sexuality, and other persistent social cleavages. Certainly any theory derived from a single case is open to criticism. But recent research in the resource mobilization tradition points to the impact that changes in consciousness have on mobilization (Klein 1984; Downey 1986; Mueller 1987; McAdam 1988).

There is a growing realization among scholars of social movements that the theoretical pendulum between classical and contemporary approaches to social movements has swung too far. Social psychological factors that were central to collective behavior theory (Blumer 1946; Smelser 1962;

Killian 1964; Turner and Killian 1972) have become the theoretical blind spots of resource mobilization theory. Ignoring the grievances or injustices that mobilize protest movements has, as Klandermans (1986) suggests, stripped social movements of their political significance. In contrast to the structural and organizational emphases of resource mobilization theory, new social movement theory attends to the social psychological and cultural discontent that propels movements. But it provides little understanding of how the injustices that are at the heart of most movements are translated into the everyday lives of collective actors. Our analysis suggests that the study of collective identity, because it highlights the role of meaning and ideology in the mobilization and maintenance of collective action, is an important key to understanding this process.

REFERENCES

Adam, Barry D. 1987. *The Rise of a Gay and Lesbian Movement*. Boston: Twayne.

Atkinson, Ti-Grace. 1974. *Amazon Odyssey*. New York: Link Books.

Baetz, Ruth. 1980. *Lesbian Crossroads*. New York: Morrow.

Barnhart, Elizabeth. 1975. "Friends and Lovers in a Lesbian Counterculture Community." In *Old Family, New Family*, ed. N. Glazer-Malbin. New York: Van Nostrand, 90–115.

Barth, F. 1969. "Introduction." In *Ethnic Groups and Boundaries*, ed. F. Barth. Boston: Little, Brown, 1–38.

Beck, E. T. 1980. *Nice Jewish Girls: A Lesbian Anthology*. Watertown, Mass.: Persephone.

Birkby, Phyllis, Bertha Harris, Jill Johnston, Esther Newton, and Jane O'Wyatt. 1973. *Amazon Expedition: A Lesbian Feminist Anthology*. New York: Times Change Press.

Blumer, Herbert. 1946. "Collective Behavior." In *New Outline of the Principles of Sociology*, ed. A. M. Lee. New York: Barnes and Noble, 170–222.

Boggs, Carl. 1986. *Social Movements and Political Power*. Philadelphia: Temple University Press.

Breines, Wini. 1982. *Community and Organization in the New Left, 1962–68*. New York: Praeger.

Buechler, Steven M. 1990. *Women's Movements in the United States*. New Brunswick, N.J.: Rutgers.

Bunch, Charlotte. 1986. "Not for Lesbians Only." In *Feminist Frontiers II*, ed. Laurel Richardson and Verta Taylor. New York: Random House, 452–54.

Califia, Pat. 1980. "Feminism vs. Sex: A New Conservative Wave." *Advocate*, February 21.

———. 1982. "Public Sex." *Advocate*, September 30.

Cassell, Joan. 1977. *A Group Called Women: Sisterhood and Symbolism in the Feminist Movement*. New York: David McKay.

Cavin, Susan. 1985. *Lesbian Origins*. San Francisco: Ism Press.

Chafetz, Janet Saltzman. 1988. *Feminist Sociology*. Itaska, Ill.: F. E. Peacock.

Chodorow, Nancy. 1978. *The Reproduction of Mothering: Psychoanalysis and the Sociology of Gender*. Berkeley: University of California Press.

Clausen, Jan. 1990. "My Interesting Condition." *Outlook* 2:11–21.

Cohen, Jean L. 1985. "Strategy or Identity: New Theoretical Paradigms and Contemporary Social Movements." *Social Research* 52:663–716.

Collins, Patricia Hill. 1989. "The Social Construction of Black Feminist Thought." *Signs* 14, no. 4:745–73.

Combahee River Collective. 1982. "A Black Feminist Statement." In *But Some of Us Are Brave: Black Women's Studies*, ed. Gloria T. Hull, Patricia Bell Scott, and Barbara Smith. Old Westbury, N.Y.: Feminist Press, 13–22.

Cruikshank, Margaret. 1980. *The Lesbian Path*. Monterey, Calif.: Angel Press.

Daly, Mary. 1978. *Gyn/Ecology: The Metaethics of Radical Feminism*. Boston: Beacon Press.

———. 1984. *Pure Lust: Elemental Feminist Philosophy*. Boston: Beacon Press.

Daly, Mary, and Jane Caputi. 1987. *Websters' First New Intergalactic Wickedary of the English Language*. Boston: Beacon Press.

Davis, Madeleine, and Elizabeth Laprovsky Kennedy. 1986. "Oral History and the Study of Sexuality in the Lesbian Community." *Feminist Studies* 12:6–26.

Devor, Holly. 1989. *Gender Blending*. Bloomington: Indiana University Press.

Downey, Gary L. 1986. "Ideology and the Clamshell Identity: Organizational Dilemmas in the Anti–Nuclear Power Movement." *Social Problems* 33:357–73.

Dworkin, Andrea. 1981. *Pornography and Silence: Culture's Revenge against Nature*. New York: Harper and Row.

Echols, Alice. 1984. "The Taming of the Id: Feminist Sexual Politics, 1968–83." In *Pleasure and Danger: Exploring Female Sexuality*, ed. Carole S. Vance. Boston: Routledge and Kegan Paul, 50–72.

———. 1989. *Daring to Be Bad: Radical Feminism in America, 1967–1975*. Minneapolis: University of Minnesota Press.

Emberley, Julia, and Donna Landry. 1989. "Coverage of Greenham and Greenham as 'Coverage.'" *Feminist Studies* 15:485–98.

Epstein, Barbara. 1990. "Rethinking Social Movement Theory." *Socialist Review* 20:35–66.

Epstein, Steven. 1987. "Gay Politics, Ethnic Identity: The Limits of Social Constructionism." *Socialist Review* 17:9–54.

Esterberg, Kristin Gay. 1990. "Salience and Solidarity: Identity, Correctness, and Conformity in a Lesbian Community." Paper presented at the annual meeting of the American Sociological Association, August 11–15, Washington, D.C.

Evans, Sarah. 1979. *Personal Politics*. New York: Vintage.

Fantasia, Rick. 1988. *Cultures of Solidarity*. Berkeley: University of California Press.

Ferguson, Ann. 1982. "Patriarchy, Sexual Identity, and the Sexual Revolution." In *Feminist Theory: A Critique of Ideology*, ed. Nannerl O. Keohane, Michelle Z. Rosaldo, and Barbara L. Gelpi. Chicago: University of Chicago Press, 147–61.

Ferree, Myra Marx, and Beth B. Hess. 1985. *Controversy and Coalition: The New Feminist Movement*. Boston: Twayne.

Ferree, Myra Marx, and Frederick D. Miller. 1985. "Mobilization and Meaning: Some Social-Psychological Contributions to the Resource Mobilization Perspective on Social Movements." *Sociological Inquiry* 55:38–61.

Fireman, Bruce, and William Gamson. 1979. "Utilitarian Logic in the Resource

Mobilization Perspective." In *The Dynamics of Social Movements*, ed. Mayer N. Zald and John D. McCarthy. Cambridge, Mass.: Winthrop, 8–44.

Freeman, Jo. 1975. *The Politics of Women's Liberation*. New York: David McKay.

Frye, Marilyn. 1983. *The Politics of Reality: Essays in Feminist Theory*. Trumansburg, N.Y.: Crossing Press.

———. 1990. "Do You Have to Be a Lesbian to Be a Feminist?" *Off Our Backs* 20:21–23.

Gamson, William A. 1975. *The Strategy of Social Protest*. Homewood, Ill.: Dorsey Press.

Gelb, Joyce, and Marian Lief Palley. 1982. *Women and Public Policy*. Princeton: Princeton University Press.

Gerlach, Luther P., and Virginia H. Hine. 1970. *People, Power, Change: Movements of Social Transformation*. Indianapolis: Bobbs-Merrill.

Gerson, Judith M., and Kathy Peiss. 1985. "Boundaries, Negotiation, Consciousness: Reconceptualizing Gender Relations." *Social Problems* 32:317–31.

Gilligan, Carol. 1982. *In a Different Voice*. Cambridge, Mass.: Harvard University Press.

Goffman, Erving. 1959. *The Presentation of Self in Everyday Life*. Englewood Cliffs, N.J.: Prentice-Hall.

Grahn, Judy. 1984. *Another Mother Tongue: Gay Words, Gay Worlds*. Boston: Beacon Press.

Hoagland, Sarah Lucia. 1988. *Lesbian Ethics: Toward New Value*. Palo Alto, Calif.: Institute of Lesbian Studies.

Hole, Judith, and Ellen Levine. 1971. *Rebirth of Feminism*. New York: Quadrangle.

Hollibaugh, Amber, and Cherrie Moraga. 1983. "What We're Rollin' Around in Bed With: Sexual Silences in Feminism." In *Powers of Desire*, ed. Ann Snitow, Christine Stansell, and Sharon Thompson. New York: Monthly Review Press, 394–405.

Jaggar, Alison M., and Paula Rothenberg Struhl. 1978. *Feminist Frameworks*. New York: McGraw-Hill.

Japenga, Ann. 1990. "The Separatist Revival." *Outlook* 2:78–83.

Jenkins, J. Craig. 1983. "Resource Mobilization Theory and the Study of Social Movements." *Annual Review of Sociology* 9:527–53.

Jenkins, J. Craig, and Charles Perrow. 1977. "Insurgency of the Powerless: Farm Workers Movement (1946–72)." *American Sociological Review* 42:249–68.

Johnson, Sonia. 1987. *Going Out of Our Minds: The Metaphysics of Liberation*. Freedom, Calif.: Crossing Press.

Johnston, Jill. 1973. *Lesbian Nation: The Feminist Solution*. New York: Simon and Schuster.

Kauffman, L. A. 1990. "The Anti-Politics of Identity." *Socialist Review* 20:67–80.

Killian, Lewis M. 1964. "Social Movements." In *Handbook of Modern Sociology*, ed. R. E. L. Faris. Chicago: Rand McNally, 426–55.

Kitzinger, Celia. 1987. *The Social Construction of Lesbianism*. London: Sage.

Klandermans, Bert. 1984. "Mobilization and Participation: Social-Psychological Expansions of Resource Mobilization Theory." *American Sociological Review* 49: 583–600.

———. 1986. "New Social Movements and Resource Mobilization: The European and American Approach." *Journal of Mass Emergencies and Disasters* 4:13–37.

Klandermans, Bert, and Sidney Tarrow. 1988. "Mobilization into Social Movements: Synthesizing European and American Approaches." In *From Structure to Action: Comparing Movement Participation across Cultures*. International Social Movement Research, vol. 1, ed. Bert Klandermans, Hanspeter Kriesi, and Sidney Tarrow. Greenwich, Conn.: JAI Press, 1–38.

Klein, Ethel. 1984. *Gender Politics*. Cambridge, Mass.: Harvard University Press.

Koedt, Anne, Ellen Levine, and Anita Rapone. 1973. *Radical Feminism*. New York: Quadrangle.

Krieger, Susan. 1982. "Lesbian Identity and Community: Recent Social Science Literature." *Signs* 8:91–108.

———. 1983. *The Mirror Dance: Identity in a Women's Community*. Philadelphia: Temple University Press.

Lewis, Sasha Gregory. 1979. *Sunday's Women*. Boston: Beacon Press.

Lockard, Denyse. 1986. "The Lesbian Community: An Anthropological Approach." In *The Many Faces of Homosexuality*, ed. Evelyn Blackwood. New York: Harrington Park Press, 83–95.

Lofland, John. 1979. "White-Hot Mobilization: Strategies of a Millenarian Movement." In *Dynamics of Social Movements*, ed. Mayer N. Zald and John D. McCarthy. Cambridge, Mass.: Winthrop, 157–66.

———. 1985. "Social Movement Culture." In *Protest*, ed. John Lofland. New Brunswick, N.J.: Transaction Books, 219–39.

Lord, Eleanor. Unpublished. "Lesbian Lives and the Lesbian Community in Berkshire County." Mimeograph.

Margolis, Diane Rothbard. 1985. "Redefining the Situation: Negotiations on the Meaning of Woman." *Social Problems* 32:332–47.

McAdam, Doug. 1982. *Political Process and the Development of Black Insurgency, 1930–70*. Chicago: University of Chicago Press.

———. 1988. *Freedom Summer*. New York: Oxford University Press.

McAdam, Doug, John D. McCarthy, and Mayer N. Zald. 1988. "Social Movements." In *Handbook of Sociology*, ed. Neil Smelser. Newbury Park, Calif.: Sage, 695–737.

McCarthy, John D., and Mayer N. Zald. 1973. *The Trend of Social Movements in America*. Morristown, N.J.: General Learning Press.

———. 1977. "Resource Mobilization and Social Movements: A Partial Theory." *American Journal of Sociology* 82:1212–41.

McNall, Scott G. 1988. *The Road to Rebellion: Class Formation and Populism, 1865–1900*. Chicago: University of Chicago Press.

Melucci, Alberto. 1985. "The Symbolic Challenge of Contemporary Movements." *Social Research* 52:781–816.

———. 1988. "Getting Involved: Identity and Mobilization in Social Movements." In *From Structure to Action: Comparing Movement Participation across Cultures*. International Social Movement Research, vol. 1, ed. Bert Klandermans, Hanspeter Kriesi, and Sidney Tarrow. Greenwich, Conn.: JAI Press, 329–48.

———. 1989. *Nomads of the Present: Social Movements and Individual Needs in Contemporary Society*. Philadelphia: Temple University Press.

Millett, Kate. 1969. *Sexual Politics*. New York: Ballantine.

Moraga, Cherrie, and Gloria Anzaldua. 1981. *This Bridge Called My Back: Writings by Radical Women of Color*. Watertown, Mass.: Persephone.

Morris, Aldon D. 1984. *The Origins of the Civil Rights Movement*. New York: Free Press.

———. 1990. "Consciousness and Collective Action: Towards a Sociology of Consciousness and Domination." Paper presented at the annual meeting of the American Sociological Association, August 9–13, San Francisco.

Mueller, Carol McClurg. 1987. "Collective Consciousness, Identity Transformation, and the Rise of Women in Public Office in the United States." In *The Women's Movement of the United States and Western Europe*, ed. M. F. Katzenstein and C. M. Mueller. Philadelphia: Temple University Press, 89–108.

———. 1990. "Collective Identities and the Mobilization of Women: The American Case, 1960–1970." Paper presented at the colloquium on New Social Movements and the End of Ideology, July 16–20, Universidad Internacional Menendez Pelayo.

Myron, Nancy, and Charlotte Bunch. 1975. *Lesbianism and the Women's Movement*. Baltimore: Diana Press.

Near, Holly. 1990. *Fire in the Rain, Singer in the Storm*. New York: Morrow.

Nestle, Joan. 1987. *A Restricted Country*. Ithaca, N.Y.: Firebrand Books.

Oberschall, Anthony. 1973. *Social Conflict and Social Movements*. Englewood Cliffs, N.J.: Prentice-Hall.

Offe, Claus. 1985. "New Social Movements: Challenging the Boundaries of Institutional Politics." *Social Research* 52:817–68.

Olzak, Susan. 1983. "Contemporary Ethnic Mobilization." *Annual Review of Sociology* 9:355–74.

Penelope, Julia. 1990. "A Case of Mistaken Identity." *Women's Review of Books* 8:11–12.

Phelan, Shane. 1989. *Identity Politics: Lesbian Feminism and the Limits of Community*. Philadelphia: Temple University Press.

Pizzorno, Alessandro. 1978. "Political Science and Collective Identity in Industrial Conflict." In *The Resurgence of Class Conflict in Western Europe since 1968*, ed. C. Crouch and A. Pizzorno. New York: Holmes and Meier, 277–98.

Ponse, Barbara. 1978. *Identities in the Lesbian World: The Social Construction of Self*. Westport, Conn.: Greenwood Press.

Radicalesbians. 1973. "The Woman Identified Woman." In *Radical Feminism*, ed. Anne Koedt, Ellen Levine, and Anita Rapone. New York: Quadrangle, 240–45.

Reskin, Barbara. 1988. "Bringing the Men Back In: Sex Differentiation and the Devaluation of Women's Work." *Gender and Society* 2:58–81.

Rich, Adrienne. 1976. *Of Woman Born*. New York: Norton.

———. 1980. "Compulsory Heterosexuality and Lesbian Existence." *Signs* 5:631–60.

Rothschild-Whitt, Joyce. 1979. "The Collectivist Organization: An Alternative to Rational-Bureaucratic Models." *American Sociological Review* 44:509–27.

Rubin, Gayle. 1984. "Thinking Sex: Notes for a Radical Theory of the Politics of Sexuality." In *Pleasure and Danger*, ed. Carol S. Vance. Boston: Routledge and Kegan Paul, 267–319.

Rule, James, and Charles Tilly. 1972. "1830 and the Unnatural History of Revolution." *Journal of Social Issues* 28:49–76.

Rupp, Leila J. 1989. "Feminism and the Sexual Revolution in the Early Twentieth

Century: The Case of Doris Stevens." *Feminist Studies* 51:289–309.

Rupp, Leila J., and Verta Taylor. 1986. "The Women's Movement since 1960: Structure, Strategies, and New Directions." In *American Choices: Social Dilemmas and Public Policy since 1960*, ed. Robert H. Bremner, Richard Hopkins, and Gary W. Reichard. Columbus: Ohio State University Press, 75–104.

———. 1990. "Women's Culture and the Persisting Women's Movement." Paper presented at the annual meeting of the American Sociological Association, Washington, D.C., August 12.

Ryan, Barbara. 1989. "Ideological Purity and Feminism: The U.S. Women's Movement from 1966 to 1975." *Gender and Society* 3:239–57.

Schneider, Beth. 1986. "I Am Not a Feminist But . . ." Paper presented at the annual meeting of the American Sociological Association, New York, September 2.

Schwartz, Michael. 1976. *Radical Protest and Social Structure: The Southern Farmers' Alliance and the One-Crop Tenancy System*. New York: Academic Press.

Smeller, Michelle M. Unpublished. "From Dyke to Doll: The Processual Formation of Sexual Identity." Ohio State University.

Smelser, Neil. 1962. *Theory of Collective Behavior*. New York: Free Press.

Smith, Barbara. 1983. *Home Girls: A Black Feminist Anthology*. New York: Kitchen Table Women of Color Press.

Snitow, Ann, Christine Stansell, and Sharon Thompson. 1983. *Powers of Desire: The Politics of Sexuality*. New York: Monthly Review Press.

Snow, David A., E. Burke Rochford, Jr., Steven K. Worden, and Robert D. Benford. 1986. "Frame Alignment Processes, Micromobilization, and Movement Participation." *American Sociological Review* 51:464–81.

Stanley, Julia Penelope, and Susan J. Wolfe. 1980. *The Coming Out Stories*. Watertown, Mass.: Persephone.

Taylor, Verta. 1989a. "The Future of Feminism." In *Feminist Frontiers*, ed. Laurel Richardson and Verta Taylor. New York: Random House, 434–51.

———. 1989b. "Social Movement Continuity: The Women's Movement in Abeyance." *American Sociological Review* 54:761–75.

Taylor, Verta, and Nancy Whittier. 1992. "The New Feminist Movement." In *Feminist Frontiers: Rethinking Sex, Gender, and Society*, ed. Laurel Richardson and Verta Taylor. New York: McGraw-Hill.

Tilly, Charles. 1978. *From Mobilization to Revolution*. Reading, Mass.: Addison-Wesley.

Touraine, Alain. 1985. "An Introduction to the Study of Social Movements." *Social Research* 52:749–87.

Treblecot, Joyce. 1979. "Conceiving Women: Notes on the Logic of Feminism." *Sinister Wisdom* 11:3–50.

Turner, Ralph H., and Lewis M. Killian. 1972. *Collective Behavior*. 2d ed. Englewood Cliffs, N.J.: Prentice-Hall.

Vance, Carole S. 1984. *Pleasure and Danger*. Boston: Routledge and Kegan Paul.

Walker, Alice. 1974. *In Search of Our Mothers' Gardens*. New York: Harcourt Brace Jovanovich.

Weigert, Andrew J., J. Smith Teitge, and Dennis W. Teitge. 1986. *Society and Identity*. New York: Cambridge University Press.

West, Candace, and Don H. Zimmerman. 1987. "Doing Gender." *Gender and Society* 1:125–51.

White, Edmund. 1980. *States of Desire*. New York: E. P. Dutton.

Whittier, Nancy. 1991. "Feminists in the Post-Feminist Age: Collective Identity and the Persistence of the Women's Movement." Ph.D. diss., Ohio State University.

Wolf, Deborah Goleman. 1979. *The Lesbian Community*. Berkeley: University of California Press.

Zinn, Maxine Baca. 1990. "Family, Feminism, and Race in America." *Gender and Society* 4:68–82.

Zita, Jacquelyn. 1982. "Historical Amnesia and the Lesbian Continuum." In *Feminist Theory: A Critique of Ideology*, ed. Nannerl O. Keohane, Michelle Z. Rosaldo, and Barbara L. Gelpi. Chicago: University of Chicago Press, 161–76.

Part 3

Sociopolitical Culture and the Persuasive Communications of Social Movement Organizations

6

Master Frames and
Cycles of Protest

David A. Snow and

Robert D. Benford

The notion that social movements hang together or cluster in some fashion is a relatively old one in the literature. The concept of general social movement, initially coined by Blumer (1951; cf. Turner and Killian 1987), suggests that specific movements within any historical era are tributaries of a more general stream of agitation. Klapp similarly points to this clustering tendency in his aptly titled *Currents of Unrest* (1972) in which he suggests the applicability of the general systems concept of "oscillation" to the analysis of collective behavior. More recently, McCarthy and Zald's (1977) concepts of "social movement organizations, industries, and sectors" provide a conceptual basis for the temporal and spatial clustering of movement activity. And the concept of "cycles of protest," elaborated by Tarrow (1983), underscores even more concretely the clustering and sequencing of collective action. Taken together these concepts and ideas bear a striking "family resemblance" (Wittgenstein 1967) in that they all direct attention, first, to the ecological and cyclical aggregation of social movements and, second, to the embeddedness of social movement organizations (SMOS) in a particular cycle or sector of movement activity.

That movement organizations and activities do indeed cluster temporally in a cyclical fashion not only is a topic of theoretical speculation but is also well documented, as evidenced by several recent empirical investigations of collective action in Western Europe (della Porta and Tarrow 1986; Shorter and Tilly 1974; Tarrow 1983; Tilly et al. 1975; Tilly 1978). Similarly, the rise and decline of collective violence in American cities during

We are indebted to Bill Gamson, Aldon Morris, Carol Mueller, William Sewell, Jr., and Sydney Tarrow for their insightful comments and suggestions. An expanded version of this chapter was translated into Italian and published in *Polis: Ricerche Estudisn Societa E Politica in Italia* 3 (April 1989): 5–40.

the 1960s and early 1970s, the sudden flowering and subsequent wilting of religious cults in the late 1960s and 1970s, and the recent eruption of collective action throughout much of Eastern Europe illustrate this cyclical pattern.

But what accounts for this clustering and apparent connection among movements within a cycle seems to be less well understood. Early collective behavior theory suggested contagion and convergence processes as possible explanatory mechanisms, but research during the past fifteen years has found that such processes tend to shroud rather than illuminate the dynamics of collective action. The more recent resource mobilization perspective focuses attention on changes in various structural factors such as social networks (Snow et al. 1980), indigenous organizational strength (McAdam 1982; Morris 1984), the structure of political opportunities (Eisinger 1973; Jenkins and Perrow 1977; Lipsky 1970), and resource pools (McCarthy and Zald 1977) as the key explanatory mechanisms that affect the waxing and waning of social movements. Although such variables are no doubt crucial to understanding the clustering of collective action, the factors that account for those changes are not unambiguously specified. Nor do purely structural explanations suffice in accounting for periodic shifts in the level of social movement activity. Why, for example, do citizens sometimes fail to act collectively on their shared grievances when the structural conditions appear otherwise ripe?

Thus, from our vantage point, two central questions are particularly problematic: first, what accounts for the temporal clustering of SMOs and activities, and second, what accounts for the cyclicity of social movement activity? We seek to advance understanding of these issues by examining theoretically the relation between cycles of protest and what we refer to as master frames. More specifically, we will elaborate and explore a number of sensitizing propositions regarding this hypothesized linkage.

We see this exercise as essentially theoretic. Our aim is not to demonstrate empirically or to verify the propositions we elaborate but to develop a framework for conceptualizing and discussing the relation between master frames and cycles of protest. This endeavor builds on and extends our earlier work on frame alignment (Snow et al. 1986) and frame resonance (Snow and Benford 1988) in two ways: it provides conceptual clarification, and it extends our analyses from the microlevel to the macrolevel. Whereas we focused before on the framing activity of individual movement organizations, here we turn to an examination of how frames function in a larger context.[1]

---

1. In attempting to illuminate the relation between master frames and cycles of protest, we focus almost exclusively on interpretive factors to the neglect of other vari-

Since our inquiry places a premium on ideational factors, we begin with a brief overview of their treatment in the literature. Next, we elaborate the characteristic features of collective action frames and then discuss master frames and cycles of protest, the two key concepts that are the focus of our inquiry. And finally, we discuss a number of sensitizing propositions regarding the relation among master frames, cycles of protest, and specific movements within these cycles.

THEORETICAL ISSUES AND CONCEPTS

Ideology, Signification, and Framing

References to ideology and its elements—values, beliefs, meanings—are commonplace in the social movement literature. The treatment of ideological factors in relation to the course and character of movements has been far from satisfactory, however. A survey of discussions of ideology in the literature suggests that the concept has been dealt with in essentially two ways. Before the emergence of the resource mobilization perspective, writers (with the exception of Turner and Killian 1987; Turner 1969) treated ideology primarily descriptively rather than analytically, and statically rather than dynamically. Some recognized its role in the social movement process, but their discussion of it seldom went beyond enumerating its functions and content, treating the latter as if it flowed almost naturally or magically from the movement's underlying strains. Description of movement ideology was seen as prefatory to the more important analytic task of ferreting out the relation between movement emergence and "structural strain" (e.g., see Smelser 1963).

Since the displacement of strain theory by resource mobilization perspectives in the mid-1970s, ideological factors have figured even less prominently in movement analyses. Indeed, the tendency has been to ignore or gloss over mobilizing beliefs and ideas, in large part because of their presumed ubiquity and constancy, which make them, in turn, relatively nonproblematic and uninteresting factors in the movement equation (Oberschall 1973, 133–34, 194–95; McCarthy and Zald 1977, 1214–15; Jenkins and Perrow 1977, 250–51; Jenkins 1983, 528). A number of critics have recently noted this oversight and have called for a broadening

---

ables such as social structure. This does not mean that we regard the latter as unimportant, nor do we seek to supplant structural explanations with an ideational framework. Rather, our purpose is to augment structuralist perspectives by calling attention to a set of heretofore neglected factors we see as crucial to developing a more thoroughgoing understanding of the ecological and temporal clustering of social movement activity.

of resource mobilization theory to include ideational factors (Ferree and Miller 1985; Gamson et al. 1982; Zurcher and Snow 1981).

Whether mobilizing ideas and meanings are treated merely descriptively or as nonproblematic constants, both tendencies strike us as misguided on two accounts. First, meanings and ideas are treated as given, as if they spring almost immanently from the events and objects with which they are associated, rather than as social productions that arise during the course of interactive processes. And second, they ignore the extent to which movements are engaged in "meaning-work"—that is, in the struggle over the production of ideas of meanings.

In the course of our fieldwork experiences with a variety of social movements (e.g., Nichiren Shoshu, Hare Krishna, the peace movement, and several urban neighborhood movements), we came to see this neglected aspect of movements as particularly interesting and also as problematic. From our vantage point, then, we do not view social movements merely as carriers of extant ideas and meanings that stand in isomorphic relationship to structural arrangements or unanticipated events. Rather, we see movement organizations and actors as actively engaged in the production and maintenance of meaning for constituents, antagonists, and bystanders or observers. This productive work may involve the amplification and extension of extant meanings, the transformation of old meanings, and the generation of new meanings (Snow et al. 1986). We thus view movements as functioning in part as signifying agents that often are deeply embroiled, along with the media, local governments, and the state, in what has been referred to aptly as the "politics of signification" (Hall 1982).

It is this signifying work that is the heart of this chapter. Consistent with our earlier work, we conceptualize this signifying work with the verb *framing*, which denotes an active, process-derived phenomenon that implies agency and contention at the level of reality construction. We refer to the products of this framing activity as collective action frames.

Characteristic Features of Collective Action Frames

The concept of frame has meaning in both everyday and academic discourse. Regarding the latter, its usage is neither discipline-specific nor particularly novel. It not only has found its way into sociology, primarily through the work of Goffman (1974), but has also been used in psychiatry (Bateson 1972), the humanities (Cone 1968), and cognitive psychology (Minsky 1975; Piaget 1954). In addition, the kindred concept of schema has been used widely and has generated considerable research in cognitive psychology (Hastie 1981; Kelley 1972; Marcus and Zajonc 1985; Neisser 1976). Throughout these works the basic referent for the concept of frame is essentially the same: it refers to an interpretive schemata that simplifies and condenses the "world out there" by selectively punctuating and encoding objects, situations, events, experiences, and sequences of actions within one's present or past environment. In Goffman's words, frames allow individuals "to locate, perceive, identify, and label" events within their life space or the world at large (1974, 21). The recent spate of research on the media and newsmaking both documents and highlights this characteristic function of frames (Gans 1979; Gitlin 1980; Tuchman 1978). Collective action frames not only perform this focusing and punctuating role; they also function simultaneously as modes of attribution and articulation.

To consider first the punctuating function, collective action frames serve as accenting devices that either underscore and embellish the seriousness and injustice of a social condition or redefine as unjust and immoral what was previously seen as unfortunate but perhaps tolerable. In either case, activists employ collective action frames to punctuate or single out some existing social condition or aspect of life and define it as unjust, intolerable, and deserving of corrective action (Gamson et al. 1982; Klandermans 1984; McAdam 1982; Moore 1978; Piven and Cloward 1977; Snow et al. 1986; Turner and Killian 1987). But the framing of a condition, happening, or sequence of events as unjust, inexcusable, or immoral is not sufficient to predict the direction and nature of collective action. Some sense of blame or causality must be specified as well as a corresponding sense of responsibility for corrective action.

This, then, takes us to the second characteristic of collective action frames: they function as modes of attribution by making diagnostic and prognostic attributions.[2] In the case of the former, movement activists attribute blame for some problematic condition by identifying culpable agents, be they individuals or collective processes or structures. And in the case of prognostic attribution, the Leninesque question is addressed by suggesting both a general line of action for ameliorating the problem and the assignment of responsibility for carrying out that action. Thus, diagnostic attribution is concerned with problem identification, whereas prognostic attribution addresses problem resolution.

In addition to their punctuational and attributional functions, collective action frames enable activists to articulate and align a vast array of

2. Our discussion is informed by the extensive literature in social psychology on attribution theory (Crittenden 1983; Hastie 1984; Heider 1958; Jones et al. 1972; Jones and Nisbet 1971; Kelley 1967, 1971, 1972; Kelley and Michela 1980; Stryker and Gottlieb 1981) as well as by the application of attribution theory to social movement conversion processes and experiences (Snow and Machalek 1983, 1984).

events and experiences so that they hang together in a relatively unified and meaningful fashion. They are signaling and collating devices that decode and "package," in Gamson's terms (1988), slices of observed and experienced reality so that subsequent experiences or events need not be interpreted anew. The punctuated and encoded threads of information may be diverse and even incongruous, but they are woven together in such a way that what was previously inconceivable, or at least not clearly articulated, is now meaningfully interconnected. Thus, what gives a collective action frame its novelty is not so much its innovative ideational elements as the manner in which activists articulate or tie them together.

Master Frames and Their Variable Features

What we call master frames perform the same functions as movement-specific collective action frames, but they do so on a larger scale. In other words, they are also modes of punctuation, attribution, and articulation, but their punctuations, attributions, articulations may color and constrain those of any number of movement organizations. Master frames are to movement-specific collective action frames as paradigms are to finely tuned theories. Master frames are generic; specific collective action frames are derivative. So conceived, master frames can be construed as functioning in a manner analogous to linguistic codes in that they provide a grammar that punctuates and syntactically connects patterns or happenings in the world. Although all master frames function in this fashion, they can also differ in a number of respects. Three of these variable features warrant attention.

The first stems from the attributional function of master frames. As suggested above, a central feature of the framing process in relation to collective action is the generation of diagnostic attributions, which involve the identification of a problem and the attribution of blame or causality. All collective action frames perform this diagnostic function, but they can vary considerably in terms of the actual specification of blame. A central finding of attribution theory is that the causes of most behavior are attributed to internal or external factors. We assume that this tendency is also operative in the case of collective action, such that its nature will vary significantly depending on whether blame or responsibility for the problem at hand is internalized.

A central issue in attribution theory has concerned the factors that account for variation in the direction of causal attributions. Among the various factors identified as affecting this process, Kelley's (1972) concept of causal schemata is particularly relevant to our concerns. He argues that causal attributions are circumscribed in part by the general conceptions people have "about how certain kinds of causes interact to produce a specific kind of effect." In some respects, this argument is similar to Mills's (1940) contention that causal attributions are derived from "vocabularies of motive." Thus, whether using the language of "causal schemata" or "vocabularies of motive," both conceptualizations suggest that causal attributions are not made in a social void but are "framed" instead by attributional algorithms of sorts that can vary situationally and temporally.

Master frames perform a similar function, albeit on a larger scale, in that they provide the interpretive medium through which collective actors associated with different movements within a cycle assign blame for the problem they are attempting to ameliorate. Thus, in the case of SMOs associated with what might be termed the "psychosalvational" frame, such as TM, Scientology, and est, the source of personal suffering and unhappiness is seen as residing within the individual rather than within the larger sociocultural context.[3] That context may be seen as suffocating and decadent, but personal rather than societal transformation is regarded as the key to change. In contrast, from the standpoint of what might be thought of as the civil rights frame, blame is externalized in that unjust differences in life circumstances are attributed to encrusted, discriminatory structural arrangements rather than to the victims' imperfections.

The second variable feature of master frames is rooted in Bernstein's (1970; 1971) idea that there are two basic linguistic codes that yield different patterns of speech and orientation. One is referred to as "the restricted code" and the other as "the elaborated code." In the case of the restricted code, speech is rigidly organized in terms of a narrow range of syntactic alternatives; it is highly particularistic with respect to meaning and social structure, and as a consequence it is more predictable and reflective of the immediate social structure. In contrast, the elaborated code gives rise to speech that is more flexibly organized in terms of a wide range of syntactic alternatives, is more universalistic with respect to meaning and social structure, and thus is less predictable and reflective of immediate structures.

Bernstein's scheme is especially relevant to the articulation function of master frames. We have noted how they function in part as modes of articulation. But not all master frames perform this function in the same fashion. Some are rigid, whereas others are more flexible and elastic. Thus it is useful to distinguish between restricted and elaborated master frames. In idea terms, the former tend to be "closed" or exclusive ideational sys-

---

3. The term *psychosalvational* was initially used by Wallis (1979) as a cover term for the array of religious and secular movements promising "individual or psycho-spiritual development and self-realization."

tems that do not so readily lend themselves to amplification or extension. As modes of articulation, they tend to organize a narrow band of ideas in a tightly interconnected fashion; as modes of interpretation, they provide a constricted range of definitions, thus allowing for little interpretive discretion. Stated more parsimoniously, restricted master frames are syntactically rigid and lexically particularistic. The nuclear freeze master frame, as we suggest below, is illustrative of a restricted one.

Elaborated master frames, on the other hand, are organized in terms of a wide range of ideas. They are more flexible modes of interpretation, and as a consequence, they are more inclusive systems that allow for extensive ideational amplification and extension. Being more syntactically flexible and lexically universalistic than the restricted frame, the elaborated master frame allows for numerous aggrieved groups to tap it and elaborate their grievances in terms of its basic problem-solving schema. The civil rights master frame, as we will discuss briefly, is clearly illustrative of an elaborative frame.

The third variable feature of master frames concerns their mobilizing potency. Potency is affected by two factors: where a master frame falls on the restricted/elaborative continuum and the extent of the frame's resonance. Regarding the first factor, we suspect that the more elaborated a master frame, the greater its appeal and influence and the more potent the frame. But potency is not assured by a highly elaborated frame. A master frame may lend itself to elaboration by various aggrieved groups across society, but such extensive elaboration may not be intensive in the sense of striking a deep responsive chord. In other words, its appeal may be only superficial or skin-deep. It follows that the potency of a master frame will also vary with the extent to which it is relevant to or resonates with the life world of adherents and constituents as well as bystanders. Hypothetically, the greater the resonance, the more potent the master frame.

Drawing on our earlier work (Snow and Benford 1988), we suggest three interrelated factors that affect the resonance dimension of potency: empirical credibility, experiential commensurability, and ideational centrality or narrative fidelity. By empirical credibility we refer to the apparent evidential basis for a master frame's diagnostic claims. Do its problem designations and attributions appear to be empirically credible from the vantage point of the targets of mobilization? To the extent that there are events that can be interpreted as documentary evidence for diagnostic and prognostic claims, a master frame has empirical credibility.[4]

4. The issue here is not whether diagnostic and prognostic claims are actually factual or valid, but whether their empirical referents lend themselves to being read as

Substantiation of designated problems does not mean that all potential constituents have firsthand experience with these problems. Some individuals may be keenly aware of social arrangements or occurrences punctuated as problematic and unjust, but those problems may be removed from their everyday life situation. For others, the problem may have already intruded into their everyday lives such that they have experienced it directly. When this is the case, the framing has experiential commensurability and, presumably, greater potency.

The final variable affecting a master frame's resonance is its ideational centrality or narrative fidelity. Following Gramsci's (1971) distinction between "organic" and "nonorganic" ideology and Rude's parallel distinction between "inherent" and "derived" ideologies, as well as previous work on belief systems (Borhek and Curtis 1975; Converse 1964), we assume that the more central the ideas and meanings of a proffered framing to the ideology of the targets of mobilization, the greater its hierarchical salience within that larger belief system and the greater its "narrative fidelity" (Fisher 1984). In other words, the frame strikes a responsive chord in that it rings true with extant beliefs, myths, folktales, and the like. When that is the case, we suspect the frame is also considerably more potent.

To summarize, we have suggested that master frames vary in terms of their attributional orientation, their articulational scope, and their potency. Regarding the issue of potency, we postulate that it is a function of a master frame's elaborative potential and its resonance, which, in turn, is affected by the frame's empirical credibility, experiential commensurability, and narrative fidelity. We suspect that at least one of these resonance variables must be operative if a master frame is to exhibit much potency and that the existence of all three translates into considerable potency.

Cycles of Protest

We now turn to the final key theoretical element: cycles of protest. Tarrow originally defined cycles of protest as sequences of escalating collective action that are of greater frequency and intensity than normal, that spread throughout various sectors and regions of society, and that involve both new techniques of protest and new forms of organization that, in combination with traditional organizational infrastructures, "determine the spread and dynamics of the cycle" (1983, 36–39). Although we accept the general thrust of this conceptualization, we think it would be

---

"real" indicators of the claims. When they are, then the claims have empirical credibility. Although this is obviously an interpretive issue, we suspect that it is easier to construct an evidential base for some claims than for others.

theoretically and empirically fruitful to modify it in several respects. First, we would extend its scope so that it could be applied to temporal variation in collective action not only at the national or sector level but also at the level of communities, regions, and the world at large. In addition, we suspect that it would be interesting to examine empirically cyclical patterns of movement industries within a larger sector or cycle, in part to assess the extent to which movement industries within the same temporal frame are affected by each other as well as similar structural factors. Finally, we think the concept of protest should be used generically, in the fashion suggested by Lofland (1985), rather than limited to noninstitutional political challenges.

THE CONCEPTS APPLIED: ILLUSTRATIVE PROPOSITIONS

With these conceptual and theoretical considerations in mind, we turn to an elaboration of sensitizing propositions that bear on the relation between master frames and cycles of protest. The first set of illustrative propositions pertains to the relation between master frames and the emergence of cycles of protest.[5] The second set concerns master frames and specific movements within a particular cycle. The third set deals with the relation between anchoring master frames and a cycle's tactical repertoire. Propositions pertaining to the relation between master frames and the shape of cycles of protest constitute a fourth set. Finally, we offer propositions associated with the relation between master frames and the decline of cycles of protest.

Master Frames and the Emergence of Cycles of Protest

Our fundamental argument is that framing activity and the resultant ideational webs that some movements spin or that emerge from the coalescence of collective action can also be crucial to the emergence and course of a cycle of protest. Since people do not act collectively without "good reason," to assert a linkage between master frames and cycles of protest may seem almost true by definition. Yet, just as the function

---

5. We have designated our preliminary statements regarding the relation between master frames and cycles of protest as "illustrative" or "sensitizing" propositions so as to differentiate our assertions from more formal propositions. Although each proposition is empirically grounded in our various fieldwork experiences and observations, we do not consider them immutable components of a unified theory. Rather, we offer them as sensitizing propositions, analogous to Blumer's (1969) notion of "sensitizing concepts," to suggest and inspire questions researchers might pursue.

of ideational elements and framing activity has not been given sufficient analytic attention by much SMO research, so it has been neglected at the macrolevel of cycles of protest. In his initial discussion of the characteristics of cycles of protest, for example, Tarrow (1983) makes only passing references to the role of mobilizing ideas and meanings in relation to the rise and decline of cycles.[6] Here we are not asserting such a linkage, but suggesting that master frames constitute an additional defining feature of cycles of protest. Thus, our orienting proposition, *Proposition 1: Associated with the emergence of a cycle of protest is the development or construction of an innovative master frame.*

The peace movement, as a movement industry, provides concrete illustration of this linkage. Randall Forsberg's proposal for a freeze on the development, testing, and deployment of nuclear weapons emerged, in 1980, as an innovative master frame that stimulated a dramatic upswing in peace movement activity throughout the first half of the decade. Previous attempts to revive the dormant peace movement had failed to generate mass mobilization. By 1963, the grim specter of nuclear holocaust had faded from the public spotlight, spawning only sporadic protests for the ensuing seventeen years (Boyer 1984), despite the fact that global strategic nuclear arsenals increased by more than eightfold during the period (Sivard 1982, 11).

Capitalizing on the bellicose rhetoric of the newly installed Reagan administration and NATO plans to deploy a new generation of nuclear weapons in Western Europe, the freeze movement amplified the severity and urgency of the nuclear threat. But it was the development of an innovative master frame that went beyond a diagnosis to include an original prognosis and a clear call to action that accounts in part for the reemergence of peace movement activity in the eighties. A bilateral, verifiable freeze provided what many felt had been *the* missing ingredient: a simple but concrete solution to the nuclear predicament (Benford 1988, 252). Hundreds of thousands of previously passive citizens were mobilized. They took to the streets in record numbers, organized lobbying campaigns, held community referenda, revived old peace organizations, and established hundreds of new ones.

These observations not only underscore the linkage between a master frame and the clustering of collective action but also suggest that in the absence of such a frame, all other things being equal, mass mobilization is unlikely. Thus, *Proposition 2: The failure of mass mobilization when structural*

6. He has since incorporated ideational and framing considerations into his discussion of protest cycles (see Tarrow 1989).

conditions seem otherwise ripe may be accounted for in part by the absence of a resonant master frame.

We noted above that the peace movement failed to generate mass mobilization throughout the 1970s, despite the fact that conditions appeared to be conducive. More specifically, the objective conditions—such as global militarism, wars, and relatively unabated increases in nuclear weapons stockpiles, as well as structural conditions including society's resource base, political opportunity structures, and organizational infrastructures—do not appear to have been any less facilitative of peace movement activity in 1975 than they were in 1980. What was lacking in the 1970s, however, was a resonant master frame that was subsequently provided by the nuclear weapons freeze campaign.

Master Frames and Specific Movements within a Cycle

If the foregoing set of propositions holds, it logically follows that at what point a specific SMO emerges within a cycle of protest affects the substance and latitude of its framing efforts. Thus, *Proposition 3: Movements that surface early in a cycle of protest are likely to function as progenitors of master frames that provide the ideational and interpretive anchoring for subsequent movements within the cycle.* Let us return to the cycle of activity associated with the peace movement in the 1980s to illustrate this proposition.

Any number of problematic events or issues could have provided the impetus for a revival of peace movement action. International confrontations, border disputes, interventionism, militarism, chemical and biological weapons developments, apartheid, and institutional and structural violence—any could have rekindled the peace movement. Yet the reemergence of peace activity in the 1980s was associated almost solely with the nuclear threat. As already suggested, this is attributable in part to the development of the freeze concept as a master frame.

The freeze campaign framed war and peace issues in a narrow and highly compartmentalized fashion. Rather than addressing the structural roots of international conflict—superpower relations, the weaknesses of international peacekeeping institutions, and the lack of nonviolent alternatives to resolving disputes between sovereign states—the freeze defined the problem in technical terms. The ever-increasing size and destructive capacities of the United States' and the Soviet Union's nuclear arsenals constituted a threat to be controlled; the idea of a nuclear freeze offered a technological solution. Most peace movement organizations followed the freeze campaign's lead and focused attention almost exclusively on "stopping hardware" (Solo 1985, 10)—on preventing the testing, production, and development of particular weapon systems that the movement considered to be the most dangerous, the most likely to increase the probability of a nuclear war.

In light of such observations, the obverse proposition is suggested. *Proposition 4: Movements that emerge later in the cycle will typically find their framing efforts constrained by the previously elaborated master frame.* Returning to the foregoing illustration, not all peace groups went along with the freeze campaign's narrow focus. National peace coalitions and traditional pacifist organizations sought to expand the boundaries of the freeze frame to encompass other peace issues and social problems. But these frame extension efforts failed to elicit popular support and were often met by staunch resistance from freeze campaign activists. Rancorous frame disputes ensued between single-issue and multi-issue groups (Benford 1989).

The foregoing set of propositions can be further illustrated with reference to the civil rights movement. Its master frame, as initially espoused by Martin Luther King, Jr., and his associates, accented the principle of equal rights and opportunities regardless of ascribed characteristics and articulated it with the goal of integration through nonviolent means. Although there was always some tension among the movement's "big four" organizations (CORE, NAACP, SCLC, and SNCC), each initially proffered frames that were consistent with integrationist goals and nonviolent philosophy. By the mid-1960s, however, CORE and SNCC shifted their framings from the integrationist and equal rights goals of the movement's master frame to a more radical black power framing. Subsequently, both organizations suffered declines in contributions and support from both external sources and constituents, in large part because of their deviation from the movement's master frame (McAdam 1982, 181–229).

Such observations suggest that though master frames do not necessarily determine the framings of SMOs that emerge later in a cycle, they do exercise considerable constraint on the content of these framings. In addition, these observations and corollary propositions point to a central reason for conflict and factionalization among SMOs within a cycle of protest. Once a movement's collective action frame has become established as the master frame, efforts to extend its ideational scope may encounter resistance from its progenitors and guardians, as well as from external supporters. In turn, deviations from the master frame may be labeled as heresy and evoke social control responses from the movement's core supporters.

Master Frames and Tactical Repertoires within a Cycle of Protest

We noted earlier that master frames not only punctuate and encode reality but also function as modes of attribution and articulation. In light of these observations, it is reasonable to suggest that the tactical derivations and choices within a cycle of protest are affected in part by the movement's master frame. A master frame implies both new ways of interpreting a situation as well as novel means of dealing with or confronting it. Hence, *Proposition 5: Tactical innovation is spawned in part by the emergence of new master frames.*

A brief examination of the emergent tactical repertoire of the civil rights movement illustrates this proposition. As already noted, the movement's leaders fashioned a master frame that articulated the ideal of equal rights and opportunities regardless of ascribed characteristics. Jim Crow laws and segregationist practices prevalent throughout the South were targeted as blatant symbolic representations of prejudice and discrimination. Tactics such as the bus boycotts and lunch counter sit-ins were developed and deployed as a means of directly challenging Jim Crow, in part by creating within specific communities a "crisis definition of the situation" (McAdam 1983, 743). Although these tactics were not the invention of the civil rights movement, this was the first time they had been applied in those settings for that cause. The freedom rides, however, were the movement's own tactical creation. Like the boycotts and sit-ins, the freedom rides created a "crisis situation" by dramatizing for the entire nation the substance of the claims articulated by the civil rights movement's master frame (McAdam 1983, 745).

Each of these tactical innovations were congruent with the master frame espoused by King and other civil rights leaders and thus flowed directly from the movement's nonviolent philosophy. Other tactical choices, such as riots, robbery, sabotage, and violence, were eschewed by nearly all the movement's organizations and participants until the mid-1960s.

These observations further underscore the relation between master frames and tactical repertoires within a cycle of protest. Hence, *Proposition 6: Movement tactics are not solely a function of environmental constraints and adaptations, but are also constrained by anchoring master frames.* In his research on "the pace of black insurgency," McAdam (1983) concludes that the civil rights movement's internal organizational and external political opportunity structures contributed to the development of innovative protest tactics and their diffusion. Moreover, he found that as rapidly as the movement devised new tactics that were effective, its opponents developed countermeasures that neutralized the tactical inventions, prompting movement leaders to devise additional novel methods of protest. We do not take exception with these conclusions, but we do suggest that movement tactics are facilitated or constrained not only by the political environment and opponents' adaptation but also by master frames.

Master frames can exercise constraining influence on the development of tactics in two ways. First, the development or use of tactics that are in-consistent with the diagnostic and prognostic components of a movement's master frame as well as with constituency values is unlikely. If movement action is inconsistent with the values it espouses or with its constituents' values, it renders its framing efforts vulnerable to dismissal.

As we indicated above, the development of nonviolent philosophy and strategy by the civil rights movement precluded the use of violent tactics. A similar observation can be made with respect to the peace movement and its nonviolent philosophy. A stark example of the movement's sensi-tivity to such constraints occurred in the summer of 1985. Just prior to the movement's annual pilgrimage to Pantex (a facility near Amarillo, Texas, where all U.S. nuclear weapons are assembled), a disarmament activist re-moved several feet of track from the railway artery serving the facility. His actions and subsequent arrest were widely publicized. Although orga-nizers of the peace pilgrimage publicly condemned the protester's tactics, their coalition's reputation and credibility were damaged. The fact that his actions had jeopardized lives contradicted the movement's most frequently amplified value and indeed its master frame. Few outside the movement, including most media representatives, differentiated the actions of the lone protester from the peace coalition (Benford 1987).

The second way in which a movement's master frame can constrain tac-tical evolution depends on the extent to which the frame is restricted or elaborated. The more restricted the movement's master frame the nar-rower the range of tactical options. In contrast, movements associated with highly elaborated master frames are likely to have greater discretion regarding tactical choices.

Again, the peace movement serves to illustrate this corollary proposition. We previously suggested that the freeze constituted a highly restricted master frame. Its prognosis, a mutual, verifiable agreement between the United States and the Soviet Union, implied the use of traditional politi-cal tactics, including lobbying members of Congress to encourage them to vote for the freeze resolution and against specific weapons bills, voting in local freeze referenda, and casting votes for and contributing to pro-freeze candidates. Other tactical choices, particularly acts of civil disobedience targeting defense contractors, were initially ruled out by the movement's mainstream activists and supporters.

Master Frames and the Shape of Cycles of Protest

Thus far we have discussed the relations among master frames and the emergence of cycles of protest, specific movements within those cycles, and their tactical repertoires. We now turn to the relation between master frames and the shape of protest cycles once they have emerged. Shape can be conceptualized in terms of two dimensional axes in which the vertical axis represents the cycle's ecological scope and the horizontal indicates its temporal span. By ecological scope, we refer to the diffusion of movement activity across different population and organizational sectors of society. Temporal span simply refers to the duration of a cycle of protest.

We have noted that one way in which master frames vary is in terms of their relative potency, and we conceptualized potency in terms of its elaborative potential and resonant capacity. We now integrate these observations with the conceptualization of shape by offering two additional propositions. The first concerns the general relation between potency and shape. Thus, _Proposition 7: The shape of a cycle of protest is in part a function of the mobilizing potency of the anchoring frame._

The civil rights movement provides concrete illustration of this proposition. Because of its considerable elaborative and resonant qualities, it is a national movement that, conceptualized broadly, has spanned several decades. More specifically, its punctuation and accentuation of the idea of equal rights and opportunities amplified a fundamental American value that resonated with diverse elements of American society and thus lent itself to extensive elaboration. Movements championing women, the disabled, the aged, and American Indians, among others, were empowered in part by the civil rights master frame. Thus, though the civil rights cycle may have peaked at the height of black insurgency in the mid- to late-1960s, the cycle's ecological scope and temporal span have extended well beyond the 1960s and the plight of black Americans.

The peace movement provides further illustrative material bearing on the relation between a cycle's shape and its underlying master frame. It is our sense that the shape of the most recent cycle of peace activity in the United States is considerably different from that of the civil rights movement. The reasons are twofold. First, as we have argued elsewhere (Snow and Benford 1988), the freeze master frame lacked the same degree of empirical credibility, experiential commensurability, and narrative fidelity, thus limiting its ecological scope in comparison to the civil rights movement. And second, the highly restrictive nature of the freeze master frame limited its potential for elaboration. We suspect that the cycle's eventual decline was attributable, in part, to proponents' failure to amplify the freeze frame in more resonant and innovative ways.

In light of this observation, it follows that the shape of a cycle is not only a function of a master frame's potency; it can also be affected by the framing work of smos within a cycle. Hence, _Proposition 8: The shape of a cycle of_ *protest is in part a function of the capacity of incipient movements within the cycle to amplify and extend the master frame in imaginative and yet resonant ways.*

This proposition alerts us to the fact that, whatever the elaborative potential of a master frame, it does not necessarily follow that it will be amplified and extended in ways that broaden the cycle's scope. Thus, the flowering of movements such as those associated with women, Chicanos, American Indians, the aged, and the disabled on the heels of the black movement was precipitated in part by the extension of the principle of equal rights and opportunities from the domain of black America to the situation of the other groups. The obvious implication of this extension of the early civil rights master frame has been the expansion of the cycle's ecological scope and temporal span.

Master Frames and the Decline of Cycles of Protest

In our first set of propositions we suggested that a crucial factor contributing to the emergence of a cycle of protest or, conversely, the failure of mass mobilization when structural conditions appear otherwise conducive is the presence or absence of a resonant master frame. If master frames are as useful as we suggest in facilitating the emergence of protest cycles, it stands to reason that they should also contribute to understanding the decline of cycles of protest. Hence, *Proposition 9: The decline or withering of an extant cycle of protest is due in part to changes in the prevailing cultural climate that render the anchoring master frame impotent.* Here we are suggesting that events can sometimes begin to pass by or overwhelm a master frame and thus erode its empirical credibility or its experiential relevance.

The decline of earlier cycles of peace movement activity is illustrative. Prior to both world wars, peace movement membership, organization, support, and activity swelled to unprecedented levels (Chatfield 1971, 1973; DeBenedetti 1980; Marchand 1972; Wittner 1969). Between 1901 and 1914, forty-five new peace organizations were established in the United States (DeBenedetti 1980, 70). Its traditional pacifist ranks expanded to include "an impressive number of the nation's political, business, religious, and academic leaders" (Marchand 1972, ix). Similarly, during the decade preceding World War II, peace activism and campaigns achieved new heights. By the mid-1930s, antiwar strikes and other demonstrations on campuses became commonplace (Wittner 1969).

In each instance, the outbreak of war reduced the movement to its pacifist core. World War I undercut peace adherents' "faith in human reason, progress, Christianity, Great Power harmony, and the need for a working peacekeeping mechanism" (DeBenedetti 1980, 79). Likewise, the rise of fascism, the onset of the Holocaust, and Pearl Harbor provided most peace adherents and sympathizers with a seemingly insurmountable challenge to the credibility of the movement's master frame. Consequently, by 1941 Americans "renounced pacifism with the same fervor with which they had previously renounced war" (Wittner 1969, 16).

Although the foregoing discussion illustrates that cycles can decline owing to changes in the cultural or political environment, their demise can also be explained in part by the emergence of frames that challenge or compete with the movement's master frame. The debates that ensue and the very existence of competing frames can chip away at the mobilizing potency of the original master frame. In light of such contingencies, we offer a final proposition. *Proposition 10: The emergence of competing frames can suggest the vulnerabilities and irrelevance of the anchoring master frame, thus challenging its resonance and rendering it increasingly impotent.*

The cycle of peace movement activity that emerged in the aftermath of World War II provides an illustration of this proposition. The gruesome effects of the war and the development of the atomic bomb led many pacifists and peace adherents to the conclusion that world government offered the only hope for the survival of our species. Although the notion of world government had been a persistent theme of earlier cycles of peace movement activity, it had constituted only one of many planks in the peace movement's platform. Following the war, however, world government emerged as a potent master frame, one that engendered widespread popular support (DeBenedetti 1980; Wittner 1969).

Its potency was short-lived, however. World government soon elicited competing frames from within the peace movement. "What the world needed," countered some traditional pacifists, "was not more authority at the top, but rather greater cooperation of peoples at the bottom in solving their mutual problems" (Wittner 1969, 179). This and other competing frames underscored for many the weaknesses of world government as a panacea for problems pertaining to war and peace. Many peace activists subsequently defected from the world government movement.

If the internal attacks on world government diminished its potency as a master frame, external attacks dealt it a deathblow. By the early 1950s, counterframing efforts led by Senator Joseph McCarthy successfully equated world government with communism (DeBenedetti 1980; Wittner 1969). In the face of such resonant frames, individuals and peace organizations could no longer afford to be associated with world government advocacy. The movement subsequently dissociated itself from the master frame, and thereafter world government remained, at best, marginal to the peace movement. Lacking a potent master frame, the peace movement suffered a period of decline.

The fifth set of propositions could just as easily have been illustrated with reference to any number of other movements. But the foregoing discussion suffices to show that extant master frames can either lose their interpretive salience owing to the profusion of events and the proliferation of alternative framings or be neutralized by the repressive tactics of more powerful groups, or both. Hence, the mobilizing potency of the master frame begins to dissipate, and the cycle with which it has been associated begins to decline.

CONCLUSION

In the preceding pages we have explored the relation between master frames and cycles of protest by enumerating ten interconnected propositions. Basing our argument on our contention that SMOs function as, among other things, signifying or framing agents actively engaged in the production of meaning and ideas, we have suggested that the products of this framing activity, which we refer to as collective action frames, can sometimes come to function as master algorithms that color and constrain the orientations and activities of other movements associated with it ecologically and temporally. Simply put, we have argued that master frames affect the cyclicity and clustering of social movement activity.

Although we realize that some scholars may take issue with the illustrative case materials employed, we reiterate that our objective here has been primarily theoretical, and, as such, we view this exercise as a springboard for systematic empirical investigation. Assessment of the analytic utility of this essay is contingent on future investigations.

Empirical reservations notwithstanding, we think several important implications flow from our conceptual framework. First, our scheme provides the conceptual tools for systematically examining the relation between existing ideologies and challenges to them and their dialectical relationship in a fashion consistent with Gramsci (1971) and Rude (1980), who, among others, regard ideational factors as important variables in the collective action equation.

A second implication pertains to ongoing sociological concern with the relation between micro- and macrostructural phenomena. Specifically, we have detailed theoretically how framing activity at the level of social movement organizations and actors can have significant implications for macrostructural phenomena such as cycles of protest.

Finally, our theoretical formulation complements and supplements resource mobilization and other structuralist perspectives in at least three ways. For one thing, the framing process and the concepts of collective action frames and master frames provide a basis for understanding the process through which collective action is inspired and legitimated. Second, these conceptual tools enable us to examine empirically rather than take for granted the process through which events and actions come to be regarded as desirable or undesirable, more or less costly, and more or less risky. And last, the analysis suggests that framing issues and processes can play an important role in affecting political opportunities, changes in the larger political environment, and the availability of resources.

REFERENCES

Bateson, Gregory. 1972. *Steps to an Ecology of the Mind*. San Francisco: Chandler.
Benford, Robert D. 1987. "Framing Activity, Meaning, and Social Movement Participation: The Nuclear Disarmament Movement." Ph.D. diss., University of Texas–Austin.
———. 1988. "The Nuclear Disarmament Movement." In *The Nuclear Cage: A Sociology of the Arms Race*, ed. Lester R. Kurtz. Englewood Cliffs, N.J.: Prentice-Hall, 237–65.
———. 1989. "Framing Disputes within the Nuclear Disarmament Movement." Paper presented at the annual meetings of the Midwest Sociological Society, St. Louis.
Bernstein, Basil. 1970. "A Socio-Linguistic Approach to Socialization." In *Directions in Socio-Linguistics*, ed. J. Gumperz and D. Hymes. New York: Holt, Rinehart, and Winston.
———. 1971. *Class, Codes and Control*. London: Routledge and Kegan Paul.
Blumer, Herbert. 1951. "Collective Behavior." In *Principles of Sociology*, ed. A. M. Lee. New York: Barnes and Noble, 99–121.
———. 1969. *Symbolic Interactionism*. Englewood Cliffs, N.J.: Transaction.
Borhek, James T., and Richard F. Curtis. 1975. *A Sociology of Belief*. New York: Wiley.
Boyer, Paul. 1984. "From Activism to Apathy: The American People and Nuclear Weapons, 1963–1980." *Journal of American History* 70, no. 4:821–44.
Chatfield, Charles. 1971. *For Peace and Justice: Pacifism in America, 1914–1941*. Knoxville: University of Tennessee Press.
———, ed. 1973. *Peace Movements in America*. New York: Schocken.
Cone, Edward T. 1968. *Musical Form and Performance*. New York: Norton.
Converse, Philip E. 1964. "The Nature of Belief Systems in Mass Publics." In *Ideology and Discontent*, ed. David Apter. New York: Free Press, 206–61.
Crittenden, Kathleen S. 1983. "Sociological Aspects of Attribution." *Annual Review of Sociology* 9:425–46.
DeBenedetti, Charles. 1980. *The Peace Reform in American History*. Bloomington: Indiana University Press.
Della Porta, Donatella, and Sidney Tarrow. 1986. "Unwanted Children: Political Violence and the Cycle of Protest in Italy, 1966–1973." *European Journal of Political Research* 14:607–32.

Eisinger, Peter K. 1973. "The Conditions of Protest Behavior in American Cities." *American Political Science Review* 67:11–28.

Ferree, Myra Marx, and Frederick D. Miller. 1985. "Mobilization and Meaning: Toward an Integration of Social Psychological and Resource Mobilization Perspectives on Social Movements." *Sociological Inquiry* 55:38–51.

Fisher, Walter R. 1984. "Narration as a Human Communication Paradigm: The Case of Public Moral Argument." *Communication Monographs* 51:1–23.

Gamson, William A. 1988. "Political Discourse and Collective Action." *International Social Movement Research* 1:219–44.

Gamson, William A., Bruce Fireman, and Steven Rytina. 1982. *Encounters with Unjust Authority*. Homewood, Ill.: Dorsey Press.

Gans, Herbert J. 1979. *Deciding What's News: A Study of CBS Evening News, NBC Nightly News, News Week and Time*. New York: Pantheon.

Gitlin, Todd. 1980. *The Whole World Is Watching*. Berkeley: University of California Press.

Goffman, Erving. 1974. *Frame Analysis: An Essay on the Organization of Experience*. New York: Harper.

Gramsci, Antonio. 1971. *Selections from the Prison Notebooks of Antonio Gramsci*, ed. A. Hoare and G. N. Smith. New York: International Publishers.

Hall, Stuart. 1982. "The Rediscovery of Ideology: Return of the Repressed in Media Studies." In *Culture, Society and the Media*, ed. Michael Gurevitch, Tony Bennett, James Curran, and Janet Woollacott. New York: Methuen, 56–90.

Hastie, Reid. 1981. "Schematic Principles in Human Memory." In *Social Cognition: The Ontario Symposium on Personality and Social Psychology*, ed. E. Tory Higgins, C. Peter Herman, and Mark P. Zanna. Hillsdale, N.J.: Erlbaum, 39–88.

———. 1984. "Causes and Effects of Causal Attribution." *Journal of Personality and Social Psychology* 46:788–98.

Heider, Fritz. 1958. *The Psychology of Interpersonal Relations*. New York: Wiley.

Jenkins, J. Craig. 1983. "Resource Mobilization Theory and the Study of Social Movements." *Annual Review of Sociology* 9:527–53.

Jenkins, J. Craig, and Charles Perrow. 1977. "Insurgency of the Powerless: Farm Worker Movements." *American Sociological Review* 42:249–68.

Jones, Edward E., D. E. Kanouse, Harold H. Kelley, Richard E. Nisbet, S. Valins, and B. Weiner, eds. 1972. *Attribution: Perceiving the Causes of Behavior*. Morristown, N.J.: General Learning Press.

Jones, Edward E., and Richard Nisbet. 1971. *The Actor and the Observer: Divergent Perspectives on the Causes of Behavior*. Morristown, N.J.: General Learning Press.

Kelley, Harold H. 1967. "Attribution Theory in Social Psychology." *Nebraska Symposium on Motivation* 15:192–238.

———. 1971. *Attribution in Social Interaction*. Morristown, N.J.: General Learning Press.

———. 1972. *Causal Schemata and the Attribution Process*. Morristown, N.J.: General Learning Press.

Kelley, Harold H., and John L. Michela. 1980. "Attribution Theory and Research." *Annual Review of Psychology* 31:457–501.

Klandermans, Bert. 1984. "Mobilization and Participation: Social-Psychological Expansions of Resource Mobilization Theory." *American Sociological Review* 49:583–600.

Klapp, Orrin E. 1972. *Currents of Unrest: An Introduction to Collective Behavior*. New York: Holt, Rinehart and Winston.

Lipsky, Michael. 1970. *Protest in City Politics*. Chicago: Rand McNally.

Lofland, John. 1985. *Protest: Studies of Collective Behavior and Social Movements*. New Brunswick, N.J.: Transaction Books.

Marchand, C. Roland. 1972. *The American Peace Movement and Social Reform, 1898– 1918*. Princeton: Princeton University Press.

Marcus, Hazel, and Robert B. Zajonc. 1985. "The Cognitive Perspective in Social Psychology." In *The Handbook of Social Psychology*, ed. Gardner Lindzey and Elliot Aronson. New York: Random House, 127–230.

McAdam, Doug. 1982. *Political Process and the Development of Black Insurgency, 1930– 1970*. Chicago: University of Chicago Press.

———. 1983. "Tactical Innovation and the Pace of Insurgency." *American Sociological Review* 48:735–54.

McCarthy, John D., and Mayer N. Zald. 1977. "Resource Mobilization and Social Movements: A Partial Theory." *American Journal of Sociology* 82:1212–41.

Mills, C. Wright. 1940. "Situated Actions and Vocabularies of Motive." *American Sociological Review* 5:404–13.

Minsky, M. 1975. "A Framework for Presenting Knowledge." In *The Psychology of Computer Vision*, ed. P. A. Winston. New York: McGraw-Hill.

Moore, Barrington. 1978. *Injustice: The Social Bases of Obedience and Revolt*. White Plains, N.Y.: Sharpe.

Morris, Aldon D. 1984. *The Origins of the Civil Rights Movement*. New York: Free Press.

Neisser, U. 1976. *Cognition and Reality: Principles and Implications of Cognitive Psychology*. San Francisco: Freeman.

Oberschall, Anthony. 1973. *Social Conflict and Social Movements*. Englewood Cliffs, N.J.: Prentice-Hall.

Piaget, J. 1954. *The Construction of Reality in the Child*. New York: Basic Books.

Piven, Frances Fox, and Richard Cloward. 1977. *Poor People's Movements*. New York: Pantheon.

Rude, George. 1980. *Ideology and Popular Protest*. New York: Knopf.

Shorter, Edward, and Charles Tilly. 1974. *Strikes in France, 1830–1968*. Cambridge: Cambridge University Press.

Sivard, Ruth Leger. 1982. *World Military and Social Expenditures, 1982*. Leesburg, Va.: World Priorities.

Smelser, Neil. 1963. *Theory of Collective Behavior*. New York: Free Press.

Snow, David A., and Robert D. Benford. 1988. "Ideology, Frame Resonance, and Participant Mobilization." *International Social Movement Research* 1:197–217.

Snow, David A., and Richard Machalek. 1984. "The Sociology of Conversion." *Annual Review of Sociology* 10:367–80.

Snow, David A., E. Burke Rochford, Jr., Steven K. Worden, and Robert D. Benford. 1986. "Frame Alignment Process, Micromobilization, and Movement Participation." *American Sociological Review* 51:464–81.

Snow, David A., Louis A. Zurcher, and Sheldon Ekland-Olson. 1980. "Social Networks and Social Movements: A Microstructural Approach to Differential Recruitment." *American Sociological Review* 45:787–801.

Solo, Pam. 1985. "A New Atlantic Alliance: European and American Peace Movement Participation." *Disarmament Campaigns* 49 (November):10.

Stryker, Sheldon, and Avi Gottlieb. 1981. "Attribution Theory and Symbolic Interactionism: A Comparison." In *New Directions in Attribution Research*, vol. 3, ed. J. H. Harvey, W. Ickes, and R. F. Kidd. Hillsdale, N.J.: Erlbaum, 25–58.

Tarrow, Sidney. 1983. *Struggling to Reform: Social Movements and Policy Change during Cycles of Protest*. Ithaca, N.Y.: Western Societies Program, Cornell University.

———. 1989. *Struggle, Politics, and Reform: Collective Action, Social Movements, and Cycles of Protest*. Ithaca, N.Y.: Western Societies Program, Cornell University.

Tilly, Charles. 1978. *From Mobilization to Revolution*. Reading, Mass.: Addison-Wesley.

Tilly, Charles, Louise Tilly, and Richard Tilly. 1975. *The Rebellious Century, 1830–1930*. Cambridge, Mass.: Harvard University Press.

Tuchman, Gaye. 1978. *Making News: A Study in the Construction of Reality*. New York: Free Press.

Turner, Ralph H. 1969. "The Theme of Contemporary Social Movements." *British Journal of Sociology* 20:390–405.

Turner, Ralph H., and Lewis M. Killian. 1987. *Collective Behavior*. 3d ed. Englewood Cliffs, N.J.: Prentice-Hall.

Wallis, Roy. 1979. "Varieties of Psychosalvation." *New Society* 20:649–51.

Wittgenstein, Ludwig. 1967 [1953]. *Philosophical Investigations*, trans. G. Anscombe. Oxford: Blackwell.

Wittner, Lawrence S. 1969. *Rebels against War: The American Peace Movement, 1941–1960*. New York: Columbia University Press.

Zurcher, Louis A., and David A. Snow. 1981. "Collective Behavior: Social Movements." In *Social Psychology: Sociological Perspectives*, ed. Morris Rosenberg and Ralph H. Turner. New York: Basic Books, 447–82.

7

Collective Identity and Activism

Networks, Choices, and the Life

of a Social Movement

D e b r a   F r i e d m a n   a n d

D o u g   M c A d a m

       In contrast to traditional grievance- or attitude-based models of activism (Block et al. 1968; Lewis and Kraut 1972; Thomas 1971; Braungart 1971; Fendrich and Krauss 1978) stand both structural and rational choice accounts of participation. Typically structural and rational choice theories have been seen as mutually exclusive (Fireman and Gamson 1979), one locating the causes of activism in structural proximity and network connections, the other in individual cost-benefit calculations. It could be argued that the strength of each position is the weakness of the other: the principal weakness of the structural explanation is its failure to be grounded in an explicit model of the individual; the principal weakness of the rational choice explanation is its failure to embed the individual in that set of relationships and group affiliations that so powerfully shape the choices she or he makes. This complementarity suggests the possibility of a fruitful merger, and in this chapter we explore new terrain at the intersection of their strengths.

    Thus, this essay grows out of a dialogue between a structural or network account of social movement activism and a rational choice account. Although we have considered many of the empirical and theoretical puzzles facing social movement scholars in this dialogue, here we focus on one outcome of this continuing exchange: our agreement about the importance of identity—collective identity—in shaping individual participation and the life of a social movement.[1]

For comments we are grateful to Roberto Fernandez, Myra Marx Ferree, Michael Hechter, Cedric Herring, Edgar Kiser, Aldon Morris, Carol Mueller, Pamela Oliver, David Snow, and members of the University of Arizona Collective Action and Social Movements Seminar.

   1. Yet collective identity is not an easy concept to capture definitionally or empirically.

The collective identity of a social movement organization (SMO) is a shorthand designation announcing a status—a set of attitudes, commitments, and rules for behavior—that those who assume the identity can be expected to subscribe to. A Polish worker who announced, "I am a member of Solidarity," gave sufficient cues to the receiver of this message that he was committed to advancing the cause of Polish workers, favored a return to representative government, and would participate in a strike upon occasion. An American who claims to be a neo-Nazi tells those who are listening that he hates blacks, Jews, and liberals and probably owns a store of firearms he can be expected to use. A collective identity is a public pronouncement of status, in the classic Weberian sense.[2]

But it is more than that. It is also an individual announcement of affiliation, of connection with others. To partake of a collective identity is to reconstitute the individual self around a new and valued identity. So to announce that one was a member of Solidarity was not simply to incur behavioral and attitudinal obligations but to claim for oneself a desired social attachment and new sense of identity. In this sense, collective identities function as selective incentives motivating participation.

If taken seriously, this insight modifies both the structural and rational choice accounts of activism in interesting ways while building common conceptual ground between them. This represents one-half of our goal in undertaking this project. The other half centers on our desire to link the concept of collective identity to the ebb and flow of activism over the life of a social movement. To anticipate a bit, we argue that the nature of the collective identities produced by movements change over time. Rooted as they are initially in existing organizations or networks, these identities function as powerful selective incentives motivating participation. This may help explain why successful movements emerge and spread as rapidly as they do. Over time, however, the very success of these movements may result in the transformation of these collective identities into public goods available to everyone. That is, movements may produce collective identities of such

---

In the first place, all identities are collective, in the sense that every identity we claim requires some degree of (collective) social approbation for it to have meaning. Collective identity is distinct from individual identity in that the latter is the sum total of collective identities that a man or woman holds; what makes an individual's identity unique is not the singularity of the constituent parts but rather the combination or configuration of those parts (Simmel 1955).

2. *Collective identity* is not a new term. Within the collective behavior–social movements literature, Orrin Klapp (1969, 1972) and Louis Kriesberg (1973) have made use of the term, although in a different way than it is used here. For them, collective identity is more akin to something like solidarity. More recently, the term has appeared in some of the "new social movements" literature (see Melucci 1986; Cohen 1985).

salience—student radical, black revolutionary, feminist—that they cease to be exclusive property of the movement, thus losing their power to compel participation. We will develop these ideas more fully in the succeeding sections.

ALTERNATIVE ACCOUNTS OF RECRUITMENT: STRUCTURAL OR NETWORK, AND RATIONAL CHOICE

Structural and network accounts seek to provide explanations of activism that locate its roots outside of the individual, relying on the insight that "however reasonable the underlying assumption that some people are more . . . susceptible than others to movement participation, that view deflects attention from the fact that recruitment cannot occur without prior contact with a recruitment agent" (Snow, Zurcher, and Ekland-Olson 1980, 789). Prior recruitment is, in fact, one of the two principal structural factors held responsible for individual participation in movement activity. In settings as diverse as peace groups (Bolton 1972), the Nichiren Shoshu Buddhist movement (Snow 1976), and the Mississippi Freedom Summer project (McAdam 1986), strong empirical support for the importance of interpersonal contacts as the key source of movement recruits has been demonstrated.

Membership in organizations has also been linked empirically to individual participation (Orum 1972; McAdam 1986; Barnes and Kaase 1979; Von Eschen et al. 1971; Walsh and Warland 1983). Belonging to a relatively larger number of organizations may encourage activism in a variety of ways. If, for instance, organizational participation produces feelings of personal efficacy (Sayre 1980; Neal and Seeman 1964), it may simply be the case that those who are organizationally more active are more likely to regard activism as potentially effective and worth participating in. Or it may simply be a matter of information: involvement in an organization increases the chance that a person will learn about movement activity. Finally, to the extent that membership in organizations expands a person's range of interpersonal contacts, it also increases their susceptibility to the kind of personal recruiting appeals that have been shown to be effective in drawing others into movements.

What is common to all structural accounts is the assumption that structural proximity to a movement, rather than any individual disposition, produces activism. Although individuals differ in their dispositions, the opportunities afforded by structural location relative to a movement determine whether they are in a position to act on these dispositions. Empirical support for these positions is unimpeachable, but deeper questions of the theoretical mechanisms and processes that support these relationships remain unanswered. Why, for instance, does contact with another activist or membership in an organization with strong ties to a movement encourage activism? Does structural proximity breed some sort of behavioral contagion? Do links to others provide information that promotes a kind of diffusion process?

Like structural theories, rational choice theories of collective action stand in opposition to accounts that rely on variations in personality characteristics to explain participation in collective action. In addition, however, rational choice theorists find structural theories lacking on the ground that all action—including collective action—can be understood only in terms of individual-level dynamics.

The rational choice theory of collective action proceeds from the assumption that individuals have given goals, wants, tastes, or utilities. Since all goals cannot be fully realized because of scarcity (of time and resources), individuals will choose between alternative courses of action so as to maximize these wants and utilities. The resulting action may be seen as the end product of two successive filtering devices (Elster 1979). The first is defined by structural constraints that limit the set of possible courses of action by reducing it to the vastly smaller subset of feasible actions. The second filtering device is the mechanism by which the actor chooses which course of action to take. Ultimately, individual action is seen to result from choices made in the face of changing structural constraints. Individuals will join in collective actions only when they expect the private benefits of participation to exceed the costs.

This proposition would be little more than commonsensical were it not for the free-rider problem. Collective actions nearly always seek collective goods for their members, ends that, once achieved, all may benefit from. The problem is that if all will benefit, regardless of whether they have participated or not, no rational actor would ever choose to contribute his or her scarce resources to help achieve such ends.

At first glance there seem to be easy solutions to the free-rider problem since certain aims intrinsically require cooperative action: no individual can, by his or her own action, form an ethnic lobby or overthrow a political regime. Individuals often have goals that cannot be satisfied through their actions alone. Nevertheless, the free-rider problem means that many people will benefit from a successful collective action, and only participants will bear the costs of failure. Conventional rational choice wisdom holds that this typically deters the rational actor from participating because individual utility is maximized by waiting on the sidelines until others have achieved the goal.

Several means have been proposed as solutions to the free-rider problem. Individuals with different levels of interest in a given goal can exchange participation and control over a range of ends (Coleman 1973), can be swayed to contribute at different points in the unfolding of a collective action or social movement (Granovetter 1978; Oliver et al. 1985), and can be convinced to act for the collective good if they are convinced that they are engaged in a continuing cooperative relationship over the long run (Taylor 1976; Hardin 1982; Axelrod 1984). The principal means of overcoming free ridership, however, is through the use of selective incentives (Olson 1965; Hechter et al. 1982; Oliver 1980).[3] Selective incentives can increase the private benefits of participation so that they sometimes outweigh the costs incurred and tip the balance in favor of activism.

There are two problems with the conventional rational choice formulation. First, for all its rigor, the theory remains largely a post-hoc *description* of behavior. There is nothing in the theory to explain why some individuals value some ends more than others or even to indicate the probable priority ranking an individual is likely to attach to a set of utilities (Emerson 1987; Friedman 1987). Without such a theory of value, it is impossible to predict when an individual will engage in collective action or to know what sorts of selective incentives will work to overcome free riding.

Just as problematic, from our point of view, is the atomistic view of the individual implicit in the rational choice model. The image is that of the atomized outsider deciding whether to join a movement or not. What this view misses is the degree to which individuals are already embedded in the movement by virtue of prior ties or group affiliations. The failure to acknowledge this embeddedness distorts the nature of the choice process and blinds the rational choice scholar to a whole class of incentives that would appear to be decisive in many instances.

Thus rational choice theory, with its overly atomistic view of the individual, is mute about the choice of ends and therefore about what sorts of selective incentives beyond material ones, or other processes, might work to overcome free riding. And structural or network theory fails to offer a plausible model of individual action and therefore a convincing mechanism by which interpersonal contacts and organizational memberships draw individuals into activism.

Each of these lacunae can be addressed not by its own perspective but by the other, and we see considerable potential payoff from theoretical

3. There is empirical evidence suggesting that material selective incentives are either (1) typically insufficient to overcome free-riding behavior or (2) less important than Olson (1965) claimed (Marwell and Ames 1980). For a review of this evidence, see Friedman and Yamagishi (1985).

fusion. From the point of view of structural or network theory, the fact that there is more collective action than rational choice theory and its free-rider problem would predict is explicable in terms of networks. Potential actors in a collective action are tied to other actors. They are embedded in networks that serve to draw individuals into activism, thereby obviating the need for extensive material incentives.

But how, precisely, *do* these networks draw individuals into collective action?[4] Here rational choice theory provides insight: they provide incentives. Refusing to respond to the call of network partners means the potential loss of all the benefits provided by that tie. These benefits may be social, such as friendship or social honor (Laumann 1973), but they may also be material. Network ties provide people with jobs (Granovetter 1970), and people are tied, network fashion, to those with whom and for whom they work. To respond to the call of an important network partner—be it for activism or some other activity—is, in this perspective, the measured response of a rational actor.

A fused perspective—made up of the strengths of each of the two accounts—suggests that the potential participants in any collective action are *rational actors embedded in networks*. Still, actors have choices to make, and any theory of collective action must address the variation in participation over time in the life of a movement. Not all embedded actors will, despite their network ties, agree to be brought in to a new collective action. Once involved, not all will participate until the goal of the movement has been attained. Among structurally similarly situated individuals, what accounts for the differential appeal of social movement activism?

To address these issues, we return to the notion of incentives, in particular, collective identity as an incentive. How do "identity incentives" affect the calculus of embedded actors who face an ongoing choice over the life of a social movement about whether to participate in collective action?

IDENTITY INCENTIVES AND THE
LIFE OF A SOCIAL MOVEMENT

For heuristic purposes we will refer to three stages in the development of a social movement in order to highlight the role of collective

4. Most structural or network studies of activism are mute on the question of what underlying sociological processes account for the robust empirical relationship between participation and network ties. One exception to this generalization is the work of Roberto Fernandez and Doug McAdam on the dynamics of recruitment in the case of the 1964 Mississippi Freedom Summer project (Fernandez and McAdam 1988; McAdam and Fernandez 1989).

identity in each. In the first stage, the emerging movement grows out of but remains dependent upon preexisting institutions and organizations. In the second stage, the existing organizations and associational networks that guided the movement initially have typically been replaced by formal social movement organizations (SMOs). It now falls to these SMOs to contend with the twin tasks of retaining old members and attracting new ones. The third stage centers on the movement in decline. Formal SMOs remain the nominal core of the movement, but increasingly the diffusion of collective identities and cultural symbols associated with the movement has blurred the boundary between the SMOs and the public.

In each of these stages, collective identity and identity incentives play a distinctive part in furthering or hindering the development of the SMO. In the first stage, the new collective identity is planted in the soil of preexisting collective identities, and to the extent it is embedded within them, it has a better chance to flower. In the second stage, the collective identities associated with the movement have typically been uncoupled from the established roles of the aggrieved community, so participants are no longer, say, church members or students but movement activists. This transformation puts pressure on the SMOs to fashion new collective identities to induce participation. In the final stage, the collective identity becomes a public good and, as such, gives rise to a full-blown free-rider problem that has till now been largely ignored by both structural and rational choice theorists of collective action.

Stage One: Why Networks Work

Typically, emerging movements grow out of and remain dependent upon established institutions and organizations. Movements as diverse as a Texas antipornography effort (Curtis and Zurcher 1973), the Populist party (Hicks 1961), the Berkeley free speech movement (Lipset and Wolin 1965), and the American civil rights movement of the 1950s and 1960s (McAdam 1982; Morris 1984; Oberschall 1973) found their impetus in existing organizations.

This kind of beginning is perhaps the single most successful strategy for launching an SMO. Its success is due to at least two mechanisms. The first crucial resource granted the emerging movement by these established organizations is the collective identity associated with them. The second is the control mechanisms that serve to tie the identity to participation and, at the same time, preclude free riding.

Successful movements usually do not create attractive collective identities from scratch; rather, they redefine existing roles within established organizations as the basis of an emerging activist identity. It is clear, for example, that the civil rights movement grew as rapidly as it did because it appropriated a highly salient role within the black community—that of Christian or church member—and used it as an incentive for promoting activism (McAdam 1982, 129–30). Following this appropriation, the movement came, in many southern towns, to control access to a role that was highly prized. Blacks in those towns, to retain their status as Christians, added civil rights activities to their other Christian duties. Similarly, in the wake of the earliest sit-ins, the role of black student came to be redefined to include participation in the movement as a necessary component (McAdam 1982, 130–31).

Examples of this fusion of prized roles and activism can be found in other movements. Among the women of the New Left, participation in the burgeoning women's liberation movement was virtually required if one was to retain one's credentials as both a woman and a radical. And the rapid growth of the 1964 free speech movement at Berkeley can be attributed to its sponsorship by a congeries of existing campus political groups. To remain a member in good standing of these groups one had little choice but to conform to the new behavioral expectation: participation in the free speech movement.

These examples contradict the traditional rational choice imagery and help explain why the vaunted free-rider problem may not be so problematic after all in the early stages of collective action. The point is that most movements do not arise because isolated individuals choose to join the struggle. Rather, established groups redefine group membership to include commitment to the movement as one of its obligations; the threatened loss of member status is usually sufficient to produce high rates of participation. As a result, the movement is largely spared the need to provide selective incentives to attract participants. As long as the movement is rooted within established organizations, appropriating their collective identities, the free-rider problem is likely to be easily overcome.

Stage Two: Retaining Existing Members and Attracting New Ones

Eventually, though, a successful movement outgrows its tentative beginnings. The mantle of leadership passes from existing organizations to newly established movement organizations. Although this transition would seem to be inevitable and ultimately beneficial to the movement, it nonetheless poses a challenge for insurgents. Uncoupling the movement from established organizations means that organizers can no longer rely upon the incentive structure of those groups to motivate participation. Here the rational choice theorists would appear to be right. At this stage of the movement, new selective incentives must be offered to retain old members and attract new ones. Early rational choice formulations erred, however, in focusing exclusive attention on material selective incentives. Subsequent research and theorizing has alerted us to the critical role played by solidary incentives in encouraging activism.

Of these incentives, the collective identity that comes to be associated with an smo is among the most important. People affiliate with groups for a variety of reasons, but they are not about to do so if the group's identity is incompatible with their image of themselves.

From the point of view of the leaders of the smo, the kind of collective identity they shape for consumption will, in large part, determine both the number and the kind of people who are likely to be attracted. The most important strategic decision to be made is one that defines the boundaries of the group: how inclusive or exclusive do the organizers want their group to be? The range, the specificity, and the action orientation are the foundations upon which the collective identity may be constructed.

A collective identity that is inclusive of a wide range of attitudes tends to make the group more rather than less exclusive. This is somewhat counterintuitive and contradicts earlier assertions. The usual view is that if an smo extends its mission—not only to promote antinuclear policies, say, but also to work for norms of justice—it casts a wider net, ensnaring those who are not necessarily committed to antinuclear policies but are concerned about how the courts treat the poor. Our view, however, is that by extending the scope of its mission, an smo actually narrows the field of potential participants.[5] When there are many attitudes and behavioral prescriptions associated with participation, it is more likely that attitude conflicts will exist between the prospective participants and the smo. A broader conception may also lead to conflict within the organization itself.

Social movement organizations that attempt to construct all-purpose collective identities may therefore appeal to a narrower audience than those that stand fast to a more limited conception. Snow et al. (1986) have noted a similar process, which they refer to as frame extension. They follow the efforts of an smo called the Austin Peace and Justice Coalition to include members of racial and ethnic minorities by extending their stance from one mostly devoted to nuclear disarmament to one inclusive of fighting discrimination. Although the success of this effort is as yet unknown,

---

5. Michael Hechter has suggested that this phenomenon—the widening of scope leading to a narrowing of the participant field—may explain the proliferation of single-issue voting coalitions.

Snow et al. do note that frame extension can often lead to "murkiness" of objectives. That murkiness may well be the result of identity conflict.

These organizations, therefore, must give careful thought to how general or specific they wish their collective identities to be. A commitment to social justice, for example, is far more general than a commitment to seek to eradicate sentencing disparities among blacks, Hispanics, and whites. Less specific collective identities leave much open to interpretation and thus appeal to a wider audience. But if individuals are in search of a ready-made, assumable identity, the amorphous nature of a general collective identity may be less powerful as a selective incentive than a highly specific one.

Finally, an smo must decide whether its collective identity has embedded within it specific implications for action. Does being a member of an antinuclear group mean showing up for demonstrations and illegal activities at military bases, or does it mean simply signing petitions and sending letters to relevant policymakers? Does being in favor of school desegregation mean merely attending meetings or does it also mean having to send one's child to public schools? Does the collective identity subsume something like an activist identity? In general, the more directive with regard to action, the more exclusive the organization.

The advantages and disadvantages of an inclusive as opposed to an exclusive collective identity are not obvious. It is the use of a collective identity as a *selective* incentive that provides clues to these advantages and disadvantages. In order to reward participants by conferring this identity, it has to be possible simultaneously to exclude nonparticipants from adopting the identity. The more inclusive the collective identity, the harder it is to control, and thus the less powerful it is as a selective incentive. Those elements, however, that serve to make participation more exclusive are also the factors that raise the cost of participation, which can serve to dissuade membership. To claim the identity of a Hare Krishna is to make a statement about the sum total of one's status, for this identity has implications for virtually all the domains of one's life, from work to family to religion to leisure. To claim the identity of a Republican has far fewer implications. Thus, smos face a quandary with respect to the nature of the collective identity they choose to offer. They might offer a range of collective identities, but why would any potential participant be inclined to adopt a more costly identity over a less costly one when both permitted the claim of membership?

The preceding discussion highlights the challenge smos face in trying to attract and retain members. But in focusing our attention exclusively on the SMO, we have distorted and minimized the nature of that challenge. The fact is that SMOs exercise far less control over the process by which the group's collective identity is established than our discussion would suggest. For one thing, SMO leaders may themselves be only dimly aware of this issue and therefore less programmatic in addressing it than we have implied. And more important, the SMO is likely to find itself confronting a variety of other groups willing to contest the organization's image. It isn't just the SMO that has a stake in defining the group's collective identity. So too do movement opponents, rival SMOs, law enforcement officials, and the media. For every partisan willing to represent the Palestine Liberation Organization (PLO) as a nonviolent spokesperson for the legitimate nationalist aspirations of an oppressed people, there will be plenty of others who will depict the group as a collection of murderers and terrorists. Huey Newton's death reminded us of just how intense the struggle was in the late 1960s to define who the Black Panthers were: courageous advocates for the welfare of ghetto residents, in one view; a bunch of violent thugs with a penchant for self-promotion, in another.

The survival chances of an SMO often rest on the outcome of just such contests for control of the group's image. Yet, in waging these contests, SMOs typically find themselves at a distinct disadvantage. The unique access to the media that movement opponents and law enforcement officials enjoy often give them a leg up on the contest. Thus, in seeking to fashion an identity that will attract and hold members, SMOs face a twin challenge. First, they must wean themselves from the stable identity incentives that accrued to the movement by virtue of its roots in established organizations in the community. And second, they must be prepared to wage a successful public relations war against a variety of well-heeled opponents. Few SMOs are able to surmount these challenges, and ironically, those that do often find themselves victims of their own success.

Stage Three: Collective Identity as Public Good and the Free-Rider Problem

The very production of a collective identity introduces an unintended consequence: once an SMO has managed to fashion an identity, it is difficult to control its consumption unless it is a highly exclusive one. In effect, the collective identity becomes a public good that all can consume without contributing to its production. For instance, by the mid-1970s, public opinion polls showed that large numbers of women (and some men) identified with or had adopted the identity of "feminist." The very attractiveness of the collective identity had led many to gravitate toward it. But the identification carried with it no obligation to join a feminist organization or to participate in forms of collective action intended to realize equal rights for women. The identity of "student radical" seems to have enjoyed much the same salience in the late 1960s. But, again, adopting the identity did not require the individual to contribute in any way to the expansion of student rights or to any related movement. Indeed, one didn't even need to be a student to adopt the identity. The black power movement may well have suffered a similar fate during this same era. For a few years in the late sixties, the identity of "black revolutionary" conferred a status and a sense of self that was highly prized by many young blacks—this despite the fact that the identity carried with it no greater requirement than that one dress and act the part.

Contemporary examples of this phenomenon are easy to come by. Anyone can call oneself a Democrat or a Republican without paying dues to the respective parties and even without voting. Jews can claim their Jewish identity without belonging to a synagogue, paying dues, or even believing in God. People's ability to assume a collective identity without contributing to the production of the collective goods that underlie that identity is anathema to the leaders and members of such organizations. It is a form of free riding that is virtually impossible to overcome.[6]

Exacerbating this is the possible problem of increasing ambiguity in the definition of collective identity. Over time, as a more heterogeneous group of individuals comes to be associated with a social movement organization, there is a tendency toward a more inclusive, and more ambiguous, definition of identity.

Therefore, SMOS would much rather restrict access to this collective identity, for it is one of the selective incentives that they can offer cheaply. But the drive to advertise and the need to differentiate themselves from other groups offering similar collective goods prevent them from restricting access. Thus, the group has lost the identity as a selective incentive as it has widened its base of membership. The leadership of a mature SMO that failed to attend to the exclusiveness issue might find itself with a great deal of apparent support but no one to pay the dues or do the work.

To the extent that the group's success depends on the wide adoption of its position, it suffers this problem more deeply. If the aim of the movement is a general change in legal or political reform, it must mobilize support among large numbers of people in order to achieve its ends. It

6. This may help account for another oft-noted phenomenon: institutionalization. Formal membership requirements are an effort to control the provision of identity. Thus, organizations outlive the movements they fuel: the NAACP lived on even after the civil rights movement died; NOW persists beyond the period of the women's liberation movement.

is worth noting that these groups do not necessarily require that people act on their convictions; in some cases it will suffice that those with power merely believe that there is a large constituency for a given course of action. The wider the adoption of a particular collective identity, the more likely this myth can be sustained. At the same time that it counts this as a success, however, it loses one of the principal weapons in its arsenal of recruitment, for there is less reason for sympathetic individuals to join. These insights provide potent clues to a long-standing empirical puzzle in the study of social movements—namely, why it is that movements often decline precipitously at what seems to be their peak of popularity.

To counteract these negative effects on membership, groups might try to institute a credentialing process. One way to do this is to insist upon observable indicators of membership, something cults often do. Although the importance of community and spiritual awareness may be shared by many people, those who join the Hare Krishna must be willing to give up their jobs and worldly possessions, don orange robes, shave their heads, and sing and dance on street corners. The Lubovitchers, in contrast to other Jewish groups, demand that their members wear distinctive traditional garb of long black robes, black hats, and *pais*. On the other hand, the credentialing process raises the cost of participation in ways that dissuade large numbers of possible constituents from joining. Thus, this avenue is unrealistic for many groups. If an existing SMO is unable to pursue such a strategy, however, it may encourage splinter groups to form. In both Britain (Bouchier 1983) and the United States (Freeman 1975), radical feminist groups were produced in the context of liberal feminist groups, with the requirements for membership becoming ever more exclusive. In the seventies in the United States, the original organizations of the women's movement were the losers.[7]

Another possibility is for an SMO to counteract the problem by tapping

---

7. Freeman (1975, 139–40) writes: "The lesbian challenge was particularly difficult for those women who were caught within the web of their own identities as radicals. Given their own personal/ideological need to be in the forefront of social change and the compelling consistency of the argument that the truly radical feminist was a lesbian, they had to conform or drop out. This is exactly what happened to two groups in Washington and Boston, both of which had been composed primarily of former New Left radicals who had been on the politico side of the politico/feminist split. They did not merely split up into separate gay and straight groups as was often the case elsewhere. Those women who were or became gay formed lesbian collectives. Those women who remained straight and still had allegiances to other radical (nonfeminist) organizations became reinvolved in general leftist politics. Those women who remained straight but did not have any other political associations went through a good deal of personal trauma. . . . They could not form or join another group because their identities as radical feminists had been destroyed. . . . those women who chose lesbian/feminism, often at great per-

a resource base other than its constituency and thereby continue to manu-facture collective identities for wide consumption. Political parties muster campaign resources from those in whose interest it is to have their can-didates elected, not just from rank-and-file Democrats and Republicans. In these kinds of situations, the resources gained from other sources can serve as selective incentives to induce participation.

The quandary is most severe in groups that depend both on a grass-roots constituency for the achievement of their ends and on that same constituency for resources. Resource-poor groups cannot counteract the free-rider problem that results from the production of the collective iden-tity as a public good because they generally lack resources to employ as selective incentives to induce participation. In these groups, their very success in disseminating the collective identity undercuts their basis of existence, and the movement may well die for lack of participation.

CONCLUSION

In tracing the role of collective identity incentives in the life of a social movement, we have sketched a synthetic perspective incorporating insights from both the structural network and rational choice accounts of activism. Scholars working in the structural network tradition have offered impressive evidence of a strong positive relationship between integration into activist networks and movement participation. Yet theirs remains fun-damentally an empirical contribution. Nowhere have they offered a theory of the individual to account for the effect of integration on activism.

For their part, rational choice theorists have elaborated just such a model of individual action, the central premise of which would seem to accord nicely with the findings noted above. Following the rational choice per-spective, we assume that activist networks are a critical source of selective incentives for those integrated into them. Where the rational choice model fails us is in its undervaluation of strictly social resources and the neces-sarily collective basis of individual choice processes.

What unites the two perspectives in our view is the concept of collective identity. As regards a social movement, collective identity refers to that identity or status that attaches to the individual by virtue of his or her participation in movement activities. One of the most powerful motivators of individual action is the desire to confirm through behavior a cherished identity. In the case of a movement, the opportunity to do so can be seen as

---

sonal cost, as a means of demonstrating their commitment, could easily perceive those who didn't as possessing less conviction, and thus not to be trusted."

a selective incentive more available to those who are integrated into activist networks than those who are not. Integration into these networks makes it more likely that the individual will value the identity of "activist" and choose to act in accordance with it.

This grants the social movement a powerful incentive to help compel participation. This is especially true in the early stages of collective action when the movement is rooted in the established organizations of the aggrieved community. Individuals are likely to participate during this phase not so much in response to the provision of new incentives as to confirm their status as a member of a community they have long valued—hence the strong empirical relationship between activism and integration into established organizations. The explication of this dynamic carries with it an important conclusion: during a movement's emergent phase, the free-rider problem is relatively easily overcome.

This does not mean it ceases to be a problem at this point. On the contrary, the problem is likely to become more serious as the movement abandons the established institutions in which it emerged in favor of specialized social movement organizations. Those SMOs can no longer rely on identification with a prized and familiar collective identity to attract prospective activists. Instead, they must fashion an identity of their own to help compel participation. But to succeed in this carries with it its own danger. Should a movement manage to create a collective identity—feminist, student radical—attractive to many, it runs the risk of losing control over the selective provision of that identity. Ironically, its very success results in the creation of a public good available to nearly everyone. To adopt the collective identity carries with it no obligation to participate in the activities of the movement. When a movement finds itself in this situation, it may already be dying.

REFERENCES

Axelrod, Robert. 1984. *The Evolution of Cooperation*. New York: Basic Books.

Barnes, Samuel H., and Max Kaase. 1979. *Political Action*. Beverly Hills, Calif.: Sage.

Block, Jean H., N. Haan, and B. M. Smith. 1968. "Activism and Apathy in Contemporary Adolescence." In *Understanding Adolescence: Current Developments in Adolescent Psychology*, ed. J. F. Adams. Boston: Allyn and Bacon.

Bolton, Charles D. 1972. "Alienation and Action: A Study of Peace Group Members." *American Journal of Sociology* 78:537–61.

Bouchier, David. 1983. *The Feminist Challenge: The Movement for Women's Liberation in Britain and the U.S.* London: Macmillan.

Braungart, Richard G. 1971. "Family Status, Socialization and Student Politics: A Multivariate Analysis." *American Journal of Sociology* 77:108–29.

Cohen, Jean L. 1985. "Strategy or Identity: New Theoretical Paradigms and Contemporary Social Movements." *Social Research* 52, no. 4:663–716.

Coleman, James S. 1973. *The Mathematics of Collective Action*. Chicago: Aldine.

Curtis, Russell L., and Louis A. Zurcher, Jr. 1973. "Stable Resources of Protest Movements: The Multi-organizational Field." *Social Forces* 52:53–60.

Elster, Jon. 1979. *Ulysses and the Sirens*. Cambridge: Cambridge University Press.

Emerson, Richard M. 1987. "Toward a Theory of Value in Social Exchange." In *Social Exchange Theory*, ed. K. C. Cook. Newbury Park, Calif.: Sage, 11–45.

Fendrich, James, and Ellis S. Krauss. 1978. "Student Activism and Adult Left Wing Politics: A Causal Model of Political Socialization for Black, White and Japanese Students of the 1960s Generation." In *Research in Social Movements: Conflict and Change*, vol. 1, ed. L. Kriesberg. Greenwich, Conn.: JAI Press.

Fernandez, Roberto, and Doug McAdam. 1988. "Multiorganizational Fields and Recruitment Contexts." *Sociological Forum* 3, no. 3: 357–82.

Fireman, Bruce, and William H. Gamson. 1979. "Utilitarian Logic in the Resource Mobilization Perspective." In *The Dynamics of Social Movements*, ed. Mayer N. Zald and John D. McCarthy. Cambridge, Mass.: Winthrop, 8–45.

Freeman, Jo. 1975. *The Politics of Women's Liberation*. New York: David McKay.

———. 1979. "Resource Mobilization and Strategy: A Model for Analyzing Social Movement Organizational Actions." In *The Dynamics of Social Movements*, ed. M. N. Zald and J. D. McCarthy. Cambridge, Mass.: Winthrop, 167–89.

Friedman, Debra. 1987. "Notes on 'Toward a Theory of Value in Social Exchange.'" In *Social Exchange Theory*, ed. K. C. Cook. Newbury Park, Calif.: Sage, 47–58.

Friedman, Debra, and Toshio Yamagishi. 1985. "Explaining Variations in Free-Riding Behavior." Paper.

Granovetter, Mark. 1970. *Getting a Job*. Cambridge, Mass.: Harvard University Press.

———. 1978. "Threshold Models of Collective Behavior." *American Journal of Sociology* 83:1420–43.

Hardin, Russell. 1982. *Collective Action*. Baltimore: Johns Hopkins University Press.

Hechter, Michael. 1987. *Principles of Group Solidarity*. Berkeley: University of California Press.

Hechter, Michael, Debra Friedman, and Malka Appelbaum. 1982. "A Theory of Ethnic Collective Action." *International Migration Review* 16:412–34.

Hicks, John D. 1961. *The Populist Revolt*. Lincoln: University of Nebraska Press.

Klapp, Orrin E. 1969. *Collective Search for Identity*. New York: Holt, Rinehart, and Winston.

———. 1972. *Currents of Unrest: An Introduction to Collective Behavior*. New York: Holt, Rinehart, and Winston.

Laumann, Edward O. 1973. *Bonds of Pluralism: The Form and Substance of Urban Social Networks*. New York: Wiley.

Lewis, Steven H., and Robert E. Kraut. 1972. "Correlates of Student Political Activism and Ideology." *Journal of Social Issues* 28:131–49.

Lipset, Seymour M., and Sheldon Wolin. 1965. *The Berkeley Student Revolt*. New York: Doubleday Anchor.

Marwell, Gerald, and Ruth E. Ames. 1979. "Experiments on the Provision of Public

Goods: I. Resources, Interest, Group Size and the Free-Rider Problem." *American Journal of Sociology* 84:1335–60.

McAdam, Doug. 1982. *Political Process and the Development of Black Insurgency, 1930–1970*. Chicago: University of Chicago Press.

———. 1986. "Recruitment to High-Risk Activism: The Case of Freedom Summer." *American Journal of Sociology* 92:64–90.

McAdam, Doug, and Roberto Fernandez. 1989. "Microstructural Bases of Recruitment to Social Movements." In *Research in Social Movements: Conflict and Change*, vol. 2, ed. Louis Kriesberg. Greenwich, Conn.: JAI Press.

Melucci, Alberto. 1986. "Getting Involved: Identity and Mobilization in Social Movements." Paper presented at the international workshop, Transformation of Structure into Action, Amsterdam, June 12–14.

Morris, Aldon D. 1984. *The Origins of the Civil Rights Movement*. New York: Free Press.

Neal, Arthur J., and Melvin Seeman. 1964. "Organization and Powerlessness: A Test of the Mediation Hypothesis." *American Sociological Review* 29:216–26.

Oberschall, Anthony. 1973. *Social Conflict and Social Movements*. Englewood Cliffs, N.J.: Prentice-Hall.

Oliver, Pamela. 1980. "Rewards and Punishments as Selective Incentives for Collective Action: Theoretical Investigations." *American Journal of Sociology* 85, no. 6: 1356–75.

Oliver, Pamela, and Gerald Marwell. 1988. "The Paradox of Group Size in Collective Action: A Theory of the Critical Mass. II." *American Sociological Review* 53:1–8.

Oliver, Pamela, Gerald Marwell, and Ruy Teixeira. 1985. "Theory of the Critical Mass. I. Interdependence, Group Heterogeneity, and the Production of Collective Goods." *American Journal of Sociology* 91:522–56.

Olson, Mancur. 1965. *The Logic of Collective Action*. Cambridge, Mass.: Harvard University Press.

Orum, Anthony M. 1972. *Black Students in Protest*. Washington, D.C.: American Sociological Association.

Pizzorno, Alessandro. 1978. "Political Exchange and Collective Identity in Industrial Conflict." In *The Resurgence of Class Conflict in Western Europe since 1968*, ed. C. Crouch and A. Pizzorno. New York: Holmes and Meier, 277–98.

Sayre, Cynthia W. 1980. "The Impact of Voluntary Association Involvement on Social-Psychological Attitudes." Paper presented at the annual meetings of the American Sociological Association, New York City.

Schelling, Thomas. 1978. *Micromotives and Macrobehavior*. New York: Norton.

Simmel, Georg. 1950. "The Metropolis and Mental Life." In *The Sociology of Georg Simmel*, trans. and ed. Kurt H. Wolff. New York: Free Press, 409–24.

———. 1955. "The Web of Group Affiliations." Trans. R. Bendix. In *Conflict and the Web of Group Affiliations*. New York: Free Press, 125–95.

Snow, David A. 1976. *The Nichiren Shoshu Buddhist Movement in America: A Sociological Examination of Its Value Orientation, Recruitment Efforts, and Spread*. Ann Arbor: University of Michigan Press.

Snow, David A., E. Burke Rochford, Jr., Steven K. Worden, and Robert D. Benford. 1986. "Frame Alignment Processes, Micromobilization and Movement Participation." *American Sociological Review* 51:464–81.

Snow, David A., Louis A. Zurcher, Jr., and Sheldon Ekland-Olson. 1980. "Social Networks and Social Movements: A Microstructural Approach to Differential Recruitment." *American Sociological Review* 45, no. 5:787–801.

Taylor, Michael. 1976. *Anarchy and Cooperation.* London: Wiley.

Thomas, L. E. 1971. "Family Correlates of Student Political Activism." *Developmental Psychology* 4:206–14.

Von Eschen, Donald, Jerome Kirk, and Maurice Pinard. 1971. "The Organizational Substructure of Disorderly Politics." *Social Forces* 49:529–44.

Walsh, Edward J., and Rex H. Warland. 1983. "Social Movement Involvement in the Wake of a Nuclear Accident: Activists and Free Riders in the Three Mile Island Area." *American Sociological Review* 48:764–81.

8

Mentalities, Political Cultures, and Collective Action Frames

Constructing Meanings through Action

S i d n e y   T a r r o w

In a recent paper, Bert Klandermans writes: "In the literature on social protest, the insight is winning ground that one's interpretations, rather than reality itself, guide political actions. . . . Interpreting grievances and raising expectations of success are the core of the social construction of protest" (1989, 121–22). The social construction of protest!— the very phrase seems to reach out from the positivism of American social scientists. But behind this opening there is less a wish to join the movement toward postmodernity than dissatisfaction with how the dominant paradigms of the last two decades of social movement research have dealt with the construction of meaning. Scholars in the 1970s and 1980s developed a great deal of theoretical sophistication and empirical evidence about the motivations of individuals mobilized into collective action. But how leaders' ideological messages are formulated and communicated to target groups and why some messages bring people into the streets while others do not have remained, until recently, outside the ken of social movement theory.

More elusive still is this question: do the belief systems and symbols that inspire protesters to take collective action possess autonomous mobilizing potential, or are they simply the mechanical expressions of material interest, political opportunity, or power? Sociologists have moved beyond the belief that only microeconomic incentives inspire people to take collective action. And recently political scientists have begun to argue once again for

This chapter is derived from my comments on David Snow and Robert Benford's contribution to the symposium on Frontiers in Social Movement Research, held at the University of Michigan in June 1988. I am grateful to Carol Mueller and Charles Tilly for the suggestions that led to the present version, and to Snow and Benford, whose theoretical work is my starting point.

the autonomy of cultural values in explaining political outcomes (Ingle-hart 1988; Wildavsky 1987). But how collective beliefs are collectively constructed and how they contribute to collective action are still unresolved problems.

This chapter will focus on two questions that follow from this growing debate. First, how do movements for change draw upon existing ideational materials? Are the latter sewn invisibly into the fabric of their ideologies? Or do they constitute a fixed repertoire of symbols and images in a political culture that constrain the construction of meaning—much as the repertoire of forms of collective action constrains leaders' tactical choices (Tilly 1978)? Second, do the ideological discourses of social movements produce *new* social understandings among a mass public? And if so, how do they do this?

I shall argue first that leaders *must* draw upon existing ideational materials in their societies, but that how they do so, and the symbols they draw upon, may run the risk of sacrificing their movement's momentum. Second, I shall argue that new social meanings—like new repertoires of contention—are products of the struggles within social movements and between them and their opponents (Mueller 1989). If we can demonstrate these processes, then we may have a key to how "culture change" occurs—not through the automatic diffusion of values through diffuse social learning processes, but from the assimilation into the general political culture of new frames of meaning from collective action.

Recently, scholars of social movements have begun to turn outside their own field to find concepts that can help them understand the construction of meaning in social movements.[1] Among them are Klandermans's "consensus mobilization," Melucci's "collective identities," and Gamson's "ideological packages."[2] Each concept has a different patrimony, holds a particular promise, and presents its own problems. I shall suggest how

---

1. A recent volume devoted fully one-third of its space to the problem of the construction of meaning: Bert Klandermans, Hanspeter Kriesi, and Sidney Tarrow, eds., *From Structure to Action: Comparing Movement Participation across Cultures*, International Social Movement Research, vol. 1 (Greenwich, Conn.: JAI Press, 1988).

2. The concept of collective identity receives ample treatment in William Gamson's contribution to this volume. For its original exposition in the social movement field, see Melucci (1985, 1988, 1989). Gamson has also pioneered in the empirical analysis of media discourse. See the references at the end of this chapter as well as his contribution to this volume. Klandermans's concept of consensus mobilization is well developed in his contribution to Klandermans, Kriesi, and Tarrow (1988) and is extended in Klandermans (1989). Though these concepts are not directly dealt with in this chapter, my debts to these authors should be obvious in what follows.

three concepts of successively declining generality and increasing purposiveness—societal mentalities, political cultures, and collective action frames—may be linked together in understanding how meaning is constructed in social movements. I shall argue that, in order to link social movement ideologies to their societies, scholars must move outward from the explicitly constructed messages of movement leaders to the broader mentalities of a society and to the culture of understandings in its political community.

MENTALITIES, OPPOSITIONAL POLITICAL CULTURE, AND MOBILIZATION: A STORY

During the 1780s, as the legitimacy of France's Old Regime was dissolving and open insurgency spreading across the country, a series of scandal trials were widely publicized (Lusebrink 1983). In the most notorious of these, the Clereaux affair, a servant who had resisted the advances of her master, a certain Thibault, was accused of robbery and hauled into court. But (pace Dickens) not only was the case decided in favor of the servant—something that might not have happened in an earlier age; a wave of popular outrage against the courts and the venal master surged through the country. The emotion that followed was described in terms typical of the period: "What violences! What tumults! What scandals! A furious multitude filled all the streets, straining to tear down the Thibault house with an ax, then threatening to burn it; covering the family with curses and outrages; almost sacrificing them to their hatred" (quoted in Lusebrink 1983, 175–76).

But like much of the collective action of the Old Regime, this was not a wild and formless jacquerie. It drew upon a known repertoire of contemporary forms of collective action and was organized around a common theme—the corruption of the courts and the innocence of the exploited. In fact, the Clereaux affair illustrates how much ideas about justice had changed in a France that was teetering on the brink of the greatest popular movement in the nation's history. As a modern interpreter has put it: "The public responses to the Clereaux Affair . . . would be inconceivable without the presence of an adequate *mental receptivity* within the contemporaneous society" (Lusebrink 1983, 375; emphasis mine).

But how widespread was this "mental receptivity" in Old Regime France and how can it be connected to collective actions like the Clereaux affair? Did such events signify a general public understanding that the courts were corrupt and householders venal, or is this merely an inference made by contemporary scholars from collective actions that may never have gone beyond passing expressions of public outrage? Apart from the evidence of outbreaks of popular collective action in the historical record, how can we know that there was any sort of consensus surrounding these causes célèbres and what role a societal mentality might have played in triggering them?

One thing we do know: most of the evidence of such a mentality comes not from the people themselves but from the popular press, from the opinions of publicists, and from the canards and popular songs that circulated during the period, from which we have inferred a popular mentality. Lusebrink (1982) tries to gauge the impact of this cause célèbre literature by compiling an exhaustive inventory of where it appeared. He shows not only that it was widely available but that it reached an extensive cross section of the public, including members of the lower middle class as well as comparatively wealthy members of the legal profession.

But if everything is a text, *le texte n'est pas tout!* Texts can be important indicators of a societal consensus, but by inferring the existence of societal consensus from such texts, we run the risk of conflating two levels and types of ideation: *societal mentalities*, which I define as popularly held values and practices about private life and behavior; and *political culture*, which I define as more clearly molded points of concern about social and political relations, containing both system-supporting and oppositional elements. Both of these should be seen as partial and interlocking foundations for the more overt and purposive level of ideation that is characteristic of social movements: the *collective action frames*, which I define as the purposively constructed guides to action created by existing or prospective movement organizers.

Why is it important to make this distinction among three levels of ideation? If the social movement research of the last two decades has shown anything, it is that grievances are not sufficient to trigger collective action, that this requires someone who can take advantage of political opportunities (Eisinger 1973; Tarrow 1989), develop organizations of some kind (Morris 1984), and interpret grievances and mobilize consensus around them (Klandermans 1988, 1989). Societal mentalities cannot carry out this function, as they are largely passive interpretations of the status quo detached from agency—and are often part of the deadening culture of poverty. Political culture is a more likely candidate, for it is organized around common points of concern and definitions of situations. But it is seldom sufficiently univocal or detached from the symbols that sustain the system to provide a firm basis for collective action against it. At best, political culture provides leaders with a reservoir of symbols with which to construct a cognitive frame for collective action. Unless we recognize and specify these three ideational levels, a yawning gap will remain between our sizable knowledge of movement organization and tactics and our relative ignorance about how meaning is constructed in social movements.

This chapter seeks to contribute to the closure of that gap. I shall turn first to the concept of mentalities, its characteristic traits and the problems it poses, before moving to political culture and then to the concept of collective action frames. I shall then try to show how the three levels can interlock and evolve during a wave of mobilization, leading to slow, halting, and contradictory changes in political culture and, thence, to the evolution of societal mentalities.

MENTALITIES IN THE NEW SOCIAL HISTORY

European social historians have tried through the concept of mentalities to provide a key to understanding popular ideologies or belief systems. In the "new social history" of the 1960s, scholars attempted to fashion concepts that could serve as an alternative to the "big" political events that dominated former historical practice. But they soon came up against the problematic status of their chosen concept, which has proven difficult to attach to actual historical agents and events—and particularly to the explanation of collective action. As a result, it is very much in question today.[3]

The concept of mentalities, mental receptivity, or mental structures, like the closely related one of "popular culture," owes much to the work of E. P. Thompson (1968, 1971) in England and that of Robert Mandrou (1964) and Michel Vovelle (1973, 1982, 1985) in France.[4] Interest in the concept reached its peak among historians in the 1960s and 1970s as the result of a particularly creative cross-fertilization among history, demography, and the social sciences (Ariès 1978, 403 ff.). One of the most refreshing characteristics of the new school was that it legitimated the use of a broader range of sources than was found in traditional historiography. Popular fetes and carnivals, songs and canards, the cheap press, data on people's eating habits, nutrition, and health, how they procreated—or tried not to—to whom or to what they left their property when they died: all of this became grist for the new historians' mill.

---

3. For several questioning or critical approaches, see the issue of *Annales* 44, no. 6 (1989), especially the contribution of Roger Chartier.

4. But it can also be dated to the first generation of *Annales* historians—Lucien Febvre and Marc Bloch—and to the work of Johan Huizinga, Mario Praz, and Henri Pirenne (Ariès 1978, 402–03).

It was typical of this school of historians that they made much use of a concept that was never rigorously or consensually defined.[5] Ariès, for example, devoted an essay of twenty-one dense pages to the concept of mentalities without ever hazarding a definition (1978, 402–23). Vovelle defined the history of mentalities as "the study of the mediations and the dialectical relationship between the objective conditions of men's lives and the way in which they tell about it and even how they live it" (1982, 17). Agulhon is scarcely less catholic, defining the field as no less than "the content of our knowledge, the way we represent reality, our sentiments— everything that is intellectual and everything that is psychological" (1986, 23). Nothing less!

Four characteristics of the new social history shaped the study of mentalities in ways that made it difficult to use as a guide to understanding collective action:

La longue durée: Following the lead of Fernand Braudel, historians of mentalities couched their construct in terms of history over the long run. In fact, as Vovelle notes, it was Braudel "who first defined the history of mentalities as the privileged site for slow evolution and inertia, in his evocation of mentalities as *prisons de longue durée* (unpublished paper, 1–2). Especially for historians influenced by anthropology, mentalities were virtually a constant; they changed so slowly as to be sometimes coterminous with the concept of culture itself. This made it hard to use the concept of mentalities—unless it was heavily mediated and carefully historicized—to analyze collective actions, which are, by definition, events of the very *courte durée*.

Consider the concept of the "moral economy," brilliantly conceived by Thompson (1971) to understand a precise historical movement—the popular reaction to a dearth of grain in seventeenth- and eighteenth-century England. The concept was soon employed to explain a wide variety of collective actions in very different social and historical contexts—sometimes without real evidence that the actors really believed in it.[6] The longue durée was not close enough to the collective action to explain behavior,

5. In France, the new history was more attentive to popular religion and to regional subcultures than to social differences (Ariès 1978, 418). Vovelle's study of wills in eighteenth-century Provence showed that secularization was present in popular culture long before the revolution (1973), and Agulhon's study of sociability in the same region showed how the social circle became a network for the diffusion of new political ideas (1982). In Britain, the social construction of class was frequently the object of historians' attention, as in Thompson's path-breaking work on the origins of the English working class (1968) and in Hoggart's richly embroidered picture of the modern English working class (1961).

6. Scott (1976) employed the concept of the moral economy to explain certain forms

except as a category so broad that it raised the question of why such events did not occur all the time.

Mentalities as resistance: Second—and this follows from the first point— 2. popular mentalities were frequently conceptualized as producing *resistance to change,* especially resistance to modernization that uprooted traditional ways. Contact with the social sciences, particularly with anthropology, reinforced this tendency, for it drew historians' attention to the internal logic of traditional societies that were facing change from outside and away from proactive movements that might have been growing within those societies. The most striking example of this tendency is found in Eric Wolf's theory of peasant revolution. In Wolf's theory, it took recourse to external organizers to explain when peasant rebellion was linked to revolution (1973).

The "resistance" construct reveals two main problems: first, that of understanding the boundary between the ordinary delinquency and *ressentiment* that suffuse rural societies and purposive collective action—a boundary that, as has been pointed out by Esman (1989), has been obscured in some recent treatments; second, that of explaining how and when *proactive* ideas and new symbols arise and are accepted among lower-class people (224). "Resistance," in the sense of "foot dragging, dissimulation, feigned ignorance, false compliance, manipulation, flight, slander, theft, arson, sabotage, and isolated incidences of violence" (Colburn 1989, ix), has always existed in rural societies. The thing is to understand the differences between the societies in which it is an accompaniment to compliance—a "prelude to submission," in Gramsci's words—and those in which organized collective action results.

The history of the people without history: The history of mentalities was 3. almost inevitably understood to be the history of the *lower* classes, following the well-justified assumption that they live furthest away from the "high culture" that is the stuff of traditional historiography. Practitioners of the new social history sometimes forgot that not only "the people, the peasants, the marginal" but also "the bourgeoisie and the intellectuals" have their collective unconscious, "their prejudices and their phantoms" (Agulhon 1986, 28). The typical producers of new ideologies and belief systems—clerics, legists, and the educated middle class—received far less attention from the new social historians than the lower orders of society.

---

of peasant resistance to modernization in Southeast Asia. It is hard to see how a concept invented to explain lower-class consumers' response to dearth in eighteenth-century England could be employed to understand subsistence producers' reaction to exploitation by landlords in mid-twentieth-century Southeast Asia.

This problem can be seen in how the new social history treated the "popular religion" that survived assaults by the church until well into the modern age. As Roger Chartier points out (1989), the sources of knowledge about popular mentalities came not from *pratiquants* of the old folkways but from official church sources who were anxious to root them out. Yet from these data, broad generalizations were made about the lower classes. If this is true of popular religion, how much more is it the case for popular collective action, the sources for which are almost invariably literate and come from forces of order dedicated to stamping it out?

The problem of agency: The shift of attention in the new social history from the actions of kings and princes to the mentalities of ordinary people produced an ambiguity about the agents responsible for historical change, for if mentalities were difficult to root in particular groups, classes, or institutions, they were even more difficult to connect to particular actions. Consider the crowd that invaded British ships docked in the port of Boston in 1775; can we understand its behavior as the outcome of a general collective mentality against unfair taxation? Perhaps we can, but only if we understand that the actions of *this* crowd were animated by the shrewd political calculus of the coalition of lawyers, publicists, and merchants who spurred it on.

The basic problem of using mentalities to understand collective action and social movements is this: whereas collective action is episodic, highly focused, and activist and results from explicit decisions by historical agents and people to take action, mentalities are long term, unfocused, and passive popular beliefs about existing society and are not oriented toward action in the public arena. As long as we are trying to understand no more than a generalized disposition toward actions, the problem is not serious; but turn to the problem of organizing social movements and the questions raised above become insoluble. What we require are intermediate concepts between the popular mentalities at the base of society and the meanings around which social movements mobilize people. Let us turn to two such concepts: oppositional political culture and collective action frames.

POLITICAL CULTURE

Almost thirty years ago, Gabriel Almond and his collaborators introduced to the field of political science a new concept—political culture—to connect the social structural bases of politics to its institutional outcomes (Almond and Verba 1964, 1–3). Their general argument was that around each political system is a greater or lesser degree of consensus toward its legitimating symbols and that citizens contribute to the maintenance of the system by their knowledge of and support for these symbols. Their more specific concern was with what they considered to be the culture necessary to *democratic* political systems, for which they deduced a construct they called the "civic culture," a mix of participant and supportive, traditional and modern, values and orientations supporting liberal democratic practices (1964, 29 ff.).

The concept of political culture enjoyed only a brief hour upon the stage of scholarly concerns,[7] in large part because of widespread disillusionment with what many thought was Almond and Verba's culture-bound set of requisites for the *civic* culture. In the resulting controversy about democratic political cultures—not all of it innocent of ideological biases—the general concept of political culture fell into disrepute as well, with only a few exceptions (Inglehart 1977, 1990). Recently, however, the concept has been revived (Laitin 1986; Wildavsky 1987; Eckstein 1988; Inglehart 1988, 1990) in part as a result of growing disillusionment with the microeconomic approaches that have become dominant in the field (Wildavsky 1987, 4–5; Inglehart 1988, 1203).

Even in its heyday, the concept of political culture was never effectively trained on explaining collective action. Almond and Verba focused only on the values they took to be requisites for democracy, turning to the concept of "subculture" to explain clusters of distinct values (1964, 26–29). Students of political culture had difficulty with collective action for three main reasons:

1. *Levels of analysis*. Studies of political culture were hamstrung by the lack of an agreed-upon level of analysis. For some, it was the sum of the politically relevant attitudes of the mass public and could best be measured by what samples of citizens believed (Almond and Verba 1964; Inglehart 1971, 1990). For others, it was found in the beliefs of those who operated the political system, and this led to an emphasis on elite political culture (Putnam 1973). For still others, it was the culturally sanctioned practices of the society that revealed its political culture, leading to the study of political ritual and repetitive interaction patterns among its members (Kertzer 1988, 1990).

None of these approaches directly attacked the problem of collective action. Surveys focused on what people *believed* were legitimate forms of political activity rather than on the activity itself (Barnes et al. 1979); elite

7. Only the briefest bibliography can be presented here. In addition to Almond and Verba (1964), the locus classicus for political culture studies is Pye and Verba, eds. (1965). Also see Almond and Powell (1966 and 1978) and Almond, Flanagan, and Mundt, eds. (1973). For a historical retrospective and critique, see the papers collected in Almond and Verba, eds. (1980).

studies seldom dealt with counterelites, and had they done so, it is doubt-ful whether they could have elicited their underlying values and predis-positions through interviews (Kriesi 1985); students of cultural practices worked predominantly with the conventional practices and rituals that could be observed through long exposure to a society and seldom with sporadic outbreaks of opposition (but see Kertzer 1988).

2. *The content of political culture.* Almond and Verba were in an awkward position when it came to understanding the core values and predisposi-tions of those who *opposed* the existing system or parts of it. Their reference point was the values they took to be requisites of liberal democracy; but the core values of opponents might result from a different set of value premises altogether. These premises might not be so much opposed to as tangential to the requisites for liberal democracy or any other system. Only an ethnographic account of the culture of opposition groups could have teased out such particularities.

Consider the values and predispositions of the communist subculture in central Italy studied by Kertzer (1990). Using the standard measures of *The Civic Culture*, these opponents scored among the highest group of participants and supporters of the requisites of democracy (Almond and Verba 1964). But when Kertzer analyzed their folkways, he found them to resonate with a culture not of Marxism-Leninism but of popular Catholi-cism (1990, ch. 6). Citizens in southern Italy also scored reasonably close to the standard value measures of the civic culture (Barnes and Sani 1974). But the cultural practices of their society, as revealed by ethnographic accounts (Banfield 1954), by voting behavior (Tarrow 1967), or by local governing practices (Putnam et al. 1985), told a very different story.

Aaron Wildavsky strikes a middle ground between the deductive theo-rizing of Almond and Verba and what he considers the nominalism of the ethnographers. He starts from the position that "what matters most to people is their relationships with other people and other people's relation-ships with them." This leads him to define political culture as shared values legitimating social relations (1987, 3) and lodged within institutional set-tings. From this he moves to the premise that "an act is culturally rational if it supports one's way of life" (5–6).

But if it is true that "an act is culturally rational if it supports one's way of life," who is to define what a way of life is? That is, even supposing that Wildavsky has chosen the most central dimensions of individuals' social situations, how can we know that these social situations are going to be interpreted by their incumbents in similar ways? Isn't an important ele-ment of culture its subjectivity, and if so, how can we know, for example, whether a Turin factory worker acts on a vision of himself as the proletarian he is, as the farm worker he used to be, or as the country gentleman he hopes to become (Sabel 1982)?

The problem is particularly acute when we try to apply Wildavsky's approach to the political culture of opposition. For example, external observers might agree that the social situation of southern Italian peasant farmers was conducive to the culture that Wildavsky calls "apathy" (e.g., "when people cannot control what happens to them . . . their boundaries are porous but the prescriptions imposed on them are severe"; p. 7). In most places and during most periods of their history, this is exactly how southern Italian peasants behaved (Banfield 1954). But in other places, and frequently in their own history, southern Italians erupted with waves of collective action: against the French occupiers in 1799; after unification with the North in the nineteenth century (Hobsbawm 1959, ch. 2); during the fascist years (Bevilacqua 1980); and after World War II, when the opportunity presented itself to seize the *latifondia* (Tarrow 1967).

In order to foster such diverse and changing behavior, the peasants' self-definition of their social situations must have been far more fluid and changeable than appears to be the case in Wildavsky's model. Perhaps we can say that apathy was their normal societal mentality, their strategy for adapting to their ordinary lot, but that rebellion was fed by an oppositional political culture that came into play only when the opportunities arose. If this is the case, then political culture should be studied not deductively or through the values expressed by respondents to surveys but through an account of people's behavior when they act collectively.

Laitin's criticism of Wildavsky's approach may be apposite: he argues that by defining culture in terms of unanimously shared values, Wildavsky may have painted himself into a narrow conceptual corner, for cultures sometimes contain enormous conflicts among values. By positing that culture is really about "how debates get framed"—rather than about common values—Laitin argues that "people with strongly opposed views can share a culture and that people with similar views can come from different cultures" (1988, 589–90). This may explain the wide diversity of behavior—from compliance to consent to rebellion—that we often find within the same culture and the sharp contrasts of interpretation that we find in the same social movements.

3. *Two faces of culture*. Another reason for this diversity comes from the discretion people have about the cultural symbols with which they identify. As Laitin argues: "people must often choose which among their religious group, language group, and so on will be their primary mode of cultural identification" (1988, 591). He bases his model of culture choice on the

concept of self-interest, writing that people's choice of an identity "is often guided by instrumental reasoning, based on the potential resources available for identifying yourself, for example, as a Catholic as opposed to a French speaker" (591).

But Laitin's criticism goes too far in one direction and not far enough in another. If the "choice" of a cultural identity, with all that it implies about one's relations to others and to the state, depended only on self-interest, it would be far more predictable and simpler than it seems to be—even assuming we could always fathom what someone's self-interest was. Although the businessman may attribute poverty to the character defects of the poor out of his own self-interest (Laitin 1988, 591), he may also attribute it to the actions of the state, to labor unions, to other actors, or to himself, depending on his personal background, with whom he interacts, and who happens to have won the last election or moved next door.

Let us return to the scandals of the Old Regime as an example of the complexities of culture choice. Those who rose in opposition to the practices of the court and the legal system in the 1780s were in good part legists, publicists, and intellectuals. They were not reflecting their self-interest in any simple way but were working out a whole new way of defining the relationship between the state and the citizen. To understand this and its effects on the culture of opposition, we would have to examine the incentive structure of people in a variety of social positions in order to predict which of them would come out against the practices of the Old Regime and which would continue to support it. And we still would not have arrived at an understanding of when such values would result in collective action. Laitin's strategic cultural analysis would have shown the widening gap between the status system of the regime and the values of the new bourgeois class in eighteenth-century France. But when that predisposition would turn to active revolt, and which sectors of the bourgeoisie would support it and which would oppose it, depended on the existence both of political entrepreneurs who were able to explain to the new class why its way of life should produce a new political culture and of opportunities in which this new definition of the situation would produce collective action.

Let me summarize where we have arrived: in order to explain the decision to participate in social movements, the construct of societal mentalities is too omnipresent, too far removed from the events of everyday life, and too wanting in agency to help us much. The concept of political culture can take us somewhat further, but if we want it to do so, we must specify its system-supporting and oppositional components and examine it with tools more sensitive than the instruments of survey research. Most important, we must understand how people choose the symbols and definitions of the situation that lead them to act collectively, and how these are proffered by real or prospective movement entrepreneurs.

When people come together in collective action it takes a very special kind of culture choice to do so. Rather than entire segments of a society reacting automatically to their social situations or choosing one culture over another, enterprising individuals and groups draw upon existing mentalities and cultures to create action-oriented frames of meaning. Like Laitin's cultural choosers, they use widely shared symbols for their instrumental ends (1988, 591), but they manipulate these symbols in order to mobilize others on behalf of their political goals. Let us turn to this concept of framing work.

COLLECTIVE ACTION FRAMES

If historians of mentalities focus on the broad sweep of historical mental constructs, and students of political culture try to understand the values and shared understandings underpinning an entire political system, students of social movements have taken a much more microscopic tack. Our research has almost always been bound by the courte durée; we have focused in detail on the organization of specific protest movements; we have studied the demands made in mobilization campaigns rather than the values or points of concern underlying them; and we have given our attention to agents of social change—social movement organizations—rather than the reception they enjoy among the population. Only recently has awareness grown of the need to place movement organizations in their broader cultural and ideological context and to try to understand how their messages get across. This volume is one response to that need.

But the problem is wrongly posed if we begin by claiming that ideology didn't matter to earlier students of movements and that to us it does. The real problem is not that earlier students didn't recognize the importance of ideation but that they concentrated only on what they could see—the grievances, demands, and symbols put forward by social movement organizations in actual mobilization campaigns—and left to one side the vague and evanescent factors that link these symbols to their societies. Since mentalities and political cultures are seldom visible in the actions of collective actors, there was little attempt to study them systematically or to link them to the strategies and successes of social movements.

The recent contributions of Gamson (1988) and his collaborators (Gamson and Lasch 1983; Gamson and Modigliani 1987, 1989) on ideological packages, of Klandermans on consensus mobilization (1988, 1989), and of

Melucci on collective identities (1988, 1989) are useful attempts to overcome this lacuna. The categories they propose are by now familiar to
specialists in the field. With some differences in approach, these scholars
attempt to conceptualize how ideological symbols are shaped by movement organizers, how effective they are in mobilizing opinion, how they
evolve over time, and how the mobilization of consensus relates to collective action. But they have been far less explicit in dealing with how the
purposive ideological symbols of social movements interact with broader
social mentalities and political cultures. It is to the latter question that I
would like to turn.

Few scholars would now question the assumption that collective action
must be undergirded by shared understandings. And almost no one believes that ideological messages are mere superstructure and are thus
isolated from people's "real" behavior. Most scholars believe—with David
Apter—that ideology serves as an economizing device with which leaders
signal a movement's goals to their adversaries, make a complex universe comprehensible to ordinary people, communicate messages among
leaders, supporters, and outsiders, and provide movements with the solidarity that enables them to maintain themselves and expand their influence in the face of repression, cooptation, or indifference (Apter et al.
1960). But instead of focusing on the content of the formal ideologies of
movement organizations, these scholars now focus on the collective identities, core discourses, and frames of meaning that link members of social
movements and movement networks to one another. In other words, they
concern themselves with how ideological messages mediate between "prefigurative" and "strategic" politics (Breines 1982; Gamson, this volume).

Since ideologies link movement leaders to others in their society, it must
follow that the content of their messages is relational—that it builds action-
oriented purposive messages out of the materials they find in their societies. Both the widely diffused mentalities studied by the historians and
the more focused symbols of political cultures must play an important
role in how leaders construct meaning within social movements. Thus far,
however, this aspect has not been well developed in the literature on social
movements. The approach identified most closely with David Snow provides a starting point for linking movement ideologies both to societal
mentalities and to political culture.

Types of Frame Alignment

In a series of papers, Snow and his collaborators argue that
there is a special category of cognitive understandings—frames—that relate to collective action (see Snow et al. 1986; Snow and Benford 1988;

Snow and Benford, this volume). Although these are latent in all cultures and are socially constructed, in modern societies social movement organizers act as the "carriers and transmitters" of these meanings and, among other things, are "actively engaged in the production of [new] meaning for participants, antagonists and observers" (Snow and Benford 1988, 198).

Snow and his collaborators have adopted Goffman's (1974) term *framing,* which they define as "schemata of interpretation" (Snow et al. 1986), to conceptualize how ideological meanings are proposed by movement organizers to would-be supporters. They argue that "by rendering events or occurrences meaningful, frames function to organize experience and guide action, whether individual or collective. So conceptualized, it follows that frame alignment is a necessary condition for movement participation, whatever its nature or intensity" (Snow et al. 1986, 464).

Snow and his collaborators use the term *frame alignment,* which they define as "the linkages of individual and SMO interpretive orientations." They identify four types of alignment, which they call "frame bridging," "frame amplification," "frame expansion," and "frame transformation" (467). They see these as different strategies of linking a movement's message to its prospective supporters. These four strategies—which may not be mutually exclusive—vary on a rough scale of the degree to which they rest, on the one extreme, on existing values and predispositions and, on the other, on alternative meanings that challenge individuals' beliefs and understandings:

Frame bridging: This is the least ambitious form of framing. It "refers to the linkage of two or more ideologically congruent but structurally unconnected frames regarding a particular issue or problem" (1986, 467).

Frame transformation: At the opposite extreme, when a movement wishes to put forward a radically new set of ideas, it must engage in "frame transformation," which implies that "new values may have to be planted and nurtured, old meanings or understandings jettisoned, and erroneous beliefs or 'misframings' reframed" (473).

In between these polar types, two intermediate processes of frame alignment are identified:

Frame amplification: This refers to "the clarification and invigoration of an interpretive frame bearing on a particular issue" (469).

Frame extension: By this process, a movement attempts to "enlarge its adherent pool by portraying its objectives or activities as attending to or being congruent with the values or interests of potential adherents" (472).

Whereas Snow and his collaborators' 1986 paper sketched the strategies that movements use to signify meanings to potential followers without reference to their potential success or failure, Snow and Benford's 1988 paper was concerned with how the success of movements' signifying efforts could be judged. In it, they identified four sets of factors that affect the mobilizing capacity of a movement's framing efforts and activities: "The first set concerns the robustness, completeness, and thoroughness of the framing effort. . . . A second set deals with the internal structure of the larger belief system with which the movement seeks to affect some kind of cognitive/ ideational alignment. The third set concerns the relevance of the frame to the life-world of the participants. The fourth set concerns . . . 'cycles of protest'" (Snow and Benford 1988, 199).

In all their efforts, Snow and his collaborators argue that movement organizers construct symbol systems designed to attract supporters to their views, but that they do not invent them out of whole cloth. On the contrary, in all but the most transformational framing efforts (that is, in at least three of the frame alignment processes they identify), organizers attempt to relate their goals and programs directly to the existing values and predispositions of their target public. They are thus in a certain sense both consumers of existing cultural meanings and producers of new meanings, which are inevitably framed in terms of organizers' reading of the public's existing values and predispositions. Collective action is thus the stage in which new meanings are produced, as well as a text full of old meanings.

In their success or failure in creating strategically successful collective action frames, movement organizers are constrained by existing cultural meanings as well; the very term *frame resonance*, which Snow and Benford use to define the potential for success of a collective action frame, implies the importance of its relationship to existing popular understandings—at least among the movement's target group. Particularly with the third condition for resonance that Snow and Benford point to—"the relevance of the frame to the life-world of the participants"—it seems clear that movement organizers must operate within the cognitive and evaluative universe that they find rather than create a new one.

In the civil rights movement in the United States, for example, the notion of "rights" derived its strategic importance from its traditional importance in American political culture, although this had most often been honored in the breach in the case of the black population. The early successes of the movement derived in part from the fact that its dominant theme rested on "frame bridging" and "frame amplification" strategies that did not require potential supporters to depart from traditional and widely shared values. In the black middle class that was the movement's main constituency, the concept of "rights" and the attendant one of "opportunity" were deeply embedded, allowing the movement to mediate between its major internal constituency and the white liberal "conscience constituents" who bolstered it from the outside.

Frames, Mentalities, and Opposition Cultures

There are four useful dimensions to Snow and Benford's concept of collective action frames for our purposes. First, frames are more flexible and situationally influenced constructs than formal ideological systems and are more easily and rapidly communicated to target groups, adapted to change, and extended to blend with other frames. In particular, frames can be adjusted to the relationships among collective actors, opponents, and third parties at a particular time. A political opportunity may crystallize an existing frame or enable movement entrepreneurs to extend it to encompass new goals or subjects.

Thus, the civil rights movement was able to profit from the changes in political alignment in the New South in the 1950s and 1960s (Piven and Cloward 1977), as well as from claims being made by the United States at the time that it supported liberation movements in the third world against colonial oppression. Similarly, the movement to oppose American intervention in Nicaragua "borrowed" symbolism from the enormous popularity of the peace movement in the 1980s, although the latter was directed mainly against the arms race in Europe.

Second, since in at least three of Snow and Benford's four frame alignment processes, leaders make use of both established and new ideational elements, new syntheses constantly emerge from the combination of these elements and there is no sharp demarcation possible between beliefs that are "within the system" and those that are "outside the system." The result is that opponents will have a more difficult time delegitimating a movement than if, for example, it proposed a totally new framework of interpretation. The implication is that a movement is far more likely to bridge, extend, or amplify existing frames in the political culture than to create a wholly new one that may have no resonance in the existing culture.

But by the same token, movements pay some costs for adapting frames that draw on societal mentalities and consensual political cultures. For example, the easy relationship between the goals of the civil rights movement and traditional American cultural understandings left the movement open to the challenges of more radical black nationalist groups who rejected the symbols of white liberalism. Moreover, once the cycle of protest had spread to new issues, the rights frame could be appropriated by others—ethnic minorities, the disabled, women, gays, animal rights advocates, even white citizens who claimed their rights were being curtailed by affirmative action (Gamson and Modigliani 1987) or those who said they represented the rights of the unborn.

A frame interacts with the political culture of a society as it is embodied in collective action, and in this way it becomes available to other groups. As the example of the civil rights movement suggests, frames are no more than that; leaders cannot control how the "common sense" of a society will guide their supporters' frames of understanding or intrude into the collective action frames they put forward. Framing is not simply the instrumental activity of social movement entrepreneurs; to use a metaphor that Tilly has employed to describe the repertoire of collective action tactics, framing is less like a completed symphony than like improvisational jazz: composers provide the initial "head" for a jam session, but the improvisations depend on a group of players over whom they have little control (1983, 463).

Third, as argued earlier, there is a fundamental divide between societal mentalities and the logic of collective action. Because movement framing is a tool for detaching people from their habitual passivity, it is founded on a preference for action. But because mentalities reflect ordinary people's attempts to understand their society, they favor quiescence over action. Therefore, a collective action frame *must* be opposed to at least some elements of existing mentalities or at least identify circumstances that justify ordinary people taking their lives into their own hands. This is why it can often profit from the existence of an oppositional political culture.

The civil rights movement solved the dilemma between the deep mentality of quiescence in the black population of the South and the need for activism by transforming quiescence into collective action. That is, rather than oppose a frame of daring and risky political activism to the acquiescent culture of southern blacks, the movement's leaders elaborated a frame of peaceful civil disobedience within the most traditional institution they possessed—the black churches. Traditional solidarities and points of concern could thus be transformed into campaigns of peaceful civil disobedience.

In this transformation of the culture of the black southern churches, the white power structure was an unwitting collaborator, for it responded to nonviolence with violence, answered the message of love with the rhetoric of hatred, turned the dogs of war on messengers of peace. The more violent and unchristian the behavior of their antagonists—as underscored and amplified by the media—the more the moral superiority of the peaceful disobedience tactic was brought home to blacks in the South and prospective allies in Washington and the North. Out of struggle, blacks invented a new collective action frame.

But the civil rights movement's solution depended upon the presence of disciplined troops, on the existence of a powerful cultural institution, and on a favorable political opportunity structure. As more radical groups sought space within the movement and as it spread from the South to the North, the peaceful disobedience frame came up against increasing attempts to transform the movement from one of assimilation into one of liberation, even separation. The result was increasing violence in both rhetoric and action and a sharp division between the movement's message and its roots in black-and-white political culture.

The evolution of the civil rights movement underscores the fourth point about collective action frames: that there are dangers for a movement in drawing too directly on dominant societal mentalities and political cultures. The alternative is for movements to draw upon oppositional political cultures—sets of values that are rejected by many but are inherited from the society's tradition of collective action and opposition. Foreign observers sometimes wondered why the civil rights movement failed to link itself to a preexisting oppositional subculture. The answer is simple but tragic: that subculture, which had seen its maximum strength during the Great Depression and the New Deal, had been largely destroyed by a McCarthyite backlash and political maneuvering during the previous two decades.

In contrast, European social movements have been able to build on still-sturdy oppositional political cultures. The peace movement again provides numerous examples—in the Netherlands (Kriesi and van Praag, Jr. 1987) and Britain (Maguire 1990), in particular. But it is in the workerist movement of the late 1960s in Italy that we can see the most striking illustration of attempts to build a new frame out of the existing materials of an oppositional political culture. Let me close with this example, which both attests to the usefulness of Snow and his collaborators' work and raises questions about the relations among frames, collective action, and culture change.[8]

WORKERISM IN THE ITALIAN PROTEST CYCLE

In an anonymously published pamphlet that appeared in 1967, a left-wing intellectual close to the Italian labor movement wrote: "Only in the factory is the social relation of production that will one day be destroyed found in the same place as the class political force . . . that will subvert and

---

8. The following discussion summarizes a longer treatment of workerism and the workers' movement of the 1960s and 1970s in Italy in Tarrow (1989). See the excellent historical synthesis in Golden (1988).

overturn it: the mole that corrodes and the gravedigger that can undermine it." The quotation encapsulates the major substantive characteristics
of the workerist frame—*ouvrierisme* in French and *operaismo* in Italian:
first, elevating the working class to the role of the potent gravedigger of
capitalism; second, denigrating political forces that are *not* rooted in the
factory; and, third drawing the implicit strategic conclusion that efforts at
social revolution must concentrate on advancing the class struggle in the
factory and not elsewhere.[9]

What the quotation fails to capture is the emotional nature of workerism: that it is the supreme "injustice" frame, which portrays the harsh
conditions of early capitalism as the necessary and sufficient cause for
vigorous and often violent collective action, that it shrugs off the complica-
tions and subtleties of parliamentary politics for the simple test of strength
of the factories, and that it draws on the most potent oppositional force
in society. The appeal of workerism goes back to the long and agonizing
history of the working class in the harsh conditions of early capitalism in
both Italy and France; to the anarchosyndicalist traditions of both labor
movements and their difficulty in gaining legal recognition and collective
bargaining rights; to their ruthless repression by fascism in Italy and by
Vichy in France; and to the social isolation that the working class still suffers in the proletarian dormitories on the outskirts of the larger cities in
both countries.

Like many collective action frames, workerism is consistent with more
than one concrete policy position (Gamson and Modigliani 1987, 143). In
its most extreme version, it is the sentiment that the proletariat is the only
fulcrum around which revolutionary activity can be organized. In a more
moderate version it is the sentiment that the basic cost that must be met
by management is labor's economic and social needs. It also has a negative connotation to elements of the Left that disagree with its tenets. For
example, workerism has been seen by an important sector of the Italian
Communist leadership as the attempt "to create a myth of the working
class and around working class struggles, obscuring the problem of alliances and obscuring the ideal, political and state dimensions of the class
struggle" (Napoletano 1978, 5).

Both the extreme and the moderate versions of the workerist frame reject the "common sense" of a capitalist society that views progress as the result of cooperation between labor and capital. But the first version focuses
opposition to capitalism centrally on the working class, whereas the sec-

---

9. For a more theoretical and historical analysis of workerism, see d'Agostini (1978),
and especially the essay by Nino Magna in that volume.

ond is compatible with attempts to expand the workerist theme to include the "ideal, political and state dimensions of the class struggle." Proponents of the more moderate view look toward alliances and try to build appeals on societal mentalities that extend beyond the industrial working class. It is obvious that proponents of the more radical version must either limit their mobilizing efforts to include only those for whom the oppositional culture comes naturally—in this case, industrial workers—or extend the meaning of the working class to other groups—for example, farm workers, low-paid service employees—or else conceive of their frame as "transformational"—for example, requiring the movement's non-working-class supporters to sublimate their own demands to those of the working class.

One of the surprising aspects of the university students' movements in both countries was their adoption of this workerist symbolism. Educated children of the bourgeoisie styled themselves workers, ideologically and physically, in an attempt to draw upon the most powerful oppositional political culture in each country's history. This symbolism began to appear in the early 1960s, when small workerist groups, to the left of the Communist parties, attempted to make contact with industrial workers. By 1966, the theme had spread to the university, as when sociology students at the new University of Trento theorized that the university is a "productive institution." The Trento sociologists' discovery of the early Marx was evident as they wrote that "students are subordinates who suffer a process of effective alienation from decisions which affect them" (quoted in Grazioli 1979, 15). Two years later, the Trento students were theorizing that the university is "one of the productive institutions of the current social system. . . . It produces a particular type of good: man as commodity, as a trained labor force or one that is in the process of being trained" (quoted in Grazioli 1979, 17–18).

Workerism was extended still further by a coalition of student groups that occupied the administration building of the University of Pisa in 1967 to protest against the government's plan of university reform (Tarrow 1989, ch. 10). But instead of seeing students as commodities, which was the Trento theory, they saw them as workers and deduced from this that they should receive a state salary. The theses of these students received national publicity when they were adopted by a faction of the UGI, the left-wing students' association, splitting the organization and eventually destroying it.

The early Marx and the traditions of an excluded working class were only one source of the attempt to bridge students and workers. There was also a strategic reason for workerism's survival among students and intellectuals. In Italy in particular, the Communists had succeeded in becoming hegemonic on the left by subordinating their support for the proletariat to a strategy of broad alliances of groups and classes (Hellman 1975; Tarrow 1967). This left a stratum of labor organizers, intellectuals, and students uncertain about the revolutionary authenticity of the major party of the Left. Many became convinced that the failure of the Left to create a socialist society could be traced to the party's failure to represent the workers' deepest needs. Workerism was the *strategic* choice of a political culture in response to this situation. This strategic theme is revealed in the same anonymous pamphlet quoted above: "In order to make the party's organization come to life materially in every factory," wrote this critic, "it will be necessary for the relations of production to come to life politically in the life of the party."

But the choice of a cultural matrix from which to construct a collective action frame does not guarantee that people will pour into the streets in response to it. In some hands, workerism became a caricature of itself: ludicrously, when the Italian Socialists, who had lost most of their working-class credentials by entering the Center-Left coalition in the early 1960s, declared themselves to be "the party of labor"; awkwardly, when elements at the base of the unions continued to insist on the primacy of wages after the economic crisis of the 1970s hit; and tragically, when it appeared in the simplistic ideologies of the terrorist groups that flourished in Italy in the mid-1970s (Tarrow 1989, ch. 11).

Just as workerism exemplifies a strategic collective action frame drawing on working-class traditions and responding to the opportunity of attacking communism from the left, it also demonstrates the vulnerabilities of collective action frames to changes in political opportunities. In Italy, at least, workerism had two major vulnerabilities as a collective action frame. First, because it was an emotional appeal to working-class activism, its leaders had to be ready to foment wildcat strikes and sit-downs and demonstrate their own prowess through rhetorical and physical violence. This made them vulnerable to the charge that workerism bred terrorism. (Indeed, the first true terrorist groups emerged in the factories, and their favorite tactic was the sequestering of managers and personnel directors.) There was enough evidence of a link between workerism and terrorism that the campaign against the latter could be used to besmirch the entire workerist left.

Workerism's second vulnerability was economics. The height of the protest cycle came at a time of economic expansion, but by the end of the period—the mid-1970s—Italy faced a major international and financial crisis. In this new context, those who placed the interests of labor above those of the collectivity could be branded with the culturally devastating label of "corporatists"—both by the government, which was ever ready to reassert the prerogatives of management, and by the Communists, who feared both a revival of fascism and a loss of electoral support among the middle class (Lange 1980).

By the late 1970s, intellectuals with a workerist past were carefully distinguishing between the centrality of the struggle in the factory and the centrality of the workers to politics (Tronti 1978, 1–7). The death knell of workerism as a rationale for collective action was marked by the disastrous failure of the Fiat strike of 1980, when thousands of assembly-line workers joined office workers in marching against the intransigence of the unions (Bonazzi 1984; Carmagnani 1984). By the late 1980s no one any longer imagined that the Italian working class shared an oppositional culture organized around workerism or would attempt to frame a mobilization campaign around its symbols.

CONCLUSIONS

The sad story of workerism in Italy allows us to draw a number of lessons and raise a series of questions about the construction of meaning in social movements.

Of the lessons, one is methodological and three are hypothetical. The methodological one is that societal mentalities are far too diffuse, too detached from actual historical agents, and too distant from collective action situations to use effectively in understanding how movements construct meaning. We will never understand, on the basis of generic constructs such as the "moral economy," "popular culture," and "resistance," how and in what circumstances collective action arises. We must turn, as movement organizers do, to the values embedded in and the points of conflict between social actors revealed in actual social situations.

Two of the hypothetical lessons can be simply stated. First, the symbols and preferences in a political culture become the guides to action of a social movement only to the extent that they can be transformed into action premises, and this excludes many of the symbols of compliance and quiescence that abound in dominant political cultures. Second, "actionable" symbols are more likely to be found in an oppositional culture— where one exists—than in the cultural bases of the existing system. When the latter are all that are available to movement organizers, the movement is vulnerable, on the one hand, to cooptation and, on the other, to outbidding, as the example of the American civil rights movement shows. A successful movement either transforms quiescent symbols into activist ones or delicately blends oppositional and consensual elements to produce a new synthesis.

The third hypothesis is perhaps the most far-reaching in trying to link cognitive frames to collective action: that although their bases lie in preexisting cultural traditions, new frames of meaning result from the struggles over meaning within social movements and from their clash with their opponents. They are elaborated not intellectually but through struggle, which is always a struggle over meaning as well as over resources (Mueller 1989, 16).

Once new collective action frames are established, much like the forms of organization or the tactics that movements employ, leaders become identified with them and construct their repertoires as variations around the themes that have animated successful struggles. Future stages of the movement depend on this initial framing process, on the policy positions they lead to, on the allies and opponents they imply, and on their actual success in mobilizing people. Success results from having the resources to organize an effective mobilization campaign, but it also depends on maintaining a delicate balance between the resonance of the movement's message with existing political culture and its promise of new departures.[10] Over time, just as repertoires of action and forms of organization are institutionalized, a given collective action frame becomes part of the political culture— which is to say, part of the reservoir of symbols from which future movement entrepreneurs can choose.

The questions raised by this analysis follow logically from these hypotheses.

First, how can collective action frames best be studied? The argument in the preceding paragraph makes plain my methodological biases. I would answer, through the study of how people struggle, against whom they struggle, and in the name of which symbols and points of concern they struggle. Only through a careful and systematic analysis of the themes that arise out of the clash between movements and their opponents—and not even through the most assiduous deconstruction of their texts—can we learn about the underlying symbols and frames of meaning in social movements.

A variety of sources and methods can follow from this approach. The ethnographic methods of Kertzer (1988, 1990) or Scott (1976, 1985); the deductive insights of DeNardo (1985) or Laitin (1986, 1988); the broad typological constructs of Wildavsky (1987; Thompson et al. 1990); the systematic time-series analyses of Inglehart (1988, 1990); the sensitive content analyses of Gamson (1988, 1989; Gamson and Lasch 1983; Gamson and Modigliani 1987); and the historical sweep of the Tillys (1975): all

10. As in much else, I am in debt to Charles Tilly for this formulation, based on his reading of an earlier version of this essay.

will contribute to our knowledge of how movements frame their collective actions and their relationship to existing and emergent political cultures.

A second question is more difficult: how can collective action frames be related empirically to political culture without an agreed-upon level of analysis for the latter concept, a common definition of its content and an adequate methodology for unearthing it? The lively debate in the *American Political Science Review* over the past few years shows that investigators are far from unanimous on this issue. At least we can take comfort from the fact that investigators are again taking cultural values and points of concern seriously, in contrast to an earlier period in which many were content to infer preferences from (economic) assumptions.

A third question is more fundamental still: how can social movement struggles, and the new frames of meaning they produce, be related to changes in political culture and societal mentalities? Only long-term analyses that embed empirical analyses in history will begin to deal with this essential problem. Here sociologists can perhaps learn from their colleagues in political science who have "taken the historical cure" (Almond et al. 1973). Only by embedding the systematic empirical analysis of social movements—at which sociologists excel—into the longer cycles of mobilization and quiescence that have marked our societies for the past two centuries can we understand how new meanings are constructed.

REFERENCES

Agulhon, Maurice. 1982. *Marianne to Battle: Republican Imagery and Symbolism in France, 1789–1880*. Cambridge: Cambridge University Press.

———. 1986. *"Leçon inaugurale: Chaire d'histoire contemporaine."* Paris: Collège de France.

Almond, Gabriel, Scott Flanagan, and Robert J. Mundt. 1973. *Crisis, Choice and Change*. Boston: Little, Brown.

Almond, Gabriel, and G. Bingham Powell. 1978. *Comparative Politics: System, Process and Policy*. Boston: Little, Brown.

Almond, Gabriel, and Sidney Verba. 1964. *The Civic Culture*. Boston: Little, Brown.

———, eds. 1980. *The Civic Culture Revisited*. Boston: Little, Brown.

Apter, David E., ed. 1964. *Ideology and Discontent*. Glencoe: Free Press.

Aries, Philippe. 1978. "L'histoire des mentalités." In J. Le Goff, R. Chartier, and J. Revel, eds., *La nouvelle histoire*. Paris: CEPL, 402–23.

Banfield, Edward. 1954. *The Moral Basis of a Backward Society*. Chicago: Free Press.

Barnes, Samuel, and Max Kaase. 1979. *Political Action: Mass Participation in Five Western Democracies*. London and Beverly Hills: Sage.

Barnes, Samuel, and Giacomo Sani. 1974. "Mediterranean Political Culture and Italian Politics." *British Journal of Political Science* 4:289–303.

Bevilacqua, Piero. 1980. *Le campagne del mezzogiorno tra fascismo e dopoguerra*. Turin: Einaudi.

Bonazzi, Giuseppe. 1984. "La lotta dei 35 giorni alla Fiat: Un'analisi sociologica." *Ricerche CeSPE*, suppl. to *Politica ed economia*, no. 11 (November).

Breines, Wini. 1982. *Community and Organization in the New Left, 1962–1968: The Great Refusal*. New York: Praeger.

Carmagnani, Fabrizio. 1984. "Il sindacato di classe nella lotta dei 35 giorni alla Fiat." *Ricerche CeSPE*, suppl. to *Politica ed economia*, no. 11 (November).

Chartier, Roger. 1989. "Le monde comme représentation." *Annales ESC* 44:1505–20.

Colburn, Forrest D., ed. 1989. *Everyday Forms of Peasant Resistance*. New York: M. E. Sharpe.

D'Agostini, Fabrizio, ed. 1978. *Operaismo e centralità operaia*. Rome: Editori Riuniti.

DeNardo, James. 1985. *Power in Numbers: The Political Strategy of Protest and Rebellion*. Princeton: Princeton University Press.

Eckstein, Harry. 1988. "A Culturalist Theory of Political Change." *American Political Science Review* 82:789–804.

Eisinger, Peter. 1973. "The Conditions of Protest Behavior in American Cities." *American Political Science Review* 67:11–28.

Esman, Milton J. 1989. "Conclusion." In F. D. Colburn, ed., *Everyday Forms of Peasant Resistance*. New York: M. E. Sharpe, 221–28.

Gamson, William. 1988. "Political Discourse and Collective Action." In B. Klandermans, H. Kriesi, and S. Tarrow, eds., *From Structure to Action: Comparing Social Movements across Cultures*. International Social Movement Research, vol. 1. Greenwich, Conn.: JAI Press, 219–46.

———. 1989. "Media Discourse and Public Opinion on Nuclear Power: A Constructionist Approach." *American Journal of Sociology* 95:1–37.

Gamson, William, and Catherine Lasch. 1983. "The Political Culture of Social Welfare Policy." In S. E. Spiro and E. Yechtman-Yaar, eds., *Evaluating the Welfare State*. New York: Academic Press, 397–415.

Gamson, William, and André Modigliani. 1987. "The Changing Culture of Affirmative Action." In L. Kriesberg, ed., *Research in Social Movements: Conflict and Change*, vol. 3. Greenwich, Conn.: JAI Press, 137–77.

Goffman, Erving. 1974. *Frame Analysis*. New York: Harper.

Golden, Miriam. 1988 "Historical Memory and Ideological Orientations in the Italian Workers' Movement." *Politics and Society* 16:1–34.

Grazioli, Marco. 1979. "Il movimento studentesco in Italia nell'anno accademico 1967–68: Ricostruzione e analisi." Thesis, Faculty of Political Science, State University of Milan.

Hellman, Stephen. 1975. "The PCI's Alliance Strategy and the Case of the Middle Classes." In D. L. M. Blackmer and S. Tarrow, eds., *Communism in Italy and France*. Princeton: Princeton University Press.

Hobsbawm, Eric. 1959. *Primitive Rebels and Social Bandits*. Manchester: University of Manchester Press.

Hobsbawm, Eric, and George Rudé. 1975. *Captain Swing: A Social History of the Great English Agricultural Uprising*. New York: Norton.

Hoggart, Richard. 1961. *The Uses of Literacy*. Boston: Beacon Press.

Inglehart, Ronald. 1971. "The Silent Revolution in Europe: Intergenerational Change in Post-Industrial Societies." *American Political Science Review* 65:991–1017.

————. 1977. *The Silent Revolution: Changing Values and Political Styles among Western Publics*. Princeton: Princeton University Press.

————. 1988. "The Renaissance of Political Culture." *American Political Science Review* 82:1203–30.

————. 1990. *Culture Shift in Advanced Industrial Society*. Princeton: Princeton University Press.

Jenkins, Craig, and Charles Perrow. 1977. "Insurgency of the Powerless: Farm Worker Movements, 1946–1972." *American Sociological Review* 42:249–68.

Kertzer, David. 1988. *Ritual, Politics and Power*. New Haven: Yale University Press.

————. 1990. *Comrades and Christians: Religion and Political Struggle in Communist Italy*. Prospect Heights, Ill.: Waveland Press.

Klandermans, Bert. 1988. "The Formation and Mobilization of Consensus." In B. Klandermans, H. Kriesi, and S. Tarrow, eds., *From Structure to Action: Comparing Social Movement Research across Cultures*. International Social Movement Research, vol. 1. Greenwich: JAI Press, 173–96.

————. 1989. "Grievance Interpretation and Success Expectations: The Social Construction of Protest." *Social Behaviour* 4:113–25.

Kriesi, Hanspeter. 1985. "The Rebellion of the Research Objects of Social Research." Paper presented to the workshop The Analysis of Social Movements, Bonn.

Kriesi, Hanspeter, and Philip van Praag, Jr. 1987. "Old and New Politics: The Dutch Peace Movement and the Traditional Political Organizations." *European Journal of Political Science* 15:319–46.

Laitin, David. 1986. *Hegemony and Culture: Politics and Religion among the Yoruba*. Chicago: University of Chicago Press.

————. 1988. "Political Culture and Political Preferences." *American Political Science Review* 82:589–93.

Lange, Peter. 1980. "Crisis and Consent, Change and Compromise: Dilemmas of Italian Communism in the 1970s." In P. Lange and S. Tarrow, eds., *Italy in Transition: Conflict and Consensus*. London: Cass.

LeRoy Ladourie, Emmanuel. 1975. *Montaillou, village occitan de 1294 a 1324*. Paris: Gallimard.

————. 1979. *Carneval de Romans: De la Chandeleur au mercredi des cendres, 1579–1580*. Paris: Gallimard.

Lusebrink, Jans-Jurgen. 1982. *Kriminalitat und Literatur im Frankreich des 18, Jahrhunderts*. Munich and Vienna: Oldenbourg-Verlag.

————. 1983. "L'imaginaire social et ses focalisations en France et en Allemagne à la fin du XVIIIe siècle." *Revue Roumaine d'Histoire* 22:371–83.

Magna, Nino. 1978. "Per una storia dell'operaismo in Italia: Il trentennio postbellico." In F. D'Agostini, ed., *Operaismo e centralità operaia*. Rome: Editori Riuniti.

Maguire, Diarmuid. 1990. "New Social Movements and Old Political Institutions: The Campaign for Nuclear Disarmament, 1979–1989." Ph.D. diss., Cornell University.

Mandrou, Robert. 1964. *De la culture populare aux dix-septième et dix-huitième siècles: La Bibliothèque blue de Troyes*. Paris: Stock.

Melucci, Alberto. 1985. "The Symbolic Challenge of Contemporary Movements." *Social Research* 52:789–816.

————. 1988. "Getting Involved: Identity and Mobilization in Social Movements."

In B. Klandermans, H. Kriesi, and S. Tarrow, eds., *From Structure to Action: Comparing Movement Research across Cultures.* International Social Movement Research, vol. 1. Greenwich, Conn.: JAI Press, 329–48.

———. 1989. *Nomads of the Present: Social Movements and Individual Needs in Contemporary Society.* Philadelphia: Temple University Press.

Morris, Aldon D. 1984. *The Origins of the Civil Rights Movement.* New York: Free Press.

Mueller, Carol. 1989. "Frame Generation in a Cycle of Protest: The Origins of 'Participatory Democracy.'" Paper presented at the annual meeting of the American Sociological Association.

Napoletano, Giorgio. 1978. "Introduzione al convegno." In F. D'Agostini, ed., *Operaismo e centralitá operaia.* Rome: Editori Riuniti.

Piven, Frances Fox, and Richard A. Cloward. 1977. *Poor People's Movements: Why They Succeed, How They Fail.* New York: Vintage.

Putnam, Robert D. 1973. *The Beliefs of Politicians: Ideology, Conflict, and Democracy in Britain and Italy.* New Haven: Yale University Press.

Putnam, Robert D., Robert Leonardi, and Raffaella Nanetti. 1985. *La pianta e le radici.* Bologna: Mulino.

Pye, Lucien, and Sidney Verba. 1965. *Political Culture and Political Development.* Princeton: Princeton University Press.

Rudé, George. 1964. *The Crowd in History: A Study of Popular Disturbances in France and England, 1730–1848.* New York: Wiley.

———. 1986. *The Crowd in the French Revolution.* Chicago: Greenwood Press.

Sabel, Charles. 1982. *Work and Politics.* New York: Cambridge University Press.

Scott, James C. 1976. *The Moral Economy of the Peasant: Rebellion and Subsistence in Southeast Asia.* New Haven: Yale University Press.

———. 1985. *Weapons of the Weak.* New Haven: Yale University Press.

Snow, David, and Robert Benford. 1988. "Ideology, Frame Resonance, and Participant Mobilization." In B. Klandermans, H. Kriesi, and S. Tarrow, eds., *From Structure to Action: Comparing Social Movement Research across Cultures.* International Social Movement Research, vol. 1. Greenwich, Conn.: JAI Press, 197–218.

Snow, David, E. Burke Rochford, Jr., Steven K. Worden, and Robert Benford. 1986. "Frame Alignment Processes, Micromobilization, and Movement Participation." *American Sociological Review* 51:464–81.

Tarrow, Sidney. 1967. *Peasant Communism in Southern Italy.* New Haven: Yale University Press.

———. 1989. *Democracy and Disorder: Protest and Politics in Italy, 1965–1975.* Oxford: Oxford University Press.

Thompson, E. P. 1968. *The Making of the English Working Class.* London: Penguin.

———. 1971. "The Moral Economy of the English Crowd in the Eighteenth Century." *Past and Present* 50:76–136.

Thompson, Michael, Richard Ellis, and Aaron Wildavsky. 1990. *Cultural Theory.* Boulder, Colo.: Westview.

Tilly, Charles. 1978. *From Mobilization to Revolution.* Englewood Cliffs, N.J.: Prentice-Hall.

———. 1983. "Speaking Your Mind without Elections, Surveys, or Social Movements." *Public Opinion Quarterly* 47:461–78.

Tilly, Charles, Louise Tilly, and Richard Tilly. 1975. *The Rebellious Century.* Cambridge, Mass.: Harvard University Press.

Tronti, Mario. 1978. "Operaismo e centralità operaia." In Fabrizio D'Agostini, ed., *Operaismo e centralità operaia*. Rome: Editori Riuniti.

Vovelle, Michel. 1973. *Piété baroque et déchristianisation: Provence au XVIIIe siècle*. Paris: Plon.

———. 1982. *Idéologie et mentalités*. Paris: Maspèro.

———. 1985. *La mentalité révolutionnaire: Société et mentalités sous la révolution française*. Paris: Editions Sociales.

———. N.d. "Histoire des mentalités: Histoire des résistances ou les prisons de longue durée." Manuscript.

Wildavsky, Aaron. 1987. "Choosing Preferences by Constructing Institutions: A Cultural Theory of Preference Formation." *American Political Science Review* 81: 3–22.

Wolf, Eric. 1973. *Peasant Wars of the Twentieth Century*. New York: Harper and Row.

Part 4

Conflict, Community, and Mobilization

9

Resource Mobilization versus the Mobilization of People

Why Consensus Movements Cannot Be Instruments of Social Change

Michael Schwartz and Shuva Paul

The absence of large-scale social upheaval in the 1970s and 1980s allowed observers of American social movements to focus on less dramatic but previously neglected phenomena. Among the most challenging of these new objects of attention were consensus movements.

In its broadest sense, the term *consensus movements* refers to social mobilizations that enjoy broad attitudinal support (80 to 90 percent of the population) and encounter "little or no organized opposition" (McCarthy and Wolfson 1988, 26). Different analysts, of course, have offered different analyses of the issues and activities undertaken by such groups. Lofland (1989), for example, emphasizes that such movements in the eighties were typically "'nonpolitical,' 'educational,' 'nonpartisan,' or 'humanitarian'" and systematically avoided the slightest conflictual entanglements.[1] Other researchers (e.g., McCarthy and Wolfson 1988 and this vol.; McCarthy and Zald 1973, 1977; McCarthy, Britt, and Wolfson, 1991) have characterized consensus movements not so much by their publicly avowed (or disavowed) ideologies as by the social infrastructures and institutional resources that shaped their emergence. In this context, consensus movements may be seen as an outgrowth of what has been called the "bureaucratization of social discontent" and the "rise of professional social movements" (McCarthy and Zald 1973, 3, 20).

All characterizations of consensus movements contain an implicit or ex-

We wish to thank Naomi Rosenthal for her help in formulating our ideas.

1. Lofland distinguishes consensus movements from Roberts and Kloss's "nonmovements." The former is like the latter, he says, in that consensus movements do not attempt to alter existing labor or property relations. Unlike nonmovements, however, which focus on psychological adaptation to social problems, consensus movements strive to bring about "mass changes in perception or consciousness" (Lofland 1989, 165).

TABLE 9.1
Mobilization Rates of Selected Social Movements

Organization	Organizing period (yrs.)	Membership increase	Number of chapters	Proportion of constituency organized
Mothers Against Drunk Driving (MADD)	7 (1978–85)	25,000	377	1/2000
Southern Farmers' Alliance	8 (1882–90)	850,000	20,000	1/4
AFL-CIO	5 (1935–40)	5,000,000	about 1,000	1/10
Students for a Democratic Society (SDS)	9 (1960–69)	100,000	2,000	1/70
American Communist party	9 (1930–39)	80,000	about 3,000	1/800
National Organization for Women (NOW)	16 (1967–83)	250,000	700	1/560
Woman's Christian Temperance Union (WCTU)	16 (1874–90)	150,000	about 2,000	1/150

plicit contrast to *conflict movements,* which can be defined as those social mobilizations that confront organized opposition in attempting to change the social structure, prevailing fundamental policies, and/or the balance of power among groups. This chapter focuses directly on this comparison: compared to conflict movements, how successful are consensus movements in mobilizing for social change?

On this question there is considerable disagreement. One group of analysts argues or implies that consensus movements carry enormous potential for generating social change and thus are the ideal vehicles for social activists (e.g., McCarthy and Wolfson 1988 and this vol.). Another group adopts the opposite view: that consensus movements have little success in managing social change (e.g., Lofland 1989). We support the latter group by focusing on those structural aspects of consensus movements that, we argue, severely limit their capacity to influence their social world.

THE PARADOX OF CONSENSUS MOVEMENTS

In table 9.1, we offer a comparison of the mobilization rates of some important social movements in the last century. The first entry in the table, the movement against drunk driving, was one of the most prominent consensus movements of the early eighties and, because of the work of McCarthy and his colleagues, is well researched. The most prominent of these organizations, Mothers Against Drunk Driving (MADD), founded in 1980, sought to raise public awareness of drunk driving issues, to push for more stringent state laws regarding drunk driving, and to provide support for victims. It was launched with considerable financial resources from the federal government, and it obtained organizational aid from local public officials and police agencies. It reaped glowing publicity in the mass media and even managed to attract (qualified) support from the alcohol industry (McCarthy, Wolfson, and Harvey 1987).

Various measures demonstrated that MADD had overwhelming public support. Many national opinion polls indicated that over 80 percent of the population endorsed its goals. It faced little mobilized opposition, and even then, opposition was aimed not at MADD's mission as a whole but only at certain of its objectives. For instance, the beer industry, though it clashed with many local MADD chapters over state legislation aimed at raising the legal drinking age, nonetheless contributed significant amounts of money and literature to other MADD efforts. It is these three factors—broad institutional support for its goals, attitudinal support from the overwhelming majority of the population, and little organized, sustained opposition— that make MADD a fitting representative of consensus movements.

Despite these advantages, MADD typifies an important and often ignored pattern in consensus movements: *its growth did not compare favorably with that of successful conflict groups.* In the five years after its emergence, MADD grew to an estimated 377 chapters nationwide, with approximately 25,000 members.[2] Compare MADD's efforts to the recruitment successes of the next two entries in table 9.1. Consider, for instance, the sensational rise of the Southern Farmers' Alliance. In what may have been the most rapid organizational expansion in American social movement history, the Alliance expanded from virtually no membership in 1882 to 850,000 in 1890. This increase brought approximately one out of four of the eligible male farmers in the South into the organization (Schwartz 1976).

This achievement is not unrivaled, however. Consider the third entry in the table. It shows the remarkable expansion of the AFL-CIO during the heyday of union organizing between 1935 and 1940. Here the increase from 3.7 million to 8.4 million represented a recruitment of one out of ten of all possible working-class constituents. Certainly, MADD, with its 377 chapters involving some 25,000 members (representing about $\frac{1}{2000}$ of its

2. Interestingly, although the capacity to achieve rapid mobilization is one of the cited virtues of consensus movements, conflicting accounts exist of the membership size of MADD (one of the most well-researched consensus organizations). Reinarman (1988) observes a constituency of 600,000, but McCarthy and Wolfson's data (1988) suggest a figure closer to 25,000. We believe that Reinarman's assessment, drawn from MADD's own literature and from newspapers, includes MADD's large mailing list constituency and that McCarthy and Wolfson's data more accurately describe MADD's chapter enrollments. Mailing list constituencies are analytically distinct from the sort of movement constituencies shown in table 9.1, for they are essentially untapped sources of interpersonal involvement in movement activities.

targeted constituency), was much smaller and more slowly growing than these two conflict movements.

Perhaps it is unfair to compare MADD only to the most successful conflict groups. More equitable comparisons can be found in the rest of the table, but even by these more modest standards, MADD did not fare well. Consider the next four entries in table 9.1. Although these groups might be called "average" among successful conflict organizations, they all accomplished more than MADD. Consider, for example, Students for a Democratic Society (SDS). Although most scholars of social movements consider SDS to have been a key actor in the 1960s, they note that its radicalism and (sometimes extreme) sectarianism limited its mass appeal and thus restrained recruitment of new members (Sale 1973; Adelson 1972). Nevertheless, during the nine years following its founding in 1960, it attracted at least 100,000 members. This meant that, among active students, it had recruited approximately one out of every seventy, clearly superior to MADD's rate.

In some sense, however, the above comparisons are unfair. Certainly, MADD was successful in the sense that the overwhelming majority of all social movements—particularly conflict groups—"die a-borning." Few of them last even one year. Still fewer spread beyond one chapter, and only a minute portion construct close to four hundred chapters, as MADD did in its first five years of existence. In this context, MADD was successful, to be sure. But the point here is to contrast those social movements that succeed in setting up shop and operating long enough to be noticed with those that become important factors in the social life of at least a part of the country. It is in this context that we see the relative weakness of consensus movements like MADD as compared to visible conflict movements like those in table 9.1.

Nor was MADD atypical: other consensus movements also have low rates of mobilization despite widespread public approval, institutional nurturance, and meager opposition. In the early 1980s, for example, the city twinning movement emerged as an exercise in "citizen diplomacy," in which many American communities formed sister-city relations with groups in the Soviet Union. It was constructed through the active participation of civic groups, schools, and churches, the endorsements of city councils, ample and favorable media attention, and generous advertising revenue from established businesses. It faced almost no sustained opposition (except from a few right-wing opponents who were usually unsuccessful in securing an audience).

The city twinning movement fits the mold of consensus movements even more snugly than MADD does. Despite all the resource advantages this movement enjoyed, it mustered only about three hundred participating communities nationwide (Lofland 1989). Clearly, all this consensus support, the lack of organized opposition, and the facilitation by institutions amounted to little actual mobilization for social change, at least when compared to the conflict movements in table 9.1.

We know of no consensus movement that pressed beyond the moderate mobilizations of MADD and city twinning. We therefore take this to be the critical paradox: consensus movements, despite popular support and ample resources, do not produce the massive mobilization found in successful conflict movements. In order to unravel this paradox, we return to the case study of MADD, relying on the comprehensive research of McCarthy and his colleagues to understand the critical dynamic issues.

There were six structural factors present in the mobilization of MADD that should have facilitated its rapid growth and influence:

1. *Movement organization.* The group's chapters were "franchises": headquarters guided and monitored their activities, provided resources and expertise, and gave them control over a specific geographical area. Because of this structure, organizational wisdom was transmitted to new chapters, together with the resources necessary for successful implementation.

2. *Alignment of infrastructural support.* The widespread approval of MADD's mission allowed it to utilize preexisting organizations to establish itself. Its chapters frequently grew out of ongoing civic, religious, and business organizations that had ready access to key resources such as meeting centers, phone banks, and buses. Thus, the networks and resources of the community became more or less the networks and resources of the movement.

3. *Extensive government support.* This included both direct monetary aid and indirect base building for the movement. The National Highway Traffic Safety Administration (NHTSA) underwrote start-up costs for MADD; it provided much of the educational literature; and state and local agencies that had managed NHTSA projects often facilitated MADD's access to public officials.

4. *Generous media coverage.* The organization's public education campaign was greatly bolstered by extensive media coverage, which aroused concern about drunk driving as well as publicizing the organization itself. It benefited not just from routine narrative coverage but also from feature stories, editorials, and press endorsements.

5. *Lavish institutional funding.* Beyond the extensive support provided by the government, MADD received ample, although unsystematic, financial support from a range of nonprofit groups and business enterprises.

6. *Broad public support.* National public opinion polls showed 80 percent and sometimes 90 percent endorsement for movement goals, including stricter penalties for drunk driving and the promotion of victim assistance programs.

The first three of these factors have been analyzed at length by McCarthy and Wolfson (1988), who argue convincingly that their confluence should have worked toward producing large mobilization gains for MADD. First, the franchise nature of the movement gave local activists visibility as part of a known national movement, crucial technical assistance in formulating strategies for collective action, and a "guaranteed local market for organizing." They found that MADD grew much faster than Remove Intoxicated Drivers (RID), one of its peers in the anti–drunk driving movement that operated as a loose coalition of local chapters. This strongly supports McCarthy and Wolfson's claims for the superiority of the franchise form of organization. Second, the availability of infrastructural resources made it less costly for MADD to mobilize. This should have resulted in a rate of mobilization faster than that for conflict movements, which must invest precious organizational energy to obtain resources. Third, extensive government support should also have facilitated the rapid growth of MADD. Government institutions defrayed the costs of organizing new chapters, underwrote research on drinking and driving, encouraged local police agencies to identify with chapter efforts, and aided MADD in framing legislative proposals. This provided the sort of social environment that conflict groups rarely have and removed one of the key impediments to growth.

The logic of McCarthy and Wolfson's arguments applies with equal force to the last three factors. It would seem, for instance, that the abundant and favorable press coverage enjoyed by MADD, by broadcasting its mission to more potential recruits than MADD's own efforts could have done, would have resulted in increased membership among the public as well as more attentiveness by lawmakers to MADD's proposals. Similarly, the lack of opposition should have removed major obstacles to MADD's efforts. The vast public approval not only gave MADD a huge base from which to recruit but enabled the movement to dispense with the often grueling (and sometimes impossible) task of winning people to its viewpoint. It could proceed directly to mobilizing them for action.

It seems clear that these factors should have facilitated mass mobilization among MADD's constituency and therefore should have produced "far more rapid social movement growth than for conflict movements" (McCarthy and Wolfson 1988, 33). Nevertheless, as demonstrated above, MADD's organizing trajectory was moderate at best.

UNRAVELING THE PARADOX

The key to unraveling the paradox lies in focusing on a signifi-
cant pattern in the six facilitating factors: the first five reflect *institutional*
rather than *constituent* support for the movement. Only the sixth factor—
favorable public opinion—pertains to the resonance of the potential membership to the goals and tactics of MADD. Moreover, even this measure-
ment of public resonance is a misleading indicator of constituent support:
opinion polls cannot tap a vital ingredient of successful mobilization—
the commitment by members to work actively for the movement (see, e.g.,
Fantasia 1988).

The significance of the pattern is this: institutional support and constituent support are *fundamentally different processes that require very different
tools of analysis* (see Morris 1981). The mobilization of monetary and infrastructural resources from established institutions (e.g., governments, the
media, businesses) and the mobilization of constituents ready and willing
to invest their time and labor to advance the cause of the movement do not
proceed in similar fashion—and they are not necessarily even correlated.

For a dramatic instance of just such a disjunction between resource and
constituent mobilization, compare the monetary resources of the anti–
drunk driving movement with those of the National Organization for
Women (NOW), with an eye to their respective recruitments (table 9.1). In
1983, NOW's budget was about 20 percent below that of the anti–drunk
driving movement in 1985—$6.5 million compared to $8 million. Yet NOW
mobilized 250,000 members as compared to 25,000 members for MADD
(Staggenborg 1988); the latter got much less "bang for the buck."

Why does this disjunction between resource mobilization and constituent mobilization occur? First, it could be a matter of differing strategies,
for MADD (and the other anti–drunk driving organizations) did not rely on
members in the same way as the other movements in table 9.1. Whereas
groups like the American Communist party obtain almost all their resources from membership dues and individual contributions, MADD had
access to a portion of the federal government's multi-million-dollar effort
to educate the public about the dangers of drinking and driving. The federal agency (NHTSA) that sponsored such programs eventually put its financial clout behind MADD (McCarthy and Wolfson 1988). In other words, the
Communist party needed to recruit members in order to obtain resources,
and MADD did not. This suggests that one should not judge the success of
consensus movements like MADD by membership size (or even mailing list
size), since they have little need for a great many (usually inactive) dues
payers. A large number of smallish chapters staffed by a core of activists

could conceivably use the organization's ample resources to accomplish the movement's tasks more effectively.

Even after taking this into consideration, however, we are left with the impression that MADD's mobilization was not commensurate with its rich supply of resources. By 1985, it had organized fewer than four hundred chapters in the whole country, far less than any other group in table 9.1, including the Communist party. But perhaps MADD did not need a large number of chapters either. Since the organization was concerned largely with public education and political lobbying, a few thoughtfully placed chapters in key towns and cities, particularly in seats of legislative action, might be its optimal strategy.[3]

We arrive, then, at a first analytic distinction between conflict and consensus organizations: conflict groups, if for no other reason than that they rely heavily on members for monetary and other resources, must attempt to sustain and enlarge their membership and geographical base. Consensus groups, however, because they can obtain resources elsewhere, are free to pursue strategies that do not involve a large membership or broad organizational presence.

This difference is part of a much larger one. Conflict organizations expect their members to take *committed* actions for the movement. Although this usually involves financial contributions, it is likely also to include large expenditures of time recruiting and maintaining membership, organizing and participating in demonstrations, and—at least for some—risking safety, security, or reputation in militant actions designed to force substantial social change. Consensus movements like MADD and its allies, absorbed as they are in lobbying and other institutionally based activities, make few such demands on members or supporters. This is the principle difference between consensus and conflict movements: *consensus groups need not (and do not) attempt to convert high attitudinal support into a committed and active rank and file.* This distinction—as table 9.1 illustrates—is the key to understanding why the very largest (and most successful) movements in American history have all been conflict-oriented in the extreme. Even the American Communist party—perhaps the quintessential conflict-oriented movement in recent U.S. history—grew much larger and faster than the anti–drunk driving movement in a comparable period of time.

---

3. This argument can be carried only so far. If the lack of effort to expand its membership base were as extreme as we are now suggesting, we could no longer consider MADD a social movement organization at all. Social movements, at the very least, try to mobilize a mass constituency and to utilize that mobilization to accomplish or resist social change. Organizations that do not do this are different creatures, more accurately described perhaps as interest groups. This will be considered at the end of this analysis.

Moreover, we believe that as long as consensus groups rely upon established institutions for nurturance, meet no organized opposition, and operate with a set of goals that displeases no more than 10 or 20 percent of the population, they *cannot* mobilize a large proportion of their supporters, even if they apply substantial resources to this endeavor. Two processes contribute to this incapacity. The first derives from the free-rider problem; the second from the lack of democracy. Although these problems can hamper conflict movements also, they have a particularly strong impact on consensus movements.

THE FREE-RIDER PROBLEM

The support that consensus groups enjoy from established institutions inspires confidence in the legitimacy and future of the movement. In the case of MADD, most people viewed the complex of institutional backers—legislators, police agencies, the media, the alcohol industry—as a sufficient base for initiating the changes necessary to handle the drunk driving problem. In this context, grass-roots organization and participation seemed superfluous. Even those who enthusiastically supported the ultimate goals of the movement did not feel compelled to join.

Such a scenario captures the essence of the free-rider problem. An individual who supports the objectives of a movement nonetheless has no incentive to join: since the individual's efforts will not alter the outcome of movement activities, the individual stands to benefit from movement successes without participating at all (see, e.g., Olson 1965; Fireman and Gamson 1979).

This argument, however, is not sufficient to explain the weak mobilization of consensus movements. It could be made about *every* social movement in table 9.1 (and every other large conflict movement) after it had achieved a certain level of success. Yet, as analyses of conflict movements and similar phenomena have shown, it is precisely at the moment of success—when the free-rider problem should become acute—that people flock in large numbers to participate (see, e.g., Granovetter 1978; Klandermans 1984). This observation allows us to recast the issue into a more analytic framework: why does the promise of success lead to the rapid mobilization of constituents for conflict organizations but to a free-rider reaction for consensus groups?

To answer this, we must understand when and why people *do not* invoke free-rider logic. This has been ably addressed by a number of researchers (e.g., Fireman and Gamson 1979; Klandermans 1984; Ferree, this vol.), but the conceptualization put forth by Fantasia (1988) is particularly illuminating in this context. Fantasia presents ethnographic data that illustrate that union solidarity arises only if two conditions are met: first, that individuals come to accept a newly unfolding group logic and think in terms of what the group *as a whole* can accomplish, and second, that potential members become convinced that movement strategies can actually succeed.

Fantasia argues convincingly that people who join a movement early are those who believe that the *group* can be successful where *individual* efforts have failed; others refrain from joining until convinced that group action is both *necessary* and *viable*. That is, if and when these others come to accept the necessity of group action, then they have cause to believe that their collective fate lies in their collective hands. The most important component in this group logic is the belief that unless large numbers join the group effort, *nobody* will benefit.

In this context each individual must also assess the potential personal losses he or she may incur by joining. This self-reflection does not operate as part of the group logic; it is an *individual* logic that sets the person apart from other members of the group. Hence, an individual could decide, "As a single mother, I cannot risk being away from my children," thus distinguishing her situation from those that other group members face and justifying her refusal to join the movement. Our single mother would not, however, say to an active participant (particularly another single mother), "I'll let you do the work, and I'll take the union wage when and if you win." This would make her a "free-loader," not just a "free-rider," and it would produce negative relationships with other people in the group. In other words, once individuals become part of the group and accept the underlying group logic—that a collective effort would benefit them—the free-rider problem falls away. They cannot deny their membership obligations, even though they may assert unique personal situations that prevent their full participation. Fantasia's study of union organizing confronts the widespread coexistence of individual cost assessment and group obligations, and it raises the key question: when does collective mobilization for a common purpose occur?

The burden of evidence is clear. Individual logic is supplanted by group logic in a context of personal relationships: friendship ties among members activate the obligations of each to the group.

More broadly, free-rider logic can best be overridden when the following four conditions are met:

1. There is an abiding sense of group fate.
2. There is a belief in the viability of group action as a strategy.

3. Individuals cannot distinguish themselves from other group members in terms of their capacity to contribute.
4. Personal ties among group members are sufficiently dense to activate group obligations in the face of free-rider impulses.

Some conflict movements fulfill all four of these conditions and are therefore structurally capable of attracting committed, active constituents. Consensus movements, however, can never fulfill all four conditions and almost inevitably fail on the second and third.

Consider the third criterion, the capacity of an individual to contribute to movement success. In the unions Fantasia studied, each member of the group had not only a more or less equal stake in victory but also a more or less equal capacity to affect the outcome. Strikes, petition campaigns, and demonstrations are basically egalitarian activities. Each individual adds the same quantum of force to the effort, and only a large number of participants can accomplish movement objectives. Although leaders almost always emerge, their value lies largely in their capacity to organize and mobilize the rank and file who do the "basic work"—collecting the signatures, shutting the factory, or disrupting the normal life of the community.

The primary work of consensus organizations, however, is carried out in legislative halls and political offices and in the mass media. Thus, MADD enlisted the aid of police personnel, mayors, and congresspeople who were especially suited to operating in these settings. Ordinary members and potential members had little to offer: they could not frame better legislation than legislators, they could not lobby better than lobbyists, and they had less influence on law enforcement policy than the mayor or police did.

These "capacity-to-contribute" shortcomings are endemic in consensus organizational structure: insofar as a group can enlist a wide array of institutional support, and insofar as its strategy relies primarily on institutional activities, it cannot convince ordinary people that their contribution is valuable or even necessary. Most people will not join such a group, no matter how fervently they support its goals, because they are, quite simply, not needed. This is a basic contradiction in consensus groups: their strength—broad institutional support—becomes their weakness.

A second contradiction derives from the viability criterion (number two above). To see this, we begin with the observation that MADD's efforts may have contributed to the changes in law enforcement between 1978 and 1985. Many states increased the minimum drinking age to twenty-one and levied stiffer criminal penalties and sentences; this led to more arrests and created "a brisk business in the treatment of drunk drivers" (Reinarman 1988, 108). But these successes did not produce a decline in alcohol-related accidents that was decisively beyond the decline that occurred through the 1970s; they were, in a sense, hollow victories.

Other consensus movements also experienced such failures. City twinning, for example, which sprung from the belief that Soviet-American relations could be improved through the establishment of sister-city contacts, was never able to claim an actual victory in improving relations between the superpowers. Indeed, the American military buildup in the 1980s began in the midst of city twinning's greatest popularity.

The absence of concrete signals that an organization's strategies are capable of realizing its goals is a critical problem for all social movements. In fact, highly demonstrable success was central to the sustenance and growth of all the conflict movements in table 9.1. Consider, for example, the AFL-CIO in the 1930s. In Flint, Michigan, in late 1936, the United Auto Workers (led by American Communist party members) called a sixty-day sit-down strike against General Motors, which produced a union contract between the largest corporation in America and a fledgling union that until then had organized no major plant. During the next year, there was an explosion in movement activity—over seven hundred sit-down strikes were staged, most of them successful. Paralleling this was a dramatic expansion in the membership of the CIO, the AFL, and the Communist party (Brecher 1972).

The Flint strike is widely seen as the turning point in the industrial union movement. When this highly publicized strike achieved success, large numbers of industrial workers in the United States became convinced that sit-down strikes would produce success for them as well. Since most of these workers already had a sense of group fate (at least within their factories and communities) and since success depended on the actions of rank-and-file membership—they had to do it themselves.

We maintain that in each of the other cases in table 9.1—and in virtually all successful social movements that have been recorded carefully— notable successes have preceded large increases in membership. For example, the Woman's Christian Temperance Union (WCTU) in 1874, after two decades of lackluster mobilization, mounted a victorious confrontation with local saloons in Hillsboro, Ohio. This sparked 250 successful temperance crusades in the next three months (Rosenthal and Schwartz 1989).

Hence, successful social movements grow at first because they have a compelling argument that their strategy will work. Until they produce success, however, they are in danger of losing this aura of viability. Although successes themselves are not enough for survival (resources are a persistent need), a movement must deliver on at least some of its promises; otherwise, it will not persuade large numbers of people to maintain a commitment to its program of action.

On this measure, both conflict and consensus organizations can be hamstrung by seemingly unworkable strategies. Although consensus groups are indeed structurally prone to such failings, we should not overlook an incontrovertible fact: *most successful conflict movements also experience, at some time or another, major failure as well.* For some, such failure did, in fact, produce movement demise (e.g., the 1960s student movements after the killings at Kent State and Jackson State). For others, it produced a decline that eventually led to new life (e.g., the labor movement in the early 1930s). For still others, failure barely set in before giving way to renewed vigor and intensified recruitment of committed members (e.g., the Southern Farmers' Alliance after the failure of the Alliance Exchange).

Initial failure, therefore, does not inevitably bring about the end of the movement. We argue that consensus organizations, however, differ sharply from conflict groups in their capacity to deal with failure. We turn now to a discussion of democracy; it is the ingredient critical to movement dynamics if strategic failure is to be a precursor to renewed vigor and success.

NEED FOR DEMOCRACY IN THE FACE OF FAILURE

The burden of evidence from social movement history suggests that the key to survival after failure is the creation of new programs and strategies that encompass the lessons learned from past defeats (Schwartz 1976; Rosenthal and Schwartz 1989). This implies the need for both a degree of flexibility and a capacity to communicate the new strategies to the rank and file, who perhaps will decide that the proposed new direction offers potential for success and will renew their commitment to the movement.

Conflict organizations are far more capable than consensus groups of creating and sustaining these processes. Consider, for example, the Southern Farmers' Alliance. It experienced tremendous growth in Texas, organizing around the initial success of the Farmers' Alliance Exchange. But when the Exchange began to fail, a debate over strategy raged within the movement. The result was a new strategy and a national organizing drive that successfully extended the group throughout the South. We maintain that it was the debate within the organization that was the critical link between the failure of the Exchange and the success of future organizing; it allowed for a thoughtful redirection of the movement toward promising new strategies to address the problems that had produced past failures (Schwartz 1976; Schwartz et al. 1981; Barnes 1987).

No comparable processes can occur in consensus movements. Consider the case of MADD once again. In 1984 and 1985 the anti–drunk driving campaign—with MADD acknowledged as its leader—was still making major headlines, but its rate of growth by chapter had begun to decline precipitously. Although it is possible that MADD's limited need for chapters contributed to this decline, there is considerable evidence that disaffection with its philosophy and tactics arose among anti–drunk driving activists. A number of local chapter leaders, for example, disaffiliated from MADD in the mid-1980s and affiliated with RID, a group that had less than .2 percent of the operating budget of MADD. Efforts by RID had included a campaign to remove alcohol advertising from the mass media. Such a strategy was eschewed by MADD because it would have antagonized both the liquor industry and the mass media, two of its most powerful institutional supports.

A shift in strategy, however, might have kept MADD's ranks from thinning. Without arguing that RID's approach would have succeeded (either in producing movement growth or in decreasing drunk driving), the absence of a change in tactics by MADD illustrates how the broad structural support for consensus movements can limit their strategic repertoire. And the experience of RID in pursuing this strategy deepens our understanding of these constraints: it was boycotted by the mass media. Because it had no alternative method of reaching potential members, it also suffered an organizing drought (McCarthy and Wolfson 1988, 29).

The structural constraints of consensus movements thus create strategic rigidity that limits their capacity to adopt new goals and tactics in light of negative experiences. Conflict movements, in contrast, may not experience the same incapacitating constraints, since they may have few, if any, institutional backers to antagonize. The example of the Communist party is particularly useful in this context. In its early years it received no institutional aid and no useful publicity from the mass media. By the 1930s (because of its limited but promising early success), it had developed an organizational infrastructure that could bring its message to potential members without the mediation of major American institutions. It could therefore advocate and adopt militant organizing tactics (like the sit-down strike) without fear of losing institutional support. The success, in turn, of these militant tactics in the 1930s laid a foundation for its rapid growth. The civil rights movement is another example of the same phenomenon. As Morris (e.g., 1984) has shown, the capacity of movement centers to communicate directly with each other was more critical to the spread of the sit-ins and other movement strategies than was the vast publicity of the mass media.

Independence from the media and other institutions conferred upon both the Communist party and the civil rights movement a degree of flexibility unavailable to MADD and RID or to other consensus groups. If a strategy can potentially antagonize powerful institutions, the price of adopting it is much greater if the movement cannot communicate or function without them. It must then choose between abandoning the strategy or weakening its organizing efforts.

During periods of crisis, when the capacity to consider the broadest strategic repertoire becomes critical, systematic constraints imposed by outside institutions greatly inhibit internal democracy. Insofar as promising strategies are incompatible with the needs or desires of supporting institutions, the social movement organization will find it difficult to explore potential options, regardless of its interest in doing so. When failure threatens retention and recruitment, such constraints often do more than simply limit available choices: they may antagonize members and supporters who perceive these limitations as proof that the whole enterprise is doomed by its incapacity (or unwillingness) to consider those options with a real chance of success.

It is true that such constraints also inhibit conflict movements. Virtually every organization in table 9.1 established a variety of encumbering relationships with outside institutions (including even the Communist party, which relied on the CIO). The AFL-CIO, for example, came to rely on the National Labor Relations Board and other sanctioning institutions; this led to the elimination of secondary strikes and a range of other tactics from its strategic repertoire (see, e.g., McDonough 1989).

Nevertheless, the very nature of consensus groups maximizes the number and power of these external constraints and therefore maximizes the number of excluded options for social action. Although many conflict groups have severely limited capacity to embrace new strategies, *all* consensus groups suffer from this handicap.

DYNAMICS OF CHANGE IN CONSENSUS MOVEMENTS

The concepts "consensus movements" and "conflict movements" are ideal-typical representations of two broad tendencies in the arena of social activism, but there is no discrete boundary between them. We are actually dealing with a continuum, one extreme of which is occupied by organizations that are relatively unencumbered and usually resource-poor and the other, by organizations that are highly encumbered and often resource-rich. Conflict groups tend to begin and remain in the unencumbered, resource-poor quadrant, though some may migrate from one location to another within the quadrant, and others, but not many, may move far into the high-encumbrance, resource-rich region.

Consensus groups *by their very nature* begin life in the highly encumbered and resource-rich quadrant, which few conflict groups ever come to occupy. As a result, they are trapped by the constraints of outside institutions and therefore will almost always be strategically rigid. This leaves them poorly equipped to respond to frustration and failure. Their prognosis for success over the course of series of campaigns in a changing environment will therefore be poor. In the end, this incapacity will make it difficult to sustain membership commitment.

Under some circumstances, however, consensus movements migrate away from outside constraint toward self-reliance, particularly under concerted pressure from a frustrated but still loyal membership. This was indeed the hope of a substantial portion of the leadership of the city twinning movement, for whom the primary purpose was to educate participants to undertake a political challenge to American nuclear and military policies. These efforts to develop a conflict strategy within a consensus framework failed; as Lofland (1989, 168) notes, these leaders, who had been "a major force in starting city twinning, [were] the least happy with what it became."

This example allows us to glimpse the possible circumstances for a successful migration along the constraint continuum. City twinning would have had to overcome a formidable string of obstacles in order to become a conflict movement: it would have had to rid itself of its dependency on business and government support, cultivate sources of funds that endorsed an attack on American military policy, develop a communication network that could carry a counterinstitutional message, and engage its members in a dense, interpersonal network of egalitarian activities that would trigger both a sense of group fate and faith in the viability of group action.

The discussion to now has addressed some of the difficulties created by the sudden lack of institutional support. Now we shall address a second problem, the process of involving consensus movement constituents in new, conflict-based activities.

An observation from city twinning is illuminating here: when it was suggested to city-twinners that their efforts could be viewed "as building blocks for alternative worldviews," Lofland reports several instances of "distress" at the thought that they might be seen as challenging "state ideology" (1989, 187). This suggests that a consensus movement, by attracting people who favor a nonpolitical, noncontroversial approach to social activism, builds its own internal barriers to the adoption of new strategies—barriers that exist in addition to the constraints imposed by outside institutions. The initial ideological stance of the members is, in a sense, structurally determined; only those who believe in the existing strategy will join.

This nonconflictual ideology is not necessarily permanent. Many social movement theorists (e.g., Schwartz 1976; Klandermans 1984; Fantasia 1988) have commented on the circumstances under which movement leaders and participants come to endorse new ideas. The most convincing of these analyses point to the presence of a dense network of personal ties and a strong sense of group identity as essential to such changes. But here again the very virtues of consensus organizations work against them. Consensus groups, by not requiring either heavy time commitments or intense interpersonal association from their members, do not lay a foundation for group-motivated changes in ideology.

Although more research is needed to understand the specific processes triggered by the setbacks experienced by consensus groups, we conclude that migration toward the conflict-mobilization approach is at least unusual. It is clear, however, that such groups face an enduring problem of holding the members they initially attract. Even those who continue to endorse an institutional-resource-dependent, nonconflictual strategy have ample impetus to depart or become inactive. Beyond the impact of free-rider logic lies the demoralization derived from defeats or hollow victories (such as the anti–drunk driving movement's failure to reduce drunk driving). Hence, there are strong tendencies for a decline in size of or participation among the existing membership.

All this suggests an illuminating comparison between consensus organizations and another type of social-activism vehicle—interest groups.[4] Unlike a social movement, which attempts to mobilize large numbers of people to directly effect social change, an interest group centers around a set of paid organizers who seek to accomplish social change through direct contact with the institutional leaders responsible for policy. The two key factors that distinguish interest groups are:

1. Interest groups *always* work with institutionally mandated authorities and follow prescribed institutional procedures for accomplishing their goal. Social movements may do this, but they may also break rules and disrupt normal processes in an effort to achieve their end.

2. Interest groups may call upon their constituency for active support, but their predominant (and perhaps exclusive) modus operandi is interaction between group leaders and responsible officials. Social

4. We thank Aldon Morris for suggesting this line of argument.

movements rely in some way on mass mobilization of their constituency to accomplish their goals, though membership action may be as moderate as petition signing.

Interest groups, because their structural locus resides in leadership and in interinstitutional negotiation, do not respond to failure by mobilizing mass protest. This not only would be difficult to organize—given the normal structure of such groups—but would also disrupt most ongoing lobbying activities, which cannot be conducted in the adversarial context normally created by protest movements.

Although here again there is no clear boundary between the two types, consensus groups show a stronger tendency to evolve into interest groups. Organizations like MADD and city twinning, with their bases of support in and funds flowing from established institutions, have immediate access to the authorities capable of addressing their objectives. They can accomplish this without mobilizing a large constituency or laboring to create democratic processes of decision making. Membership action is not central to the organization's strategic plan. Even initially, these groups have difficulty attracting membership commensurate with their resources, since the free-rider problem creates a daunting barrier to mobilization. But even modest membership is difficult to sustain, since the inevitable middle-range defeats are not redressed through the sort of democratic processes that forestall demoralization and declining participation. In this context, leaders are forced to rely even more on the organization's institutional backers and to develop strategies that will not jeopardize ties to established authority. This not only further constrains the group; it further reduces the incentive to participate in its activities. The logical consequence of this cycle is a classic interest group that relies exclusively on direct connections to policymakers and not at all on large-scale mobilization.

REFERENCES

Adelson, Alan. 1972. *SDS.* New York: Scribner's.

Barnes, Donna. 1987. "Strategy Outcome and the Growth of Protest Organizations: A Case Study of the Southern Farmers' Alliance." *Rural Sociology* 52:165–86.

Brecher, Jeremy. 1972. *Strike!* Boston: South End Press.

Fantasia, Rick. 1988. *Cultures of Solidarity: Consciousness, Action, and Contemporary American Workers.* Berkeley: University of California Press.

Fireman, Bruce, and William Gamson. 1979. "Utilitarian Logic in the Resource Mobilization Perspective." In *The Dynamics of Social Movements,* ed. M. N. Zald and J. D. McCarthy. Cambridge, Mass.: Winthrop, 8–44.

Granovetter, Mark. 1978. "Threshold Models of Collective Behavior." *American Journal of Sociology* 83:1420–43.

Klandermans, Bert. 1984. "Mobilization and Participation: Social-Psychological Expansions of Resource Mobilization Theory." *American Sociological Review* 49: 583–600.

Lofland, John. 1989. "Consensus Movements: City Twinning and Derailed Dissent in the American Eighties." In *Research in Social Movements: Conflict and Change*, vol. 11. Greenwich, Conn.: JAI Press, 163–96.

McCarthy, John D., David W. Britt, and Mark Wolfson. 1991. "The Institutional Channeling of Social Movements in the Modern State." In *Research in Social Movements: Conflict and Change* 13:45–76.

McCarthy, John, and Mark Wolfson. 1988. "Exploring Sources of Rapid Social Movement Growth: The Role of Organizational Form, Consensus Support, and Elements of the American State." Paper presented at the workshop on Frontiers in Social Movement Theory, Ann Arbor, June 8–10.

McCarthy, John D., Mark Wolfson, and Debra Harvey. 1987. "Chapter Survey Report: Project on the Citizens' Movement against Drunk Driving." Washington, D.C.: Center for the Study of Youth Development, Catholic University of America.

McCarthy, John D., and Mayer N. Zald. 1973. *The Trend of Social Movements in America: Professionalization and Resource Mobilization*. Morristown, N.J.: General Learning Press.

———. 1977. "Resource Mobilization and Social Movements: A Partial Theory." *American Journal of Sociology* 82:1212–41.

McDonough, Terrence John. 1989. "The Construction of Social Structures of Accumulation: The Resolution of Economic Crisis in American History." Ph.D. diss., Department of Economics, University of Massachusetts, Amherst.

Morris, Aldon D. 1981. "The Black Southern Sit-In Movement: An Analysis of Internal Organization." *American Sociological Review* 46:744–67.

———. 1984. *The Origins of the Civil Rights Movement*. New York: Free Press.

Olson, Mancur. 1965. *The Logic of Collective Action*. Cambridge, Mass.: Harvard University Press.

Reinarman, Craig. 1988. "The Social Construction of an Alcohol Problem: The Case of Mothers Against Drunk Driving and Social Control in the 1980s." *Theory and Society* 17, no. 1:91–120.

Rosenthal, Naomi, and Michael Schwartz. 1989. "Spontaneity and Democracy in Social Movements." In *Organizing for Change: Social Movement Organizations in Europe and the United States*, ed. Bert Klandermans. International Social Movement Research, vol. 2. Greenwich, Conn.: JAI Press, 33–59.

Sale, Kirkpatrick. 1973. *SDS*. New York: Random House.

Schwartz, Michael. 1976. *Radical Protest and Social Structure: The Southern Farmers' Alliance and Cotton Tenancy, 1880–1890*. New York: Academic Press.

Schwartz, Michael, Naomi Rosenthal, and L. Schwartz. 1981. "Leader-Member Conflict in Protest Organizations: The Case of the Southern Farmers' Alliance." *Social Problems* 29:22–36.

Staggenborg, Suzanne. 1988. "The Consequences of Professionalization and Formalization in the Pro-Choice Movement." *American Sociological Review* 53:585–605.

10

Communities of Challengers
in Social Movement Theory

Clarence Y. H. Lo

During the past two decades resource mobilization theory, in particular the work of John McCarthy and Mayer Zald, has become the leading paradigm used to analyze social movements. McCarthy and Zald have emphasized how contemporary movements have become large-scale organizations that gather economic resources, compete with one another, and interact with other organizations much as large business firms do. Many social movement organizations utilize a professionalized bureaucracy to sell memberships to a mass market of isolated consumers. Thus, McCarthy and Zald theorize about recent social movements by applying concepts that have been used to describe advanced capitalist economies.

In this chapter, I contend that McCarthy and Zald have based their theorizing on the latter stages of social movements that have been accepted as regular participants in the political system. What needs more attention are the political challengers who had to resort to protest and disruption in order to gain any influence with government. These political challengers mobilize resources using processes much different from the market-managerial mechanisms described by McCarthy and Zald. In order to break into the polity, challengers do not need membership dues from a mass audience; rather, they need substantial personal commitments from a limited group for a specific conflict. I argue that challengers tend to get their resources not from market exchanges but from commitments embedded in the social relations of a community.

My arguments build upon variants of the resource mobilization approach other than McCarthy and Zald's and are part of a more general

I wish to thank the editors of this volume and John McCarthy for their detailed comments and encouragement.

call to understand social movements by using historical approaches emphasizing the origins and development of movements. Historical studies have shown that in communal settings, artisans and other small-scale producers arose in protests that shaped key features of the modern world—the kinds of social classes formed, their consciousness, and the political representation they won. I suggest that concepts derived from historical research can be revised so as to contribute to theories about recent social movements. The challengers of today, like those of the past, also mobilize in communities, but now in communities of consumers rather than the small-scale producers of old. Today, the contention for power in communities still shapes the challengers' aims and ideologies and their very consciousness of inequality and class.

In short, I argue that theorizing about recent social movements could benefit from a historical approach that utilizes the concepts of challengers, community, and early capitalism as a counterweight to the present emphasis on polity members, market organization, and late capitalism. I begin in the next section with the premise that social movement theory should focus on political challengers. This was, after all, the agenda of classical social movements research, which developed theories about insurgency distinct from theories of conventional politics. Resource mobilization theory sought to explain both challengers *and* conventional politics. McCarthy and Zald analyzed movements that had become members of the polity. They then developed a variant of resource mobilization theory with a characteristic (and problematic) imagery of the advanced capitalist economy.

SOCIAL MOVEMENTS
AND CONVENTIONAL POLITICS COMPARED

In the early 1960s, social scientists developed separate analyses for social movements and for conventional politics. Theories of social movements were based on studies of revolutions, protests, and other non-institutionalized events, such as riots, fads, and panics, in contrast to more routine political activities, such as interest group lobbying.

Smelser's theorizing about unconventional collective behavior emphasized how it differs from routine behavior. Collective behavior, short-circuiting the routine small and gradual adjustments, is a drastic action to change society. According to Smelser (1962, 8), a major defining characteristic of collective behavior is that "it is not institutionalized behavior. According to the degree to which it becomes institutionalized, it loses its distinctive character." Other leading scholars of the period also contrasted social movements to institutions that slowly implement change. Although Turner and Killian (1972, 252, 404) recognized that some movements eventually solidify into institutions, they emphasized that social movements undergo frequent changes—the turnover of membership, the succession of leaders, and the formulation of new beliefs.

These "classical" theories, which had been built around the distinction between social movements and institutionalized groups, were criticized by the scholars of the 1970s. For example, Gamson (1975) argued that revolutions could be studied using the same approaches that had been used to analyze interest group activity. Both a rebellion and a business association, according to Gamson, develop political goals, devise means to accomplish goals, and sometimes make mistakes. The 1970s critics condemned the notion that participants in protest movements are irrational, disturbed, or alienated individuals. The critics sought to uphold political protesters as reasonable, sociable citizens. Oberschall (1973) argued that protesters deciding to commit themselves to a movement are comparable to ordinary people making economic decisions about working or spending money.

Thus, the resource mobilization approach began with the premise that the same general model of human behavior could be used to analyze both protests and conventional politics. Some researchers went further and attempted to build a common theory of collective action that would apply to both protests and routine politics. Tilly, for example, linked protests and institutionalized politics in a theory of historical development. In his book *From Mobilization to Revolution*, Tilly (1978) applied the concepts of interests, opportunity, and threat to both revolutions and orderly electoral campaigns, and to both violent strikes and the institutionalized collective bargaining that later evolved.

MOVEMENT INTEREST GROUPS
AND ECONOMISTIC CONCEPTS

The important work of McCarthy and Zald (1973, 1977) has sought to develop a common theory of social movements and conventional politics, emphasizing that movements have come to resemble bureaucratized interest groups. McCarthy and Zald utilize concepts that have been devised to analyze contemporary business corporations, and they apply economistic analogies to social movements.

McCarthy and Zald focus on movement organizations that by the mid-1970s had evolved into interest groups, such as Common Cause, the National Association for the Advancement of Colored People (NAACP), the American Civil Liberties Union, the National Organization for Women

(NOW), the Sierra Club, and Ralph Nader's Public Interest Research Group (McAdam 1982, 25). These formally structured *movement interest groups* wield influence by lobbying public officials, preparing reports, and shaping public opinion. In order to raise money, interest groups solicit funds in nationally directed campaigns and utilize the latest advertising techniques, computer technology, and professional fund-raising strategies.

Movement interest groups, in short, rely on contributions of money. For many of these groups, the contributors are individuals scattered throughout the nation. Most of the members of interest groups with such an "isolated structure," rather than being tied into locally based chapters, receive mail solicitations directly from the national office (McCarthy and Zald 1977, 1227). Mobilizing contributions from isolated constituents entails collecting a resource, money, that is readily exchangeable because it is a universal measure and store of value. With this conceptualization of resource mobilization as a market exchange, McCarthy and Zald then make use of concepts borrowed from economic theory (Perrow 1979, 201).

For McCarthy and Zald (1977, 1230), the potential members of a movement interest group are consumers in a market. They are portrayed as making individual consumer choices about whether to have a fish dinner, buy a new fishing lure, or join the National Wildlife Federation. To analyze the buying of interest group memberships, McCarthy and Zald use an economic model of consumer purchases of competing products, highlighting such factors as discretionary personal income, advertising, and name recognition. Consumer demand for an interest group's memberships can be analyzed as a function of membership price. Just as consumer loyalty to a product makes for more inelastic demand, so too loyal members will still join despite high dues. In movements as well as markets, there is "the possibility of offering slight changes in products in order to capture some of the increased potential market" (Zald and McCarthy 1980, 7).

According to McCarthy and Zald, members are "consumers," and hence movement leaders are "managers" selling a product in competition with other interest groups. Movement organizations with the same general goals compete to obtain money from adherents. Interest group managers exercise their skills in manipulating images through the mass media. And just as conglomerate corporations diversify to remain competitive, movement interest groups, so the argument goes, introduce "new product lines"—additional campaigns and causes. For example, Ralph Nader's groups took on the issues of nuclear power and tax reform in addition to auto safety and gained a better "market position" among competitors.

McCarthy and Zald continue using the metaphors of advanced, bureaucratic capitalism to describe the relations between movement interest groups and larger trends in society. Just as individual business firms are grouped together into an *industry* selling similar products and are further aggregated into a *sector* of the economy, McCarthy and Zald (1977, 1219) aggregate movement organizations into a "social movement industry" (SMI) sharing similar goals and combine industries into the "social movement sector," consisting of all SMIs in a society. Zald and McCarthy (1980, 12, 18) propose that a social movement industry can be analyzed like an industry in the economy. One can study the interlocks between boards of directors of movements and "the differences in industry structure—the number, size, and market locations of SMOs [social movement organizations] in an industry." Competing corporations develop industry structures whereby some firms dominate a market and others develop specialized niches; similarly, social movement organizations produce changing patterns of dominance and differentiation (see Zald, this vol.). Large corporate organizations are closely interrelated with government agencies, spending, and policies; so too, social movement organizations obtain aid and encouragement from the government (McCarthy and Zald 1973).

McCarthy and Zald argued in two articles in 1973 and 1977 that the market-managerial mode of resource mobilization—the solicitation of scattered supporters by advertising and direct mail—caused much of the upsurge of social movement activity in the 1960s (1977, 1228). But a 1987 article by McCarthy questions whether such mobilizations of isolated members have been as effective as previously thought. He notes that the prochoice movement weakened because of its reliance on solicitations of isolated supporters—its "infrastructure deficit." McCarthy traces the strength of the opposing right-to-life movement to a dense network of local infrastructures—the church congregations, Catholic schools, and chapters of the Knights of Columbus that have organized fund-raisers and demonstrations. Although some parts of the right-to-life movement rely on computer-generated mailings, the main strength of the movement is its fifteen hundred community-based "right-to-life committees," which claim a total membership of around eleven million (McCarthy 1987, 52–53).

Going further than McCarthy's refinements, I develop below two major criticisms of the McCarthy-Zald model: its theory of the structures of resource mobilization and its political sociology.[1] I will extend McCarthy's notion of thick infrastructure and argue that a major modification of resource mobilization theory is needed to conceptualize the significant flows

---

1. The criticisms of McCarthy and Zald in this chapter are meant to apply only to the specific works cited and are not meant to characterize the work of either author as a whole.

of resources from communal rather than associative or market settings. In the movements of the 1960s and other eras, a key resource was not so much money or other exchangeables from markets but rather a community's willingness to participate in disruptive activities.

This particularly holds true for an important category of movements, political challengers, who receive neither recognition nor advantages from authorities. According to an article by Zald (1987), however, challengers are rare in economically developed societies. He comes to this startling conclusion by way of his and McCarthy's earlier arguments that movement interest groups have proliferated in the United States. Rising personal incomes give individuals the discretionary funds to buy memberships in movement interest groups. Increased numbers of professional workers provide movements with skilled volunteers with flexible time schedules. McCarthy and Zald argue that in the era of advanced capitalism, large organizations and government bureaus multiply funding opportunities for movements.

Zald (1987) goes further to note that movements have arisen to defend, as a matter of conscience, the interests of even the politically weakest of groups—whales, dogs, and laboratory animals. Among humans, political rights have become so widespread that any group can publicly raise its issues as a member of the polity. Thus, Zald concludes that "diverse interests are easily and continuously represented. . . . This is an assertion that basic access to the polity of societal members is easily achieved. . . . The issue of political rights, however, has been central to a[nother] perspective on social movements that sees them as arising, in a sense, by societal members *outside* of the polity" (1987, 321, 329, 336). This chapter supports such a perspective.

In contrast to Zald's view that movements easily become polity members, I argue in the next section that theory now needs to focus on the numerous movements who were or still are excluded from the polity. For these challengers, McCarthy and Zald's economistic analysis is inappropriate. Challengers obtain resources not from transactions in a market but from actions embedded in the social relationships of a community. Rather than analyzing challengers in terms of the concepts of "industrial structure" and "professional management" borrowed from studies of advanced capitalism, the theorist can usefully turn to concepts derived from an earlier era—when petty capitalism prevailed and artisans in villages confronted the newly expanding state.

But today, are there any political challengers in democratic societies? Or is the concept of "challenger" useful only for the conflicts of the last century, when the lower classes were truly deprived of their rights?

BRINGING THE CHALLENGERS BACK IN

Challengers can be contrasted to established interest groups such as the American Medical Association, which can be termed *polity members*. Members of the polity regularly consult with governmental authorities, and they routinely provide input into decision-making bodies and have some effect on the policies adopted. As Tilly (1978, 52–54, 117) defines it, polity members have a high rate of return in their dealings with government, expending few resources to gain influence and win large benefits. Tilly argues that there is a sharp distinction between polity members and the challengers who lack access, win few advantages, and, in short, have much less power.

Challengers become members of the polity only when they have gained *acceptance* and have won new *advantages*. Following Gamson's (1975, 28–37) definitions, I argue that acceptance of a movement occurs when any one of its antagonists recognizes the movement, appoints its leaders to official positions, or consults with or negotiates with the movement. Movements win advantages when they gain significant concessions, partly fulfilling at least one of the movement's goals (even if nothing is gained for other goals). Challengers, in contrast, are mobilizing to enter the polity but have gained neither acceptance nor advantages.

Gamson's research into social movements in the United States before 1945 uncovered thousands of challenging movements, a sizable minority of which ceased to exist without ever entering the polity. But more recently, has polity membership been granted to practically all groups, as Zald contends? As individuals, of course, American citizens enjoy political rights such as the franchise. The polity, however, is best conceptualized not as isolated individuals with abstract rights but as political groups competing for recognition and limited government resources. Although an individual has the civil liberty to express an opinion, the person might also be a member of a challenging group, which cannot win regular consultations or concessions and is therefore not a polity member. Tilly emphasizes that polity members are not only tolerated and granted civil liberties; they have significantly greater power than challengers, "and power itself consists of a group's making its interests prevail over others." To be a polity member, a group must sometimes win roll-call votes in Parliament, say, or affect the expenditures of government (Tilly 1978, 125–33).[2]

A challenger can obtain an invitation to speak at a House subcommittee

---

2. Adopting Tilly's definition of the polity, Zald's views about widespread political rights would be translated not as "Most groups are polity members" but as "Most groups

hearing. But an infrequent presentation, granted through a maverick congressional representative or arranged to round out the views on a panel, is not the same as the established pattern of consultations a polity member enjoys. Furthermore, even though the nuclear freeze campaign succeeded in winning advisory referenda in seven states, the freeze movement never became a polity member because it was never taken seriously by Reagan administration officials. Independent of the movement's efforts, the administration concluded a missile treaty with the Soviet Union, a policy change in a direction sought by freeze advocates. In a case like this, when events other than a movement's campaigning lead to policies favored by the movement but when the movement itself never wins consultations with authorities, the movement can be called a "preempted challenger."

More difficult to fulfill is the second criterion for polity membership—winning advantages and favorable policy decisions. The Clamshell Alliance and the Abalone Alliance (who opposed nuclear power plants at Seabrook, New Hampshire, and at Diablo Canyon, California) did not become members of the polity because the plants became operational and no significant concessions were made. Environmental groups like the New England Coalition on Nuclear Pollution can be termed "recognized challengers" because even though they did not win advantages, they were formally accepted as intervenors presenting expert testimony before the Nuclear Regulatory Commission.

Particularly in the federal government arena, few challengers become polity members, as noted by theories that emphasize the selectivity of policy-making. Schattschneider (1960), for example, conceptualizes the political system as a series of filters that exclude possibilities and narrow down options into agendas and more specific policies. To make policy is to reject many alternatives and the groups that advocate them. Foreign and defense policy in the executive branch, especially, is an elitist and secretive process on which the demands of challengers have little impact.

In short, I have developed a typology of social movements that distinguishes between movements that are challengers and movements that have become members of the polity (see table 10.1). Movements also vary as to the types of social relations that mobilize resources, as I will argue in the following section. I will distinguish between movements that mostly gain resources from a staff soliciting a market, and movements that mostly obtain resources from ongoing relationships in a community. McCarthy and Zald argue that most social movements can now be categorized in

---

are contenders." Zald (1987, 321, 336) does recognize that some contenders have little power (McCarthy and Zald 1977, 1226).

TABLE 10.1
Polity Membership by Social Movement Organization

| | TYPE OF RESOURCE MOBILIZATION | |
	market-managerial	communal
polity members	1. movement interest groups: NAACP, environmental lobbying groups, NOW, Common Cause, ACLU	2. community action: antibusing movements
challengers	3. challengers with isolated adherents: nuclear freeze (preempted challenger), intervenors against nuclear power (recognized challenger)	4. communal protests: urban social movements, environmental protests

box 1 in table 10.2 because the trend of social movements in the United States (see dotted line) is resource acquisition from professionally managed appeals to isolated constituents.

Highlighting an important trend of the time, McCarthy and Zald's papers in 1973 and 1977 provided insights into the leftist movements of the 1960s, which evolved into the lobbying organizations of the 1970s. A longer historical perspective, however, can build a more comprehensive theory of power and resources in social movements. True enough, polity members are numerous in the advanced capitalist democracies; some challengers do indeed become polity members. But the polity does not develop in a unilinear trend toward all-inclusive membership (or market-managerial resource mobilization); rather, political groups display diverse and complex patterns of evolution that involve exiting as well as entering the polity at different times.

For decades, a movement can consist of both challengers and polity members. The radical feminist movement coexists with established women's organizations, and direct-action environmental protests with groups lobbying for conservation. Political challengers sometimes receive direct support from more established polity members, as exemplified by the NAACP's support of civil rights protesters. Although some movements quickly evolve into polity members, they can nonetheless revert to being challengers later. For example, the right-to-life movement by the late 1980s had developed many recognized and influential national organizations; nevertheless, a militant fraction, Operation Rescue, attempted to disrupt abortion clinics. Gaining neither consultations nor changes in

TABLE 10.2
Evolutionary Paths for Social Movements

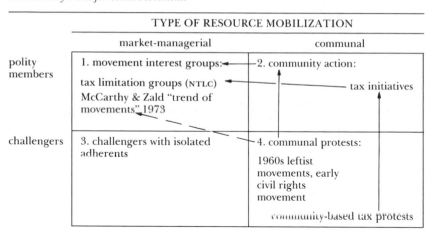

	TYPE OF RESOURCE MOBILIZATION	
	market-managerial	communal
polity members	1. movement interest groups:◄─────2. community action: tax limitation groups (NTLC) ◄──────── tax initiatives McCarthy & Zald "trend of movements" 1973	
challengers	3. challengers with isolated adherents	4. communal protests: 1960s leftist movements, early civil rights movement community-based tax protests

policy, Operation Rescue instead met with a repressive response—arrests and lawsuits. Moves toward polity membership can spark a conscious countertrend. When a few leaders in the Ku Klux Klan decided to run for elective offices and claim respectability, dissenting leaders broke away and formed sects emphasizing imminent racial war, military training and weapons stockpiling, and violent racial confrontations.

Before they first became polity members, many movements spent long years as challengers, totally excluded from the polity and denied even the most fundamental citizenship rights. Before the 1960s, southern blacks were prevented from registering and voting; those younger than age twenty-one did not have the right to vote. But even with the possession of voting rights, some groups still faced major barriers to government access. Although white, middle-class property owners thought of themselves as upstanding citizens who deserved to have government solve their problems, they were outside the polity when they formed movements such as the property tax revolt. Government repeatedly ignored their protests, despite growing militancy.

For example, in suburban Cook County near Chicago in the late 1970s, hundreds of homeowners flocked to community meetings to denounce increased property assessments; some sixty thousand joined a tax strike and refused to pay their taxes. Southern Californian suburbanites had been protesting property taxes since the 1950s. During a period of only thirty days in 1957, sixteen thousand protesters attended mass meetings throughout Los Angeles County. Representatives from thirty-six communities formed a coalition to recall the county assessor. In 1966 as property tax bills continued their steep climb, angry homeowners attended twenty-five mass meetings throughout southern California and organized a tax strike. Fourteen communities, including many in the San Fernando Valley where property tax bills had doubled, erupted in the protests of 1976 that drew twelve thousand to meetings in just one month's time (Lo 1990).

For decades, government failed to meet demands to lower tax bills, and tax protesters remained challengers. Although an individual had the right to appeal a tax bill, the county assessor had little discretion to lower appraisals, because assessments were pegged to current market values and these were rapidly rising. After the protests of 1957 in Los Angeles, officials formed two study committees and declared a temporary hiring freeze. The activists in 1966, however, gained nothing, and in 1976 they won only a seventy-dollar per household tax reduction. Politicians, interested as they were in keeping their budgets growing, were unwilling to make the changes the protesters demanded.

In short, after World War II many political groups in the United States continued as challengers or became challengers. Some of them, in accord with McCarthy and Zald's trend of social movements, mobilized resources through market-managerial modes and became recognized interest groups. (Other market-managerial mobilizers, like the nuclear freeze referenda campaigns or the movement to teach creationism in public schools, still remain outside the polity; see box 3 in table 10.1.) McCarthy and Zald's theory, however, does not adequately analyze the civil rights movement, urban social movements, and the student movement, which fought to enter the polity and in some cases succeeded *because of* protests based in communities (see solid arrows in box 4 in table 10.2).

For example, recent research has shown that the civil rights movement won early key victories by using indigenous resources from the black community. Only after these initial successes did funds begin to flow from largely white institutions such as foundations, churches, businesses (Morris 1984), and the War on Poverty and VISTA programs of the federal government, and only later did some civil rights groups successfully solicit large numbers of individual white sympathizers.

The tax revolt is another example of a movement that turns to market-managerial resource strategies after it wins key victories using communal resources. The revolt achieved national prominence after 1978, when voters in California by a two-to-one margin passed Proposition 13 and slashed their property taxes. But up to the time that 1.5 million signatures were gathered to place the proposition on the ballot, the movement in California had no paid staff and no professional managers. The tax revolt and many other social movements, as I argue below, became polity members by mobilizing contributions from communal rather than market ties (boxes 2 and 4 in table 10.2). Only after 1978 did the National Tax Limitation Committee (NTLC) emerge, which solicited contributions from sympathetic business elites and isolated constituents, in accord with the McCarthy and Zald market-managerial model (see box 1 in table 10.2). Lacking local chapters, the NTLC contacted donors by utilizing three public relations firms and computerized mailings totaling tens of millions of pieces annually (Lo 1990, 193).

Let us turn now to the movements in box 4 of tables 10.1 and 10.2. What tactics did they resort to, and what kinds of resources were needed to sustain these tactics?

Protest Tactics and Communal Resources

Challengers attempt to fight their way into the polity by using unconventional tactics. They show their unity of purpose through demonstrations and assemblies. They stop their normal routines of life—refusing to work, pay rent, buy goods, pay taxes, or serve in the military—and try to hold out until the authorities capitulate. They may seek to disrupt the activities of others, making them unable to transact business. To undertake these protests, a challenger needs types of resources quite different from the twenty-five dollars for membership dues that interest groups thrive on.

A challenger usually depends more on communal resources compared with market-managerial resources (McCarthy and Zald 1977, 1228). McCarthy and Zald make it clear that the central tendency for contemporary social movements is the market-managerial model. I contend, however, that another ideal-type model, that of communal resources, needs to be elaborated. These two models—not just the market-managerial model—define the range of variation among contemporary social movements. Between the poles of 100 percent market-managerial resources and 100 percent communal resources is a continuum along which particular movements evolve and change.

For example, the Committee in Solidarity with the People of El Salvador (CISPES) consisted mostly of decentralized local groups. Utilizing community resources, CISPES chapters organized demonstrations supporting leftist movements in Central America and protesting speeches by U.S. government officials. Later in its history, however, CISPES organized national fund-raising campaigns; a related group, the National Sanctuary Defense Fund, raised over $2 million through mass solicitations (Gosse 1988, 25, 36, 40).

Whereas a movement interest group solicits great numbers of geographically dispersed donors for small individual monetary contributions to a general cause, a challenger usually seeks more resources from a *limited group,* mobilizing *substantial personal commitments* for a *specific conflict.* Since challengers do not obtain much favorable publicity in the national media at first, they are unable to tap mass markets for contributions, so they are forced to rely on localized constituencies. Even when they are protesting conditions and trends of national scope, typically these larger issues first become salient through a localized conflict. The issue of toxic chemical pollution, for example, was first dramatized by the Love Canal Homeowners Association, a group representing eight hundred families in a community near Buffalo, New York.

Protest actions require participants to give much to the movement. The jailings, beatings, and murder that activists risked in the early years of the civil rights movement are now legendary. Even after some civil rights organizations became polity members, activists in other groups that remained challengers, such as the Black Panther party, continued to face grave risks. To remain active despite high penalties requires intense personal commitment made not by isolated individuals responding to a media message but by community members who can meet face to face to affirm their loyalty. Market-managerial mobilization can keep an established interest group functioning, but it does not attract the highly committed persons needed for protest actions. As McCarthy (1987, 62) admits, direct-mail solicitations produce lists of relatively uncommitted members, many of whom do not even renew memberships. Of the members of the Environmental Defense Fund, 58 percent thought of membership as merely sending in a check to obtain a newsletter, and 79 percent of the members of Common Cause indicated that they did not want to become more active in the organization.

Taking a disruptive action requires resources at a definite location rather than exchangeable liquid resources. The sit-down strike at the Flint, Michigan, General Motors plant in 1936 depended on commitments from five thousand workers to concentrate their numbers physically at one location, seize a building, and live in it. A challenger's mobilization of resources in a particular locale contrasts to an interest group's mobilization of money, which can be easily collected from one contributor and spent thousands of miles away.

Challengers need a different type of resource—highly committed activists whose availability matches the ebb and flow of specific local confrontations. Challengers usually cannot use market-managerial mobilization because it is a high-overhead operation with a different pattern of resource flow. Administrative staff, computers, postage, and advertising are costly, and the movement interest groups that use them must have large and increasing revenues generated through constantly expanding membership sales. Groups excluded from the polity typically have little money to begin with. Nor can challengers obtain many resources from organizations or elites in society. Hence, challengers cannot make the large initial investments needed to gain further resources from market mechanisms such as mass sales of memberships.

Challengers thus require a type of resource mobilization that sharply contrasts with the market-managerial model portrayed in the McCarthy and Zald article of 1977, with its emphasis on advanced capitalism, consumer markets, and individual purchases of movement memberships. For market-managerial mobilizations, money is the key resource—a universal liquid resource that is relatively easy to detach from contributors via checks or credit cards. But for challengers, this model is inappropriate, as is the accompanying economistic imagery of late capitalism. The localized social relations that challengers use to mobilize their deep and specific commitments are analogous not to the rationalized markets of advanced capitalism but to exchanges in early capitalism when economic relations were embedded in social relations.

The notion that economic resources are embedded in social life (Granovetter 1985) was perhaps best articulated by Karl Polanyi (1944), who criticized models of gainful market exchange for failing to deal with social forces—tradition and the yearning for security, status, and community—that motivated and patterned economic activity. Polanyi analyzed the early years of the industrial revolution, when work relations were embedded in communal relationships and preindustrial and moral traditions held sway. Artisans regulated their production, taking into account the standards and needs of the community (Thompson 1963). Important social movements in England at the time—Chartism (franchise extension) and Luddism (machine breaking)—were also embedded in the social relationships of communities (Calhoun 1982). Tilly (1978), Oberschall (1973, 129), and others have captured this feature of early modern Europe in their studies of communal movements of peasants and workers who revolted against the expanding powers of the central state.

My arguments about political challengers and embedded resources are consistent with the research whose common theme is that movements develop out of preexisting social ties. For the case of contemporary challengers, what needs to be specified is the type and scale of social ties that most contribute to mobilization. (By comparison, for some religious movements that require high commitment, recruitment takes place through acquaintance ties.) Interactions in small affinity groups have mobilized resources for civil disobedience actions against nuclear facilities; small groups also helped the feminist movement survive in the 1950s and expand in the 1960s.

McAdam, McCarthy, and Zald (1988, 709) use the term *micromobilization contexts* to describe the networks of groups and informal associations that sustain a movement. Micromobilization contexts are intermediate in level and scale between the individual who joins a movement and the historical trends in society. McAdam, McCarthy, and Zald rightly point out that processes at this mesolevel determine how movements arise and develop. I argue that scholars have neglected processes at the mesolevel that are slightly larger than micromobilization contexts and can best be conceptualized by using the concept of community.

BRINGING COMMUNITY BACK IN

Political challenges utilize not only networks among friends and small groups but also the ties in the somewhat larger context of a community. A community is a population ranging from several thousand to tens of thousands of persons residing in or otherwise having ties to a specific geographical location. The physical contiguity of community members allows them to engage in face-to-face interactions and develop some form of commitment, even if limited, to other community members. The notion of a limited community grounded in interpersonal interaction, first articulated by Janowitz (1951), implies that through interactions, residents define the very existence of community—its physical boundaries and its common identity. Katznelson (1981) and others have demonstrated the importance of such demarcated ethnic communities, for example, in local politics.

Most communities at a given time do not produce political challenges. But throughout history, many challengers utilizing unconventional tactics have drawn on resources embedded in territorial communities. Castells (1983) has argued that many political challengers—such as the Paris Commune in 1871, the Spanish socialists of the 1970s, and protesters against urban renewal in U.S. cities—were community-based movements attempting to create cultural identity, find social roots, and publicly determine the utilization of space. And most leftist political challenges in the United States have been supported by subgroups with strong community ties in certain geographic locales. The Communist party in New York City in the 1930s, a militant challenger, was based in a local network of Communist unions in workplaces, along with housing projects, restaurants, schools, and recreational groups organized by party members (Flacks 1988, 138, 188).

Another challenging group, ACORN, organized the poor to confront welfare agencies and government officials for improved benefits. The organization won its first victories in Arkansas and then grew rapidly because it encouraged grass-roots leaders to convene neighborhood meetings where residents organized political actions that further developed community awareness and participation. By 1984, ACORN had mobilized sixty thousand members in communities in twenty-seven states. Eighty percent of ACORN's budget came from communal sources such as door-to-door canvassing, chapter members' dues, and local fund-raising events (Delgado 1986).[3] Similarly, Massachusetts Fair Share in the 1980s organized community groups in blue-collar areas.

Community-based movements have also arisen to protest hazardous substance dumps, spills, and treatment facilities. The Love Canal Homeowners Association was a challenger because state and federal agencies initially did not consult with community residents and did not act to ameliorate toxic chemical contamination in homes. Tens of thousands of other toxic chemical dumpsites have produced hundreds of local challengers (Lo 1985). These community-based protest groups received few resources from established environmental groups, who were polity members committed to lobbying federal and state governments. Not only challengers of the left but also important right-wing movements in the United States such as the Ku Klux Klan and the John Birch Society were organized around community-based chapters—klaverns and cells.

Thus, community-based movements of challengers have persisted in advanced capitalist societies like the United States. The contribution in the early stages of capitalist development of communal resources to political protests has been studied by historical sociologists like Charles Tilly. Tilly, however, misses the extent to which communal protests remain a feature of contemporary societies. Instead, he argues that as societies have modernized, there has been a gradual transformation in the forms of collective action. *Communal* protests with reactive goals gave way to *associative* movements with proactive goals.

In the seventeenth century, Tilly (1978, 1986) argues, numerous communal protests did arise from villages, households, and guilds. Localized

3. Movements that rely on communal organization can be decentralized or centralized, and can be autonomous or instigated by professional staffs, vanguards, or other outsiders to the community. Thus, my critique of McCarthy and Zald, which emphasizes *communal* rather than *market*, differs from other critiques of McCarthy and Zald emphasizing the *decentralized* character of movements. Canvassing neighborhoods for funds can be part of either a communal challenge or a market-managerial strategy. Many community-based movements use the canvass in combination with Saul Alinsky's strategy of protests to confront authorities.

protests had the reactive goals of regulating commerce, defending existing rights to use common lands, and maintaining an accustomed livelihood— thereby resisting the new demands of state officials, landowners, or traders who sought to impose taxes, military service, or higher food prices. But by the nineteenth century, Tilly argues, communal protests had faded, making way for actions conducted by nationwide, centralized *associations* such as political parties, trade unions, and interest groups. Rather than defending traditional rights from incursion, associations pressed new claims for voting rights, higher pay, and government services.

Tilly's portrayal of major historical trends, however, misses important features of twentieth-century movements in the United States. Even in the era of late capitalism, communal protests such as the civil rights movement and the student movement have arisen. Furthermore, these communal movements have articulated not merely reactive goals but also proactive ones—seeking new political rights to vote and participate (Thompson 1963). Tilly's argument that political modernization has extinguished communal protests misses the extent to which segments of society remain peripheral and resist the institutions of bureaucratic late capitalism, even in the most advanced nations. As Gusfield (1975) and other critics of modernization theory have pointed out, the communal persists despite the master trends of rationalization and economic development.

True enough, the guild and the household and their social relations are no longer the locus for the material production of goods in an advanced capitalist economy. Gone are the small, tightly knit, independent communities of producers in the early nineteenth century that Calhoun (1982) describes. These forms of community have been eclipsed, and even where they have persisted, as in agriculture in the rural South, the terrain has been inhospitable for social movements. In the place of traditional communal relations there has arisen in the contemporary period not the stark uniformity of rational association but a more modern form of communal relation. The transition from early to late capitalism has not been marked by the elimination of communal relations and the universality of associative relations. Rather, there has been a transformation in the character of communal relations themselves.

Community Consumerism

The traditional villages of a thousand inhabitants have faded into history, and production now takes place as part of an interdependent global economy. In advanced capitalist societies, what activities are based in communities? Contemporary communities encompassing about thirty thousand residents are still the locale for personal acquaintanceships and friendships, and they entail the social relations of consumerism.

The largest single item of consumer spending for most households is the home, whether bought or rented. The purchase and use (consumption) of shelter is a communal phenomenon; the character of one's neighborhood, for example, helps determine the value of one's property. Many consumer items are centered in the home, and grocery stores, restaurants, dry cleaners, and child-care facilities are located nearby. The character of goods and services available in a community depends upon the consumers living there. The style of life of one's neighbors becomes the social context for one's own life-style. Sometimes consumerism is based in an ethnic or racial community; residents dwell among those of the same group and pursue a congenial life-style (Lo 1990, 52). These status communities frequently share a common future—as political decisions and economic trends subject residents to the same conditions (Gusfield 1975).

Residential communities are also the base for churches and cultural organizations, which draw participants from the community or nearby areas. Consumerism is enhanced by neighborhood improvement associations, who press for zoning and government services to enhance the quality of life. Schools provide services and, when government run, can be characterized as social consumption.

Community consumerism and related cultural and ethnic activities, which Max Weber discussed under the rubric of status, usually take place every day unnoticed and without controversy. But occasionally conflicts over community functions give rise to social movements whose strength is grounded in the consumption and status relationships in communities. Compared to the relationships within the self-sufficient villages of the early nineteenth century (Calhoun 1982), the social relationships of a modern community are less intense and systematic and are diffused over a larger territory. But contemporary communities can still generate political challenges, as the following examples suggest.

Local cultural institutions such as churches have been the meeting places where ethnic or racial communities constituted themselves as political challengers (Zald and McCarthy 1987, 69–71). In Birmingham, Alabama, in 1963, churches held mass gatherings to raise funds and plan nonviolent actions to end the segregation of public transit. Strong community ties had been developed through the indigenous religion and culture, investing the challengers with inspiration and vision (Morris 1984, xii, 69). Similarly, during a corn-mill strike in Clinton, Iowa, a minister in the community vigorously supported the strike through sermons, collections for the strike fund, and prayer vigils at the picket line (Fantasia 1988, 196–225). Local churches, temples, and alternative spiritual communities heightened the commitments of those who personally obstructed the workings of nuclear weapons facilities (Epstein 1988, 81–86). Other social movements developed around colleges that were the focuses of cultural and residential communities, as, for example, the university towns of Berkeley, California, and Madison, Wisconsin, were at the time of the antiwar movement.

Community-based protests against factory closings are further evidence of the importance of residential communities of consumption, even in conflicts involving the workplace. The main opponents to a plant closing are often not national trade union leaders, who may be reluctant to champion the cause of a particular local. Instead, the protests may come from those in the community who depend upon the workers spending their paychecks locally. Store owners, city officials dependent on workers' tax payments, and churches needing workers' contributions form community-based coalitions to stop plant shutdowns.

Another example of frustrated consumerism that has led to communal-based protest is the property tax revolt. High property taxes increased housing costs and cut into other consumer expenditures. To reduce their taxes, homeowners turned to neighborhood groups that had been organized around issues of consumption in their community such as zoning permits, traffic, and local government services. In the Los Angeles suburbs of the San Fernando Valley alone, homeowners organized through eighteen associations and another seven community-based groups specializing in tax fighting (Lo 1990, 52).

The building blocks of tax protests were not equivalent individuals on an open market (as in the market-managerial model) but the households in specific communities that had been reassessed. The protests utilized resources that were embedded in the social relations of those communities.[4] A tax protest might begin with an informal living-room meeting among neighbors. Volunteers would then go door-to-door in their neighborhoods and gather petition signatures at a nearby supermarket. Tax protest leaders had not made a profession out of organizing movements (as in the McCarthy and Zald model). Nor did they have an interest in perpetuating the bureaucracy of an organization.

If the McCarthy and Zald model of market-managerial mobilization cannot fully explain communally based challengers, then another major approach—the theorizing about "new social movements"—also misunderstands the nature of community in contemporary society. This theory, which focuses on the new associations and countercultures that transform social life (Offe 1985), neglects preexisting communities of residence and the importance of tradition in developing radical communal challenges.

---

4. Communal resources are mobilized not only by challengers but also by polity members. An example is Mothers Against Drunk Driving (MADD), which could be placed in box 2 of table 10.1.

Advanced capitalism, in short, is an inappropriate concept for analyzing the mobilization of challengers. McCarthy and Zald's bureaucratic version of advanced capitalism or the postindustrialism of new social movement theory may characterize contemporary society in which movements arise. But advanced capitalism does not adequately characterize the mesolevel interactions that are crucial in explaining the origin of political challenges. Petty capitalism is a more applicable concept.

Seeing the social movements of the twentieth century as communal has allowed us to examine the history of the *form* of movements. Movement resources continue to stem from social ties found in communal infrastructures, which have changed as residential communities evolved into centers of economic and cultural consumption rather than production.

The way in which movements mobilize communal resources affects the *content* and ideology of movements. Challengers change their goals over time as they mobilize communal resources to enter the polity. My approach, which shows how movement goals are transformed by processes in communities, differs from the literature that emphasizes how goals evolve in a conservative direction because of processes in highly bureaucratized organizations (Michels 1949).

Whether challengers become conservative and pro-business depends upon how they mobilize to break into the polity, as can be seen in the history of the tax revolt. Protesting homeowners in suburban communities initially did not have sufficient resources to win government recognition or changes in policy. Homeowners had been demanding drastic solutions—slashing the tax rate or changing the constitutional provisions on assessments—that would force strict limits on government spending. Homeowners achieved their first major victory—gathering the million and a half petition signatures that placed Proposition 13 on the California ballot—only when they formed an alliance with small business leaders in their communities. These business owners collected signatures from their customers, arranged for publicity in community newspapers, donated office space, and set up phone banks. Local real estate brokers' boards asked their agents to gather signatures as they showed property (see box 2 in table 10.2; Lo 1990, 169).

The resources that tax protesters needed to enter the polity were grounded in geographic communities. Small retail businesses tapped their network of customers, who typically lived nearby. Realtors and apartment owners also had a stake in property in a specific location.

The case of the tax revolt shows how challengers can initially try to exert power, fail, and then continue to contend for power using communal resources. The interaction between a community-based challenger and the state forces the challenger to define itself and specify the programs and interests it advances. The tax revolt began with protests in working-class and lower-middle-class neighborhoods of homeowners unable to pay their tax bills (Lo 1990, 70). These local protests initially proposed reducing taxes on homes but not businesses; some even favored increasing taxes on oil companies to pay for homeowners' tax relief. But as leading small businesses helped tax protesters to mobilize resources, the platform of the challengers was modified to include not only a tax cut for homeowners but an even larger tax cut for businesses. This was the program that was placed on the California ballot as Proposition 13. Its two-to-one electoral victory gave a boost to the cause of pro-business, conservative tax reduction, which became so influential in the Reagan administration.

The pro-business content of the tax limitation movement, then, emerged from a challenge by small property owners—from the petty-bourgeois character not only of small businesses in the production sector but also of homeowners in the consumption sector. Community consumerism in the United States, centered as it is around the home, is based in petty-capitalist relations—buying or renting a home, furnishing it, and making improvements and repairs.

Community challengers that arise in this terrain differ from the militant European trade unions that arose with large-scale capitalist production. If there is any analogy to be found between contemporary American challengers and trade unions, it will not be with the unions of advanced capitalism but those of early nineteenth-century communities in the United States among tailors, stone cutters, and other artisans in small workshops producing for the local consumers (Wilentz 1984). In the context of petty-capitalist relations, the artisans of a century and a half ago, like tax protesters today, developed a political consciousness of the virtues of limited republican government.

CONCLUSION

This chapter has advocated a historical approach to studying recent social movements. A historical perspective is important, first, because it reveals that the immediate antecedents of contemporary movement interest groups were political challengers who were not immediately accepted into the polity. But it is perhaps more important to probe even further backward in time. Historical analysis of the challengers of a century ago can generate concepts that clarify the politics of Western democracies.

A major political issue of the nineteenth century was how workers would develop the organizations to contend for their interests, thereby shaping their economic conditions and the larger political order. The social life of artisans and workers, particularly their ties in residential communities and their ethnic identifications, produced the demonstrations and strikes that so influenced the process of industrialization. Communities existed long before modern class identifications (Katznelson and Zolberg 1986); in fact, communities generated political actions that helped determine the consciousness of the working class and how classes would be represented through political parties, trade unions, and other institutions of society.

Challengers today operate in an advanced capitalist system created in part by the conflicts of the previous century. As present-day movements pursue their own challenges, their actions too stem from resources embedded in the social life of communities. How they mobilize communal resources affects their class identifications and their influence upon state institutions. Although "community" is not an apt metaphor for all of society, communities nevertheless continue to generate the few but persistent challengers who seek to change political rules so that citizens may better shape their society and its future.[5]

REFERENCES

Calhoun, Craig. 1982. *The Question of Class Struggle*. Chicago: University of Chicago Press.

Castells, Manuel. 1983. *The City and the Grassroots: A Cross-Cultural Theory of Urban Social Movements*. Berkeley: University of California Press.

Delgado, Gary. 1986. *Organizing the Movement: The Roots and Growth of ACORN*. Philadelphia: Temple University Press.

Epstein, Barbara. 1988. "The Politics of Prefigurative Community: The Non-Violent Direct Action Movement." In *Reshaping the U.S. Left: Popular Struggles in the 1980s*, ed. Mike Davis and Michael Sprinker. London: Verso, 63–92.

Fantasia, Rick. 1988. *Cultures of Solidarity: Consciousness, Action, and Contemporary American Workers*. Berkeley: University of California Press.

Flacks, Richard. 1988. *Making History: The Radical Tradition in American Life*. New York: Columbia University Press.

Gamson, William A. 1975. *The Strategy of Social Protest*. Homewood, Ill.: Dorsey.

Gosse, Van. 1988. "'The North American Front': Central American Solidarity in the Reagan Era." In *Reshaping the U.S. Left: Popular Struggles in the 1980s*, ed. Mike Davis and Michael Sprinker. London: Verso, 11–50.

Granovetter, Mark. 1985. "Economic Action and Social Structure: The Problem of Embeddedness." *American Journal of Sociology* 91:481–510.

Gusfield, Joseph. 1975. *Community: A Critical Response*. New York: Harper.

Janowitz, Morris. 1951. *The Community Press in an Urban Setting*. Glencoe, Ill.: Free Press.

5. This vision of a democratic community whose members participate in dialogues and action to shape their future differs from the view of politics expressed by Zald (1987, 330), who describes a polity wherein institutionalized associations defend the interests of those who cannot speak for themselves, including children, fetuses, and nonhumans.

Katznelson, Ira. 1981. *City Trenches: Urban Politics and the Patterning of Class in the United States*. Chicago: University of Chicago Press.

Katznelson, Ira, and Aristide Zolberg, eds. 1986. *Working Class Formation: Nineteenth-Century Patterns in Western Europe and the United States*. Princeton: Princeton University Press.

Lo, Clarence Y. H. 1985. "Community Based Protests against Toxic Chemical Pollution." Manuscript, Department of Sociology, University of California at Los Angeles.

―――. 1990. *Small Property, Big Government: Social Origins of the Property Tax Revolt*. Berkeley: University of California Press.

McAdam, Doug. 1982. *Political Process and the Development of Black Insurgency*. Chicago: University of Chicago Press.

McAdam, Doug, John D. McCarthy, and Mayer N. Zald. 1988. "Social Movements: Building Macro-Micro Bridges." In *Handbook of Sociology*, ed. Neil Smelser. Beverly Hills, Calif.: Sage, 695–737.

McCarthy, John D. 1987. "Pro-Life and Pro-Choice Mobilization: Infrastructure Deficits and New Technologies." In *Social Movements in an Organizational Society*, ed. Mayer N. Zald and John D. McCarthy. New Brunswick, N.J.: Transaction Books, 49–66.

McCarthy, John D., and Mayer N. Zald. 1973. *The Trend of Social Movements in America: Professionalization and Resource Mobilization*. Morristown, N.J.: General Learning Press.

―――. 1977. "Resource Mobilization and Social Movements: A Partial Theory." *American Journal of Sociology* 82:1112–41.

Michels, Roberto. 1949. *Political Parties*. Glencoe, Ill.: Free Press.

Morris, Aldon D. 1984. *The Origins of the Civil Rights Movement*. New York: Free Press.

Oberschall, Anthony. 1973. *Social Conflict and Social Movements*. Englewood Cliffs, N.J.: Prentice-Hall.

Offe, Claus. 1985. "New Social Movements: Challenging the Boundaries of Institutional Politics." *Social Research* 52:817–68.

Perrow, Charles. 1979. "The Sixties Observed." In *The Dynamics of Social Movements: Resource Mobilization, Social Control, and Tactics*, ed. Mayer N. Zald and John D. McCarthy. Cambridge, Mass.: Winthrop, 192–211.

Polanyi, Karl. 1944. *The Great Transformation*. Boston: Beacon Press.

Schattschneider, E. E. 1960. *The Semi-Sovereign People: A Realist's View of Democracy in America*. New York: Holt, Rinehart, and Winston.

Smelser, Neil. 1962. *Theory of Collective Behavior*. New York: Free Press.

Thompson, E. P. 1963. *The Making of the English Working Class*. New York: Vintage.

Tilly, Charles. 1978. *From Mobilization to Revolution*. Reading, Mass.: Addison-Wesley.

―――. 1986. *The Contentious French*. Cambridge, Mass.: Harvard University Press.

Turner, Ralph H., and Lewis M. Killian. 1972. *Collective Behavior*. 2d ed. Englewood Cliffs, N.J.: Prentice-Hall.

Wilentz, Sean. 1984. *Chants Democratic: New York City and the Rise of the American Working Class, 1788–1850*. New York: Oxford University Press.

Zald, Mayer N. 1987. "The Future of Social Movements." In *Social Movements in an*

Organizational Society, ed. Mayer N. Zald and John D. McCarthy. New Brunswick, N.J.: Transaction Books, 319–36.

Zald, Mayer N., and John D. McCarthy. 1980. "Social Movement Industries: Co-operation and Conflict among Social Movement Organizations." *Research in Social Movements: Conflicts and Change* 3:1–20.

———. 1987. "Religious Groups as Crucibles of Social Movements." In *Social Movements in an Organizational Society*, ed. Mayer N. Zald and John D. McCarthy. New Brunswick, N.J.: Transaction Books, 67–96.

Part 5

Mobilization, Quiescence, and Consensus

11

Mobilizing Technologies
for Collective Action

Pamela E. Oliver and

Gerald Marwell

Activists are at the core of most collective action. Sometimes they act alone, but often they seek to draw others into collective action. This chapter is about how a committed and highly motivated activist (or small group of activists) tries to mobilize collective action by a larger group of interested, but less committed and motivated people. It closely examines the choices activists face and the consequences of those choices. We argue that the problems involved in getting other people to support collective action directly affect the kinds of goals activists pursue and the tactics they choose.

The processes we analyze arise in social movements, charitable causes, some kinds of politics, and voluntarism. This is the collective action sector: parents volunteer time in their children's schools and lobby their school boards for more money; some march in the streets for civil rights, and others walk door to door for the Heart Fund; people hold neighborhood fairs and national telethons. Of course, there are important differences between protest actions and voluntarism, but we should not permit these differences to obscure their similarities.

Movement activists and nonmovement volunteers often arise from the same cultures and subcultures and draw on a set of shared knowledge about collective action. This cultural knowledge base will be a pervasive theme in our analysis. Although the theme is general, our empirical examples will be drawn from white middle-class activists in the United States in the late twentieth century. This group has been the backbone of many social change movements and charities. But we do *not* choose them because of their role in "the sixties." We are more interested in understanding participation during "normal times," when most people are busy with their jobs, families, and ordinary routines. The sixties represent a different, if not unique, kind of historical period, one in which a population collectively develops the belief that change is necessary and possible and experiences a heightened level of mobilization. During such periods, people almost mobilize themselves. Activists are busy trying to keep up with the masses rather than prodding them to action (see Oliver 1989a for a theoretical analysis of such periods). In such times of excitement, many of the fundamental processes and relationships described in this chapter should hold, but the overall higher level of mobilization would also make the texture of action very different from the descriptions we paint.

COLLECTIVE ACTION AS AN ORGANIZATIONAL PROBLEM

This chapter concerns what people *do* in social movements, not *why* they join. We define activists as people who care enough about some issue that they are prepared to incur significant costs and act to achieve their goals, and we take their existence as a given.[1] Each activist is defined with respect to a specific issue and might well be a nonactivist on other issues. We assume that people can and do care about *collective* goals and act on them as if they were personal benefits. We take the goals as subjectively determined and often linked to important elements of people's self-identities. This assumption is in line with virtually all available empirical evidence about collective action participants.

Even though activists are highly motivated and willing to spend their own time and money on an issue, they have to worry about costs and benefits, about whether the resources they begin with are enough to accomplish their goals. Because they incur real costs and sacrifices through their actions, they must consider whether their sacrifices will make a significant difference in the things they care about.

Sometimes activists have sufficient time and money of their own to accomplish their goal and may not try to mobilize others. Social movement scholars often ignore these kinds of cadre actions when they think about social movements, even though they are actually a very important part of any movement. Here, however, we assume that the activists do not start with enough resources and must spend time and money on mobilization and organization, hoping that this investment will attract enough time or money from others to accomplish the goal.

We also assume that *non*activists will *not* contribute unless explicitly

1. For the record, however, we do *not* believe that instrumentalist cost/benefit considerations explain activist commitment. In general, we believe that activist commitment comes from the creation of an activist identity through a progressive socialization process involving the creation of solidary ties (see Oliver 1983, 1984; McAdam 1986; John Wilson 1973).

asked by an activist or implicitly "asked" by an event (usually generated by an activist) that presents an occasion for decision making (Collins 1981). Nonactivists never initiate action. They may respond to opportunities created by activists, but it is not certain that they will contribute.

The most important thing to understand about nonactivist contributions is that they are *small*: a ten-dollar contribution to the Sierra Fund; a call to a member of Congress; an hour on an informational picket line. Because it is so small, each contribution produces only a small difference in the outcome, most often a difference so small that it is technically "unnoticeable" (see Olson 1965). The *cost* of the contribution, though large enough to be technically noticeable to the contributor, is also typically small enough to range from trivial to minor. Often the largest components of the cost are the ancillary details that affect the convenience or comfort involved in making the contribution. Is a preaddressed envelope provided? Is it raining? Are one's friends participating? Even when the cost is very small, however, a cost-benefit calculus would say that contributing is not worthwhile since the cost is compared to an even smaller increase in benefit. Mobilizing nonactivist contributions is thus always plagued by the noticeability problem.

On the other hand, the very fact that the cost of a contribution is low means that it can often be overcome by other incentives, such as wanting to feel good about oneself or not wanting to argue with an acquaintance. Furthermore, because the contribution is not very consequential for either its costs or its benefits, the person is not likely to spend much time thinking about the decision or worrying about whether it is the best or most reasonable decision given his resources and values. In short, nonactivist contributions tend to be "flaky": they are not strongly determined by consistent principles but are highly subject to the impact of a wide variety of extraneous and idiosyncratic factors.

To simplify matters, we conceive the population of nonactivists as composed of three subgroups: those with zero, low, and high probabilities of contributing. The zero-probability group contains people who oppose the collective goal or who are decidedly indifferent to it. Their behavior is well determined: they will *not* contribute.

The high-probability group comprises people who do attach a significant positive value to the collective good and are willing to make small contributions to it. These individuals have an interesting dynamic. They can be said to be motivated by "purposive incentives" (James Wilson 1973)— that is, by the incentive of feeling like the right kind of person who contributes to the right collective goods (see Oliver and Furman 1990). Making these contributions often reaffirms a central self-identity such as radical, conservative, feminist, or socially conscious humanist. The strong positive feeling they have about making the contribution easily exceeds its cost.

The problem is that this kind of person is frequently asked to make contributions and cannot respond positively to *all* these requests without making large sacrifices. For all their self-identity as people who care about collective goods, these nonactivists are not willing to give all their money away to good causes. Nor are they willing to give up all their leisure time and reduce their commitments to their jobs or families. If they were, they'd be activists. Thus, the high-probability group must choose among requests for their small contributions, and their choices will be underdetermined and unpredictable.

Finally, the low-probability group supports the goal but has no strong identity with it. Normally they are classic free riders. Deterred by the noticeability problem, they will usually not contribute. But because they nominally support the goal and the cost of contributing is low, even small incentives for giving, such as persuasive or personal appeals or recent news events, can tip the balance.

Activists face two key uncertainty problems in mobilizing nonactivists. First, they often lack sufficient information to sort a population accurately into the zero-, low-, and high-probability groups. Second, even among the high-probability group, they rarely know exactly who will contribute to a given appeal, so that mobilization usually involves wasted effort. Uncertainty and incomplete information are central problems for activists trying to mobilize others and central to a theory of mobilization.

The fact is that activists rarely know in advance how a mobilization will turn out. The decisions of nonactivists are so underdetermined that it may be impossible accurately to predict even the aggregate outcome from a large population with a known proportion of high contributors. For the activist, this adds up to potential frustration if contributions are much lower than anticipated. The activists, who care deeply, know that other people also support the issue. They often find it hard to understand why all these supporters are not contributing.

Many common features of mobilization are best understood as ways to manage or contain this uncertainty. But there are always surprises, and the ultimate success of a movement campaign often is due more to luck or the ability to react quickly than to planning. This does not mean that activists give up planning. Quite the contrary. Real activists spend much of their time planning events, making predictions about consequences, and, if they are wise and experienced, making contingency plans for a wide range of possible results of their efforts.

Knowledge and Technology

Activists cannot just throw abstract time and money at a goal, nor can they abstractly mobilize others' time and money: they have to pursue a specific course of action. They must choose from among those actions they know how to do and perceive as options. Thus, knowledge is central to the matter of how activists act. Although we are putting a slightly different theoretical slant on the data, it is well established empirically that the existing state of knowledge sharply constrains collective actions, and the discovery or invention of a new way of doing things can suddenly alter activists' choices (see James Wilson 1973; John Wilson 1973; Tilly 1978; McAdam 1983; Marwell and Oliver 1984; Oliver 1989a for related arguments).

Useful knowledge about how to do collective action comes in packages we call *action technologies*—sets of knowledge about how to do a particular action and what its consequences are likely to be. The word *technology* is important, because it connotes knowledge that may not be generally available. We use the term *technology* in the anthropological or cultural sense, in which everyone has some technological knowledge. We do not mean that technologies are held only by experts. We do assert, however, with what we believe is strong empirical support, that *some* kinds of technologies found in social movements *are* held only by experts, and we discuss the significance of this pattern when it holds.

For analytic purposes we distinguish between two types of action technologies. *Production technologies* are sets of knowledge about ways of achieving goals, such as lobbying, demonstrations, strikes, or attending a public hearing. *Mobilization technologies* are sets of knowledge about ways of accumulating the resources (such as time and money) necessary for production technologies. The distinction between production and mobilization is useful analytically even when the two are confounded in practice. We will show how and why the available mobilization technologies can often constrain the possible production technologies available to a cultural group.

Most collective action theory takes the goal toward which these technologies are directed as a given (e.g., Olson 1965; Oberschall 1973; Oliver, Marwell, and Teixeira 1985), but this is very misleading. Activists are usually committed to something more broad and diffuse than a specific policy goal. They are committed to world peace, women's rights, ending racism, or helping the homeless. Even a goal like "achieving quality education at Crestwood Elementary School" is actually rather diffuse. We can use the term *collective issue* for each of these goals, precisely because it is broad and ill defined.[2] For any collective issue, there are a large number of more specific goals that concerned activists would consider relevant, such as passing a pay equity bill or requiring the arrest of spouse abusers. Some of these goals are themselves broad and subsume a variety of even more proximate goals, such as reducing the weight of seniority in determining pay equity. Everyone who cares about the issue might consider most of these goals worthwhile, but there might be disagreement about priorities. For other goals, there may be disagreement about whether they are worthwhile, useless, or even counterproductive. Feminists have disagreed in the past about protective legislation and in the present about whether maternity leave should be different from paternity leave and whether divorce laws should be gender-neutral.

It must be recognized that specific goals, production technologies, and mobilization technologies are chosen together, as packages. An activist's selection of a particular goal within a broad issue domain is always based in part on her knowledge of a production technology that she believes has a chance of achieving that goal. Similarly, her choice of a production technology usually depends on her knowledge of a mobilization technology that she thinks can provide the required resources. Without doing violence to its common use, we may use the term *strategy* for the whole package of a goal, a production technology, and a mobilization technology. The strategy package is limited by constraints on each of its elements. Constraints on or choices about mobilizing translate directly into constraints on goals and tactics.

The production technology also defines the amount and kind of resources that need to be mobilized. We have previously shown the importance of the form of the "production function" (Oliver, Marwell, and Teixeira 1985) relating inputs of resources to outputs of the collective goal. On the low end, it matters whether there is some threshold level of contributions that must be achieved before the collective action can have a positive effect. If so, there is both a risk of wasting activist and nonactivist resources on an action that accomplishes nothing and a bandwagon effect once the threshold is exceeded. On the high end, it matters whether the function has some saturation point beyond which contributions are less worthwhile. Collective actions oriented toward well-defined goals are usually closed-ended. Mobilizations of money, especially by professionalized organizations seeking to justify their permanent existence, are often

2. This is very similar to McCarthy and Zald's (1977) definition of a social movement as a set of preferences. We have argued elsewhere (Marwell and Oliver 1984; Oliver 1989a) that social movements should be viewed as sets of actions, not as attitudes, and thus need a term for the general attitude that a social movement is oriented toward.

for more open-ended goals like curing cancer, feeding the hungry, or achieving world peace.

Time and Money as Resources

A production issue that has received scant attention previously concerns the vast difference between time and money as resources for collective action. Resource mobilization theory and our own collective action theories have typically confounded the two, assuming that they are more or less interchangeable. But time and money have markedly different analytic properties.

Time is the ultimate resource for collective action. The entire collective action sector is labor-intensive. Incidental amounts of money may be needed for supplies and rents, but the basic production activities always involve people doing things. When money is raised for collective action, it is used mostly to buy time.[3] Thus, we need to understand time as a resource and the nature of the relation between time and money.

Analytically, time is not at all like money. Money is perfectly fungible; it doesn't matter from whom it comes or in what amounts. You can spend it on anything you want. If you have a thousand dollars, it doesn't matter whether one person contributed all of it or twenty people contributed fifty dollars or one thousand people contributed one dollar each. You can spend your thousand dollars on paper, hourly wages for labor, or long-distance telephone charges.

Time is very different. There really is no such thing as abstract time. It always matters *who* is participating, and a time contribution can never be physically removed from the giver. This has several consequences. First, different people have different skills, different acquaintances, different levels of status or influence. The performance of any job is affected by who does it, although, for example, the effect is smaller for envelope stuffing than for speech making. Second, given the finite nature of time, there is a true physical limit to how much time a person can spend on collective action. Third, in some technologies it is better if fewer people make larger contributions than if many make smaller contributions. Lobbying is an example. Effective lobbying requires getting to know people and establishing trust. One person working full time is much more effective than twenty working two hours a week. Creative intellectual tasks such as writing and research are best done by fewer people making larger contributions. Finally, the opposite holds in other technologies: in mass actions

3. This statement is particularly true for social movements, the subject of this book. There are charitable groups who use money more directly, but they are not our central focus here.

such as marches, petition signing, or voting, each person can make only the same small contribution, and what matters is how *many* have contributed. One person marching for a thousand hours is not the same as a thousand people marching for one hour.

Economists, and those influenced by economists, imagine that time and money are equivalent because you can pay people for their time. But, at least for collective action, they are wrong. The substitutability between time and money in collective action is highly constrained, and these constraints are a central force shaping the forms of collective action that are possible. Of course, volunteer labor can substitute for some paid services, as when volunteers save postage by delivering leaflets. And there are some jobs that can be done by either paid workers or volunteers, such as staffing phone banks.

The problem is that purchased time has to be in the form of jobs. On the demand side, the central work of most collective action requires long-term ongoing involvement and cumulative experience and knowledge, not occasional labor. On the supply side, most people want well-defined permanent full- or half-time jobs, not a couple of hours of work a week on an irregular basis. Although collective action often involves the sporadic need for low-skill activities that can be performed by either volunteers or hired help, within white middle-class circles, the promise of payment is often ineffective in finding someone to do the work. Donating your time to a worthy cause can be satisfying. Being offered a wage well below your regular wage to do a job with lower status than your regular job is an insult, not an inducement.

The ability to attract volunteers always signals the attractiveness and power of a cause, and for many kinds of participation payment would delegitimate the action. Even if one could mobilize a mass demonstration by offering to pay every participant twenty dollars, the fact of payment would destroy the demonstration's political impact. It is clear that canvassers would collect less money if the public were aware that they are paid.

For these reasons, money cannot be easily converted into time when the technology requires many people making small contributions. Such technologies usually require the direct mobilization of volunteer time or the restructuring of many small tasks into larger ongoing jobs for which people can be paid regularly. On the other end of the continuum, it is very difficult for unpaid volunteers to handle the kinds of jobs that require large ongoing commitments. They can do it only if they do not have paid jobs occupying their time, and they can afford to be full-time volunteers only if they have alternate sources of support. Thus, there is a strong pull for the big jobs to be done by full-time paid staff.

The processes that lead nonactivists to participate and give time are usually different from those that elicit contributions of money. The nature of the costs that activists incur in mobilizing time on the one hand and money on the other differs, and it is usually difficult to do both at the same time with the same technology. (See Oliver and Furman 1990 for related arguments.) Thus, quite different technologies have been developed for the two tasks. Each available technology imposes constraints on strategies.

HOW MOBILIZING TECHNOLOGIES
CONSTRAIN STRATEGIES

We turn now to a survey of the empirical terrain of currently available mobilizing technologies for white middle-class Americans, showing how each necessarily imposes constraints on the possibilities for action.

Mobilizing Money

The decision to rely on money as a resource propels activists into a world dominated by professionals, moderation, and ritual. McCarthy, Britt, and Wolfson (1990) show that most ways of raising money require tax-exempt status, which itself sharply constrains production technologies. Social movement and protest organizations find themselves constrained to act like charities. Apart from this very general (and very important) constraint, the specific technology chosen for fund-raising adds more constraints.

Regardless of the issue, be it conventional or radical, when white middle-class activists need to raise money, they do it in a small number of well-defined ways that fall into two groups. The first consists of highly professionalized technologies: large-donor fund-raising, seeking grants and contracts, direct mail solicitation, paid canvassing, and telemarketing. Payroll check-off plans, religious fund-raising, and the use of 900 numbers in phone solicitation belong in this group as well. In the second group are technologies that typically use volunteer labor. These include fairs, rummage and bake sales, brunches, car washes, walk- or runathons or other versions of the same idea, volunteer canvassing and telephoning, raffles, ad books, and selling items on commission. Also in this group are benefit concerts, fun runs or walks, and social events such as dances or dinners. The volunteer technologies are more diverse than the professional, and we may have missed a few, but the list is still short. People raise money for charities and social movements in virtually identical ways. Organizations may be radical or conservative at the level of ideology and program, but in their fund-raising approaches, they are more similar than different.

Professionalized Technologies. The professionalized technologies all involve a great deal of highly specialized information that is largely independent of the issue or goal. One may see evidence of this in the proliferation of for-profit consulting and marketing firms serving the nonprofit sector.[4]

The important analytic divide among professionalized technologies is whether contributions are solicited from a few large donors or from many small contributors. The former requires less overhead, but large contributors tend to exert control over what is done with their money. The technologies for getting money from many small contributors are more expensive, more risky, and more shaped by marketlike processes (McCarthy and Zald 1977), but they produce a pool of money with virtually no strings attached. All professionalized technologies seek to damp down uncertainty by creating a fund-raising system that provides a stable and reliable baseline income. One approach to reducing uncertainty is to employ a mixture of fund-raising techniques. But because these techniques are so specialized, this mixed approach can be used only by organizations large enough to have many professional employees with expertise in different specialities. Larger, older organizations are better able to do this, but none is immune from risk.

Large-donor fund-raising and seeking grants and contracts are similar techniques, differing primarily in whether the donor is a person or an organization (foundation, company, government agency) and whether a written proposal is required. These technologies have relatively low overhead. One person can handle them on a part-time basis, and a relatively high proportion of available time and money can be channeled into the group's program. Large-donor fund-raising can be performed by inexperienced activists if they are bold, and some organizations fund sketchy proposals from novices with interesting ideas. Nevertheless, most grants and large contributions go to activist groups employing professionals experienced with one or another technology.

Dependence on large donors usually forces activists to change strategies as elite concerns and resources shift. Even though it is very common for activists to have goals other than those they can sell in a proposal and to try to divert resources into their other goals, reporting and accounting procedures increasingly constrain them to do what the donor was willing to pay them to do. Thus, these technologies can support only goals and production technologies that appeal to wealthy individuals or organizations.

---

4. E.g., see the paid advertisements in the *Chronicle of Philanthropy,* "The Newspaper of the Non-Profit World."

The technologies that depend on small contributions have the opposite configuration. Small contributors wield essentially no control over the activists and their choice of strategies, but all technologies for obtaining small contributions involve high overhead costs.

Direct mail solicitation is an old technology that has been professionalized and elaborated by the computer revolution. The technology draws directly on advances in direct mail advertising. It is used by almost every kind of group—political movements on the right and left, pro- and anti-abortion groups, colleges, medical charities, organizations to save children in the third world. All the major social movement organizations use direct mail including NAACP, NOW, Sierra Club, SANE/Freeze, and so forth.

The key to direct mail success is a good list of high-probability contributors. Unselective mailings usually lose money. Larger well-established organizations have their own lucrative mailing operations, but smaller or new organizations must rely on someone else's list and thus usually contract their mailing out to for-profit firms working on commission. In the highly professional business of direct mail, the "rich get richer," and many of those who are getting rich are the professional mailers.

Direct mail contributors may be called members, but they exert little or no control over the organization, except indirectly through refusing to give more money. In some cases they may have a strong identification with their organization and may gain a sense of participation and satisfaction in loyally contributing when asked. These loyal contributors provide the large direct mail organizations with a relatively stable funding source that permits them to hire large staffs and pursue long-term strategies. In the social movement sector, direct mail as a mobilizing technology tends to be most compatible with national lobbying and public education as production technologies. Both can be conducted by professional staffs in national offices. Some of the strongest direct mail organizations also have active local chapters, and among many of these, the local chapter receives a share of the money given by contributors in its area. But national offices cannot create or sustain chapters, which depend on the entirely different dynamics of voluntarism (Oliver and Furman 1990).

Less depersonalized is paid door-to-door canvassing for social movement organizations, a complex technology that was invented in 1973 by Mark Anderson, the founder of Citizens for a Better Environment. It was an explicit application of the technology of door-to-door encyclopedia sales to organizations seeking to benefit the public. The key innovations are organizational: setting up the canvass as a year-round full-time occupation, paying the canvassers a commission or bonus for the money they raise, and firing canvassers who fail to collect a specified minimum amount of money every day. Canvassing diffused through environmental and consumer movement organizations to the peace movement and other groups (Oliver 1989b).

Because canvassing unselectively targets every household in its geographic area, it is very inefficient and costly. It succeeds at all only because a person on the doorstep is much more persuasive and has a much higher probability of obtaining a contribution than does an impersonal piece of junk mail. Its cost is also somewhat compensated for by the fact that it can find new high-probability contributors. Canvasses are often linked with direct mail or telemarketing operations, which can take advantage of these new contacts. Paid canvassing has not spread into the charitable sector, partly because it is considered unethical and partly because it is so financially inefficient. In spite of its extremely high overhead (which often approached 100 percent by the late 1980s), however, it can support a large cadre of trained grass-roots organizers. Canvassers not only solicit money and tell people about the organization's goals and activities but ask them about their needs and concerns and reactions to the organization. Canvassing organizations have often been able to mobilize simple mass actions like postcard mailings, and canvassers have sometimes acted as organizers of local groups to participate in demonstrations or direct action campaigns. Canvassers are trained in exactly the skills needed for electoral canvassing, so that political candidates often "borrow" them.[5] Thus canvassing combines mobilization and production. This can be clearly seen in one variant, in which professional community organizers support themselves by canvassing part time.

Telemarketing is exploding everywhere in the nonprofit sector. Most telephone solicitation uses lists of high-probability contributors, although some issues with mass appeal can be sold to the general population. Some telephone solicitors are volunteers, but these are usually for short-term annual drives. Most are paid, and telemarketing is increasingly performed by specialized for-profit businesses that sell their services on commission to nonprofit organizations. Telephone solicitors sell almost anything including Citizens Action–type environmental groups, Mothers Against Drunk Driving, peace initiatives, and religious causes, along with every conceivable variety of charitable and political cause, from conservative to radical.

Our analytic framework makes the reason for the telemarketing boom transparent. It is much less costly than door-to-door canvassing but has almost the same appeal of a real person making the request. Telemar-

---

5. Because tax-deductible organizations cannot be involved in electoral politics, lending out canvassers requires laying them off so that someone else can hire them.

keting can be either selective or unselective and thus can be tailored to an issue. Exotic causes can be sold to specialized lists; those with broader appeal (like Mothers Against Drunk Driving) can be marketed to the general population. The telemarketing business is booming, and the only cloud on the horizon is increasing consumer resistance as many people are coming to define calls at home as an invasion of privacy.

We can only briefly mention the three other professionalized fundraising approaches. There is a long-standing tradition in virtually every organized religion of soliciting offerings or requiring tithes, which has reached an apex of professionalism with televangelism. Although not directly raised by activists, the money derived from religious offerings supports many kinds of collective actions including charitable groups, community organizing, and certain political causes and issues, such as anti-abortion groups, peace groups, anticommunist groups, the Sanctuary movement, and certain political candidates.

The United Way raises money for a wide variety of charitable causes through payroll deductions. For existing charities, obtaining a share of the United Way budget is a form of large-donor fund-raising, since it involves writing an application to a governing board. In a few locales, more politicized groups have fought for and won the right to have alternative funds listed as options on payroll deduction forms. Once they have won the right to be on a form, the member organizations of a fund obtain money for relatively little cost, as long as they can successfully negotiate agreements about how to divide it up.

The newest professionalized technology, 900 numbers, appeared while we were preparing this chapter, and we do not know all its implications. Widespread advertising induces the public to call a 900 number; the call itself automatically entails a charge, and an additional contribution, to be included in the caller's telephone bill, is solicited. It appears to be a technology for the large well-funded national organizations.

Professionalized technologies raise large amounts of money, but all impose severe constraints on collective action. To be tax-deductible, and virtually all are, they must file for 401-3-c status and promise not to be disruptive or to seek to influence elections or legislation. Large-donor fundraising depends on the whims of the wealthy or powerful. Direct mail and telephone solicitation are subject to the vagaries of market processes and are increasingly controlled by for-profit firms. Canvasses require extraordinarily high overhead and can remain solvent only by strictly enforcing daily quotas of money to be raised.

Professionalized technologies tend to be designed to raise as much money as possible on an indefinite time horizon. They require open-ended strategies with diffuse and long-term goals that are unlikely to be immediately realized. Goal displacement is ubiquitous, in that the top priority of paid staffs becomes ensuring that the organization has a stable funding source. Each type of professionalized fund-raising approach calls for a different kind of specialist and a different kind of organization. Once these are in place, an organization is committed to a particular type of mobilizing technology and cannot easily change it. Thus, in ongoing organizations, the mobilizing technology is usually taken as a given, and new goals and production technologies are chosen in large measure for their compatibility with the way the organization raises money.

Volunteer Fund-Raising.   The list of fund-raising methods that use volunteer labor is longer and more diverse, but it is still short. Although successful new technologies rapidly diffuse, people rarely invent whole new ones. They use existing technologies, perhaps adapting or modifying them a little. People easily recognize the basic technologies and the principle of modifying them. If someone asks you to buy a frozen pizza for world peace, you know what they mean, even if it sounds a bit bizarre. Once you've filled out a pledge card for a runathon or bike-athon, you understand the idea. Now we have bowl-athons and hop-athons, cartwheel-athons and, probably, sing-athons.

All these technologies have the same general structure. Core activists spend resources to create some event with well-defined roles that can be played by volunteer participants. The activists spend more resources mobilizing nonactivist participants for these roles. Nonactivists then pay to participate in the event. After expenses for rents, insurance, and so on are deducted, the profits are used to fund the collective action. Activists keep expenses low, partly by soliciting in-kind donations of food, raffle prizes, or whatever else is needed, so that there is little risk of losing much money. The volunteer participants get involved in the organization and actually do something that helps achieve the group's goals. Although even in this sector there are professionals who run fund-raising events on commission, all-volunteer events are still common.

Activists pick a particular technology the first time because they have learned of it elsewhere and think it is feasible. They usually encounter inefficiencies or make mistakes, but if the event basically works, the activists are motivated to build on that experience and use the same technology again. Organizations tend to ritualize their fund-raising events, holding annual fairs or raffles, for example. Ritualized events are much less costly, because the activists can draw on their own experience or the codified experience of their predecessors. Volunteers and customers are easier to mobilize because they already understand the event and the roles they are to play.

In contrast with the professionalized fund-raising technologies, these volunteer-based technologies raise relatively little money and sometimes require a large expenditure of volunteer labor. Whereas the professional-ized technologies often gross millions of dollars, the volunteer technologies gross in the thousands of dollars and sometimes much less. To some extent, this comparison is unfair, since the professionalized technologies are ongoing year-round operations, and the volunteer-based fund-raiser is a single event. But the groups involved usually consider the amount they raise adequate. Organizations that do not have paid staff, or whose staff is supported by a grant or another organization, do not need much money. What they usually need more of is time.

Mobilizing Time

Collective action always requires the mobilization of time. In professionalized collective action, money is mobilized from nonactivists to pay activists to do the collective action. Here we discuss the technologies for mobilizing participation by nonactivist volunteers in activities like at-tending meetings, marching in demonstrations, circulating petitions, or helping with fund-raisers.

Technologies for mobilizing time from nonactivist volunteers are much less professionalized and much less well defined and elaborated than those for mobilizing money. Although the term *technology* comfortably fits fund-raising, it is awkward when applied to inducing people to participate be-cause the knowledge involved is more diffuse and less specialized. But it is knowledge nonetheless, or at least shared cultural understandings about who can ask other people to do something under what circumstances. In this section, we attempt to subject the obvious to analysis.

Limited and Open Requests for Participation.   Being asked to spend two hours attending a protest demonstration or working at a school fair may sound the same as being asked to attend a two-hour orga-nizational meeting: both involve two hours and apparently differ only in people's taste for one kind of activity versus another. But attending a meet-ing, especially an organizational meeting, implies a willingness to attend future meetings and to participate in the group's projects. That is, it is tantamount to becoming an activist on the issue in question and implic-itly involves a much greater time commitment—a commitment that is of uncertain extent and indefinite duration.

For this reason, a lot of the technological knowledge about mobilizing volunteer time is about organizing and dividing labor and structuring events and jobs so that people can be invited to participate in well-defined and limited ways. The technology of direct action organizing provides information about how to create well-defined dramatic protest actions that can accomplish a goal in an exciting way and leave participants wanting to do more. The general technology of voluntary fund-raising events involves subdividing jobs into well-defined units like organizing the food concession or bringing six dozen cookies to a bake sale. A technology often used in the charitable sector but only occasionally used in social movements involves creating long-term jobs that involve only a few hours a week, such as calling for Jewish charities for three hours every Tuesday night or being on call for the rape crisis center three nights a month. Many people who are unwilling to make the major short-term open-ended commitment that activism entails are quite willing to make a long-term commitment to a well-defined task. They also are aware that failing to keep their commitment will cause a noticeable problem for the event or the organization's mission.

Technologies for Communicating the Request.   If activists are to mobilize volunteer participants, they have to invite them to participate, most commonly by explicitly asking for their cooperation, although sometimes by creating a visible event that by its existence invites others to participate. After deciding what to ask participants to do, activists must decide whom to ask and how to ask them. There is technology and cultural knowledge implicit in this decision, even if sometimes it is so mundane that one is essentially naming the obvious. But let's work through the possibilities anyway. The first is to contact personally and ask for help unselectively from all available nonactivists or a random sample of them. This approach is so expensive and inefficient that it is almost never used for requesting time contributions for anything more demanding than signing a petition. Its use represents an absence of technological knowledge in extremely uninformed novice activists, or it can reflect desperation after the more usual approaches have failed. It is, however, a useful baseline against which technologies for mobilizing volunteers can be measured.

The second choice, and the first real technology, is to ask the people you have some personal acquaintance with or those on some list of high-probability contributors, such as members of the organization sponsoring the action or people who live near the site of a proposed toxic waste dump. Those who are both acquaintances and high-probability contributors will have very high probabilities of agreeing to contribute and are always the starting point for this technology. If this group does not provide enough contributors, the next choice between other acquaintances and other high-probability contributors varies a great deal depending on the nature of the issue, the subculture of the activist and potential participants, and the social organization of the two groups.

Mobilizing time requires being willing to ask people to do things and knowing something about the people you are trying to mobilize. The personal link is very important. It is easier to ask a friend for help than a stranger. It is considered legitimate in most white middle-class circles to ask for participation from a stranger whose interest in an issue can be taken as publicly known, although even here there are etiquette barriers. Strangers cannot politely be asked to do things that would violate stereotyped gender roles, for example. Strangers also find it relatively easy to provide excuses for refusing the request.

This technology, "ask the people you know or who you know are interested," is efficient but inherently limited. It is so efficient that we can safely predict that if the pool of activists' acquaintances or known high-probability contributors will yield enough participation for the production technology, all mobilization efforts will be limited to these groups. But it is limited, because it ignores everyone who is not already known to the activists, either personally or by virtue of being on the high-probability list. And one's friends tend to become exhausted by repeated requests.

A second technology activists commonly use for large marches and demonstrations is federated mobilization. This involves personally approaching the leaders of existing organizations, who are persuaded to solicit the participation of their members. For example, many actions in the civil rights movement were coordinated this way through black churches (Morris 1984). Although the principle is not difficult to understand, federated mobilization is not part of the general cultural knowledge of nonactivists; it is usually something people learn through experience. Federated mobilization expands the scope of mobilization, but it depends on the cooperation of other leaders and reaches only those who are members of the contacted organizations.

An example of a highly specialized form of federated mobilization is the technology for organizing a large demonstration. Demonstration initiators negotiate with established organizations to form an ad hoc sponsoring coalition. A compromise platform and speakers' list is drawn up. The coalition partners take responsibility for getting their own members to attend and, sometimes, for trying to bring in other participants. If the march is national, coordinators in each locale make arrangements for group transportation. The initiators take responsibility for general publicity, obtaining permits, training marshals, and the host of other details that are part of the contemporary technology of demonstrations.

Direct or federated, most mobilization of time involves contacting people already known—"preexisting channels of communication." Only personal contact through an established social relation has a high probability of obtaining a nonactivist's contribution of time. The obvious constraint imposed by this technology is that it is very difficult to transcend existing social relations and forge new ones.

Activists often try to escape this constraint through written communication in an appropriate mass medium. The possibility of doing this is part of the common culture, and naive activists often try it. What those who lack technological knowledge do not know is that this approach usually fails. Written communications from unknown others have very low credibility. Credible publicity most often comes from objective news stories, so activists attend classes to learn how to write press releases that will get printed or stage media events that will attract television reporters.

More specialized impersonal media sometimes successfully mobilize volunteers. These include mass media public service announcements about upcoming events of presumed general interest, "volunteers needed" columns or bulletin boards utilizing much the same format as help-wanted advertisements for paid jobs, and newsletters or memos sent to members of an organization with a known interest in the issue. These impersonal mass communications can sometimes pull in new participants who are not known to the original activists. The response rate to these approaches is always very low, but even a low response can provide a significant cadre of workers, especially when prior organization creates well-defined roles to fill. These approaches depend upon prior organization and communication channels and a shared cultural understanding of the concept of volunteering for a common cause or attending a public event.

It is worth stressing that these impersonal channels occasionally strike an unexpectedly responsive chord. Publicity can sometimes lead people generally to start talking among themselves about an event and the issues involved. Occasionally, these conversations snowball and lead to a widespread collective understanding that whole networks of people will participate. The problem for the activists is that they cannot create these conditions or even know in advance whether they exist. Thus, when this happens, activists are usually caught off guard and are overwhelmed with the unexpected numbers of participants who strain their plans and resources.

Professional Organizing.   There is not room here to provide any serious analysis of professional organizing, but we can indicate where it fits in the picture. An organizer creates an organization (formal or informal), a structure within which others can participate as activists or nonactivists. Although there are many volunteer organizers, there are also many paid professional organizers, who principally organize labor unions or community groups. Once a formal organization exists, a person may keep the title "organizer" for the job of organizational maintenance. Many books and schools teach the subject. The concept of technology clearly fits this arena, and there are a number of competing theories and ideologies of organizing. The usual theory is that the professional organizer has no goals of his own but rather seeks to learn people's interests and concerns and helps them define their own goals. Various schools of organizing differ in the extent to which they believe organizers need to raise the consciousness of people and give them new ways of understanding what their interests are.

Organizers spend much of their time fostering or creating new social relations so that the effective personalized technologies for mobilization can transcend initial social barriers. They also transfer technology and teach people how to raise money or create structures that can effectively use volunteer time. Depending on their orientation, they may also spend a great deal of time in "political education," talking to people with the goal of persuading them to reinterpret their circumstances and interests.

The ideology of organizing sharply distinguishes the organizer from indigenous leaders, asserting that leaders should make policy and organizers help to execute policy. But, in fact, organizers and paid staff often function as leaders, and when indigenous leaders are strong, they can conflict with the staff. Professional organizers usually create organizations that depend on the continuing presence of paid staff, although in some instances the paid staff members are indigenous to the group, and outside organizers leave the scene. Thus, professionally organized groups are propelled into the world of fund-raising and its constraints.

CONCLUSIONS

Our central thesis is that technologies for mobilizing resources impose tight constraints on the forms of action that are possible. Once a person or group is using one technology, it is not easy to switch to another. Groups that are structured to raise money are not well structured to mobilize volunteers, and vice versa. Raising money through direct mail tends to concentrate power in a central national office; raising money through canvassing creates large cadres of canvassers in local areas who must be managed and motivated. Volunteers mobilized for a protest demonstration are not usually available for fund-raising.

Within technologies, activists talk the language of this chapter. Professional activists worry about mailing lists, market saturation, labor costs, and the mass appeal of issues and programs. Volunteer activists try to think up new attractive events or execute the ritualized ones well. They mobilize through the people they know: the same people go to the same events, and they exchange the currency of mutual obligation—I went to your event, so you come to mine.

This is not the stuff of transcendent social change, not the stuff of revolution or upheaval. This is the world as it looks most of the time, in the nonturbulent troughs in a protest cycle (Tarrow 1989). As far as we can tell, the volunteer world looks about the same as it always has in relatively quiet times. The walkathons are fairly new, but fairs and sales and benefit concerts have been around for years. Cultural information passes readily between protest or social change organizations and charitable organizations. Actions are organized primarily through preexisting social networks. Much activity is cyclical and ritualized, and most innovation takes the form of applying old models to new circumstances or making small changes in existing models.

On the professional side, however, there are enormous differences between the present and the past. There have always been some paid activists (see Oliver 1983 for a review), but the past thirty years have seen a proliferation of professionalized technologies and professional activists. For the individuals involved, the pull into professional activism is (or at least was initially) an ideological commitment to social change and a self-identity as an activist. But the technologies have clearly taken on lives of their own and have seemingly become virtual ends in themselves, especially for the private firms serving the sector.

We do not want in any way to imply that professionalized mobilization has replaced spontaneous grass-roots mobilization. Our arguments have made it clear that we do not think professionalized mobilizations can create grass-roots mobilizations of volunteers, because mobilizing money is usually inconsistent with mobilizing action. But the processes through which new actions emerge are still in place and operating, although we seem to be in a quiet period. It is nevertheless worth asking whether these professionalized organizations will prove to be irrelevant to grass-roots mobilization, supportive of it, or competitive with it.

REFERENCES

Collins, Randall. 1981. "On the Microfoundations of Macrosociology." *American Journal of Sociology* 86:984–1014.

Klandermans, Bert. 1984. "Mobilization and Participation: Social-Psychological

Expansions of Resource Mobilization Theory." *American Sociological Review* 49 (October):583–600.

Klandermans, Bert, and Dirk Oegema. 1987. "Potentials, Networks, Motivations, and Barriers: Steps Towards Participation in Social Movements." *American Sociological Review* 52 (August):519–31.

Marwell, Gerald, and Pamela Oliver. 1984. "Collective Action Theory and Social Movements Research." *Research in Social Movements: Conflicts and Change* 7:1–27.

Marwell, Gerald, Pamela E. Oliver, and Ralph Prahl. 1988. "Social Networks and Collective Action: A Theory of the Critical Mass. III." *American Journal of Sociology* 94:502–34.

McAdam, Doug. 1983. "Tactical Innovation and the Pace of Insurgency." *American Sociological Review* 48:735–54.

———. 1986. "Recruitment to High-Risk Activism: The Case of Freedom Summer." *American Journal of Sociology* 92:64–90.

McCarthy, John D. 1987. "Pro-Life and Pro-Choice Mobilization: Infrastructure Deficits and New Technologies." In *Social Movements in an Organizational Society*, ed. Mayer N. Zald and John D. McCarthy. New Brunswick, N.J.: Transaction Books.

McCarthy, John D., David W. Britt, and Mark Wolfson. 1991. "The Institutional Channeling of Social Movements in the Modern State." In *Research in Social Movements: Conflict and Change* 13:45–76.

McCarthy, John D., and Mayer Zald. 1973. *The Trend of Social Movements in America: Professionalization and Resource Mobilization.* Morristown, N.J.: General Learning Press.

———. 1977. "Resource Mobilization in Social Movements: A Partial Theory." *American Journal of Sociology* 82:1212–39.

Morris, Aldon D. 1984. *The Origins of the Civil Rights Movement.* New York: Free Press.

Oberschall, Anthony. 1973. *Social Conflict and Social Movements.* Englewood Cliffs, N.J.: Prentice-Hall.

Oliver, Pamela. 1983. "The Mobilization of Paid and Volunteer Activists in the Neighborhood Movement." In *Research in Social Movements: Conflict and Change* 5:133–70.

———. 1984. "If You Don't Do It, Nobody Else Will: Active and Token Contributors to Local Collective Action." *American Sociological Review* 49:601–10.

———. 1989a. "Bringing the Crowd Back In: The Nonorganizational Elements of Social Movements." In *Research in Social Movements: Conflict and Change* 14:1–30.

———. 1989b. "Selling the Movement on Commission: The Structure and Significance of Canvassing by Social Movement Organizations." Paper presented at the annual meeting of the Society for the Study of Social Problems.

Oliver, Pamela, and Mark Furman. 1990. "Contradictions between National and Local Organizational Strength: The Case of the John Birch Society." *International Social Movements Research* 2:155–77.

Oliver, Pamela E., and Gerald Marwell. 1988. "The Paradox of Group Size in Collective Action: A Theory of the Critical Mass. II." *American Sociological Review* 53 (February):1–8.

Oliver, Pamela, Gerald Marwell, and Ruy Teixeira. 1985. "A Theory of the Critical Mass, I. Interdependence, Group Heterogeneity, and the Production of Collective Goods." *American Journal of Sociology* 91:522–56.

Olson, Mancur. 1965. *The Logic of Collective Action*. Cambridge, Mass.: Harvard University Press.

Snow, David A., Louis A. Zurcher, Jr., and Sheldon Ekland-Olson. 1980. "Social Networks and Social Movements: A Microstructural Approach to Differential Recruitment." *American Sociological Review* 45 (October):787–801.

Tarrow, Sidney. 1989. *Struggle, Politics, and Reform: Collective Action, Social Movements, and Cycles of Protest*. Western Societies Program, Occasional Paper no. 21. Center for International Studies, Cornell University.

Tilly, Charles. 1978. *From Mobilization to Revolution*. Reading, Mass.: Addison-Wesley.

Wilson, James Q. 1973. *Political Organizations*. New York: Basic Books.

Wilson, John. 1973. *Introduction to Social Movements*. New York: Basic Books.

12

Consensus Movements, Conflict Movements, and the Cooptation of Civic and State Infrastructures

John D. McCarthy and

Mark Wolfson

Much recent work on social movements has demonstrated how collective action emerges from and is shaped by preexisting patterns of social relations among the adherents of social movements. The leaders of social movement organizations often direct their efforts at gaining access to, or "coopting," these civic and political infrastructures, which were originally created for other purposes. In this chapter, we develop a distinction between consensus movements and conflict movements as a means of achieving a better understanding of the conditions that favor or discourage the success of cooptation efforts.

Conflict movements have long been the focus of most research and, as a consequence, the source of our major theoretical insights about the emergence, mobilization, and change of social movements in modern societies. Conflict movements—such as the labor movement, poor people's movements, the feminist movements, and the civil rights movement—are typically supported by minorities or slim majorities of populations and confront fundamental, organized opposition in attempting to bring about social change. *Consensus movements,* on the other hand, are those organized movements for change that find widespread support for their goals and

David Baker, MaryAnna Colwell, John Crist, Roberto Fernandez, Debra Harvey, Doug McAdam, Clark McPhail, Robert Mitchell, Tony Oberschall, Brian Powers, Maryellen Schaub, and Mayer Zald all provided important criticism of earlier drafts of this chapter. We appreciate their assistance, though we did not always follow their sage advice. We also thank the National Science Foundation (Grant no. SES-8419767) for its support of a portion of the research on which this chapter is based. Mark Wolfson also received support for this research from a National Institute of Mental Health Postdoctoral Training Grant awarded to Stanford University as well as a National Institute of Alcohol Abuse and Alcoholism Postdoctoral Training Grant awarded to the Alcohol Research Group (No. AA-07240).

little or no organized opposition from the population of a geographic community.[1] We explore some of the unique features of consensus movements as contrasted to conflict movements in an effort to draw out their differing impacts upon cooptation efforts.

The cooptation of civic and state structures by social movements, when successful, can greatly facilitate collective mobilization. When a movement is able to coopt an existing civic structure such as the Moral Majority's use of the Baptist Bible Fellowship alliance structure (Liebman 1983), its ability to mobilize people and resources is likely to be greatly enhanced. Similarly, when a movement can coopt a segment of the state, such as the interconnection between the United Farm Workers and California Rural Legal Assistance (an arm of the federal government's Legal Services Corporation; Casper 1984), the difficulties of mobilization are likely to be reduced. Earlier analyses have demonstrated the centrality of both civic and state structures to the understanding of many modern movements, but they have rarely gone much beyond simply identifying and illustrating their importance. By comparing the consequences of cooptation efforts by actors in consensus movements and conflict movements, we can specify more clearly the varying conditions that affect the success of these efforts.[2] In this way we begin to link the analysis of modern social movements with analyses of the structure of civic organizational fields, elements of the modern state, and their intersection.

CONSENSUS MOVEMENTS

A consensus movement is a social movement in which the opinions and beliefs of a geographically bounded population supporting its suggested changes approach total consensus: perhaps 80 to 90 percent of the population in the community supports it, and it confronts little or no organized opposition.[3] The main features of this definition follow

1. The notion of consensus has been a red flag to the sociologists who anchor their theoretical assumptions in contrast to the previously paradigmatic "functionalism" that assumed societalwide consensus on basic issues as a central condition of societal integration (e.g., Williams, 1959). Our use of the idea of consensus has nothing in common with these earlier uses.

2. Of course, many other factors besides these affect the likelihood of mobilization (McAdam et al. 1988). Our analysis particularly assumes constant levels and unvarying sophistication of effort aimed at mobilization, factors whose variable consequences have received extensive attention (e.g., Jenkins 1983; Klandermans and Oegema 1987; Klandermans 1988).

3. We use the idea of consensus movement here in a manner somewhat different from John Lofland's (1989), but our understanding of the concept is implicit in his original use

from earlier definitions of social movements and countermovements. "A *social movement* is a set of opinions and beliefs in a population representing preferences for changing some elements of the social structure or reward distribution, or both, of a society. A *counter-movement* is a set of opinions and beliefs in a population opposed to a social movement" (McCarthy and Zald 1977, 20).

Consensus movements are, by our definition, geographically delimited, and generally are subsocietal or subnational. They may be neighborhood-based, they may be rooted in a part of a community, or they may be communitywide. Local ethnic enclaves, freeway opposition groups, and some anti–toxic waste groups illustrate the variation of consensus movements across ever-larger segments of local geographical communities. Consensus movements may be broader than the local community but still subnational. Regional consensus movements, based on a variety of social differences between geographical areas (e.g., language, culture), have been common in many nations. Consensus movements are typically subnational, but a few may achieve, for short periods of time, consensus at the national level.

For a variety of reasons, consensus movements (aside from nationalist movements) are probably rare at the national level. First, the likelihood of diversity of all kinds increases with community size (Wilson 1986), and nations are typically large. As a result, we would expect a small likelihood of consensus on any issue in very large communities. Second, it is probably unusual that a mobilized social movement at the national level does not soon generate an organized opposition, if it does not immediately spawn one.[4] And that probability increases as a result of newly emergent technologies. No matter how small the minority opposition may be, modern techniques of interest aggregation (Godwin 1988) create opportunities for issue entrepreneurs to generate the resources to form organized opposition groups.

Consensus movements, when they emerge, are probably a rather un-

---

of it. Lofland says, "Consensus movements are distinguished from conflict movements in terms of the degree to which each recognizes and acts on oppositions of objective social interests and seeks in direct and detailed fashion to change social policy" (1989, 163). He goes on to spell out what he views as correlated features of consensus movements. This is not the place to dispute his hypothesized cluster of features of consensus movements.

4. Hayes (1981) developed a typology of legislative policy processes that depends on a distinction between consensual and conflictual issues (or in his terms, demand patterns) that is quite similar to the one we have developed here. Besides the substance of issues, the important factor for him in distinguishing between these types of public policy issues is whether or not there is an organized opposition.

stable movement form.[5] We know that both the nature of organized efforts at social change and the extent and shape of support of all social movements are affected by a variety of internal and external factors (Zald and Ash 1966).[6] Consensus movements may evolve into conflict movements, and conflict movements may, now and then, evolve into consensus movements. For instance, the ways in which social change goals are symbolically presented by movement leaders and the ways in which they are perceived to affect previously organized groups can have important effects upon the shape of support across ever-wider geographic communities. Shifts in the framing of the goals of an ongoing movement may substantially alter the size and location of its actual and potential constituencies (Snow and Benford 1988; Gamson and Modigliani 1989).

The work of Clarence Lo (1984) provides an example of a shift from a conflict toward a consensus movement. Lo showed that a change in concrete goals resulted in a substantial broadening of community support for the tax revolt movement in southern California. Initially, the goals of the movement included tax relief for homeowners and the poor, with the corporate sector targeted as the economic loser. Support for changes in the property tax law was narrow, and organized opposition was substantial. But when the goals were redefined to include relief for corporations, organized opposition declined, and community support widened. This shift is seen as the backdrop to understanding the massive community support that developed in California for the tax revolt movement, accounting in part for the movement's rapid mobilization (see also Lo 1990).

The transition of newly emergent consensus movements into conflict movements is probably the more typical trajectory. The change goals of many consensus movements are characterized by "their *lack of specificity*

5. This is one of the reasons they have been largely ignored recently by observers of social movements. In addition, widely shared theoretical assumptions of the centrality of conflict to social movement processes is also an important factor. Nelson says that consensus or "valence" issues "have largely been overlooked in agenda-setting research by [political scientists], in part because so much of the research is rooted in the interest group tradition, which stresses the conflictual nature of agenda setting (1984, 27).

6. This assumption underscores the difficulties of typing movements. We have chosen to speak in typological language here for parsimony. Both the distribution of opinion on any social change question, varying between high levels of conflict of various shapes to complete consensus, and the extent of organized opposition obviously can vary along specifiable dimensions. Research questions, examples of which are developed below, must obviously be stated in variable form, e.g., "The greater the consensus and the smaller and more resource poor an organized opposition, then . . ." We recognize that the two criteria we have named for identifying consensus movements may not necessarily vary together as we have assumed for purposes of exposition.

and their attempt to *reaffirm the ideals of civic life*" (Nelson 1984, 28).[7] The former characteristic of consensus movement change goals may be undermined both by the development of an organized opposition—a countermovement—and by the normal processes of the "issue attention cycle" (Downs 1972). The goals of movements become increasingly specific during the process of mobilization and the efforts to influence public policy. As movements encroach upon the densely populated public arenas intersecting with the modern state, they are more likely to be seen as threats to entrenched interests and in conflict with organized groups' previously negotiated positions on public issues.

Such a trajectory of change is illustrated by the ongoing evolution of the citizens' movement against drunken driving. During its early period of rapid growth, it was a good example of a consensus movement (McCarthy and Wolfson 1988; Lofland 1989) since, as we will see below, it was widely supported and found almost no organized opposition. Early leaders of this movement saw the issue of automobile fatalities almost exclusively within the framework of the social control of the drinking driver (Gusfield 1988), and they received widespread support for their activities. Since then, the movement has increasingly focused its attention on structural reform. National and local movement organizations have, over the past few years, advocated the twenty-one-year-old drinking age, mandatory seatbelt use legislation (Wolfson 1988, 1989), strong restrictions on alcohol advertising, and hefty increases in alcohol (especially beer) taxes. To the extent that strategies such as these are advocated, the groups increasingly come into conflict with powerful, organized corporate interests, especially alcohol advertisers, producers, retailers, and their allies. This conflict seriously threatens the relatively broad consensus support of the movement that existed in most local communities when simply criminalizing drunken driving was seen as its primary aim.

A salient example of this can be seen in the events of the Conference on Drunk Driving convened in 1988 by Surgeon General C. Everett Koop (Office of the Surgeon General 1989). At the conference, which included many activists of the movement, panelists recommended restricting alcohol advertising aimed at young people and increasing alcohol taxes (in order to reduce consumption among the young). The alcohol and advertising industries and their allies sought unsuccessfully to halt the conference

7. It is exactly these features of the stated goals of many consensus movements that led John Lofland to characterize them as "timid rebellion," "disguised politics," and "derailed dissent" (1989). Clarence Lo (1988) has labeled them "Pollyanna" movements on similar grounds.

in order to suppress the anticipated recommendations (McCarthy 1988). In the process, the debate about the promise of radically different solutions to the drinking-driving problem became the focus of public attention. To the extent that these kinds of approaches are adopted by national and local movement organizations, the groups are likely to find themselves in direct conflict with highly organized and affluent corporate actors. That conflict is certain to have significant consequences for the extent and locus of community support for the groups.

Although national and state-level consensus movements are normally short-lived, more localized consensus movements can be quite stable. Consensus movements depend not only on the extensity of support but also on the structure of group and community solidarity for their mobilized support, as we will argue below. As a result, shifts in public opinion may not necessarily turn them into conflict movements, especially at the more local levels. Thus, the most fruitful empirical comparisons between consensus and conflict movements may be over time at the national level and across communities and groups at the local level.

We turn, first, to the social organization of citizen support before we discuss the processes by which solidarity and authority constrain or facilitate the mobilization of groups and elements of the state under varying conditions of consensus within their boundaries. We follow these discussions with illustrations of the processes and their consequences in groups and in elements of the state.

THE SOCIAL ORGANIZATION OF MOVEMENT SUPPORT

Support for social change is seldom universal. It is sometimes widely dispersed, or it may cluster within segments of either or both of two universally important dimensions of community organization—civic infrastructure and geopolitical structure.

Scholars have sought to understand movements in modern societies by studying their emergence out of preexisting clusters of solidarity that are organized associationally (Freeman 1975; Morris 1984; McAdam 1982). A wide agreement has developed around the importance of social infrastructures in explaining the likelihood of the formation and extent and rate of growth of social movement organizations (smos) at the local level. Systematic evidence from a variety of movements suggests that the use of preexisting networks of relations between supporters of social movements makes mobilization both more likely and less costly (see McCarthy 1987). Since these networks were generated for other social purposes, smo leaders must determine whether they are available to the movement for collective action. If they can be coopted, their formally and informally organized networks and the resources they control can be appropriated. Those resources may include buses, telephones, mailing lists, office facilities, personnel, and the like. One example of this process is the prolife movement's growth (in significant part) out of local structures of the Catholic church, fundamentalist Protestant congregations, and, increasingly, evangelical seminaries (Wills 1989). Similarly, the civil rights movement grew out of the black churches, traditionally black colleges and universities, and segmented voluntary associations, such as the National Association for the Advancement of Colored People (see McAdam 1982; Morris 1984). In large part, the movement against the war in Vietnam grew out of a number of religious groups and elite university settings. These typical patterns of infrastructural utilization by conflict movements reflect some level of consensus within certain organized social networks and account in part for the networks' availability for manipulation by social movement activists.

It has been widely noted that modern communities are more likely than traditional ones to be organized along the lines of civic infrastructures that are not coterminous with the geographic boundaries of community (Oberschall 1973). The bases of communal mobilization, on the other hand, are circumstances in which "the collectivity might be integrated and organized along viable traditional lines based on kinship, village or tribal organization, or other forms of community, with recognized leaders and networks of societal relations extending to its boundaries" (Oberschall 1973, 119). Collective action based upon geographically bounded consensus may have been more common in less modern societies, but it certainly is not uncommon in modern societies. For our purposes, however, the most important feature of the geographical boundaries of consensus is its articulation with structures of the modern state. In the same way that the structures of associationally concentrated consensus may be cooptable for other purposes, so too may geographically bounded consensus be cooptable through structures of the state. Just as civic leaders (those who can make binding decisions within organized groups) must acquiesce or actively participate in lending preexisting structures to social change purposes, political authorities (those who can make binding decisions within geographical boundaries) can acquiesce or actively participate in making structures of the state available to facilitate or constrain social movement mobilization. The importance of the cooptation of diverse state structures by the activists of conflict movements has been widely noted (McCarthy and Zald 1973; Bennett and DiLorenzo 1985). But a systematic consideration of the mechanisms of cooptation of civic structures and the broader conditions of its likelihood of success has not been attempted. We briefly explore the process of cooptation and some of the general conditions that facilitate or constrain movement efforts to coopt civic and state structures before we more closely examine some examples of cooptation under varying conditions of consensus support.

ELEMENTS OF A THEORY OF
COOPTABLE SOCIAL STRUCTURES

If we assume some degree of competent individual and organizational agency aimed at social change, as well as consensus support for it, the cooptation of groups or elements of formal authority for its pursuit is not problematic. By examining mobilization under conditions of declining consensus we can illuminate the processes that affect both cooptability and the emergence of organized opposition to cooptation within a social structure. These include, at a minimum, the forms and processes of authority and solidarity *within* social structures (both civil and political), the forms and processes of authority and interelement relations *between* local and extralocal structures, and the cooptation process itself. Each of these may facilitate or constrain the cooptation of social structures.[8]

To understand cooptation is first to understand the conditions under which members of groups or functionaries of state elements who are initially opposed or neutral to cooptation eventually cooperate with it, or at least refrain from creating organized opposition to it. We ask here not how groups are formed explicitly to pursue collective social change goals but how groups constituted for one purpose are redirected toward other purposes that their members do not unanimously support. Thus, we frame not another version of the free-rider problem but the costly rider problem: what structures and processes internal to groups and state elements influence the likelihood that members who do not view change goals as in their interest will nonetheless allow the collective pursuit of them, a portion of whose costs they must bear?[9]

Group solidarity is certainly one process that affects these likelihoods, whether we conceive of it as the consequence of group processes, such as

8. Zald and Berger (1987) develop a comprehensive approach to accounting for changes in the leadership of organizations. Cooptability for social change purposes, as we address it here, is typically more narrow, though it can sometimes involve the change of leadership.

9. We focus here upon the possibilities of group cooptation rather than the possibilities of a group's successfully encouraging its members to become directly active in other groups explicitly pursuing *only* social change goals. Though similar to cooptation, that is the process of "bloc recruitment" discussed by Oberschall (1973).

ritual and extensity of interaction (Collins 1982; Fireman and Gamson 1979), or as the consequence of rational choice processes (Stinchcombe 1975; Hechter 1987). Whatever the origin of loyalty to group or state element, the more widespread it is the less likely the opposition to cooptation by dissident members.[10]

Internal political and social structures are also important in understanding cooptability under conditions of diminishing consensus. The distribution of power, hierarchies of status, and standard processes of decision making also affect the likelihood of cooptation when consensus is less than complete. The extent to which resources have been invested in creating individual loyalty (Stinchcombe 1975) and the ability of leadership to sanction potential dissidents (Hechter 1987) are other important internal factors.

Finally, the articulation of the structure of sentiments and the social and political structure of the group or state element can be expected to inhibit or facilitate internal dissent. For instance, individual and organized opposition to cooptation attempts should be more likely to the extent that the opponents of cooptation are also a well-organized minority faction within a group or state element.

Thus, there are several internal factors that, in addition to the levels of support for and the extent of organized efforts at cooptation, are important in explaining the ability of movements to appropriate resources located within social structures.

Although the likelihood of cooptation is partly based on the internal processes we have sketched above, few groups or elements of modern states can act without taking into consideration their many ties with other groups and authority structures. These formal and informal relations of solidarity and authority with external entities also serve to constrain as well as facilitate local opportunities for successful cooptation. Groups and state elements are tied both horizontally and vertically to many other groups through formal transactions (Laumann and Knoke 1987), formal and informal coalitions (Stinchcombe 1975), and functional arenas (Scott and Meyer 1983). Groups and elements of the state are also linked through the interpersonal networks of individuals (Rosenthal et al. 1985; Mintz and Schwartz 1985).

Sometimes the importance of these extralocal ties for inhibiting cooptation are based upon the formal obligations of authority, such as those

10. We should note that our view of the effects of loyalty or solidarity are not universally held. Hirschman (1970, 121), e.g., argues that vocal dissent (or "voice") is more likely in institutions marked by high levels of solidarity, such as families, tribes, and churches.

that exist between superordinate and subordinate units of state elements, churches, and voluntary associations. But the solidity of these ties can also be based upon intragroup solidarity built out of past histories of group relationships as well as dense, overlapping, interpersonal networks that sometimes link groups to one another. Thus, it is more likely that the greater the number and density of links with other groups and state elements, the greater the likelihood that local cooptation will be constrained because of the increased likelihood that some of the external groups with which a group is linked will come to know of it and oppose it.

Cooptation is inherently a difficult process since it entails using group resources for purposes *other than those for which they were originally created*. A local Knights of Columbus chapter choosing to invest extensive effort in an antipornography crusade, a local labor union choosing to devote great effort and resources toward the problem of homelessness, and a professional association choosing to commit itself and its resources publicly to the prochoice movement are very important group choices that are open to challenge by dissenting members on a number of grounds. As a result, the actual likelihood of cooptation should decline rapidly as consensus declines. We have already sketched some of the internal and external con ditions that can be expected to govern its occurrence. In addition, several elements of cooptation campaigns are also likely to be important in determining whether or not they succeed.

Cooptation is an ongoing process that is more or less reversible at any point in time. Initial attempts at cooptation may be spurned, or a group or state element may stop lending its resources to social change efforts after a period of having done so. We suspect that the continuation of cooptation is less problematic than its initiation. Once a group or a state element becomes publicly committed to a social change effort, its sunk legitimacy costs are likely to make withdrawal of support difficult. Nevertheless, withdrawal is not uncommon when the unfolding implications of cooptation become increasingly obvious to group members or state functionaries.

Several attributes of mobilization agents should affect the movement of groups and state elements through the potential stages of initial cooptation, continuation of support, and withdrawal of support. For example, movement proponents who are members of the group or state element and are higher in the authority hierarchy are more likely to succeed in their cooptation attempts than individuals not so favorably situated, all other things being equal. Illustrations of this principle are seen in the work on the diffusion of innovations (Rogers 1983) and the leadership role on civil rights issues by liberal clergy in white Protestant congregations (Hadden 1969; Wood 1981). The forthrightness of cooptation advocates is a somewhat more complex factor. In cases where sentiment in favor of a movement's goals is lukewarm or strong norms against the diversion of group resources exist, a surreptitious approach is probably most effective. Such an approach may backfire, however. In cases where sentiments in favor of a movement's goals are strong and diversion of resources is not objectionable, a forthright approach is likely to be most effective.

Characteristics of the resources that are the goal of cooptation efforts should also affect the chances of their appropriation. The availability to movements of infrastructures, material resources, and labor power is affected by both their level and the extent to which they have been previously committed or are "slack" (Gamson 1968).

Finally, movement proponents can expect to encounter a series of logics of resistance to cooptation that are rooted in internal processes and in the structure of external relations of the group or state element. A small minority that chooses to resist cooptation must do so with accounts that have varying degrees of legitimacy with other participants. The simplest resistance logic is "we do not aim to do that," or "our constitution does not allow that." But more elegant logics stem from external ties. Commonly heard arguments are "we are not allowed to do that" because of formal external obligations to groups and elements of the state, or "we shouldn't do that" because of long-standing solidarity with others who would strongly disapprove of the actions. Logics based upon legal rules of SMO procedure, such as those governing organizational forms and protest tactics, are also common (McCarthy et al., 1991).

Concerted attempts to coopt preexisting social structures for the pursuit of social change are waged within these groups and elements of the state and are affected both by internal structures and processes and external forces. The way in which these campaigns are waged is probably of minor but some significance to their success. In the following sections we illustrate these points with examples of cooptation processes at various levels of consensus.

PROCESSES OF COOPTATION IN AND AMONG SOCIAL INFRASTRUCTURES

Religious groups and worker combinations (labor unions and professional associations) are the most typical formal civic infrastructures in the United States.[11] Cycles of efforts at cooptation by movements wash

11. Kinship and less formal friendship-acquaintance networks are the most widespread form of civic infrastructure.

across them as activists attempt to use the resources of these infrastructures for waging collective action. As a result, these are probably the most common sites of conflict over cooptation. Religious groups have been identified as central for cooptation for many movements, such as civil rights, the New Right, and prohibition. But the availability for cooptation of these infrastructures may change over time, as Wuthnow (1983) illustrates for evangelical groups. Labor unions have varied greatly in their commitment to bread-and-butter issues over more general issues of working-class life. And modern professional groups have wavered in their willingness to speak to issues beyond their technical competence (McCarthy 1987).

Consensus Cooptation

In conflict movements, only certain infrastructural locations are available for cooptation—those in which movement supporters are located. As a result, the range of infrastructures that are central to conflict mobilization is typically quite narrow. But in consensus movements, the range of available infrastructures should largely mirror the universe of social groupings in geographical communities. This is exactly the pattern in a number of such movements.

An amazingly wide variety of types of infrastructure have been utilized by the activists of the citizens' movement against drunken driving. For example, our research has found local anti–drunken driving SMOs nested in preexisting friendship groups, in networks that developed on the job, and in those developing out of consumption, such as a group of women who patronized the same beauty parlor. Some of the friendship groups developed informally from common residence patterns, although one local group developed out of a more formal neighborhood association (McCarthy et al. 1987).

As would be expected (Zald and McCarthy 1987), many groups developed out of religious organizational structures, including Protestant, Catholic, and Jewish congregations and their social action and social concern committees. In addition, several of the preexisting friendship groups were based in common worship. Many groups grew out of voluntary associations, including Junior Women's clubs, a league of mothers, a chapter of the Order of the Eastern Star, an airline pilots' club, several Rotary clubs, and a Lions Club. Others were nested in a local bicycle club, a little theater group, and several 4-H clubs. One developed out of a bereaved parents' group, another out of a local political party structure, and several out of alcohol and drug abuse groups. A number of groups grew out of businesses, such as insurance companies and an ambulance company.

This range of associational and communal infrastructural sites is extremely broad in comparison with those typical of more conflict-oriented movements. The pattern supports our expectation that as support for a social movement approaches consensus levels in communities, almost the entire range of preexisting social groups becomes available for cooptation.

The pattern we have described for the movement against drunken driving seems typical of other consensus movements, such as the city twinning movement described by Lofland (1989), an antipornography crusade (Zurcher and Kirkpatrick 1976), many local movements opposing the siting of toxic waste dumps (Mitchell and Carson 1986), and some local movements resulting from "suddenly imposed grievances," such as the Three Mile Island nuclear incident, in a subset of affected communities (Walsh 1988), and the Santa Barbara oil spill (Molotch 1970; Molotch and Lester 1975). All these cases showed extremely heterogeneous sources of associational support for their attempts to mobilize.

Conflict Cooptation

We have sketched the conditions that we believe govern the co-optability of social structures in general. Many have noted the importance of these structures for mobilization, but no one has empirically assessed the variable importance of the features of these social infrastructures as predictors of the likelihood of cooptation. As a consequence, we can illustrate the importance of only a few of the factors in accounting for the likelihood of conflict movements' cooptation of social infrastructures.

A fruitful example of several of the processes governing cooptation can be seen in the recent use of religious infrastructures of the Roman Catholic church by the prolife movement. American Catholics are divided on the issue of abortion. Even though regular worshipers are more prolife than Catholics in general, a significant minority of regular worshipers do not support the strong restrictions on abortion typically advocated by the activists of the prolife movement. Regardless of the consequent lack of consensus at the local parish level, however, many parishes lend their resources to elements of the prolife movement. There is very little evidence of local opposition to such cooptation. The acquiescence of dissident parishioners can be attributed to parish solidarity ("our church is prolife, so we expect you to go along") and by the social pressures within the parish ("the pastor expects . . ."). The power of both forces for conformity within local groups is also seen in the participation in the prolife movement of many Catholics who are themselves ambivalent about restrictions on the availability of abortion (McCarthy 1987).

The likelihood of the cooptation of parishes in support of the movement can also be seen as the result of pressure from above, emanating from the extralocal structures of authority and solidarity that characterize the church (in the early phases of the prolife movement, the American bishops actively encouraged parish-level mobilization in support of the prolife movement). On the other hand, the isolated local prochoice collective action that has emerged among Catholics has occurred in peripheral structural sites (such as religious orders and ad hoc groups of lay and religious Catholics) and has encountered aggressive social control efforts by the church hierarchy.

The differential success of efforts by gay and lesbian activists and their allies to coopt local religious infrastructures reflects differences between the Catholic episcopal structures and the more loosely coupled denominational structures of many Protestant groups. Little enduring success at cooptation has occurred within Catholic infrastructures, whereas important successes have been seen within some local congregations and national Protestant denominational structures (D'Emilio 1983). The possibility of the development of consensus in support of gay or lesbian activism at the level of the local worship community is relatively remote in geographically organized Roman Catholic structures, and more likely in congregations that can form on the basis of likemindedness without similar geographical constraints, such as those in congregational Protestant denominations. Moreover, the existence of less constraining ties between local congregations and extralocal denominational structures means that local religious groups are more autonomous, and hence more cooptable. Catholic bishops who initially sympathized with local efforts at cooptation of certain resources of the church by gay activists (e.g., allowing the use of facilities and other resources by Dignity, an association of gay Catholics) were eventually constrained by the tightly coupled structure of the church.

There are a variety of avenues by which cooptation can proceed. In more tightly coupled hierarchical structures, top-down cooptation efforts are extremely likely to succeed. We have noted the successful efforts of bishops to mobilize parishes in support of the prolife movement. A similar pattern is seen in the cooptation of the lay Catholic voluntary association, the Knights of Columbus, in support of an antipornography crusade. Zurcher and Kirkpatrick (1976) describe how one local chapter was persuaded to wage an antipornography campaign as the result of encouragement and direction from the national organizational office. Sympathetic local group leaders may also choose to allow activists from the outside easy access to their membership without necessarily lending the facilities and material resources of the group to the cooptation efforts. For example, during the second wave of Ku Klux Klan organizing across the Midwest, sympathetic local pastors often allowed Klan organizers to address their congregations in efforts to recruit members (Alexander 1965), as they did also for the organizers of the Anti-Saloon League (Kerr 1985).

We have conceived of cooptation as an ongoing process. Social infrastructures may be only temporarily available to social change causes; usually the continuity of such availability is rather fragile. Zurcher and Kirkpatrick (1976) show that a number of local groups who initially supported an antipornography campaign withdrew because they found the activists of the campaign to be "too flamboyant." Since cooptation entails some level of diversion of the efforts of ongoing social groups, a variety of logics can be expected to prevail in opposing it, either initially or once it is underway. As noted above, the diversion of group efforts from their main focus will be a central logic of resistance to cooptation. Similarly, arguments that stress the costs to the group of diversion, such as the potential loss of favorable tax advantages as a result of known cooptation (McCarthy et al. 1991), can be compelling.

PROCESSES OF COOPTATION
IN AND AMONG STATE ELEMENTS

It is generally recognized that state power in the United States is (at least formally) widely diffused. The subdivision of the state by function (executive, legislative, judicial) and by level (federal, state, county, city) results in a scattering of state authority, responsibility, and power. In recent times, the massive growth of the executive branch of the state at all levels (witnessed in the array of newly created executive agencies with wide social responsibilities) has resulted in further diffusion of the authority of the state. The functionaries of these agencies are often vested with wide latitude of statutory authority (Lowi 1969; Nordlinger 1981). Although this characteristic of the modern U.S. state has been the focus of criticism (Lowi 1969), it is precisely this feature that creates the potential for widespread and disconnected facilitation of social movements by diverse elements of the state.

Many observers have noted the benefits of direct and indirect state support for the mobilization of movements (McCarthy and Zald 1973, 1977; Walker 1983; Jenkins and Perrow 1977; Helfgot 1974; Bennett and DiLorenzo 1985). Rather than the variable origins and conditions of such support, however, the timing and consequences of state and other elite support for social movements have been the subjects of the most lively debate. Most argue that support by authorities normally follows rather than precedes the emergence of grass-roots collective action (McAdam 1982; Jenkins and Eckert 1986), and as a consequence they see it as being of secondary importance. Others have argued that elite (especially state) facilitation routinely results in the cooptation or channeling of movements into the adoption of moderate goals and tactics (Piven and Cloward 1977). Although we subscribe to the view that state support for social movements is often a critical factor in determining their impact, we are interested here in a different question: how is the patterning of state support related to the consensus or conflict nature of a movement? We explore this question below.

Consensus Cooptation

Just as there are diverse locations of potential support in community infrastructures, the differentiated, loosely coupled federal state also holds manifold possibilities for cooptation by movements. Earlier we posed the question of heterogeneity of infrastructural support for consensus movements. Similarly, we may ask whether such movements are more likely than conflict movements to enjoy support from a variety of positions within the state.

A number of case studies of conflict movements suggest that even when such movements enjoy support from one location within the state, they frequently are actively opposed by other state agencies. For example, the Boston antibusing movement enjoyed substantial support from local authorities but was opposed by the federal government to whose actions the movement was actively opposed (Useem 1980; Taylor 1986). Similarly, the conflicting positions of the federal, state, and local governments have been seen as important in shaping the outcomes of the civil rights movement of the 1960s (Barkan 1984; McAdam 1982; Garrow 1978). In addition to these conflicts among different levels of the state, a number of analysts have examined the effects of divisions between branches of government (often the executive and judicial branches) on social movements (Handler 1978; Barkan 1985).

By definition, consensus movements are not strongly opposed by any significant location within the state. But do such movements enjoy support from a diverse set of locations? We would argue that there is an important reason to believe that movements approaching the consensus type often do enjoy at least some degree of heterogeneity of state support. In contrast to the criticism from partisan and grass-roots sources that is likely to follow from known governmental facilitation of conflict movements, similar attempts to aid the mobilization of consensus movements are almost certain to generate legitimacy, and perhaps even resources, for the beneficent unit of the state. The managers of state agencies, then, can be expected to see major advantages in aiding the activists of a consensus movement. The result of this confluence of the interests of social movement activists and state functionaries should be high levels of state facilitation of consensus movements.

Case studies of several consensus movements provide some support for this argument. For example, the contemporary anti–drunken driving movement has enjoyed substantial direct and indirect support from a diverse set of locations within the federal, state, and local governments. State and federal highway agencies, as well as state and local police departments, have been particularly important in providing both tangible and symbolic support to many of the constituent groups of this movement (McCarthy and Wolfson 1988; McCarthy et al. 1987; Wolfson 1988, 1989).

In some areas the patterning of government support for the movement of activists opposing the reopening of the Three Mile Island nuclear reactor also seems to resemble that of a consensus movement (Walsh 1988, 70–74). Several of the surrounding communities had significant numbers of individuals with close ties to the facility (e.g., as workers or suppliers). This seemed to act as a check on the extent to which government officials could criticize the utility and provide support to activists opposing its reopening. But Newberry Township, which was physically remote from Three Mile Island (it lacked any direct bridge connection), had few such individuals with close ties to the facility. As a result, support for the opposition viewpoint appeared to approach consensus. And, as we would expect, many of the infrastructures of the small (and presumably relatively undifferentiated) township government were opened to the movement. The local SMO (the Newberry Township Steering Committee) was started by a township supervisor, first met in a township building room, and later met at the township school hall. Local politicians and government employees were active members of the group, and two township leaders even took a course in civil disobedience in preparation for a possible direct action. When the state police began to investigate the activities of local activists, both individual supervisors and the Board of Supervisors (in an official action) voiced a protest.

Several other case studies provide evidence of heterogeneous locations of state support under conditions of apparent consensus. For example, the local movement opposing the reopening of offshore oil drilling in Santa Barbara, which appeared to enjoy near-consensus support, received substantial and symbolic support from a wide variety of local government structures (Molotch 1970). Also, local environmental movement struggles in Japan have sometimes achieved the heterogeneity of local government support that we argue is characteristic of consensus movements (McKean 1981). Finally, the city twinning movement described by Lofland (1989), whose framing of its goals made public opposition virtually impossible, benefited from the support of a panoply of government agencies.

These several cases of apparent heterogeneity of state support of consensus movements would seem to provide some evidence for our argument. It also suggests several limitations to the potential heterogeneity of state infrastructural support. Consensus support for a movement, as we argued above, tends to exist within relatively narrow geographic boundaries. National-level consensus movements tend to be rare, and all consensus movements tend to be short-lived. Thus, heterogeneous state support for consensus movements tends to be contained within the geopolitical units in which consensus exists. State units outside of the local boundaries of consensus may in some cases support the local consensus movements (just as they may support conflict movements). But the incentives to do so are substantially diminished as any gains of legitimacy become increasingly problematic. Moreover, the presence of constituencies likely to oppose cooptation means that powerful disincentives may exist. Finally, overt opposition by state agencies becomes more likely under such circumstances, as witnessed by the actions of the Pennsylvania State Police vis-à-vis the Newberry Township activists.

A second constraint on heterogeneity of state support under conditions of consensus involves the scale of governmental units. Local state structures—particularly those of small communities—tend to lack the variety of locations of higher levels of government (state and federal). Thus, heterogeneity of support has a somewhat different meaning in small communities.

Conflict Cooptation

Political scientists have extensively chronicled the evolution of intimate ties between governmental bodies and the emergent SMOs of conflict movements (Lowi 1971; Gais et al. 1984). Sometimes a governmental agency will strive to create organized collective action in order to legitimate its existence, and sometimes an agency is created in response to collective action. The important facilitating consequences of the relationship between the U.S. Women's Bureau and the emergent women's movement during the early 1960s in the United States yet again illustrate the importance of such ties (Duerst-Lahti 1989). But only some collective actors are successful in developing working relationships with such governmental structures.

We argued above that solidarity and authority processes within nonstate infrastructures could check or counterbalance the process of declining cooptability under conditions of declining consensus. Are there comparable processes within state locations—processes that can ensure continuing co-optability under conditions of increasing conflict? Perhaps the analogue of solidarity within civic infrastructures is legitimacy within state infra-structures. Even when many staff members of an agency privately oppose cooptation by a particular movement, they may accede to agency leaders who support cooptation because of the perceived legitimacy of the leader's claims. Similarly, authority processes within state agencies—the capacity of agency leaders to coerce subordinates—can ensure continuing coopt-ability under conditions of declining consensus.

Just as civic infrastructures are constrained by their location within net-works of other organizations, state agencies are similarly constrained. A particularly important constraint is higher levels of government in the U.S. federal system. Superordinate levels of government can use moral suasion, incentives and disincentives, and, at times, direct authority to in-fluence subordinate levels to continue support for a movement, even when increasing levels of conflict are evident at these lower levels.

A clear example of this process comes from the anti–drunken driving movement. Historically, the movement's focus on the individual drunken driver tended not to threaten established interests. But when the move-ment became involved in advocating, at the federal and state levels, a twenty-one-year-old drinking age, it came up against the powerful inter-ests of alcohol producers, distributors, and retailers, as well as the less powerful interests of eighteen-to-twenty-year-old college students (Wolf-son 1988, 1989). State legislatures, which had been receptive to the move-ment's effort to enact laws aimed at controlling individual drunken drivers through traditional methods of deterrence, might have balked at legisla-tion, such as the twenty-one-year-old drinking age, that threatened sig-nificant economic interests within their states. The federal government, however, enacted legislation threatening to withhold significant amounts of federal highway funds from states that did not establish the twenty-one-year-old drinking age. This proved to be an important incentive in spurring states to pass such a law (Wolfson 1988, 1989).

Another example of the same process was the conflict between local communities that passed ordinances restricting the location or manufac-ture of nuclear materials within their jurisdictions. Although many such ordinances are mostly symbolic, more than 160 local communities have passed them (New York Times 1989). Typically, such ordinances are the suc-cessful result of efforts by antinuclear activists to coopt all elements of the state where high levels of local consensus in support of their goals exist. When the ordinances directly impinge upon the policies of higher-level state authorities, however, they are likely to draw attempts at overturning them. An example of this is the case of Oakland, California, where the federal government has, through the federal courts, asserted its authority on this question at the local level (*New York Times* 1989; Bishop 1989). The likelihood of the assertion of federal power in the more loosely coupled American system is probably substantially smaller than in more tightly coupled political systems, such as that of Japan (McKean 1981).

Potential Lines of Contrast
between Consensus and Conflict Movements

The logic of our general approach to understanding the co-optation of civic and state infrastructures should be applicable to other institutions, such as businesses and, in particular, media firms and alliances among them. We suspect that consensus movements are especially able to garner favorable media coverage, the city twinning movement (e.g., Lofland 1989) and the movement against drunken driving (McCarthy and Wolfson 1988) being notable examples. To the extent that consensus declines, however, the dense connections that characterize the environment of media firms should strongly reduce their cooptability.

Other hypothesized differences between conflict and consensus movements, such as the importance attributed to self-awareness for success that Lofland (1989) sees as central to consensus movements, can provide the bases of comparison. Our earlier thinking led us to argue that consensus movements were characterized by more rapid membership mobilization than conflict movements (McCarthy and Wolfson 1988), but Michael Schwartz (1988) convinced us that our expectation was open to question. Once we worked through the logic of consensus movements, it became clear that formal membership in consensus movement organizations is not as important as it is in conflict movement organizations, where membership numbers are perceived to some extent as dissident citizen votes that are therefore worth mobilizing. It is likely that consensus movements as a consequence put a lower premium upon formal membership recruitment and require fewer resources to achieve noticeable impacts (Wolfson 1988, 1989).

Finally, the bracing consequences of conflict, formalized so eloquently by Coser (1956), suggest a line of analysis that compares the combat readiness and mobilization efficiency of movements of the two types. The leaders of consensus movements probably are subject to less scrutiny for their actions than the leaders of conflict movements. If this is so, we should expect to find more corruption and greater overhead costs among smos in consensus movements as compared with conflict movements.

In consensus movements there is little incentive for movement activists or leaders of civil or state infrastructures to disguise cooptation. On the other hand, many conflict cooptation attempts are surreptitious because they are potentially controversial. Most consensus cooptation is wide open to observation, whereas much conflict cooptation is veiled or hidden. As a result, studying consensus movements can help us better understand conflict movements.

REFERENCES

Alexander, Charles C. 1965. *The Ku Klux Klan in the Southwest*. Louisville: University of Kentucky Press.

Barkan, Steven E. 1984. "Legal Control of the Southern Civil Rights Movement." *American Sociological Review* 49, no. 4:552–65.

———. 1985. *Protestors on Trial*. New Brunswick, N.J.: Rutgers University Press.

Bennett, James T., and Thomas J. DiLorenzo. 1985. *Destroying Democracy: How Government Funds Partisan Politics*. Washington, D.C.: Cato Institute.

Bishop, Katherine. 1989. "Oakland Battles to Be Nuclear-Free." *New York Times*, December 22, p. B6.

Casper, Ellen. 1984. "A Social History of Farm Labor in California with Special Emphasis on the United Farm Workers Union and California Rural Legal Assistance." Ph.D. diss., New School for Social Research.

Collins, Randall. 1982. *Sociological Insight*. New York: Oxford University Press.

Coser, Lewis A. 1956. *The Functions of Social Conflict*. New York: Free Press.

D'Emilio, John. 1983. *Sexual Politics, Sexual Communities*. Chicago: University of Chicago Press.

Downs, Anthony. 1972. "Up and Down with Ecology: The Issue Attention Cycle." *Public Interest* 28 (Summer):38–50.

Duerst-Lahti, Georgia. 1989. "The Government's Role in Building the Women's Movement." *Political Science Quarterly* 104, no. 2:249–68.

Fireman, Bruce, and William A. Gamson. 1979. "Utilitarian Logic in the Resource Mobilization Perspective." In *The Dynamics of Social Movements*, ed. Mayer N. Zald and John D. McCarthy. Cambridge, Mass.: Winthrop, 8–44.

Freeman, Jo. 1975. *The Politics of Women's Liberation*. New York: Longman.

Gais, Thomas L., Mark A. Peterson, and Jack L. Walker. 1984. "Interest Groups, Iron Triangles and Representative Institutions in American National Government." *British Journal of Political Science* 14:161–85.

Gamson, William. 1968. *Power and Discontent*. Homewood, Ill.: Dorsey Press.

Gamson, William A., and Andre Modigliani. 1989. "Media Discourse and Public Opinion on Nuclear Power." *American Journal of Sociology* 95 (July):1–37.

Garrow, David. 1978. *Protest at Selma*. New Haven: Yale University Press.

Godwin, R. Kenneth. 1988. *One Billion Dollars of Influence: The Direct Marketing of Politics*. Chatham, N.J.: Chatham House.

Gusfield, Joseph R. 1988. "The Control of Drinking-Driving in the United States: A Period of Transition?" In *Social Control of the Drinking Driver*, ed. Michael D.

Laurence, John R. Snortum, and Franklin E. Zimring. Chicago: University of Chicago Press, 109–35.

Hadden, Jeffrey K. 1969. *The Gathering Storm in the Churches*. Garden City, N.Y.: Doubleday.

Handler, Joel. 1978. *Social Movements and the Legal System*. New York: Academic Press.

Hayes, Michael T. 1981. *Lobbyists and Legislators: A Theory of Political Markets*. New Brunswick, N.J.: Rutgers University Press.

Hechter, Michael. 1987. *Principles of Group Solidarity*. Berkeley: University of California Press.

Helfgot, Joseph. 1974. "Professional Reform Organizations and the Symbolic Representation of the Poor." *American Sociological Review* 39, no. 4:475–91.

Hirschman, Albert O. 1970. *Exit, Voice and Loyalty*. Cambridge, Mass.: Harvard University Press.

Jenkins, J. Craig. 1983. "Resource Mobilization Theory and the Study of Social Movements." *Annual Review of Sociology* 9:527–53.

Jenkins, J. Craig, and Craig M. Eckert. 1986. "Channeling Black Insurgency: Elite Patronage and Professional Social Movement Organizations in the Development of the Black Movement." *American Sociological Review* 51 (December):812–29.

Jenkins, J. Craig, and Charles Perrow. 1977. "Insurgency of the Powerless: Farm Worker Movements (1946–1972)." *American Sociological Review* 42, no. 2:249–68.

Kerr, K. Austin. 1985. *Organized for Prohibition: A New History of the Anti-Saloon League*. New Haven: Yale University Press.

Klandermans, Bert. 1988. "The Formation and Mobilization of Consensus." *International Social Movements Research* 1:173–96.

Klandermans, Bert, and Dirk Oegema. 1987. "Potentials, Networks, Motivations and Barriers: Steps toward Participation in Social Movements." *American Sociological Review* 52:519–31.

Laumann, Edward O., and David Knoke. 1987. *The Organizational State: Social Choices in National Policy Domains*. Madison: University of Wisconsin Press.

Liebman, Robert C. 1983. "Mobilizing the Moral Majority." In *The New Christian Right*, ed. Robert C. Liebman and Robert Wuthnow. New York: Aldine, 50–74.

Lo, Clarence Y. H. 1984. "Mobilizing the Tax Revolt: The Emergent Alliance between Homeowners and Local Elites." *Research in Social Movements: Conflicts and Change* 6:293–328.

———. 1988. "Remarks." Workshop on Frontiers in Social Movement Theory, University of Michigan, Ann Arbor, June 8–11.

———. 1990. "Small Property versus Big Government." Berkeley: University of California Press.

Lofland, John. 1989. "Consensus Movements: City Twinning and Derailed Dissent in the American Eighties." *Research in Social Movements: Conflicts and Change* 11:163–96.

Lowi, Theodore J. 1969. *The End of Liberalism*. New York: W. W. Norton.

———. 1971. *The Politics of Disorder*. New York: Basic Books.

McAdam, Doug. 1982. *Political Process and the Development of Black Insurgency*. Chicago: University of Chicago Press.

McAdam, Doug, John D. McCarthy, and Mayer N. Zald. 1988. "Social Movements: Building Macro-Micro Bridges." In *Handbook of Sociology*, ed. Neil Smelser. Beverly Hills, Calif.: Sage, 695–737.

McCarthy, Coleman. 1988. "When It Comes to Alcohol, Broadcasters and Advertisers Don't Know When to Stop." *Philadelphia Inquirer*, December 31, p. 8A.

McCarthy, John D. 1987. "Pro-Life and Pro-Choice Mobilization: Infrastructure Deficits and New Technologies." In *Social Movements in an Organizational State*, ed. Mayer N. Zald and John D. McCarthy. New Brunswick, N.J.: Transaction Books, 49–66.

McCarthy, John D., David W. Britt, and Mark Wolfson. 1991. "The Institutional Channeling of Social Movements in the Modern State." In *Research in Social Movements: Conflict and Change* 13:45–76.

McCarthy, John D., and Mark Wolfson. 1988. "Exploring Sources of Rapid Social Movement Growth: The Role of Organizational Form, Consensus Support and Elements of the American State." Paper presented at the workshop on Frontiers in Social Movement Theory, University of Michigan, Ann Arbor, June 8–11.

McCarthy, John D., Mark Wolfson, and Debra Harvey. 1987. "Chapter Survey Report on the Citizens' Movement against Drunk Driving." Washington, D.C.: Center for the Study of Youth Development, Catholic University.

McCarthy, John D., and Mayer N. Zald. 1973. *The Trend of Social Movements in America: Professionalization and Resource Mobilization*. Morristown, N.J.: General Learning Press.

———. 1977. "Resource Mobilization and Social Movements: A Partial Theory." *American Journal of Sociology* 82, no. 6:1212–41.

McKean, Margaret A. 1981. *Environmental Protest and Citizen Politics in Japan*. Berkeley: University of California Press.

Mintz, Beth, and Michael Schwartz. 1985. *The Power Structure of American Business*. Chicago: University of Chicago Press.

Mitchell, Robert C., and Richard T. Carson. 1986. "Property Rights, Protest, and the Siting of Hazardous Waste Facilities." *American Economic Review* 76 (May):285–90.

Molotch, Harvey. 1970. "Oil in Santa Barbara and Power in America." *Sociological Inquiry* 40, no. 1:131–44.

Molotch, Harvey, and Marilyn Lester. 1975. "Accidental News: The Great Oil Spill as Local Occurrence and National Event." *American Journal of Sociology* 81, no. 2:235–60.

Morris, Aldon D. 1984. *The Origins of the Civil Rights Movement*. New York: Free Press.

Nelson, Barbara J. 1984. *Making an Issue of Child Abuse*. Chicago: University of Chicago Press.

New York Times. 1989. "U.S. Seeks to Overturn Oakland Nuclear Ban." September 8, p. A10.

Nordlinger, E. A. 1981. *On the Autonomy of the Democratic State*. Cambridge, Mass.: Harvard University Press.

Oberschall, Anthony. 1973. *Social Conflict and Social Movements*. Englewood Cliffs, N.J.: Prentice-Hall.

Office of the Surgeon General. 1989. *Surgeon General's Workshop on Drunk Driving: Background Papers*. Rockville, Md.: U.S. Department of Health and Human Services.

Piven, Frances F., and Richard A. Cloward. 1977. *Poor People's Movements: How They Succeed, How They Fail.* New York: Vintage.

Rogers, Everett M. 1983. *Diffusion of Innovations.* New York: Free Press.

Rosenthal, Naomi, M. Fingrutd, M. Ethier, R. Karant, and D. McDonald. 1985. "Social Movements and Network Analysis: A Case Study of Nineteenth-Century Women's Reform in New York State." *American Journal of Sociology* 90, no. 5:1022–54.

Schwartz, Michael. 1988. "Far from the Madding Crowd." Paper presented at workshop on Frontiers in Social Movement Theory, University of Michigan, Ann Arbor, June 8–11.

Scott, W. Richard, and John W. Meyer. 1983. "The Organization of Societal Sectors." In *Organizational Environments: Ritual and Rationality,* ed. John W. Meyer and W. Richard Scott. Beverly Hills, Calif.: Sage, 129–53.

Snow, David A., and Robert D. Benford. 1988. "Ideology, Frame Resonance, and Participant Mobilization." In *From Structure to Action: Social Movement Participation across Cultures,* ed. Bert Klandermans, Hanspeter Kriesi, and Sidney Tarrow. International Social Movement Research, vol. 1. Greenwich, Conn.: JAI Press, 197–217.

Stinchcombe, Arthur L. 1975. "Social Structure and Politics." In *Handbook of Political Science,* ed. Fred I. Greenstein and Nelson W. Polsby. Vol. 3. Reading, Mass.: Addison-Wesley.

Taylor, D. Garth. 1986. *Public Opinion and Collective Action: The Boston School Desegregation Conflict.* Chicago: University of Chicago Press.

Useem, Bert. 1980. "Solidarity Model, Breakdown Model and the Boston Anti-Busing Movement." *American Sociological Review* 45:357–69.

Walker, Jack L. 1983. "The Origins and Maintenance of Interest Groups in America." *American Political Science Review* 77:390–406.

Walsh, Edward J. 1988. *Democracy in the Shadows.* New York: Greenwood Press.

Williams, Robin M., Jr. 1959. *American Society.* New York: Knopf.

Wills, Gary. 1989. "Evangels of Abortion." *New York Review of Books* 36 (June 15):15–18.

Wilson, Thomas C. 1986. "Community Population Size and Social Heterogeneity: An Empirical Test." *American Journal of Sociology* 91, no. 5:1154–69.

Wolfson, Mark. 1988. "The Consequences of a Social Movement: An Organizational Analysis of the Impact of the Citizens' Movement against Drunken Driving." Ph.D. diss. Washington, D.C.: Department of Sociology, Catholic University.

———. 1989. "The Impact of Social Movement Organizations: The Role of Resources, Age, Lobbying and Interorganizational Networks." Paper presented at the annual meeting of the American Sociological Association, San Francisco, August 9–13.

Wood, James R. 1981. *Leadership in Voluntary Organizations.* New Brunswick, N.J.: Rutgers University Press.

Wuthnow, Robert. 1983. "The Political Rebirth of American Evangelicals." In *The New Christian Right,* ed. Robert C. Liebman and Robert Wuthnow. New York: Aldine, 168–87.

Zald, Mayer N., and Roberta Ash. 1966. "Social Movement Organizations: Growth, Decline and Change." *Social Forces* 44 (March):327–40.

Zald, Mayer N., and M. A. Berger. 1978. "Social Movements in Organizations:

Coup d'Etat, Insurgency and Mass Movement." *American Journal of Sociology* 83 (January):823–61.

Zald, Mayer N., and John D. McCarthy. 1987. "Religious Groups as Crucibles of Social Movements." In *Social Movements in an Organizational Society*, ed. Mayer N. Zald and John D. McCarthy. New Brunswick, N.J.: Transaction Books, 67–96.

Zurcher, Louis A., and R. George Kirkpatrick. 1976. *Citizens for Decency: Antipornography Crusades as Status Defense*. Austin: University of Texas Press.

Part 6

When Paradigms Collide

Resource Mobilization versus Breakdown Theories

13

Normalizing Collective Protest

Frances Fox Piven and

Richard A. Cloward

Over the past two decades, resource mobilization (RM) analysts have emphasized the importance of institutional continuities between conventional social life and collective protest.[1] There is much about this interpretation with which we agree. It is a corrective to some of the malintegration (MI) literature in which movements are portrayed as mindless eruptions lacking either coherence or continuity with organized social life. Nevertheless, we shall argue that RM analysts commit a reverse error. Their emphasis on the similarities between conventional and protest behavior has led them to understate the differences. They thus tend to normalize collective protest.

Blurring the distinction between normative and nonnormative forms of collective action is the most fundamental expression of this tendency, as if rule-conforming and rule-violating collective action are of a piece. To be sure, RM analysts are obviously aware that some forms of protest violate established norms and are therefore illegitimate or illegal. Indeed, a good deal of their work deals with electrifying examples of defiance of normative structures. Nevertheless, in the course of examining the institutional continuities between permissible and prohibited modes of collective

---

1. This contemporary development in the literature on protest follows a similar but much earlier development in the literature on property crime, or crimes against persons with income as the goal. Consider that Edwin H. Sutherland thought that "the processes which result in systematic criminal behavior are fundamentally the same in form as the processes which result in systematic lawful behavior" (1939, 4) and thus that "criminal behavior is a part of human behavior, has much in common with non-criminal behavior, and must be explained within the same general framework as any other behavior" (1947, 4). For a comparative analysis of these kindred but sequential theoretical perspectives in the study of crime and protest, see Piven and Cloward, "Crime and Protest" (forthcoming).

action, they often allow this distinction to disappear. But an exposition of the similarities between the structure of everyday life and the structure of protest is not an explanation of why people sometimes live their every-day lives and other times join in collective defiance. And it is, of course, precisely this theoretical problem that is central to the MI analyses that RM analysts disparage; it is nonnormative collective action—disorder and rebellion—that MI analysts want to explain.

Other problems in the RM literature are consistent with this normaliz-ing tendency. Protest is often treated by RM analysts as more organized than it is, as if conventional modes of formal organization also typify the organizational forms taken by protest. And some RM analysts normalize the political impact of collective protest, as if the processes of influence set in motion by collective protest are no different than those set in motion by conventional political activities.

These criticisms, which are discussed in this chapter, do not detract from the generalization that institutional arrangements pattern both con-ventional and unconventional collective action. Still, the differences must be explained. And once the problem of explaining differences is brought back into view, the wholesale rejection of the MI tradition by RM analysts may be seen as premature.

NORMATIVE AND NONNORMATIVE COLLECTIVE ACTION

In his recent appraisal of theories of civil violence, Rule says RM analysts define violent action as "simply a phase in other forms of collective action, caused by the same forces that move people to other, 'normal' assertions of collective interest" (1988, 170–71). Thus the Tillys object to "sociological interpretations of protest, conflict, and violence that treat them as occurring outside of normal politics, or even *against* normal politics" (1975, 240). It is true, as the Tillys say, that protest is a form of politics. But does it really make sense to treat protest and violence as if they were simply "normal" politics? To do so is to ignore the powerful role of norms in the regulation of all social life, including relations of domination and subordination.

Ongoing struggles for power continually stimulate efforts by contenders to promulgate and enforce rules that either proscribe the use of specific political resources by their antagonists or define conditions limiting their use (e.g., the conditions under which labor can be withheld in industrial conflict or sexual access withheld in mating conflict). Thus conceived, rule making is a strategy of power. Moreover, it is a strategy that creates new and lasting constraints on subsequent political action. Once objectified in a system of law, the rules forged by past power struggles continue to shape ongoing conflicts by constraining or enhancing the ability of actors to use whatever leverage their social circumstances yield them. That is why new power struggles often take the form of efforts to alter the parameters of the permissible by challenging or defying the legitimacy of prevailing norms themselves (Piven 1981). Nevertheless, protest is indeed "outside of normal politics" and "against normal politics" in the sense that people break the rules defining permissible modes of political action. Of course, the distinction between normative and nonnormative is not always easy to draw because norms themselves are often ambiguous, and no more so than when they become the focus of conflict and renegotiation. Still, a riot is clearly not an electoral rally, and both the participants and the authorities know the difference.

There are several important ways in which some RM analysts direct attention away from rule violations. One is to treat collective protest as if it were merely interest group politics, a proclivity that marks the work of McCarthy and Zald (1977; see also McCarthy et al., in press, on citizen organizing against drunk driving). Another is to conflate the normative and nonnormative. Even Tilly, whose work shows appreciation of the distinctive features of protest, frequently lumps normative and nonnormative collective action together. His definition of *contention* covers all "common action that bears directly on the interests of some other acting group," such as collective violence ("that sort of contention in which someone seizes or damages persons or objects"), and conventional political action, such as electoral rallies and campaigns (1986, 381–82). His classification of contemporary forms of collective political action includes strikes, demonstrations, electoral rallies, public meetings, petition marches, planned insurrections, invasions of official assemblies, social movements, and electoral campaigns (1986, 393). A similar conflation occurs in the survey essay on social movements prepared by McAdam, McCarthy, and Zald for Smelser's *Handbook of Sociology*, where they define virtually all forms of collective action as "social movements"—from mass civil disobedience to "burial societies" and "PTAs" (1988, 704).[2]

A still further expression of this normalizing tendency occurs when analysts focus on those aspects of protest that are normative and even ritual-

---

2. Rule is quite critical of the work on collective behavior by Park (1921), and especially by Turner and Killian (1957), for failing "to distinguish between collective and 'normal' behavior" (1988, 102). He also claims that the problem of distinguishing "collective behavior from the rest of social life" is one of two central questions with which he will be preoccupied in his book (1988, 115). But in his extensive and sympathetic discussion of RM work, Rule does not note that RM analysts also blur this distinction.

ized (thereby illuminating the continuities between everyday institutional processes and collective protest) but then make much less of the non-normative aspects (thereby obscuring the discontinuities between everyday institutional processes and collective protest). Here, for example, is Tilly's characterization of preindustrial food riots:

> If we ignore the intimate relation of the food riot to the politics of the old regime, we shall neglect the coherent political action the riot represents. Far from being impulsive, hopeless reactions to hunger, bread riots and other struggles over the food supply took a small number of relatively well-defined forms. . . . The work of the crowd embodied a critique of the authorities, was often directed consciously at the authorities, and commonly consisted of the crowd's taking precisely those measures its members thought the authorities had failed their own responsibility to take—inventorying grain in private hands, setting a price, and so on. (1975, 386)

But as this description makes clear, humble villagers did not just act in the traditional role of the authorities; they usurped their powers. Surely this feature of their action demands explanation.[3] Yet even when Tilly and his collaborators provide such dramatic examples of defiance, it is the socially patterned character of such protest events that commands their theoretical attention.

Finally, consistent with their predisposition to think of collective violence as normal politics, some RM analysts characteristically deemphasize violence by protesters and instead single out violence by the authorities. On the basis of their historical studies, the Tillys claim that most

> collective violence will ordinarily grow out of some prior collective action which is not intrinsically violent: a meeting, a ceremony, a strike. . . . To an important degree, the damage to objects and, especially, to persons *consisted* of elite reactions to the claims made by ordinary people: troops, police, and thugs acting under instructions from owners and officials attacked demonstrators, strikers, and squatters. (Tilly et al. 1975, 49 and 288)

Similarly, Snyder and Tilly conclude that "where governments have substantial force at their disposal, in fact, these specialists ordinarily do the

---

3. Elsewhere, Tilly acknowledges this extraordinary normative violation: "The frequent borrowing—in parody or in earnest—of the authorities' normal forms of action . . . often amounted to the crowd's almost literally taking the law into its own hands" (1981, 161). Nevertheless, it is the role of norms in shaping the modes of defiance, not the defiance of norms as such, that is emphasized.

major part of the damaging and seizing which constitutes the collective violence" (1972, 526). This leads to their generalization that "collective violence should rise and fall with the nonviolent political activity" (527). Granted that government is the *main* perpetrator of violence, this does not warrant the implication that people themselves do not engage in various forms of nonnormative collective action, including violence against persons and property. And if that is so, then governmental repression should also rise and fall partly in reflection of the amount of defiant behavior in which protesters themselves engage.

THE PACE AND TIMING OF COLLECTIVE PROTEST

A critical reason for calling attention to these normalizing tendencies is that they invalidate much of the work by RM analysts that deals with the prerequisites of protest—with the conditions under which people are led to defend or advance their interests by taking defiant actions that violate rules and risk great reprisals. We first criticize the grounds on which RM analysts have rejected traditional MI explanations of protest origins; then we show that the RM explanation, which emphasizes socially structured opportunities for protest, is inadequate.

Grievances and Protest

One insignia of RM work is the argument that there is little or no relationship between variations in relative deprivation and the pace and timing of collective protest. Oberschall asserts that "grievances and disaffection are a fairly permanent and recurring feature of the historical landscape" (1978, 298), suggesting a "constancy of discontent" (McAdam et al. 1988) that in turn justifies shifting "from a *strong* assumption about the centrality of deprivation and grievance to a *weak* one" in explanations of collective protest (McCarthy and Zald 1977, 1215). It is largely on this ground that RM analysts claim to have won the debate with MI analysts: "Useless Durkheim," Tilly says (1981, chap. 4).[4]

The empirical basis for this claim rests in no small degree on the widely accepted evidence presented by Tilly and his collaborators, especially their

---

4. This overall conclusion seems illogical even within the RM framework that postulates continuity between normal and defiant political activity. It is well established, e.g., that worsening economic conditions lead to voting shifts, imperiling incumbents and sometimes causing dramatic political realignments (see, e.g., Tufte 1978). Since economic deterioration produces changes in conventional political behavior, the logic of the RM analysis would lead one to expect a similar correlation between worsening economic conditions and protest.

time-series studies of the relationship between "breakdown" variables, such as intensified hardship or rapid urbanization, and the pace and timing of collective protest. But MI analysts do not claim that breakdown is a necessary precondition of normative forms of group action. What they emphasize instead is that breakdown is a precondition of collective protest and violence, of riot and rebellion. Any effort to test breakdown theories must therefore employ a dependent variable in which normative and nonnormative forms of collective action are disaggregated, which Tilly and his collaborators do not do. In effect, the MI tradition is being dismissed for an argument it never made.

Shorter and Tilly's study of strike frequencies in France illustrates this problem. They claim that strike rates correlate with good times and not with economic downturns, thus presumably invalidating the hardship variant of the relative deprivation version of the MI tradition. But strikes were legal in France beginning in 1865 (Tilly et al. 1975, 73) and thus for the entire 1865–1965 period of the Shorter and Tilly study. Or at least Shorter and Tilly do not separate out legal strikes from strikes that include illegal activity (e.g., violence and sabotage or other strike actions initiated by workers that violate government regulations or wildcat strikes that violate union contracts). Taken as a whole, this corpus of research does not answer the question of the conditions under which ordinary people do in fact resort to violence or defiance, and the findings cannot therefore be taken to refute the MI perspective.

We quickly acknowledge that time-series studies that distinguish between normative and nonnormative action will be more difficult to conduct. Not only is the distinction itself sometimes elusive, but norms change over time, in part as the result of successive challenges that produce new balances of power, reflected in new structures of rules. Forms of collective action impermissible in one period may be permissible in another, or the reverse. Moreover, caution has to be exercised in aggregating collective actions that occur in different institutional contexts, simply because different norms may apply, as when land occupations by urban squatters acquire tacit legitimacy and factory takeovers usually do not.

This problem and the obfuscation it creates is worsened by the fact that normative collective action occurs much more frequently than nonnormative action, and perhaps more so in the modern period with the granting of political rights and the vast increase in permissible forms of conflict. The sheer quantity of conventional political action overwhelms the episodic incidents of unconventional protest. Electoral rallies occur with great frequency, for example, but riots are infrequent. For this reason, unless normative and nonnormative forms are disaggregated, the conventional

will overwhelm the unconventional, thus blotting out any possible relationship between breakdown and collective protest. The point is that collective
violence and defiance must be operationalized in ways that are true to the
MI argument, however difficult that may be, if the relevance of MI ideas
to the origins of collective violence and defiance is to be fairly tested.

A second and equally fatal source of confounding results from a criticism we made earlier—the failure to distinguish between violence initiated
by protesters and violence initiated by the authorities. The MI tradition
seeks to predict violence by the former, not violence by the latter. Consider Lodhi and Tilly's time-series analysis of collective violence in France
between 1830 and 1860, which has generally been accepted as punctur-
ing MI explanations by showing that the pace and timing of collective
violence does not increase with "the rate at which social ties are being
dissolved" through urbanization (1973, 316). Their dependent variable includes "771 incidents of collective violence occurring in France from 1830
to 1860, consisting of every event involving at least one group of 50 persons or more in which some person or object was seized or damaged over
resistance" (305). But Lodhi and Tilly do not go into "the nature of the
actions" that compose their "grand totals of collective violence," limiting
themselves instead to "aggregate levels . . . of collective violence" (305)
measured by "the number killed, wounded or arrested" (298–99). And
these data, they say, "measure, in effect, how rigorously police and troops
put down protests and demonstrations" (306). The same problem arises in
the Snyder and Tilly time-series study on hardship and collective violence
in France during the same years. Again, the dependent variable is "the extent of governmental repression" (1972, 520), indicated by the number of
killings and arrests by the authorities. The question, then, is what is being
measured? Is it resort to violence by ordinary people, or is it violence in-
flicted by the authorities? But this question cannot be answered because
the dependent variable is clearly not an uncontaminated measure of the
extent to which people themselves initiated violence prior to governmental
responses.

In sum, given both the failure to disaggregate normative and nonnormative collective action and the failure to distinguish between the perpetra-
tors of violence, none of these studies can be taken as refuting the MI
tradition. Hardship and dislocation may yet be shown to correlate with
what Kerbo calls "movements of crisis" (1982; see also Kerbo and Shaffer
1986). Moreover, malintegration ideas are now enjoying a certain renaissance among some RM analysts. What seems to be provoking this shift is
the contradiction between the theoretical dismissal of the breakdown tradition, on the one hand, and the empirical descriptions of the actual con-

ditions preceding protest episodes that RM analysts themselves describe, on the other. Their accounts almost always begin by identifying precisely the sorts of antecedent conditions to which MI analysts attribute stress. These conditions—far from being recurrent, permanent, and ubiquitous, as RM analysts usually insist—are often awesome, new, and fearsome. For example, preindustrial food rioters, land squatters, and machine smashers were reacting to social and economic forces of such transforming scale as to threaten the destruction of their way of life. And perhaps for just this reason, some RM analysts are now breaking ranks over this issue. Thus there is a growing tendency in the RM literature to reintroduce terms like "intensified grievances" and "suddenly imposed grievances" (Walsh 1981), together with renaming traditional concepts such as legitimacy and delegitimacy with terms like "cognitive liberation" (McAdam 1982) and "ideological anger" (Exum 1985, 14).

Lateral Integration and Protest

We come now to the RM quarrel with the social disorganization strand in the MI tradition. Because protest grows out of everyday social organization, which creates collective capacities, RM analysts claim that it is normal. Tilly takes this argument to its logical extreme. Following White's use of the term *catnet* to define *organization*—that is, the degree of organization depends on the extent to which *cat*egories of people (e.g., blacks) are bound together by internal *net*works (e.g., religious)—Tilly argues that the more categories are laced with networks, the more they can "in principle, mobilize" (1978, 64). Hence, one of the RM school's most fundamental causal propositions: "The greater the density of social organization, the more likely that social movement activity will develop" (McAdam et al. 1988, 703).

But even as social integration is exalted in explanation of protest, so too is its absence. Protest is attributed sometimes to the fact that people are integrated in the social order and sometimes to the fact that they are not. On the one hand, if social categories of people lack a "veritable lattice work" of internal networks (McAdam et al. 1988, 711), their "infrastructure deficits" impede mobilization (McCarthy 1987). On the other hand, multiple group memberships impose role obligations, thus raising the costs of participation in movements. Consequently, McCarthy and Zald (1973) direct attention to the disproportionate participation in the movements of the 1960s by persons with few social ties, or what are called the "biographically available": students and "autonomous" professionals, for example. Students in particular are singled out because their preexisting ties to the social order are no longer binding, nor have they formed new and enduring ties. Thus students could be drawn to the Freedom Summer project during the civil rights movement because they were "remarkably free of personal constraints that might have inhibited participation" (McAdam 1988, 83). Much the same point could be made for ghetto rioters who were predominantly young and at best loosely involved in the usual array of marital, occupational, and related roles.

The proposition that the probability of protest varies directly with the degree of lateral integration is badly flawed for another reason: although collective defiance is episodic and infrequent, the lateral integration requisite to protest is ubiquitous. By not seeing this, RM analysts end by using a double standard in evaluating the MI tradition. On the one hand, they fault MI analysts for failing to concede that grievances do not necessarily lead to protest. Thus the Tillys accuse relative deprivation analysts of using a constant to explain a variation, since they give in to

> the temptation . . . to ignore the places, times, and populations in which nothing happened. When conflict is at issue, why waste time writing the history of harmony? The simple answer: an explanation of protest, rebellion, or collective violence that cannot account for its absence is no explanation at all; an explanation based only on cases where something happened is quite likely to attribute importance to conditions which are actually quite common in cases where nothing happened. That is the characteristic defect of many theories being bandied about today which treat rebellion as a consequence of frustrated rising expectations without specifying how often (or under what conditions) rising expectations are frustrated without rebellion. (1975, 12)

On the other hand, RM analysts also use a constant to explain a variation, since they too "ignore the places, times, and populations in which nothing happened." Tilly (1986) has culled four centuries of French history for episodes of collective protest, but he has not told us about those that should have erupted but did not. Here is a population of people; they had sufficient solidarity to act on their grievances, and protest might not have been met with outright repression; nevertheless, they remained inert. Surely such occasions were numerous. But the opposite impression is conveyed when these four centuries of French protests, or a century of protests in Italy, Germany, and France (Tilly et al. 1975), are compressed between the covers of a single book. Gamson's (1975) study of "challenging groups" in America suffers from the same defect. He tells us about those groups who protested but not about those who could have but did not.

This illogic pervades the RM literature. Wilson and Orum claim that "conventional psychological theories," such as relative deprivation, do not explain the ghetto riots of the 1960s, and that instead "social bonds . . . i.e., friendship networks, drew many people to become active participants" (1976, 198), but they do not wonder why riots before the 1960s were so rare or why there have been so few since, despite pervasive friendship bonds in both periods. Similarly, McAdam, McCarthy, and Zald suggest that the concentration of students in institutions of higher education has created the "organizational potential for chronic student movements . . . even if [the student movement of the 1960s] has presently waned" (1988, 712). The student movement certainly did wane; it has turned out to be anything but chronic. Most of the time most people try to make their ordinary lives, not to make history (Flacks 1988).

These analysts are led away from this problem because they overstate the structural requisites of protest. To be sure, people have to be related to one another; they must have some sense of common identity, some sense of shared definitions of grievances and antagonists, some ability to communicate, and so on. But these requisites do not depend on the dense and enduring lateral relationships posited by the RM school. On this point, Oberschall agrees: "collective protest actions . . . are possible even in a state of disorganization. . . . the minimum requirements for collective disturbances are shared sentiments of collective repression and common targets of oppression" (1973, 133). Consequently, some forms of protest are more or less universally available. Arson, whether in the fields of the preindustrial world or in the streets of the urbanized world, re-quires technological rather than organizational resources, and not much of the former, either. Riots require little more by way of organization than numbers, propinquity, and some communication. Most patterns of human settlement, whether the preindustrial village or modern metropo-lis, supply these structural requirements. In fact, the movements of the 1960s and 1970s often mobilized people who were previously only weakly or fleetingly related to one another, whether student activists or direct action participants in the peace and environmental struggles. And the ghetto rioters may not have been riffraff, but neither were they drawn from the highly integrated sectors of the black community.

Moreover, the minimal structural requirements for protest are likely to be available even during the periods of rapid social change to which Durk-heimians attribute breakdown and collective disorder. In this sense, RM analysts may have overstated breakdown ideas, as if what is meant is the total shredding of the social fabric, making it akin to complete atomization. Durkheim spoke of the way the suicide rate varies with degrees of cohesion (rural versus urban; married versus single, widowed, and divorced; and so forth). Bonds are strong, moderate, or weak; whether Durkheim also meant to suggest that bonds can disappear altogether is debatable. But whatever he intended, the point is that total atomization, if it ever exists, is at most a fleeting phenomenon: where there are human beings, there are networks. Because people are averse to being alone, they construct relationships even under the most disorganized conditions, and they do so rapidly. In short, lateral integration, however fragile, is ubiquitous, thus making opportunities for protest ubiquitous.

These observations also suggest that the generalization that the forms of protest change as societies change is overstated, and for the same reason: the requisite degree of lateral integration is overstated. The Tillys claim that urbanization and industrialization caused the small-scale, localistic, and diffuse modes of preindustrial collective protest to give way to large-scale, associational, and specialized forms. Thus from the eighteenth "to the nineteenth century either in Europe or America, we discover significant further changes in the prevailing forms of contentious gatherings. We notice the food riot, machine breaking, invasions of common fields, and their companion forms of collective action peaking and then disappearing. We find the demonstration, the strike, the election rally, the public meeting, and allied forms of action taking on more and more prominence" (Tilly 1981, 99). The main generalization follows: "The organizational revolution reorganized violence" (Tilly et al. 1975, 49).

Since at least some forms of protest require only minimal integration, however, these protest forms display remarkable continuity. "The riot," for example, "is the characteristic and ever-recurring form of popular protest" (Rude 1964, 6). More generally, preindustrial food riots, grain seizures, land invasions, and machine smashing have rough parallels in the modern period with urban riots, mob looting, squatting, sit-downs, sit-ins, rent strikes, and industrial sabotage. This suggests that Tilly's argument that repertoires of protest change as societies change—old forms out, new forms in—needs qualification. Even as changing modes of social organization bring into being new forms of protest, certain persisting features of social organization facilitate continuities in other protest forms.

Finally, the predictive value of lateral integration is weakened because the same structural capacities provide people with more than one way of reacting to their lot in life. The factors to which RM analysts attribute various forms of contention—interests, organization, mobilization—are also associated with the rise of religious movements, for example, or of organized racketeering. Consider the social bonds of friendship: Wilson and Orum (1976) attribute ghetto riots to them, and Ianni (1974) notes that blacks, lacking the ethnic-familial solidarities that make the Italian Mafia possible, nevertheless developed a Black Mafia because of friend-ship solidarities forged in street gangs and prisons. And perhaps there is even an interactive effect between crime and protest: the rise and spread of organized networks of drug entrepreneurship and consumption may help explain the low level of protest in the black ghettos since the 1960s. In other words, social integration does not dictate that people will seek solutions to felt grievances in politics at all, whether by conventional or unconventional means.

In general, then, *organizational capacity does not predict anything*—except that the violation of rules *might* take collective form and, if collective, that it *might* take political form.[5] We have elsewhere referred to this as the problem of "indeterminancy"—that given objective conditions, such as structural opportunity, do not necessarily determine given behavioral out-comes (Cloward and Piven 1979, 654; 1989). Plainly, the question of the correlates of the pace and timing of collective protest remains open.

Vertical Integration and Protest

People who are organized laterally are also typically connected to other groups vertically. But hierarchical bonds usually constrain collec-tive protest, and that is still another reason lateral integration does not predict protest. Tocqueville noted that it was only with the weakening of ties between nobility and peasantry that the French Revolution became possible. Moore subsequently analyzed variations in the "institutional links binding peasant society to the upper classes" and argued that weaker link-ages were more conducive to peasant revolution (1966, 477–78). Ober-schall also follows this line of thinking by suggesting that protest potential is enhanced when societies are "segmented" so that lower-stratum col-lectivities have "few links and bonds" to higher-stratum groups—for ex-ample, when landlords are absentee owners, or when forms of colonial rule generate "few links between colonizer and colonized," or when self-contained farm belts are "cut off from the power centers . . . except for

5. And even if people are in fact inclined to seek solutions to their problems through politics, variations in social integration may predict the forms of protest better than the incidence of it: e.g., disciplined civil disobedience occurred more often in the South and rioting occurred almost exclusively in the North during the 1960s. A possible explana-tion is that northern ghettos were less cohesive than southern black communities, making it more difficult to promote disciplined protest, especially in the face of provocations by the police.

market relations." In contrast, Oberschall continues, if there are strong "vertical social and political bonds between upper and lower classes, mobilization into protest movements among the lower classes is not likely to take place" (1973, 119–20).[6]

Because hierarchical integration is more the rule than the exception, the important problem is to identify the conditions under which its constraining influence weakens. On this point, the ideas of MI analysts may be relevant. Vertically integrated institutions probably become settings for protest only under exceptional conditions—when grievances intensify or when linkages weaken.

Prior to the advent of the RM school, the black church, with its "other-worldly" oriented clergy who were dominated by white influentials, was thought to divert people from political action, as indeed it did. But RM analysts have since rehabilitated the black church by arguing that it provided a crucial nexus for the civil rights mobilization, and indeed it also did that. The same point can be made for the Catholic church in Latin America whose centuries-long alliance with the landed oligarchies has only recently begun to give way. And a similar shift of the church's role occurred in Poland. It was probably constituency discontent that forced the shift to activist theologies by the black churches in the South and by the Catholic churches in Latin America and Poland. Otherwise, church leaders risked the loss of legitimacy in the eyes of their parishioners. Similarly, the shift by white Protestant fundamentalist clergy in the United States from a theological doctrine prescribing the separation of religion and politics to one calling for secular political protest in the name of maintaining religious values (e.g., civil disobedience at abortion clinics) may reflect, at least in part, rising discontent among many parishioners in the face of threats to their traditional way of life raised by greater cultural permissiveness (Ginsberg 1989; Piven 1984).

Electoral institutions also illustrate the dual effects of institutional integration. The ideology of democratic political rights, by emphasizing the availability of legitimate avenues for the redress of grievances, delegitimizes protest; and the dense relationships generated by electoral politics also divert people from protest. Rising popular discontent, however, sometimes sets in motion a process that, at least temporarily, transforms electoral politics itself. For instance, when deteriorating economic circumstances produce voter volatility, the short-term concerns of political

6. On this point, see also Eric Wolf's (1969) discussion of the constraining effect of clan ties that crossed class lines in prerevolutionary China.

leaders with reelection may lead them to cope with unstable majorities by symbolically identifying with the grievances of discontented groups, thus fueling anger and legitimating protest (Piven and Cloward 1977, 18).

In many situations, protest becomes possible only when vertical controls weaken owing to large-scale processes of social change. In the 1930s, the craft unions associated with the dominant American Federation of Labor (AFL) issued charters to industrial workers who were clamoring for unions, but the AFL oligarchs were less than enthusiastic in welcoming their new constituents. Given their level of discontent and their loose ties to the AFL, industrial workers broke free, and strike waves followed. A similar process occurred in company unions that had been established to inhibit protest, particularly in the steel industry. And only as strikes escalated did a few enterprising union leaders, sensing the possibilities of the moment, create organizing committees to form industrial unions (Piven and Cloward 1977, 153). On this point, Hobsbawm agrees: "Mass union organization, in the US of the 1930s as in all analogous 'explosions' of labor unionism with which I am familiar, was the result of worker mobilization and not its cause" (1978). Another example of breakout is provided by the post-war drives by public employees for the right to unionize and strike. They gained this right only after the historically close ties between civil service associations and local political parties had weakened (Piven 1969). And the postwar black protest movement was not imaginable until the modernization of the plantation system led to mass evictions of blacks from the land and from a system of semifeudal controls (Oberschall 1973; Piven and Cloward 1977).[7] In short, breakdown is often prerequisite to breakout. Perhaps Durkheim is not so useless after all.

NORMALIZING PROTEST ORGANIZATION

Some among the Durkheimians tend to think of collective protest as purposeless disorder, but RM analysts think it has purpose, and that it is political—the effort to exercise power in contests with other groups. In this large sense, protest is normal because politics is normal, as we would agree. In recasting collective protest as politics, however, RM analysts have normalized both the organizational forms typically associated with protest, especially with lower-stratum protest, and the political processes generated by protest.

Both of these tendencies appear in Tilly's work and are linked to his

7. For further examples of this general point and the literature bearing on it, see Kerbo (1982, 652).

understanding of historical change as progress. Thus, in the preindustrial world, the possibility of exerting influence depended on "the willingness of [challenging groups] to inflict and endure harm," but the "grant of legality [to many previously proscribed forms of political action] lowers the group's costs of mobilization and collective action" (Tilly 1978, 167). Consequently, what now "tells more" than inflicting and enduring harm is "the group's capacity to organize, accumulate resources, and form alliances," especially within the electoral system (Tilly et al. 1975, 285). The implication is that ordinary people can now form organizations to pursue their goals through normal politics.

This conclusion strikes us as altogether too sweeping. True, with the grant of legality, the risk of repression no longer inhibits many forms of mobilization. At the same time, however, legalization increases the costs of mobilization because it imposes additional resource requirements. Tilly himself implies as much in his discussion of the way legalization transformed strikes: elements of "standardization," "routinization," and "bureaucratization" were introduced, and "spontaneity" declined (1978, 161). Moreover, legalization "muzzles" or "encapsulates" strike power (Piven and Cloward 1977, 155–75), as McCammon reminds us in her update of the way U.S. labor relations law "severely crippled, if not negated," the power of the strike (1990, 225). In other words, to use conventional methods of influence effectively, people have to be able to muster the resources both to organize bureaucratically and to overcome the influence of other groups in regular political contests. Those resources, Tilly says, are "the economist's factors of production: land, labor, capital, and perhaps technical expertise as well" (1978, 69). By these criteria, however, lower-stratum challengers are obviously left with serious resource deficits (Piven 1963).

Although RM analysts have tried to solve this problem in two ways, each method has failed. One approach has been to treat formal organization as if it compensates for lack of political resources. Unfortunately for lower-stratum groups, organization is a pale substitute for resources. Gamson's check list of what it takes for a group to become "combat-ready" shows why. Since the antagonists are bureaucratically organized, challengers must create parallel organizations with three characteristics: (1) a constitution, (2) an internal division into officers, committees, and rank and file, and (3) a formal membership list. In addition, it is important that there be sufficient centralized authority to quell factionalism in the group or, if the group is more decentralized, some other mechanism to control internal dissension. "Each of these variables—bureaucracy, centralization of power, and [the limiting of] factionalism—makes a contribution to success. . . . There are, then, definite advantages for a challenging group, inevitably engaged in conflict with an organized antagonist, to organize itself for facility in political combat" (1975, 108).

Gamson derives these conclusions from his study of fifty-three challengers in American history between 1800 and 1945, all of which were formally organized groups existing on an average of eight years. Two-fifths of them were occupationally based, mainly unions; one-third were assorted reform groups, including abolitionists, political parties, civil rights organizations, and peace groups; another fifth were socialist groups, such as the International Workingmen's Association; and the remainder were right-wing or nativist groups, such as the German-American Bund (1975, 20).

Protest actions that were not sponsored by formally organized groups did not turn up in the sample.[8] "Perhaps that tells us something," Gamson says, thereby implying that collective protest episodes are always sponsored by organizations (personal communication). But even the most casual perusal of collective action events—whether the ghetto riots in the American cities of the 1960s or the mass demonstrations in Eastern Europe or the food riots in Latin America—makes clear how dubious that thesis is, and especially how dubious it is for the kinds of collective protest and disorder that are of concern to Durkheimians. (Of course, formal organizations do often come to be associated with protest events in various ways, sometimes because outside observers erroneously attribute these events to preexisting formal organizations and sometimes because protests stimulate the founding of organizations by social movement entrepreneurs who are then given credit retroactively for the protests themselves.)

Protest is also depicted as overorganized in a good many RM case studies. The rise of movements is signified by organizational paraphernalia, such as the formation of social movement organizations with leaders who make demands and call for demonstrations or lobbying. Absent these manifestations, RM analysts often do not recognize the existence of movements. Thus the two major recent RM accounts of the civil rights movement barely touch on riots: Morris (1984) does not mention them (except for a brief reference to the riot in Birmingham), and McAdam (1982) ignores the question of why they occurred. Similarly, in a survey of the social movement literature by McAdam, McCarthy, and Zald (1988), riots are mentioned only once, nor do many other modes of disruptive protest figure much in their survey. Their discussion of social movement organizations ranges across

8. "In theory," Gamson says, "a collective behavior listing might have yielded a challenging group, in the absence of any other appropriate organizational listing, but this, in fact, never occurred. Thus all of our final sample listings are organizations" (1975, 156).

such issues as inclusivity and exclusivity, federation and chapter structures, and competition within social movement industries, which exerts pressure for "product differentiation." The "professional social movement organization" is singled out; in "pure" form, its distinguishing characteristic is that it "communicates with adherents or members through the mails or the mass media" (1988, 716–18).

These portrayals may well have validity for groups that have the resources to construct enduring formal organizations and still further resources that can be converted into political power. But can those with few resources form influential organizations successfully? Indeed, do they even have the resources to form stable formal organizations, influential or not? Lower-stratum groups often act as though they think so, and they do their best to adopt constitutions, elect officers, divide responsibilities among committees, compile membership lists, hold conventions, seek alliances, and garner external financial and expert resources. But such formal organizations cannot be wished into existence; it takes resources to create them and especially to sustain them. Labor organizations solve this problem with mechanisms to coerce membership and contributions—such as the union shop and dues checkoff—but lower-stratum groups typically lack the capacity to coerce participation. Consequently, efforts by lower-income people to build formal organizations generally fail, as the most cursory reading of the history of poor people's organizations reveals. Naison's account of tenant organizing in New York City during the 1930s ends by noting that the citywide structure that coordinated local tenant organizations "proved fragile":

> Never did City-Wide's fund raising produce over one thousand dollars per year. . . . The slum tenants . . . lacked the resources to subsidize it, or the political skills and inclinations to build the kind of stable organizations that could give City-Wide real permanence. City-Wide survived on the politically-motivated idealism and skills of underemployed professionals, both of which were vulnerable to shifts in political climate and improvements in the economy. (1986, 127)

The same point can be made for welfare rights organizing in the 1960s: the National Welfare Rights Organization lasted only about five years because local groups throughout the country could not sustain themselves once external resources from the antipoverty program, such as organizers drawn from the ranks of VISTA volunteers, began to contract. A serious defect of Gamson's sample is that the vast number of failed organization-building episodes by lower-stratum people is not represented, since most such efforts never resulted in fully formed organizations, or the resulting organizations were so puny and short-lived that they were not available to be sampled. Had there been a way to sample these episodes, Gamson might not have been so quick to advance a formal organization prescription, especially for lower-stratum groups. In short, the resources necessary to develop permanent mass-based bureaucratic organizations are not equally distributed in the class structure. The preoccupation with formal organization thus inadvertently contributes to the class bias in the work of RM analysts that has been remarked upon by Kerbo (1982).

The RM analysts have also tried to solve the problem of lower-stratum resource deficits by emphasizing the importance of coalition politics in which "third parties" make up for resource deficiencies.[9] Here the problem is not so much that lower-stratum groups lack resources to form stable organizations as that their organizations, even when formed, command few of the kinds of resources that can be converted into regular political influence. Organization, in short, is not necessarily a source of power.

The role of third parties in making up for the lack of political influence by lower-stratum groups was highlighted by Lipsky in his analysis of the 1963–64 New York City rent strike (1968, 1970). He concluded that the essence of the politics of protest is "showmanship" or "noise" in which leaders curry sympathy and support from potential "reference publics." His findings, which have been widely accepted, are summarized by the Tillys: "Lipsky makes a strong case that the strike movement owed what success it had (which was not enormous) to the fact that dramatic protests activated powerful third parties who then put pressure on responsible authorities to respond to the grievances of the protestors" (1975, 294). None of this was true. The so-called rent strike movement consisted of a mere flurry of rent-withholding activity between November 1963 and March of the next year. The only sense in which the episode was "dramatic" was that Jesse Grey, the citywide strike leader, knew how to attract press coverage by announcing (inaccurately) that thousands of buildings were about to go on strike and by conducting tenement tours for sympathetic reporters who wrote stories deploring housing conditions. As a factual matter, no powerful third parties put pressure on anyone (Piven and Cloward 1967).[10]

9. Morris (1984) has taken exception to this view in his discussion of the civil rights movement by summoning evidence of the substantial resources the black community itself supplied, but his own data make clear that these internally generated resources, including especially leadership resources, were contributed mainly by middle-class blacks.

10. The strike failed to rally significant third-party support because the organizers followed Gamson's prescription: they first built tenant committees. Then, together with tenant leaders, they tried to induce tenants to use the procedures for legal redress laid out by the housing agencies. They canvassed apartments for housing violations, filled

How then can people without conventional political resources exert influence? In our own work on unemployed and labor movements, rent strikes, welfare rights organizing, and the civil rights movement, we have tried to show that lower-stratum protesters have some possibility of influence—including mobilizing third-party support—if their actions violate rules and disrupt the workings of an institution on which important groups depend.[11] When lower-stratum groups form fragile formal organizations and employ conventional political strategies, they can easily be ignored. But institutional disruptions cannot so easily be ignored: they provoke conflict, they arouse an array of third parties, including important economic interests, and they may even contribute to electoral dealignment and realignment. To restore institutional stability and to avoid worsening polarization, political leaders are forced to respond, whether with concessions or with repression. To suppose that normal or conventional political strategies can have these effects is to underestimate the maldistribution of political resources and to trivialize the consequent realities of power.

Even when the resources are available to create them, formally organized groups are not likely to undertake disruptive protests. Gamson's formal organization prescription ignores the problems that disruptive or rule-breaking protests create for formal organizations. It is not that disruption and violence are never employed by formally organized groups; it is that, in general, organization constrains such tactics. Protests can provoke severe repression, which formal organizations will not usually risk (secret or underground organizations are better positioned in this respect). This is a point made by E. P. Thompson when he speaks of the English crowd's

> capacity for swift direct action. To be of a crowd or a mob was another way of being anonymous, whereas to be a member of a continuing organization was bound to expose one to detection and victimisation. The 18th century crowd well understood its capacities for action, and its own art of the possible. Its successes must be immediate, or not

---

out official forms, scheduled visits by building inspectors to record hazardous violations, checked to be sure the inspectors actually filed these forms, arranged for rents to be placed in escrow, contacted lawyers, and shepherded tenants through the courts, not once but over and over again in the face of delaying tactics by landlords. And for all that, only a few victories were won. As tenants and organizers were increasingly overwhelmed and worn down by these procedures, the strike faltered and then collapsed only a few months after it began (Piven and Cloward 1967).

11. The essential importance of institutional disruptions for the exercise of political influence by resourceless groups is set out in Piven (1963) and in Cloward and Piven (1966). For theoretical elaborations and applications to particular social movements, see Piven and Cloward (1967, 1977) and Cloward and Piven (1968). The role of disruption is debated in Gamson and Schmeidler (1984) and Cloward and Piven (1984).

at all. It must destroy those machines, intimidate those employers or dealers, damage that mill . . . before troops come on the scene. (1974, 401)

Scott puts the same point this way: "Mob action . . . may represent a popular tactical wisdom developed in conscious response to political constraints realistically faced. Spontaneity and a lack of formal organization then become an *enabling* mode of protest rather than a reflection of the slender political talents of popular classes" (n.d.). And Oberschall again breaks with the main RM currents of thought to argue that "the degree of organization varies inversely with the magnitude of violence in confrontations" (1973, 340).

Protest is also inhibited by constraints that result from the vertical integration upon which organizational maintenance by relatively resourceless groups often depends. Thus McAdam, McCarthy, and Zald claim that "a principal goal of [RM analysts] is understanding how emergent movement organizations seek to mobilize and routinize—frequently by tapping lucrative elite resources of support—the flow of resources, which ensures movement survival" (1988, 697), without acknowledging that this dependency generally turns movement organizations away from protest. This is a problem we have tried to address in our own work (1977, especially the introduction to the paperback edition), but McAdam dismisses as "pessimistic" our conclusion that organization (in the sense of formal organization) tends to militate against the use of disruptive tactics (1982, 54). Nevertheless, McAdam concludes his own discussion of these issues in words that could have been our own: "the establishment of formal organizations . . . sets in motion . . . the destructive forces of oligarchization, cooptation, and the dissolution of indigenous support . . . [all of which] tames the movement by encouraging insurgents to pursue only those goals acceptable to external sponsors. . . . The long list of movements that have failed to negotiate these obstacles attests to the difficulties inherent in the effort" (1982, 55–56).

NORMALIZING POLITICAL INFLUENCE

In democratic polities, whether protesters win or lose depends on the interaction between disruptive political tactics and electoral politics. But the influence resulting from the interaction between institutional disruptions and the electoral system cannot be understood by the usual mode of analysis that focuses, as the Tillys do, on the forming of alliances (1975, 285).

Lower-stratum disruptive movements tend to emerge at junctures when larger societal changes generate political volatility and dealignment and new political possibilities. On this point, we agree with the line of analysis in much RM literature that attributes protest from below in part to the opportunities generated by the fragmenting of elites and by realigning processes. Still, the impact of protest during these periods is not simply that it contributes to subsequent coalition building and realignment. What needs to be understood is that disruptive protest itself makes an important contribution to elite fragmentation and electoral dealignment. Indeed, we think the role of disruptive protest in helping to create political crises (or what we have called "dissensus politics") is the main source of political influence by lower-stratum groups (Cloward and Piven 1966, 1968; Piven and Cloward 1967, 1977, chap. 4; Piven and Cloward 1988, introduction).

The sharp contrast between our dissensus politics analysis and a good number of RM analyses can be illustrated by examining explanations of civil rights successes. For example, McAdam correctly emphasizes that a "significant disruption of public order" was essential to ensure federal responses to the civil rights movement (1982, 221). Despite this promising beginning (and despite its clear difference from Lipsky's "noise" and "showmanship"), McAdam goes on to explain federal responses in the usual coalitional terms: protesters won because of the growing influence of the black vote coupled with the support of sympathetic northern white liberals. Something like this coalitional process did indeed happen. It was not more important, however, than the fact that the tactics of the civil rights movement helped cleave the Democratic party's North-South alliance. This alliance was already weakening owing to southern opposition to New Deal labor and social welfare policies and owing to the expansion of the white middle class generated by economic modernization in the South during the postwar period. The result was to stimulate neopopulist movements and to revive the southern wing of the Republican party. Democratic leaders tipped decisively toward supporting civil rights legislation only when it became clear that black protests were *also* helping to swell the volume of southern white defections to the Republican party. With the white South alienated, it was finally in the interests of the national Democratic party to enfranchise blacks in an attempt to rebuild its shattered southern wing. For McAdam, however, the Democratic party's southern regional base was "a relatively small, politically expendable segment of the population" (1982, 215), which did not figure in the calculations of national Democratic party strategists. Of course, the South was not expendable and national Democratic party leaders knew it was not, which is why they resisted civil rights concessions for as long as they did. But civil rights protests—by activating northern liberals and the growing concentrations of black voters in the northern cities, *and especially by enlarging the tide of southern white defections*—changed the political calculus. Generally speaking, then, disruptive tactics force concessions not by enlarging and consolidating coalitions but by exacerbating electoral dissensus during periods when electoral divisions are already widening (Cloward and Piven 1966, 1968; Piven and Cloward 1967, 1977, chap. 4; Piven and Cloward 1988, introduction).

After two decades of work by analysts associated with the RM school, protest by lower-stratum people is as marginalized and deviant as it ever was. Despite a substantial volume of work on the civil rights movement, for example, we know little more than we did before about the riot of May 11, 1963, in Birmingham—perhaps the single most important episode in the black movement to that date—or of the subsequent riots in which 169 were killed, 7,000 wounded, and 40,000 arrested, except that the participants were not "riffraff."

When RM analysts talk about these riots, they reveal the biases of a normalized, overorganized, and conventionalized conception of political protest. The riots are not so much analyzed as regretted. McAdam considers that Jacobs and Landau "accurately summed up the situation" when they explained that "neither SNCC nor any other group has found a form of political organization that can convert the energy of the slums into political power" (quoted in McAdam 1982, 191). But if such efforts to organize the black lower class had been undertaken—at least if they had been undertaken early enough and forcefully enough in the 1960s—there might have been no riots. As it was, the main role played by various social movement leaders during the rioting was to try to quell it, and RM analysts unfailingly approve. Morris says that when riots broke out in Birmingham in June 1963, civil rights leaders "hit the streets at once in order to persuade members of the black community not to engage in violence" so as to "save the agreement" with the economic elites of Birmingham. With the rioters subdued, "the agreement stood, and the planned exercise of 'people power' had been successful" (Morris 1984, 273). McAdam correctly notes that the early riots triggered a veritable northward stampede by movement leaders to establish organizational footholds in the ghetto as a means of regaining control over a movement that was "slipping away from them" (1982, 191). And Oberschall expresses the same outlook when he concludes that "the single most important failure of the middle-class blacks and the civil rights organizations was their failure to mobilize and to organize the lower-class community" (1973, 213).

So there we have it again. Like many malintegration analysts before them, resource mobilization analysts have also reduced lower-stratum protest politics to irrational and apolitical eruptions.

REFERENCES

Cloward, Richard A., and Frances Fox Piven. 1966. "A Strategy to End Poverty." *Nation*, May 2. Reprinted in Richard A. Cloward and Frances Fox Piven, *The Politics of Turmoil*. New York: Pantheon, 1974.

———. 1968. "Dissensus Politics: A Strategy for Winning Economic Rights." *New Republic*, April 20. Reprinted in Richard A. Cloward and Frances Fox Piven, *The Politics of Turmoil*. New York: Pantheon, 1974.

———. 1979. "Hidden Protest: The Channeling of Female Innovation and Resistance." *Signs* 4:41.

———. 1984. "Disruption and Organization: A Rejoinder to Gamson and Schmeidler." *Theory and Society* 13:587–99.

———. 1989. "Why People Deviate in Different Ways." In *New Directions in the Study of Justice, Law and Social Control*, ed. the Arizona State University School of Justice Studies Editorial Board. New York: Plenum.

Exum, William H. 1985. *Paradoxes of Black Protest: Black Student Activism in a White University*. Philadelphia: Temple University Press.

Flacks, Richard. 1988. *Making History: The Radical Tradition and the American Mind*. New York: Columbia University Press.

Gamson, William A. 1975. *The Strategy of Social Protest*. Homewood, Ill.: Dorsey.

Gamson, William A., and Emilie Schmeidler. 1984. "Organizing the Poor: An Argument with Frances Fox Piven and Richard A. Cloward, *Poor People's Movements: Why They Succeed, How They Fail*." *Theory and Society* 13:567–85.

Ginsberg, Faye. 1989. *Contested Lives: The Abortion Debate in an American Community*. Berkeley: University of California Press.

Hobsbawm, Eric J. 1978. "Should the Poor Organize?" *New York Review of Books* 25, no. 4 (March 23).

Ianni, Francis A. J. 1974. *Black Mafia: Ethnic Succession in Organized Crime*. New York: Simon and Schuster.

Kerbo, Harold R. 1982. "Movements of 'Crisis' and Movements of 'Affluence': A Critique of Deprivation and Resource Mobilization Theories." *Journal of Conflict Resolution* 26, no. 4 (December).

Kerbo, Harold R., and Richard A. Shaffer. 1986. "Unemployment and Protest in the United States, 1890–1940: A Methodological Critique and Research Note." *Social Forces* 64:1046–56.

Lipsky, Michael. 1968. "Protest as a Political Resource." *American Political Science Review* 62:1144–58.

———. 1970. *Protest in City Politics: Rent Strikes, Housing and the Power of the Poor*. Chicago: Rand McNally.

Lodhi, Abdul Qaiyum, and Charles Tilly. 1973. "Urbanization and Collective Violence in 19th-Century France." *American Journal of Sociology* 2 (September).

McAdam, Doug. 1982. *Political Process and the Development of Black Insurgency, 1930–1970*. Chicago: University of Chicago Press.

————. 1988. *Freedom Summer: The Idealists Revisited.* New York: Oxford University Press.

McAdam, Doug, John D. McCarthy, and Mayer N. Zald. 1988. "Social Movements." In *Handbook of Sociology*, ed. Neil J. Smelser. Beverly Hills, Calif.: Sage.

McCammon, Holly J. 1990. "Legal Limits on Labor Militancy: Labor Law and the Right to Strike since the New Deal." *Social Problems* 37, no. 2.

McCarthy, John D. 1987. "Pro-Life and Pro-Choice Mobilization: Infrastructure Deficits and New Technologies." In *Social Movements in an Organizational Society*, ed. Mayer N. Zald and John D. McCarthy. New Brunswick, N.J.: Transaction Books.

McCarthy, John D., Mark Wolfson, David P. Baker, and Elaine M. Mosakowski. In press. "The Foundations of Social Movement Organizations: Local Citizens' Groups Opposing Drunken Driving." In *Ecological Models of Organization*, ed. Glenn R. Carroll. Cambridge, Mass.: Ballinger.

McCarthy, John D., and Mayer Zald. 1973. *The Trend of Social Movements in America: Professionalization and Resource Mobilization.* Morristown, N.J.: General Learning Press.

————. 1977. "Resource Mobilization and Social Movements." *American Journal of Sociology* 82:1212–41.

Moore, Barrington. 1966. *The Social Origins of Dictatorship and Democracy: Lord and Peasant in the Making of the Modern World.* Boston: Beacon Press.

Morris, Aldon D. 1984. *The Origins of the Civil Rights Movement.* New York: Free Press.

Naison, Mark. 1986. "From Eviction Resistance to Rent Control: Tenant Activism in the Great Depression." In *The Tenant Movement in New York City, 1904–1984*, ed. Ronald Lawson, with the assistance of Mark Naison. New Brunswick, N.J.: Rutgers University Press.

Oberschall, Anthony. 1973. *Social Conflict and Social Movements.* Englewood Cliffs, N.J.: Prentice-Hall.

————. 1978. "Theories of Social Conflict." In *Annual Review of Sociology*, 4. Beverly Hills, Calif.: Sage.

Piven, Frances Fox. 1963. "Low-Income People and the Political Process." A report published by Mobilization for Youth. Reprinted in Richard A. Cloward and Frances Fox Piven, *The Politics of Turmoil*. New York: Pantheon, 1974.

————. 1969. "Militant Civil Servants." *Transaction* 7, no. 1 (November). Reprinted in Richard A. Cloward and Frances Fox Piven, *The Politics of Turmoil*. New York: Pantheon, 1974.

————. 1981. "Deviant Behavior and the Remaking of the World." *Social Problems* 28, no. 5:489–508.

————. 1984. "Women and the State: Ideology, Power and the Welfare State." In *Gender and the Life Course*, ed. Alice Rossi. New York: Aldine.

Piven, Frances Fox, and Richard A. Cloward. 1967. "Rent Strike: Disrupting the Slum System." *New Republic*, December 2. Reprinted in Richard A. Cloward and Frances Fox Piven, *The Politics of Turmoil*. New York: Pantheon, 1974.

————. 1977. *Poor People's Movements.* New York: Pantheon.

————. 1988. *Why Americans Don't Vote.* New York: Pantheon.

————. Forthcoming. "Crime and Protest: Discovery and Rediscovery."

Rude, George. 1964. *The Crowd in History.* New York: Wiley.

Rule, James B. 1988. *Theories of Civil Violence*. Berkeley: University of California Press.

Scott, James. N.d. "The Hidden Transcript of Subordinate Groups." Department of Political Science, Yale University.

Shorter, Edward, and Charles Tilly. 1974. *Strikes in France, 1830 to 1968*. New York: Cambridge University Press.

Snyder, David, and Charles Tilly. 1972. "Hardship and Collective Violence in France, 1830–1960." *American Sociological Review* 37.

Sutherland, Edwin H. 1939. *Principles of Criminology*. 3d ed. Chicago: University of Chicago Press.

———. 1947. *Principles of Criminology*. 4th ed. Philadelphia: Lippincott.

Thompson, E. P. 1974. "Patrician Society, Plebian Culture." *Journal of Social History* 7, no. 4.

Tilly, Charles. 1975. "Food Supply and Public Order in Modern Europe." In *The Formation of National States in Western Europe*, ed. Charles Tilly. Princeton: Princeton University Press.

———. 1978. *From Mobilization to Revolution*. Reading, Mass.. Addison Wesley

———. 1981. *As Sociology Meets History*. New York: Academic Press.

———. 1986. *The Contentious French*. Cambridge, Mass.: Harvard University Press.

Tilly, Charles, Louise Tilly, and Richard Tilly. 1975. *The Rebellious Century*. Cambridge, Mass.: Harvard University Press.

Tufte, Edward R. 1978. *Political Control of the Economy*. Princeton: Princeton University Press.

Walsh, Edward. 1981. "Resource Mobilization and Citizen Protest in Communities around Three Mile Island." *Social Problems* 29:1–21.

Wilson, Kenneth L., and Anthony M. Orum. 1976. "Mobilizing People for Collective Political Action." *Journal of Political and Military Sociology* 4:187–202.

Wolf, Eric. 1969. *Peasant Wars in the Twentieth Century*. New York: Harper and Row.

14

Looking Backward to Look Forward

Reflections on the Past and Future of the

Resource Mobilization Research Program

M a y e r   N.   Z a l d

Social scientists follow the news, especially when their scholarly interests are linked to and resonate with the moral, political, and practical concerns of the larger society. But they do more than just follow the news; they engage in an ongoing conversation and debate within their specialty areas and with the surrounding intellectual community. The emergence of the modern civil rights movement at the end of the Eisenhower era, followed by the War on Poverty, the anti–Vietnam War movement, and the flowering of other social causes, represented the external catalyst for a renewed concern with social movements. Within the scholarly community, debates about the adequacy of grievance models and the growth of models of collective action that presented alternatives to the apolitical and irrationalist cast of some versions of collective behavior theory fed into a search for a new framework for social movement theory. What has been called collective action or resource mobilization (CA or RM) theory emerged out of that context.

Here I reflect upon the scholarly developments of the last two decades. In the first section, I briefly review the perspectives dominant before the rise of activism in the 1960s, and in the second, I examine how those events challenged those perspectives. I then discuss the core assumptions of the various resource mobilization approaches. The most interesting issue, however, is not where we have been but where we are going. The next section attempts to evaluate the strengths and weaknesses of RM-related research with an eye to identifying major lacunae. And the last section asks whether there are problems unsolved and unsolvable within

I am indebted to Aldon Morris, Doug McAdam, and John McCarthy for their critical readings of an earlier draft of this chapter.

RM/CA theory and whether there are significant challengers to the theory.

My central argument is as follows: in its various manifestations, resource mobilization/collective action theory provided a detailed framework that both integrated and supplanted earlier lines of research. Fresh, provocative, and iconoclastic in 1970, as Morris and Herring (1987) have demonstrated in a content analysis of journal articles, RM theory by 1980 had become the dominant paradigm. It had become so dominant that its assumptions have often been assimilated as the routine and unstated grounds of much contemporary work.

The theory was useful not only because it challenged outmoded approaches but because it created a space for new perspectives not necessarily directly tied to core elements of RM theory. That is, it sharpened the boundaries of analysis, made critical disaggregating distinctions, and challenged many earlier assumptions. By turning the unproblematic into the problematic, it has helped us develop both more sophisticated social psychological analyses and, what barely existed before in American sociology, a serious foray into the macrosociology of social movements.

Although RM theory itself is becoming old hat, there are a number of important problem areas that have not received the attention they deserve. These include the relation of class and identity formation to mobilization, political opportunity, and state structure as determinants and constraints on social movement mobilization and outcomes, the microfoundations of risk and rationality, the role of demonstration effects, and the intersection of cultural crisis and social movement activity. Although there are current challengers to RM theory, there are none, in my opinion, that can effectively supplant it. Instead, the exciting task is to integrate the challengers.

SOCIAL MOVEMENT
AND COLLECTIVE BEHAVIOR TRADITIONS

Several approaches to the study of social movements and collective behavior had developed in sociology prior to the upsurge of activism in the 1960s, and there was little integration among them. Four major lines were most prominent: (1) the mass society approach (Fromm 1941; Hoffer 1951; Kornhauser 1959), which combined Le Bonian assumptions and images of massification with a horror of fascism, provided a diagnosis of the transformed nature of social movements in modern times (this approach had structural and psychological versions); (2) the political geography-sociology approach (Heberle 1951; Lipset 1950), which linked social class and social relations of production to voting behavior, party mobilization, and political power; (3) the Chicago school (Park and

Burgess 1921; Park 1967; Fuller and Meyers 1941; Turner and Killian 1957; Lang and Lang 1961), which analyzed the forms of collective behavior and the social construction of collective action (in contrast to the political-sociology approach, which ignored the elementary forms of collective behavior, this school played down political links and structure); and (4) the institutionalist approach (Selznick 1952; Gusfield 1955; Messinger 1955), which drew on themes in Weber and Michels and was concerned with the routinization of charisma, organizational adaptation, and the iron law of oligarchy. Of course, these approaches were not sealed off from one another. For instance, Lipset contributed to both political geography analysis and to institutional analysis.

Looking back, one notes that at least one of these approaches has almost completely vanished—mass society analysis, in both its sociological and its psychological guises. Shorn of its metaphysical pathos, Kornhauser's emphasis upon the linkage of masses and elites through associations resonates with current work on movement infrastructures and with the analysis of civil society. Yet contemporary work has so distanced itself from the civilizational diagnosis upon which mass society theory was based that it has thrown out the whole package. It is possible that one of the limits of RM/CA writings is that they do not contribute explicitly to societal diagnoses (I will return to this later).

It is also worth noting that the preoccupation of the institutionalists with the Weber-Michels emphasis on routinization and bureaucratization shifts in the hands of later students to a debate about the effectiveness of organizations and tactics (see Piven and Cloward 1977; Gamson 1975).

Finally, and most important, these earlier approaches all more or less assumed an increase in grievances as the major engine of social movements, without paying attention to costs and alternatives forgone as shaping action potential. Of course, the importance of that psychological assumption varied in different writings, and the Chicago school treated grievance manufacture as part of its problematic.[1]

Since many analysts explained collective action in terms of an upsurge in grievances, let me comment on how the concept was employed. Much of the sociological work involved an ex post facto examination of the outcropping of collective action, without systematically asking whether grievances

---

1. The Chicago school of collective behavior analysis was rooted in the symbolic interactionism of George Herbert Mead and W. I. Thomas. As such, they were early social constructionists. Unfortunately, they tended not to take symbols seriously as objects of analysis. Interestingly, many current students of social movements who analyze cognitive framing and symbols are tied to Mead through the works of Erving Goffman more than through the students of collective behavior.

at the individual or aggregate level had systematically changed. For instance, after racial conflict occurred, a scholar would examine previous changes in local conditions and precipitating incidents related to race. Moreover, little comparative work was done, so it was difficult to examine changes in grievance level as an explanation in comparison to the role of other potential explanatory factors.

An emphasis upon grievances was bolstered by the then current frustration-aggression theory. In its simplified form it asserted a direct link between deprivation (frustration) and action. Although the American soldier studies and the Merton-Kitt (Alice Rossi) interpretation usefully had led us to look at relative deprivation rather than absolute deprivation, it still focused on grievances, not situated action. A deprivation or relative deprivation model of social movements became explicit in the works of Gurr (1970) and Davies (1963, 1969).

Three brief comments about the research schools of the 1950s that have relevance for the future: first, several scholars have come to believe that a major new initiative is needed linking class analysis to social movement theory (see Fantasia 1988; McNall 1988). Although we are in position to do a more sophisticated analysis now, that initiative was anticipated by Lipset and Heberle.[2] Second, the organizational-institutional approach, shorn of its preoccupation with the Weber-Michels problematic, remains a viable part of the agenda of the future, even if its imagery leads to an overly formal and bureaucratized view of social movement organizations (smos). Recent work by Lofland (1985) and by McCarthy (1987) has begun to reinvigorate organizational analysis.

Third, although the early efforts of some of those working in the Chicago school now seem soft and lacking in rigor, they emphasized some phenomena not well treated in RM/CA. Resource mobilization approaches do not deal well with enthusiasm, spontaneity, and conversion experiences, or with the link between public opinion climates and social movement mobilization and outcomes. Although one might not want to put as much emphasis on spontaneous processes and events as was the practice, and one would want to get away from Le Bonian overtones, an analysis of spontaneity

---

2. It should be obvious that social movement theory and class analysis have much to say to each other. The exclusion of Marxist analysis from the American academy until the middle of the 1960s and the tendency of Marxists to submerge social movement mobilization and tactics in the analysis of class relations have limited the contribution of Marxists to social movement analysis, even though practical Marxists had much to say about tactics of mobilization and the dilemmas of participation in party politics. On the other side, sociologists of social movements separated their objects from concrete social formations; they undertheorized the link of movements to social structure.

and enthusiasm adds much to the hyperrationality that can develop in RM theory (see Rosenthal and Schwartz 1989). The social movement energy released through enthusiasm is generated through feelings of solidarity and communal sharing and wholeness, not just by the decline in costs of participation or the escalation of expectations of achieving group goals. Enthusiasm and spontaneity become a resource as well as an outcome of social movements. Similarly, RM/CA approaches may well underestimate the importance of changes in public opinion and attitudes for the attainment of movement goals, especially in such movements as the antismoking movement or the women's movement, where attainment of goals depends upon the change of individual behavior and attitudes. The general point is that the scholarly tendency to sharpen analytic distinctions between forms of collective behavior and social movement phenomena may have led us to ignore some of the rich complexity and interconnectedness of empirical reality.

THE CHALLENGE OF THE
SIXTIES TO SOCIAL MOVEMENT THEORY

The social conflicts and social movements that came to dominate domestic politics in the 1960s provided a catalyst for a renewed interest in the study of social movements and a challenge to existing approaches. Writings in the early part of the decade modified, but did not severely challenge, the major approaches. Smelser's *Theory of Collective Behavior* (1962) combined Chicago school analyses of the forms of collective behavior with a Parsonian analysis of normative orientations and societal controls. Zald and Ash (1966) continued the line of analysis of the institutionalists but, by examining a wider range of movement outcomes and processes, challenged the metaphysical pathos inherent in that model. They argued that oligarchization and conservatism are not inherent in smos. Increasingly, however, the activism and radicalization of the decade challenged social scientists' interpretations of American society and the theoretical paradigms used to study society and social movements. Remember, before the upsurge of activism and radicalism, the American public seemed quiescent; we were supposed to have become a middle-class, affluent society. Some scholars even predicted the end of ideology (Bell 1960).

There were several interpretations given for the increased radicalization of politics in the United States and Europe. One approach, based on a Maslowian view of motivation, located the change in postindustrial and antimaterialistic values (Inglehardt 1971). Affluence was said to have transformed the industrial world, allowing higher values to become central. Radicalization was only the implementation of those values. A second but related theory was more specific to America. Activism in the context of drugs, sex, and rock and roll, tied to the "greening" of America, was a reflection of the revaluation and dissaffiliation from bourgeois-industrial society. Culture shift led to activism.

A third approach focused on the student movement. Since college students were active in several of the specific movements of the days—the cultural movement of sex, drugs, and rock and roll, the civil rights movement, and the antiwar movement—explaining their behavior became important (Feuer 1969). A socialization to radicalism interpretation—the "red diaper" theory—was advanced as one interpretation of student activism (Flacks 1967). Another, more structural, approach treated college students as an emerging protoclass: the growth of mass higher education and increased credentialism blocked mobility channels and created student solidarity.

Often these interpretations of increased activism presented a motivational or value change approach to the rise of social movements. That is, changes in values confronted with a static social system led to a grievance against the status quo. But these interpretations of the sixties did not challenge the received paradigms of social movement analysis. They were explanations of historically specific events, not changes in theoretical assumptions.

The revival of Marxist analysis, which interpreted the sixties as a manifestation of the contradictions of capitalism, assimilated the events of the decade into a general theory of social change. But though the contradictions of American capitalism may help explain the typical forms of social conflict in a given period, they tell one little about the specific dynamics of mobilization.

The events of the 1960s provided a catalyst for social movement theory in several ways. For one, issues of power, conflict, and the variable distribution of political resources came to center stage. Since many social scientists sided with the activists and were debating issues of strategy and tactics, the irrationalist assumptions of the collective behavior approach seemed outmoded. Collective action was seen as part and parcel of political action, not something discrete and separate (Weller and Quarantelli 1973). Social movements were pursuing political goals with means appropriate to their situation. For another, in contrast with a view of America as a homogeneous middle-class society, the enduring role of class and racial cleavages as generators of inequality was drummed home in both the War on Poverty and the civil rights movement. Yet, since class and race were enduring, their variable manifestation in activism demanded explanation.

Why now and not earlier? What caused cycles and trends? Why were some movements more successful than others in gaining their ends?

THE EMERGENCE OF RESOURCE
MOBILIZATION/COLLECTIVE ACTION THEORY

Beginning their work as a critique of earlier approaches and drawing upon several streams in the social sciences, a number of scholars converged on what has become the RM/CA approach. I briefly trace the development of the approach, discuss its core assumptions, and indicate its status as a theoretical research program (see Morris and Herring, 1987, for a fuller discussion).

The resource mobilization perspective began to emerge in the late 1960s. Olson published his seminal book *The Logic of Collective Action* in 1965. Leites and Wolf published a rational choice analysis of peasant involvement in guerrilla warfare in 1970. Lipsky's paradigmatic article "Protest as a Political Resource," which schematically shows how violence and protest have indirect as well as direct effects on authorities, was published in 1968. So too was Gamson's *Power and Discontent*, with its emphasis on the consequences of the differential distribution of political access and resources for strategies of influence. Oberschall's text and the first McCarthy and Zald article were published in 1973. Tilly and his colleagues (among them, Shorter) and students (Snyder, Aminzade) were developing their collective action and strike analysis program in the early 1970s. By 1977, when a conference sponsored by the National Science Foundation and organized by McCarthy and Zald (1979) was held at Vanderbilt University, the core of the program was in place.

Different contributors to resource mobilization research may well specify different core assumptions for the perspective. The contrasts with the assumptions of earlier work are easily summarized (see Morris and Herring 1987). First, behavior entails costs; therefore grievances or deprivation do not automatically or easily translate into social movement activity, especially high-risk social movement activity. The weighing of costs and benefits, no matter how primitive, implies choice and rationality at some level. Mobilization out of the routines of social and family life, out of work and leisure, is a problematic. Second, mobilization of resources may occur from within the aggrieved group but also from many other sources. Third, resources are mobilized and organized; thus organizing activity is critical. Fourth, the costs of participating may be raised or lowered by state and societal supports or repression. And fifth, just as mobilization is a large problematic, so too are movement outcomes. There is no direct or one-to-one correspondence between amount of mobilization and movement success.

Although other writers might disagree with this phrasing, I think most scholars working within an RM frame would come somewhat close to this statement of core assumptions. They might add a couple of assumptions or orienting statements to tie these general statements to their own specific interests. I myself would add that social movement struggle involves not only authorities and partisans but bystander publics and reference elites who view the movement through a media filter. (This is the Lipsky expanded model, which I will draw upon later to highlight some of the gaps in our current research.)

By the middle of the decade 1970–80 it was apparent that a paradigm shift had occurred. Indeed, it might be claimed that a theoretical research program had been established. It is clear that though the major theoretical statements overlapped, they varied in their emphases. Oberschall focused upon risk-reward and mobilization problems (not mobilization outcomes) in the context of group and organizational embeddedness. Micromobilization was at the center of his agenda, not the dynamics of organizations or of tactics in relation to the state. Indeed, the distinction between collective behavior and social movements is not critical to much of his analysis. (The same is true for a later major contribution, that of Oliver, Marwell, and Teixeira 1985.) For McCarthy and Zald, the variant takes off from the point of view of the smo or the movement entrepreneur, looking outward for resources and reflexively looking at constituents and the authorities for tactics and opportunities. In *The Strategy of Social Protest* (1975), Gamson was oriented to the role of tactics and organization in outcomes, but in *Encounters with Unjust Authority* (1982), Gamson, Fireman, and Rytina directed their attention to the first problematic, micromobilization.

Another variant of RM/CA focused upon political opportunities and the relationship of social movements to the state (Perrow 1979; McAdam 1982). For Tilly (1964, 1969, 1978, 1984) especially, collective action is deeply tied to the growth and transformation of the state. State action pushes into the local context, generating resistance, and it legitimates or delegitimates repertoires of contention. Although Tilly's theoretical stance deeply involves state action, his methodological program, especially in the early research, focused on dimensions of collective action incidents—number of participants, duration of incident, intensity (tactics and costs).

There is little doubt that the RM/CA program came to dominate American studies of social movements. Moreover, Olson's work has had enormous impact on political scientists' work on interest groups. It can be argued that the RM/CA framework now frames the study of the mobilization of interests (see Walker 1983; Gais, Peterson, and Walker 1984).

Although the RM/CA program has stimulated a large amount of research, like much of social science research, the gap between theory and data has sometimes been wide—Rule (1988) has argued that overall, it has been extremely wide. Nevertheless, a rich program has developed.

STRENGTHS, WEAKNESSES, AND OPPORTUNITIES

In what areas have we made substantial progress? What are some of the major gaps in the literature as it has developed? To explore these questions, it will be useful for us to think of the program as specifying micro-, meso-, and macroproblems.[3]

Micromobilization

It is clear that here is where we have made the most progress. We now have a good sense of the important advantages of block mobilization of activists, of how networks are used for recruitment by different kinds of movements, and of the conditions under which people with favorable and neutral attitudes become active participants.

We also have a literature that takes the Olson problematic seriously, detailing free-rider effects and arguing about the role of solidarity and selective incentives offered by entrepreneurs in overcoming any free-rider problems (Fireman and Gamson 1979; Walsh and Warland 1983; Mitchell 1979). Recruitment issues can be framed more generally than free-rider problems, since analysts are often interested in examining recruitment to organizations, such as religious sects and voluntary associations, that are not strictly in the business of attempting to provide public goods; thus the two bodies of literature are slightly disjunctive. Nevertheless, we have made great progress in the area of recruitment to activism. The research is cumulative, weaves back and forth between theory and data, and has made our understanding more precise.

We know much more about how active participants are recruited than about why they stay or leave. Since the balance of incentives changes over time as people participate in groups, those topics deserve greater atten-

---

3. A more complete review of strengths and weaknesses can be found in McAdam, McCarthy, and Zald (1988).

tion (see Gornick 1977). We do, however, have a growing literature on the effects of participation on *later* political and social movement activity (Fendrich and Turner 1989; McAdam 1988; Whalen and Flacks 1989).

The literature on micromobilization is largely concerned with the recruitment of participants for events and for chapter memberships. We know much less about the recruitment of individual financial donors. Who gives, how often, and to what overlapped set of causes remain unexplored questions, for the most part. (But see the chapter by Oliver and Marwell in this volume.) On the other hand, we do know something about fund-raising from individuals as a marketing problem (Johnston 1980; Sabato 1981; Godwin and Mitchell 1984). We also have a sense of how philanthropic institutions allocate funds and some idea of the relation of foundation grants to the course of movements. Jenkins and Eckert (1986) conclude that in the case of the civil rights movement the increase in grants has followed the growth of protest action, rather than leading it, and has gone to more moderate elements among the movement organizations.

The work on micromobilization, then, has taken us far. But note that the underlying psychological decision model has been a utilitarian model of cost/benefits. Unfortunately, research has not taken advantage of the important advances in understanding risk-taking judgments that has radically changed decision theory. (For a representative collection of studies, see Kahneman, Slovic, and Tversky 1982.) This work represents a vast extension beyond Herbert Simon's theories of decision making, which were founded on notions of bounded rationality, limited search, and preference biases. The ideas of decision heuristics and of biasing effects in the presentation of information for decisions need to be systematically incorporated into social movement research. Among other findings, we now know that observations of the world that in a statistical sampling frame ought to be treated as fluctuations from the mean are often treated as deterministic parameters. And we know that events of similar risk-reward outcomes will trigger different behavioral outcomes, depending on the cognitive frame in which they are embedded. These framing effects might be thought of as "half full" or "half empty" frames in which the manner of presentation leads the actor to focus upon the likelihood of negative versus positive outcomes. Since most people are risk-averse, negative frame events are perceived as having greater expected disutility than the same event framed positively. These works have penetrated deeply into the technical literature on the evaluation and framing of risk and risk aversion. Since rationality in action is actually psychorationality, we ought to incorporate a more sophisticated view of rationality into our work.

Micro-meso Linkages

It is important to specify the organizational and institutional intermediate linkages through which much social movement activity occurs. Data collection problems limit advances, because in order to make progress one needs implicit or explicit comparison between meso-situations and structures. Micro-meso linkages are usually studied as a set of contrasts between SMOs within a movement (Snow, Zurcher, and Ekland-Olson 1980) or as a contrast between the infrastructures of movement and countermovement (see McCarthy 1987).

A systematic attack on micro-meso linkages would develop research on careers of mobilization, retention, and disaffiliation as these intersected with activities and movement organizations of different kinds. Movement activities vary in their risk and potential for reward. Movements and SMOs may be tightly linked to other organizations and structures of societies, as in consensus movements (see McCarthy and Wolfson, this vol.), or be quite conflict-laden and segregated activities within the social structure.

Meso-Studies

Because we have a long tradition of SMO analysis and this analysis is tied to a major field of sociological theory, organizational analysis, RM theory has borrowed heavily from organizational theory. Unfortunately, organizational theory presents us with a language that, because it is oriented toward bureaucracy and formal structure, may warp the analysis of the more unbounded and fragile forms of organization often found in social movements. Organizational theory is most developed for organizations based on material incentives, whereas SMOs bind people with solitary and purposive incentives. Lofland (1985) has attempted to develop a typology of group structures found in social movements, and McCarthy and Wolfson (1989) have recently rethought the issue of national-chapter relations utilizing the analogy to franchising in the retail sector.

Movement organizations must be seen in the context of movement industries. Radical organizations develop their structures and tactics partly in response to those of the dominant mainline organizations. Moreover, the overall targets of action and resource procurement problems for a movement industry may limit the options for the organizations within it. Movements aimed at changing laws in individual states must develop a different structure and tactics than movements aimed at national-level targets. Movements aimed at consciousness change must have different structures and tactics than movements aimed at overthrowing governments.

Although there is still much to be learned about the internal operations of SMOs—in particular, about the processes of schisms or mergers—I do not think that it is a major gap in our knowledge. But such a gap *does* exist in our understanding of social movement industries. It was common in the older tradition to identify a single SMO with a whole movement. Thus, industry structure and relations were ignored. Drawing upon the burgeoning interest in interorganizational analysis in the study of complex organizations, scholars during the past two decades have treated this topic in some depth. Barkan (1986) and Morris (1984) have each discussed interorganizational relations in the civil rights movement. Haines (1988) has addressed the effects of a radical flank on fund-raising in the civil rights movement. Staggenborg (1986) has discussed coalitional work in the modern women's movement, and Rupp and Taylor (1987) have looked at the organizational conflicts and divisions in the women's movement of the late 1940s and 1950s.

Because most studies of interorganizational relations are movement-specific and often limited to a short time period, theoretical and comparative analyses have been relatively neglected. But recent developments in the analysis of the relation between firms and industry change could facilitate a comparable analysis of the dynamics of social movement industries. Tushman and Romanelli (1985) note that product industries develop stable structures of competition, dominance, and differentiation. When major market shifts or technology shifts occur, the structures are displaced. For example, think about the changing structure of the automobile industry as international competition increased, shaking up the old patterns of dominance among Ford, General Motors, and Chrysler. Some organizations rise, some fall, during the shakeout period. If the industry restabilizes at a different market and product level, the old pattern of differentiation and competition will have changed. For almost any movement, using a historical canvas gives a very different picture than using only a short period of maximum movement mobilization. The effects of a radical flank are part of a dynamic of growth and decline that has not been well specified. Tarrow's (1989) landmark study of protest and politics in Italy between 1965 and 1975 shows what can be accomplished when an overall cycle of protest is combined with an analysis of organizations in different parts of a movement.

The Media and the Social Movement Message

The central innovation of the Lipsky model was that it expanded our analysis of social movement relationships between partisans and authorities to include bystander publics and reference elites as filtered through the media. Although we have had several good books and articles on the role of the media in filtering social movement activity (Gitlin 1980; Molotch and Lester 1975; Molotch 1979) and now assume that activists and authorities play to the media, we do not have an extensive literature on the effects of media presentation on bystander publics. The best analysis of bystander effects is still Turner's article, "The Public Perception of Protest" (1969).

Because there are no detailed controlled studies, it is easy to fall into what Aldon Morris calls media determinism, the assumption that media portrayals determine movement outcome. That is peculiar, given that the standard assumption of communication research has been that media presentation has little effect on changing behavior (though not perceptions).

Although the media serve as a linkage and arousal system, from the point of view of both activists and authorities what is at stake is their *perception* of public concern, not necessarily the actual amount of public concern. Their perception shapes movement and authority response. Moreover, movement action and authority response are likely to change public support only at the margin, since public support is tied to deeper identities and social positions.

As we develop a comprehensive literature on movements and the media, it is important to remember that both are nested in a larger political and institutional arena. First, the media's portrayal of and preoccupation with issues shape the agenda of authorities, who have only limited time and cognitive capacity. Media attention, however, though it functions as an agenda shaper, is not necessarily a sure guide to the directions of public opinion. Second, media portrayal of movement-authority relations is part of a larger contest for institutional and ideological legitimacy. If we believe that a quest for legitimacy is involved when partisans and authorities confront each other through the media, then the media contest represents a potential indirect link to the stability and transformation of authority.

There *is* a literature on the media and movements that is hardly known to sociologists: that published in communications journals (Kielbowicz and Scherer 1986). But aside from crossing disciplinary boundaries, it has been hard to assimilate within the mainstream of RM theory for two reasons. First, most research out of the RM/CA framework focuses upon adherents, activists, and their interaction with authorities. A focus on the media necessarily leads an analyst to look at the indirect linkage processes. Second, the media deal in symbolic coin, and until recently, the analysis of symbols and meaning was not high on the sociologists' agenda.

Macro-Issues

In the 1960s, the state and its relation to social movements was not a problematic. Even as we dealt with the relation of partisans to authorities, the short time span of our analyses and our usual preoccupation with one movement in one society led us to treat polity structure as a constant.

Charles Tilly, more than anybody else, changed all that. Not only did the forms and incidence of collective action change as the nation-state intruded into local life, but the demands and requirements of the state affected everything from taxes to concepts of liberty and law. The state generates many of the issues with which social movements wrestle; as well, the state facilitates or hinders movements, lowering or raising the costs of collective action, operating in coalition with the movement or opposing it.

Of course, social movement analysts have often been concerned with the seizure of power, the enactment of legislation, and the support of politicians favorable to the movement. But we have been less concerned with the internal workings of government and its transformation as it facilitated or hindered movements. Jenkins's (1985) treatment of the factors that shaped the federal government's response to the farm workers' unionizing efforts represents an important departure in this respect, for it shows how internal political processes shaped specific responses. McCarthy, Britt, and Wolfson (1990) have shown how postal regulations and the Internal Revenue Service's treatment of nonprofits shape the economy and tactics of smos.

Until very recently, we have not been much concerned with the broader comparative aspect of how national social systems shape and channel demands for change. But new studies are addressing this issue. A volume edited by Klandermans, Kriesi, and Tarrow (1988) contains a number of comparative papers that examine similar movements in different countries. Studies by Kitschelt (1986), Gale (1986), and others have explored social movement processes and alliances in terms of administrative structure and implementation of policy, rather than simply their engagement in the legislative arena. Nevertheless, we have barely opened up this area for analysis. A liaison with political scientists and historians is necessary if we are to realize our potential.

To mention only one fundamental issue at the juncture of political science and political sociology, social movements have a symbiotic relation to political parties. They become parties, and they influence parties; the shape and solidity of the party system in turn impinge upon the organizational form that social movements take. Yet, although some scholars have dealt with this issue (Kitschelt 1989; Spitzer 1987), there is no overarching framework that captures the range of possibilities and structural relationships. (For one attempt at spelling out these relationships, see Garner and Zald 1985.)

To summarize, the RM/CA theoretical research program has made substantial progress. In many areas a cumulative and rich research agenda has been pursued, and there are a number of areas where exciting research problems remain. Thus, RM theory is still a vital and provocative program. This does not mean that some specific empirical claims have gone unchallenged. For instance, some assertions about the role of professionals or the timing and dependence on external resources have been hotly disputed.

The issue of program viability and vitality depends partly upon internal matters, the ability of the framework to generate interesting and researchable problems, and partly on external matters, the existence of alternative theoretical programs or of problems of moment not easily assimilated into the program. Are there significant challengers to RM/CA theory? And what problems can it not readily address?

DIFFICULT PROBLEMS AND CHALLENGERS

The physicist Ernst Mach is supposed to have said that adherents of disproved theories are not converted or convinced; they just die. Is RM theory about to be supplanted by a rival framework? Will it vanish from disuse? At the moment I see no major competitor to RM theory as an overarching frame for the study of social movements. It is possible, however, that it will become simply part of the routine grounds used as a backdrop for problem formulation. In that case, were theoretical assumptions to become more implicit than explicit, the connection of research to underlying core assumptions would become ambiguous and the program might lose coherence. There are several issues that are not easily assimilated into the RM framework. I shall discuss two important ones.

Meaning and Social Movements

Roy D'Andrade (1986) states that there are three kinds of science: physical sciences in which there are mathematically described relations among elements; natural sciences, including much of the biological, geological, and social sciences, where the mode of explanation is the understanding of the working connections among systemically related components; and semiotic sciences, those that deal with meaning. D'Andrade argues that within a system of meanings, much of social science can proceed as a natural science. Capitalism, for instance—assuming self-interest and assuming labor as a commodity—can be examined as a natural system. But, of course, neither self-interest nor labor as a commodity is a natural object. Both have had to be constructed.

Once the objects of valuation for public discourse are created, RM theory proceeds as natural system theory, but the objects of public discourse have to be created. Concepts of justice, of freedom, of rights, are part of a civilizational stock, subject to cultural change. On a less grand scale, the definition of nuclear power as a threat, the issue of fetal life, the notion of welfare chiselers, the identification of smoking and evil, are each part of a symbolic discourse fundamental to the growth and potency of social movements.

How symbols and meaning change can be treated historically and descriptively. That, however, though necessary, is not a very powerful intellectual mode. Here is where semiotics and symbolic and social constructionist approaches must supplement and articulate with our natural system analyses. Gamson and Modigliani's (1989) work using frame and script analysis to examine the creation of key metaphors and symbolic packages for a variety of contemporary political issues is one major attack on the problem. In an exhilarating piece, Oberschall (1989) has built upon the work of Louis Dumont in showing how large-scale worldviews and discrete ideologies are combined and reflected in concrete action. Everyday local conflict combines elements of long-term civilizational ideologies. Best (1989) has used a constructionist approach to examine the images of issues, and Gusfield (1981) has drawn on dramatistic and rhetorical analyses to show how the public discourse about alcoholism has been shaped.

These new approaches to the analyses of meaning are very important in understanding social movement activity. Recognizing, as RM theory does, that social movement entrepreneurs have a stake in rhetoric and that they attempt to manipulate and define ideologies and symbols does not mean that RM theory has any purchase at all on the linguistic-cognitive-emotive conditions of meaning systems, for either the long or short haul. Of course, the issue plagues all instrumental theories, of which RM theory is but one.

Cultural Crisis: An Interpretation

Resource mobilization theory may be useful in explaining single social movements and even how one movement creates repertoires and definitions used by others. But is it useful in examining whole epochs? We might treat the sixties as a kind of rolling sea of movements—each one mobilizing, creating political opportunities and discontents, being reflected in the media, and incurring responses from authorities. Some of the waves have elements of and connections with earlier waves; others seem more autonomous. In this metaphor, the seventies and eighties were dominated by the countermovement undertow. But though RM/CA theory could be used for understanding this particular rolling sea of social movements, it does not explain the orientation, the central thrust, of every major epoch.

How are we to explain the orientation of movement epochs? If you argue that there was a crisis of the American capitalist state in the sixties overlaid by a cultural crisis of modernism and authority (a conjunction of imperial state, racist state, and generational conflict), the movements become the outpouring, the manifestation of the cultural crisis. Such a theory, however, lacks agency, a gap RM theory can fill. But the methodology and indicators of such an interpretation begin in the realm of ideas, contradictions within institutions, and large historical events. That approach to the rise and fall of periods of massive unrest may potentially be a strong competitor. Garner and Zald (1985) present a political economy approach to the orientation and scope of the social movement sector that links the larger social structure to epochal crises. But since institutional contradictions are not always resolved through social movement emergence, the approaches may in fact be complementary. The intersection of macrotheories of change and RM theory requires further development.

It is clear that RM/CA theory is strong and vital. Yet it does not begin to have all the answers or pose all the important problems. Moreover, many students of social movements do not use it or find it helpful. Students of the so-called new social movements in Europe, who often root their analyses in consciousness (Melluci 1980; Touraine 1981), and students of urban social movements as a locus of class conflict (Castells 1982) tend to work outside of RM/CA theory. Similarly, some scholars who work in the tradition of the Chicago school believe that RM/CA theory is but a misspecification of that older tradition. Ultimately, the test of the value of a framework is its use in a conversation among scholars. Its staying power depends upon its contribution to the warranting of truth in such a conversation (McCloskey 1985; Rorty 1983). Although no one can speak to the lasting value of RM/CA theory to that conversation, its short-run contribution nevertheless has been substantial.

REFERENCES

Barkan, Steven E. 1986. "Interorganizational Conflict in the Southern Civil Rights Movement." *Sociological Inquiry* 56:190–209.

Bell, Daniel, ed. 1960. *The End of Ideology*. Glencoe, Ill.: Free Press, chap. 14 and epilogue.

Best, Joel, ed. 1989. *Images of Issues: Typifying Contemporary Social Problems*. New York: Aldine De Gruyter.

Blumer, Herbert. 1949. "Collective Behavior." In *A New Outline of the Principles of Sociology*, ed. A. M. Lee. New York: Barnes and Noble, 167–219.

Castells, Manuel. 1982. "Urban Social Movements and the Struggle for Democracy: The Citizen Movement in Madrid." *Urban Praxis* 18.

Caute, David. 1988. *The Year of the Barricades: A Journey through 1968*. New York: Harper and Row.

Curtis, Russell L., and Louis A. Zurcher, Jr. 1973. "Stable Resources of Protest Movement: The Multi-organizational Field." *Social Forces* 52, no. 1:53–60.

D'Andrade, Roy. 1986. "Three Scientific World Views and the Covering Law Model." In *Metatheory in Social Science: Pluralisms and Subjectivities*, ed. Donald W. Fiske and Richard A. Shweder. Chicago: University of Chicago Press, 61–81.

Davies, James C. 1963. *Human Nature in Politics: The Dynamics of Political Behavior*. New York: Wiley.

———. 1969. "The J-Curve of Rising and Declining Satisfaction as a Cause of Some Great Revolutions and a Contained Rebellion." In *Violence in America: Historical and Comparative Perspectives*. Washington, D.C.: U.S. Government Printing Office.

Fantasia, Rick. 1988. *Cultures of Solidarity*. Berkeley: University of California Press.

Fendrich, James M., and Robert W. Turner. 1989. "The Transition from Student to Adult Politics." *Social Forces* 67, no. 4 (June):1049–57.

Fernandez, Roberto, and Doug McAdam. 1987. "Multiorganizational Fields and Recruitment to Social Movements." In *Organizing for Social Change: Social Movement Organizations across Cultures*, ed. Bert Klandermans. Greenwich, Conn.: JAI Press.

Feuer, Lewis. 1969. *The Conflict of Generations: The Character and Significance of Student Movements*. New York: Basic Books.

Fireman, Bruce, and William H. Gamson. 1979. "Utilitarian Logic in the Resource Mobilization Perspective." In *The Dynamics of Social Movements*, ed. Mayer N. Zald and John D. McCarthy. Cambridge, Mass.: Winthrop, 8–45.

Flacks, Richard. 1967. "The Liberated Generation: An Exploration of the Roots of Student Protest." *Journal of Social Issues* 23:52–75.

Fromm, Erich. 1941. *Escape from Freedom*. New York: Rinehart.

Fuller, Richard C., and Richard R. Meyers. 1941. "The Natural History of a Social Problem." *American Sociological Review* 6, no. 2 (June):320–29.

Gais, Thomas L., Mark A. Peterson, and Jack L. Walker. 1984. "Interest Groups, Iron Triangles and Representative Institutions in American National Government." *British Journal of Political Science* 14:165–85.

Gale, Richard. 1986. "Social Movements and the State: The Environmental Movement, Counter-Movement, and Governmental Agencies." *Sociological Perspectives* 29 (April):202–40.

Gamson, William. 1968. *Power and Discontent*. Homewood, Ill.: Dorsey Press.

———. 1975. *The Strategy of Social Protest*. Homewood, Ill.: Dorsey Press.

Gamson, William, Bruce Fireman, and Steven Rytina. 1982. *Encounters with Unjust Authority*. Homewood, Ill.: Dorsey Press.

Gamson, William, and André Modigliani. 1989. "Media Discourse and Public Opinion on Nuclear Power." *American Journal of Sociology* 95, no. 1 (July):1–37.

Garner, Roberta, and Mayer N. Zald. 1985. "The Political Economy of Social Movement Sectors." In *The Challenge of Social Control*, ed. Gerald Suttles and Mayer N. Zald. Norwood, N.J.: Ablex.

Gerlach, Luther P., and Virginia H. Hine. 1970. *People, Power, and Change: Movements of Social Transformation*. Indianapolis: Bobbs-Merrill.

Gitlin, Todd. 1980. *The Whole World Is Watching*. Berkeley: University of California Press.

Godwin, R. Kenneth, and Robert C. Mitchell. 1984. "The Implications of Direct Mail for Political Organizations." *Social Science Quarterly* 65 (September):829–39.

Gornick, Vivian. 1977. *The Romance of American Communism*. New York: Basic Books.

Gurney, J. N., and K. T. Tierney. 1982. "Relative Deprivation and Social Movements: A Critical Look at Twenty Years of Theory and Research." *Sociological Quarterly* 23:33–47.

Gurr, Ted. 1970. *Why Men Rebel*. Princeton: Princeton University Press.

Gusfield, Joseph R. 1955. "Social Structure and Moral Reform: A Study of the Woman's Christian Temperance Union." *American Journal of Sociology* 61:221–32.

———. 1981. *The Culture of Public Problems: Drinking and Driving and the Symbolic Order*. Chicago: University of Chicago Press.

Haines, Herbert H. 1984. "Black Radicalization and the Funding of Civil Rights: 1957–1970." *Social Problems* 32:31–43.

———. 1988. *Black Radicals and the Civil Rights Mainstream, 1954–70*. Knoxville: University of Tennessee Press.

Heberle, Rudolph. 1951. *Social Movements: An Introduction to Political Sociology*. New York: Appleton-Century-Crofts.

Hoffer, Eric. 1951. *The True Believer: Thoughts on the Nature of Mass Movements*. New York: Mentor.

Inglehart, Ronald. 1971. "The Silent Revolution in Europe: Intergenerational Change in Post-Industrial Societies." *American Political Science Review* 65:991–1017.

Jenkins, J. Craig. 1983. "Resource Mobilization Theory and the Study of Social Movements." *Annual Review of Sociology* 9:527–53.

———. 1985. *The Politics of Insurgency: The Farm Worker Movement in the 1960s*. New York: Columbia University Press.

Jenkins, J. Craig, and Craig M. Eckert. 1986. "Channeling Black Insurgency: Elite Patronage and Professional Social Movement Organizations in the Development of the Black Movement." *American Sociological Review* 51:812–29.

Johnston, Hank. 1980. "The Marketed Social Movement: A Cast Study of the Rapid Growth of TM." *Pacific Sociological Review* 23:333–54.

Kahneman, Daniel, Paul Slovic, and Amos Tversky, eds. 1983. *Judgement under Uncertainty: Heuristics and Biases*. Cambridge: Cambridge University Press.

Kielbowicz, Richard B. and Clifford Scherer. 1986. "The Role of the Press in the Dynamics of Social Movements." In *Research in Social Movements: Conflicts and Change*, ed. Louis Kriesberg. Greenwich, Conn.: JAI Press, 71–96.

Kitschelt, Herbert P. 1986. "Political Opportunity Structures and Political Protest." *British Journal of Political Science* 16:57–85.

———. 1989. *The Logic of Party Formation: Ecological Politics in Belgium and West Germany*. Ithaca, N.Y.: Cornell University Press.

Klandermans, Bert. 1984. "Mobilization and Participation: Social-Psychological Expansions of Resource Mobilization Theory." *American Sociological Review* 49:583–600.

———. 1986. "New Social Movements and Resource Mobilization: The European and the American Approach." *Journal of Mass Emergencies and Disasters* 4:13–37.

Klandermans, Bert, Hanspeter Kriesi, and Sidney Tarrow, eds. 1988. *From Struc-*

ture to Action: Comparing Social Movement Research across Cultures. International Social Movement Research, vol. 1. Greenwich, Conn.: JAI Press.

Kornhauser, William. 1959. *The Politics of Mass Society.* Glencoe, Ill.: Free Press.

Lang, Kurt, and Gladys Lang. 1961. *Collective Dynamics.* New York: Crowell.

Leites, Nathan, and Charles Wolf, Jr. 1970. *Rebellion and Authority: An Analytic Essay on Insurgent Conflicts.* Chicago: Markham.

Lipset, Seymour M. 1950. *Agrarian Socialism.* Berkeley: University of California Press.

Lipsky, Michael. 1968. "Protest as a Political Resource." *American Political Science Review* 62:1144–58.

Lofland, John. 1985. *Protest: Studies of Collective Behavior and Social Movements.* New Brunswick, N.J.: Transaction Books.

McAdam, Doug. 1982. *Political Process and the Development of Black Insurgency, 1930–1970.* Chicago: University of Chicago Press.

———. 1983. "Tactical Innovation and the Pace of Insurgency." *American Sociological Review* 48:735–54.

———. 1986. "Recruitment to High-Risk Activism: The Case of Freedom Summer." *American Journal of Sociology* 92:64–90.

———. 1988. *Freedom Summer: The Idealists Revisited.* New York: Oxford University Press.

McAdam, Doug, John McCarthy, and Mayer N. Zald. 1988. "Social Movements." In *Handbook of Sociology,* ed. Neil J. Smelser. Newbury Park, Calif.: Sage.

McCarthy, John D. 1987. "Pro-Life and Pro-Choice Mobilization: Infrastructure Deficits and New Technologies." In *Social Movements in an Organizational Society,* ed. Mayer N. Zald and John D. McCarthy. New Brunswick, N.J.: Transaction Books, 49–66.

McCarthy, John D., David W. Britt, and Mark Wolfson. 1991. "The Institutional Channeling of Social Movements in the Modern State." In *Research in Social Movements: Conflict and Change* 13:45–76.

McCarthy, John D., and Mark Wolfson. 1989. "Freestanding Locals, Coalitions, Franchises and Outlets: The Importance of Social Movement Organizational Form." Paper presented at the annual Asilomar Conference on Organizations, Pacific Grove, Calif., April 23–25.

McCarthy, John D., and Mayer N. Zald. 1973. *The Trend of Social Movements in America: Professionalization and Resource Mobilization.* Morristown, N.J.: General Learning Press.

———, eds. 1979. *The Dynamics of Social Movements: Resource Mobilization, Social Control, and Tactics.* Cambridge, Mass.: Winthrop.

McCloskey, Donald N. 1985. *The Rhetoric of Economics.* Madison: University of Wisconsin Press.

McFarland, Andrew F. 1977. *Public Interest Lobbies.* Washington, D.C.: American Enterprise Institute.

———. 1984. *Common Cause: Lobbying in the Public Interest.* Chatham, N.J.: Chatham House.

McNall, Scott. 1988. *The Road to Rebellion: Class Formation and Kansas Populism, 1865–1900.* Chicago: University of Chicago Press.

Melluci, Alberto. 1980. "The New Social Movements: A Theoretical Approach." *Social Science Information* 19:199–226.

Messinger, Sheldon L. 1955. "Organizational Transformation: A Case Study of a Declining Social Movement." *American Sociological Review* 26:3–10.

Mitchell, Robert C. 1979. "National Environmental Lobbies and the Apparent Illogic of Collective Action." In *Collective Decision-Making Applications from Public Choice Theory*, ed. Clifford S. Russell. Baltimore: Johns Hopkins University Press, 87–121.

Molotch, Harvey. 1979. "Media and Movements." In *The Dynamics of Social Movements*, ed. Mayer N. Zald and John D. McCarthy. Cambridge, Mass.: Winthrop, 71–93.

Molotch, Harvey, and Marylin Lester. 1975. "Accidental News: The Great Oil Spill as Local Occurrence and National Event." *American Journal of Sociology* 81:235–60.

Morris, Aldon D. 1984. *The Origins of the Civil Rights Movement*. New York: Free Press.

Morris, Aldon D., and Cedric Herring. 1987. "Theory and Research in Social Movements: A Critical Review." In *Political Behavior Annual*, ed. Samuel Long. Norwood, N.J.: Ablex.

Oberschall, Anthony. 1973. *Social Conflict and Social Movements*. Englewood Cliffs, N.J.: Prentice-Hall.

———. 1989. "Culture Change and Social Movements." Paper presented at the annual meeting of the American Sociological Association, San Francisco.

Oliver, Pamela. 1984. "If You Don't Do It, Nobody Will: Active and Token Contributors to Local Collective Action." *American Sociological Review* 49:601–10.

Oliver, Pamela, Gerald Marwell, and Ruy Teixeira. 1985. "A Theory of Critical Mass." *American Journal of Sociology* 91, no. 2 (November):522–56.

Olson, Mancur. 1965. *The Logic of Collective Action*. Cambridge, Mass.: Harvard University Press.

Park, Robert E. 1967. *On Social Control and Collective Behavior*, ed. Ralph H. Turner. Chicago: University of Chicago Press.

Park, Robert E., and Ernest W. Burgess. 1921. *Introduction to the Science of Society*. Chicago: University of Chicago Press.

Perrow, Charles. 1979. "The Sixties Observed." In *The Dynamics of Social Movements: Resource Mobilization, Social Control and Tactics*, ed. John D. McCarthy and Mayer N. Zald. Cambridge, Mass.: Winthrop.

Pickvance, C. G. 1975. "On the Study of Urban Social Movements." *American Sociological Review* 23:29–49.

Piven, Frances Fox, and Richard A. Cloward. 1977. *Poor People's Movements*. New York: Pantheon.

Reich, Charles A. 1971. *The Greening of America*. New York: Bantam.

Rochford, E. Burke. 1982. "Recruitment Strategies, Ideology, and Organization in the Hare Krishna Movement." *Social Problems* 29:399–410.

Rorty, Amelie Oksenberg. 1983. "Experiments in Philosophic Genre: Descartes' Meditations." *Critical Inquiry* 9 (March):545–65.

Rosenthal, Naomi, and Michael Schwartz. 1989. "Spontaneity and Democracy in Social Movements." In *Organizing for Change: Social Movement Organizations in Europe and the United States*, ed. Bert Klandermans. International Social Movement Research, vol. 2. Greenwich, Conn.: JAI Press.

Rule, James B. 1988. *Theories of Civil Violence*. Berkeley: University of California Press.

Rupp, Leila, and Verta Taylor. 1987. *Survival in the Doldrums: The American Women's Rights Movement, 1945 to 1960*. New York: Oxford University Press.

Sabato, Larry J. 1981. *The Rise of Political Consultants*. New York: Basic Books.

Selznick, Philip. 1952. *The Organizational Weapon*. New York: McGraw-Hill.

Simons, Herbert W. 1970. "Requirements, Problems, and Strategies: A Theory of Persuasion for Social Movements." *Quarterly Journal of Speech* 56:1–11.

———. 1981. "The Rhetoric of Political Movements." In *Handbook of Political Communication*, ed. Dan Nimmo and Keith Sanders. Beverly Hills, Calif.: Sage, 417–44.

Simons, Herbert W., E. W. Mechling, and H. Schreier. 1985. "Function of Communication in Mobilizing for Collective Action from the Bottom Up: The Rhetoric of Social Movements." In *Handbook of Rhetorical and Communication Theory*, ed. C. Arnold and J. Bowers. Boston: Allyn and Bacon.

Smelser, Neil. 1962. *Theory of Collective Behavior*. New York: Free Press.

Snow, David A. 1986. "Organization, Ideology and Mobilization: The Case of Nichiren Shoshu of America." In *The Future of New Religious Movements*, ed. D. G. Bromley and P. E. Hammond. Macon, Ga.: Mercer University Press.

Snow, David A., Louis A. Zurcher, Jr., and Sheldon Ekland-Olson. 1980. "Social Networks and Social Movements: A Microstructural Approach to Differential Recruitment." *American Sociological Review* 45, no. 5: 787–801.

Snyder, David, and William R. Kelly. 1979. "Strategies for Investigating Violence and Social Change: Illustrations from Analyses of Racial Disorders and Implications for Mobilization Research." In *The Dynamics of Social Movements*, ed. Mayer N. Zald and John D. McCarthy. Cambridge, Mass.: Winthrop, 212–37.

Spitzer, Robert J. 1987. *The Right to Life Movement and Third Party Politics*. Greenwich, Conn.: Greenwood.

Staggenborg, Suzanne. 1986. "Coalition Work in the Pro-Choice Movement: Organizational and Environmental Opportunities and Obstacles." *Social Problems* 33 (June):374–90.

Tarrow, Sidney. 1989. *Democracy and Disorder: Protest and Politics in Italy, 1965–75*. Oxford: Clarendon Press.

Tilly, Charles. 1964. *The Vendee*. Cambridge, Mass.: Harvard University Press.

———. 1969. "Collective Violence in European Perspective." In *Violence in America: Historical and Comparative Perspectives*, ed. Hugh D. Graham and Ted R. Gurr. Washington, D.C.: U.S. Government Printing Office.

———. 1978. *From Mobilization to Revolution*. Englewood Cliffs, N.J.: Prentice-Hall.

———. 1984. "Social Movements and National Politics." In *Statemaking and Social Movements: Essays in History and Theory*, ed. Charles Bright and Susan Harding. Ann Arbor: University of Michigan Press.

Touraine, Alain. 1981. *The Voice and the Eye: An Analysis of Social Movements*. New York: Cambridge University Press.

Turner, Ralph. 1969. "The Public Perception of Protest." *American Sociological Review* 34:815–31.

Turner, Ralph H., and Lewis M. Killian. 1957. *Collective Behavior*. Englewood Cliffs, N.J.: Prentice-Hall.

Tushman, Michael L., and Elaine Romanelli. 1985. "Organizational Evolution: A Metamorphosis Model of Convergence and Reorientation." In *Research in Organizational Behavior*, ed. Barry Staw and L. L. Cummings. Vol. 7. Greenwich, Conn.: JAI Press, 171–222.

Walker, Jack L. 1983. "The Origin and Maintenance of Interest Groups in America." *American Political Science Review* 77:390–405.

Walsh, Edward J. 1981. "Resource Mobilization and Citizen Protest in Communities around Three Mile Island." *Social Problems* 29:1–21.

Walsh, Edward J., and Rex H. Warland. 1983. "Social Movement Involvement in the Wake of a Nuclear Accident: Activists and Free Riders in the Three Mile Island Area." *American Sociological Review* 48:764–81.

Weller, Jack, and E. L. Quarantelli. 1973. "Another Look at Collective Behavior." *American Journal of Sociology* 79, no. 3 (November):665–85.

Whalen, Jack, and Richard Flacks. 1989. *Beyond the Barricades: The Sixties Generation Grows Up.* Philadelphia: Temple University Press.

Zald, Mayer N., and Roberta Ash. 1966. "Social Movement Organizations: Growth, Decay and Change." *Social Forces* 44:327–41.

Part 7

Conclusion

15

Political Consciousness and Collective Action

Aldon D. Morris

must include agency

Human action cannot be reduced to social structures and impersonal social forces. From birth to death, human beings are embedded within cultural contexts that provide them with belief systems that help guide their actions and infuse them with meaning and comprehensibility. But neither are they simply detached cultural actors, given that they are also embedded within structural contexts that shape their actions and limit their options. To understand human action, therefore, attention has to center on the intersection between culture and structure. This is especially true in the study of collective action because it focuses on a human enterprise in which culture and structure function as both constraints and promoters of social change. Indeed, one central message of this volume is that culture must be brought back into social movement analyses if such analyses are to be parsimonious and free of structural determinism. This chapter is concerned with how consciousness and structure affect collective action. Analysis of class consciousness is the logical place to begin this inquiry, for this concept has been central in discussions of collective action and it embodies both structural and cultural phenomena.

CLASS CONSCIOUSNESS AS SOCIAL PROCESS: EUROPEAN TRADITION

Empirical studies using diverse methodologies and conceptual frameworks have demonstrated that class consciousness has developed in

I should like to thank Carol Mueller, Robert Newby, Myra Marx Ferree, Barbara Reskin, and Charles Tilly for comments on an earlier version of this chapter. Special thanks to Michael Schwartz, whose searching critique of this essay influenced my arguments significantly.

a variety of societies and historical periods and that it has affected major revolutions and social movements. Indeed, class consciousness has been one of the key determinants of social and historical change. *The Making of the English Working Class* (1966) by E. P. Thompson was a landmark study on the formation of social class and class consciousness. One of Thompson's major contributions is his conceptualization of both class and class consciousness as dynamic processes rather than the more typical mechanistic formulations whereby class consciousness automatically emerges from a reified class structure. Thus, Thompson defined class as a happening that occurs "when some men, as a result of common experiences . . . , feel and articulate the identity of their interests as between themselves, and as against other men whose interests are different from (and usually opposed to) theirs." He argued that "the class experience is largely determined by the productive relations into which men are born—or enter involuntarily" (Thompson 1966, 9). Thompson defined class consciousness as the way in which these class experiences are handled in cultural terms: that is, embodied in tradition, value systems, ideas, and institutional forms (16). He treats class consciousness as a variable, arguing that the class experience appears to be determined, whereas class consciousness does not. Thompson concludes that "consciousness of class arises in the same way in different times and places, but never in just the same way" (10). From this vantage point societies in different times and places can be examined to see how class consciousness developed and operated substantively.

The best starting point is Thompson's classic account of the rise of class consciousness in Britain between 1790 and 1830. Early in this period the Industrial Revolution crystallized, creating the conditions out of which arose a new structural group—the modern working class. It was a distinctively new structural formation composed of urban-based wage earners similarly situated within the productive relations of Britain's economy. As wage earners, these workers were severely exploited economically and oppressed socially both by the capitalist class who owned the means of production and by the state. Indeed, members of the working class were subjected to a demanding factory-oriented discipline imposed on them by capitalists concerned with extracting maximum profits. This new externally organized mass of humanity labored under harsh and unsanitary conditions. They lived in self-contained and clearly identifiable neighborhoods that suddenly sprang up in close proximity to the new industrial factories. Because of their social location in the productive sphere, modern English workers collectively accumulated common experiences rooted in mass production and tempered by human suffering.

The objective aspects of this new formation are clear. This social arrangement brought into existence millions of workers with a common class interest. Second, because workers were forced to enter into exploitative class relations with capitalists and oppressive political relations with the state, a new system of human oppression developed, best captured by the concept "class domination." Third, as a result of class domination, the workers' common class interests were opposed to the interests of the dominant class and the state. Finally, the formation of the working class gave rise to new identifiable social structures, central to which were the large industrial factories in which a vast set of productive activities and social relations emerged, and to new densely populated neighborhoods that housed the workers. All of these were objective phenomena whether or not they were recognized or understood by workers caught within their grip.

But now the questions became, how would workers understand, conceptualize, articulate, and ultimately respond to these objective phenomena? How would they handle these objectively generated shared experiences in psychological, political, and cultural terms?

At this juncture enters the concept "class consciousness," which Thompson developed meticulously. First, it took English workers approximately forty years to develop mature class consciousness (1790–1830). During this period, workers engaged in numerous confrontations with the capitalist class and the state. These confrontations were usually characterized by limited goals, initiated by only particular segments of workers and not guided by a coherent social and political vision. Thus, working-class consciousness emerged slowly through a process of concrete social and political struggle, information sharing, and organization building. More precisely, these recurring struggles gave rise to working-class leaders; radical orators; radical newspapers that collectively constituted a radical press; intellectually and politically charged reading societies, coffeehouses, bookstores, and pubs; political meetings and street theater; a variety of social and political doctrines; and especially worker associations and mutual aid societies. In other words, it was the concrete struggles themselves from which class consciousness developed and matured within the English working class during the late eighteenth and early nineteenth centuries.

From Thompson's account emerges the view that over these forty years of struggle, the objective social structures—working-class neighborhoods with their myriad institutions, along with factories and their vast numbers of embedded social relationships—became infused with highly charged debates concerning the nature of worker exploitation, worker rights, and the place of workers in the overall social order. Workers disseminated, dissected, and internalized social and political doctrines and analyzed, debated, and rethought class confrontations. Remarkably, a great deal of this intellectual and political culture was generated and consumed by barely literate workers, often assisted by orators and those with enough educational skills to read aloud.

According to Thompson, by 1830 this tremendous body of fragmented worker thoughts, theories, feelings, shared knowledge, experiences, values, and suffering—all rooted in a network of worker organizations and institutions—had coalesced into an important social force: class consciousness. This consciousness enabled workers, first, to form "a picture of the organization of society, out of their own experience and with the help of their hard-won and erratic education, which was above all a political picture" (Thompson 1966, 710). Indeed, workers learned to see their own lives as part of a general history of conflict between classes. Second, there developed "a consciousness of the identity of interests between working men of the most diverse occupations and levels of attainment, which was embodied in many institutional forms" (407). Third, there developed "a consciousness of the identity of the interests of the working class, or 'productive classes,' as against those of other classes; and within this there was maturing the claim for an alternative system" (807). Finally, this mature class consciousness did not result automatically from impersonal structural forces. Rather, "the working class made itself as much as it was made" (194).

The development of such class consciousness was not unique to nineteenth-century England. Sewell (1980) has documented the emergence of a French working-class consciousness strikingly similar to that analyzed by Thompson. In France, this consciousness emerged through years of class struggle, reaching its maturity in 1833. By that year French workers had established a working-class press, an autonomous workers' discourse informed by an authentic working-class point of view, revolutionary rhetoric and class language, and working-class leaders. But most important, they had developed working-class organizations known as workers' associations. These were the structures through which class consciousness became an institutionalized independent force. It was these associations that forged the strong link between analysis and action, enabling workers to create a unified and class-conscious workers' movement. Thus, in a passage reminiscent of Thompson, Sewell declared that "the agitations and conceptual innovations that took place between 1830 and 1834 constituted the first stage in the making of the French working class" (282).

Bonnell (1983) has provided an account of the flowering and maturing of working-class consciousness among Russian workers in St. Petersburg and Moscow from 1900 to 1914 that is remarkably similar to the English and French cases. Over this period, Russian workers developed workers' associations and trade unions, working-class leaders assisted by outside intellectuals, and new ideas and images about who they were and their overall place in the social order. Like the British and the French, these workers united social analysis with organization building and concrete collective action. In the process, Russian workers by 1914 had developed a mature class consciousness deeply rooted in a social and political vision that stressed "proletarian solidarity, the irreconcilability of class interest, and the interconnection between economic and political struggle" (453).

Nor is the development of class consciousness limited to the eighteenth and nineteenth centuries. Touraine (1983) found class consciousness to be evident among Polish workers active in the Solidarity movement in 1980. He wrote that "the activity of the trade union was constantly defined in terms of class struggle" (41). Polish workers focused on class exploitation, worker alienation, and better working conditions. Indeed, the majority of Polish workers "simply thought of belonging to the working class and having direct experience of social relations within the factory as being the firmest and most fundamental guarantee for an effective defense of their interests" (43). Touraine concluded that "Solidarity is a trade union, but it is also, more broadly, a workers' movement, animated by class consciousness" (44). The evidence, therefore, suggests that Thompson was correct in his claim that class consciousness develops in different times and places. It is a real social and historical force.

CLASS CONSCIOUSNESS AS PERCEPTIONS AND IMAGES: THE AMERICAN TRADITION

Social scientists have differed over whether class consciousness, in contrast to the European tradition, has ever played a major role in the social and political life of Americans. Indeed, a significant stream of social scientists, along with the popular press, have persistently claimed that Americans—especially workers—have failed to develop and express class consciousness. This lack of class consciousness, characterized as American exceptionalism, has been attributed to many factors, including American prosperity, egalitarianism, and the absence of a feudal past. If there is anything to be learned from recent scholarship on class consciousness, it seems to be that the American exceptionalism thesis is misleading. Empirical studies by Centers (1949), Leggett (1968), Jackman and Jackman (1983), Wright (1985), Vanneman and Cannon (1987), and Fantasia (1988) have all found that Americans are indeed class conscious. Although I will say more about this later, I argue here that most studies of

American class consciousness suffer from weak conceptual formulations in which workers' opinions and perceptions are highlighted rather than their concrete actions and that these studies tend to be ahistorical because of their overreliance on survey research methodology. Fantasia's work is a major exception in this respect. The bulk of these studies, however, are still sufficient to challenge the American exceptionalism thesis, given that this thesis was based on studies utilizing similar methodology and conceptualizations. A brief examination of several representative studies will demonstrate this point.

Vanneman and Cannon's central proposition is "that Americans do perceive class in American society—true classes: not just vague status distinctions between the elegant and the uncouth but actual conflict groups that are divided by opposing interests in the capitalist organization of society" (1987, 14). After examining the views of a wide variety of workers, they conclude, "what we discovered—over and over again—was that American workers are amazingly clear on the shape of the American class system and their place within it" (283). Jackman and Jackman, after analyzing a national survey of Americans, conclude that "about eight out of ten Americans feel at least somewhat strongly about their identification with a social class, and as many as five out of ten feel very strongly about it" (1983, 40). Moreover, they found that most Americans view class interests as mutually opposed (66). Finally, Wright, relying on survey research conducted in the United States and Sweden, found that in both countries workers tended to identify with working-class interests and capitalists identified with capitalist interests. He also found that in both countries workers tended to identify with and locate themselves within the working class (1985, 263).

Even though Wright, Jackman and Jackman, and Vanneman and Cannon define social class quite differently and disagree over the meaning of workers' perceptions, they all reach the same conclusions: Americans are very cognizant of social class and are able to sort people and occupational positions into class categories with considerable clarity. The exceptionalism thesis finds no support in these studies, given their revelation that class consciousness affects the lives of Americans in fundamental ways.

CLASS CONSCIOUSNESS AND AMERICAN SOCIOLOGY: A CRITIQUE

Studies of class consciousness in America tend to be ahistorical and divorced from real group struggle. This approach stands in sharp contrast to the European tradition. In those studies we see how class consciousness emerged as a social process and became organizationally anchored in the context of class confrontations. We get a concrete sense of the kinds of ideas, leaders, organizations, institutions, and worker solidarity that came into existence as a result of class consciousness and class struggle. Thus, speaking of the class consciousness that animated English workers between 1790 and 1850, Jones argued that "one of the most striking features of the social movements . . . had been the clarity and concreteness of their conception of the state. . . . It had been seen as a flesh and blood machine of coercion, exploitation and corruption. The monarchy, the legislature, the Church, the bureaucracy, the Army and the police had all been occupied by 'bloodsuckers,' 'hypocrites,' 'placemen,' etc. The aim of popular politics had been to change the form of state" (1983, 238). This consciousness propelled by worker solidarity made an important contribution to the mobilization and outcomes of revolutions, social movements, the establishment of the rights of public demonstrations and of freedom of the press. In contrast, from studies such as those of Wright, Jackman and Jackman, and Vanneman and Cannon, what emerges are the images, perceptions, and opinions that individuals may hold about class dynamics and class structure at one point in time unhitched to either real historical or contemporary struggles.

Much is lost from this ahistorical approach to class consciousness. In particular, it is exceedingly difficult to determine or measure how class consciousness actually affects collective action if it is not analyzed in the context of real struggles during which actors must draw on a form of consciousness that guides their strategic choices in terms of who is identified as the opposition, which interests are considered paramount, and how class efficacy is assessed. This problem is prevalent in survey research analyses of American class consciousness and leads to limited conceptual strategies. Thus, for example, Vanneman and Cannon write, "our analysis throughout this book depends on a crucial distinction. . . . studies of American workers must distinguish the opinions of the workers themselves (their class consciousness) from the forms that the class conflict eventually takes (such social structures as union and political parties)" (19 14). They therefore argue, "instead, we must investigate that conscio ness independently from the structural outcomes and then test whetl the consciousness actually explains the results of the conflict" (15).

This strategy reveals a conceptual narrowness. Class consciousness conceptualized here as simply the opinion of workers, not a process ge erated and shaped by class interactions. More important, how can cl consciousness be investigated independently of the forms that class confl eventually take and the structural outcomes of that conflict? Class co sciousness is important precisely because it influences the very nature class conflict and helps determine the kinds of social structures—unions, political parties, workers' associations—that will be erected and that affect the outcome of class conflict. Indeed, it seems that a more fruitful approach would be to investigate class consciousness within the social and historical context of class interactions so that its relative weight can be assessed. If treated independently and given a life of its own, the concept of class consciousness ceases to be conceptually sensitive and assumes an ad hoc character.

Moreover, the most serious limitation of class consciousness research, and especially research dealing with American society, is exactly this—its conceptual narrowness. The assumption usually underlying such studies is the view that there exists an uncluttered class consciousness in the mental and cultural worlds of human beings that operates according to a unique class logic. In this approach the boundaries of class consciousness are not treated as analytically problematic. Stated differently, the real possibility that class consciousness is only one kind of political consciousness and cannot be understood or properly assessed apart from a larger interactive system of political consciousness has received scant attention in the literature. Most scholars implicitly assume the existence of a clear bounded class consciousness. Wright's work (1985) is useful in this respect because this assumption is stated in explicit terms. By examining it, we understand more clearly how this conceptual narrowness plagues class consciousness research generally.

In *Classes* (1985), Wright states, "class consciousness is to be understood in terms of the class content of perceptions, theories, and preferences that shape intentional choices" (250). He argues that "the explanatory problem in the analysis of class consciousness is to elaborate the processes by which such class content is determined and the effects it has on the patterns of class formation and class conflict" (250). For Wright, class consciousness is based in what he calls the objective properties of the class structure. It is class experiences that shape consciousness rather than personal attributes such as race, gender, ethnicity, and age (251). Thus, for Wright, "pure class consciousness" that affects class interests and class struggles actually exists. It is a distinct realm of consciousness whose boundaries can be delineated and effects measured.

What Collins has appropriately labeled "either/or" dichotomous thinking (1990, 28) characterizes this genre of research, which assumes that class consciousness is an entity unto itself and bounded. For example, given that race is such a persistent reality in the American context, researchers in this tradition have investigated whether blacks identify with their class or their race. In this "either/or" stance Vanneman and Cannon, who are sensitive to the possible conceptual limitations of splitting streams of political consciousness, nevertheless write about a "race" rather than a "class" consciousness (1987, 237). Similarly, Jackman and Jackman (1983), throughout their volume, speak of racial identity outweighing class feelings among blacks (187) and claim that blacks exhibit greater racial bonds than class bonds in contrast to whites (48–50). In short, most researchers proceed on the assumption that class consciousness is of a different objective order than other forms of consciousness presumed to be attached to and driven by personal attributes. As a consequence, they employ the "either/or" approach or ignore other forms of consciousness altogether.

But this conceptually narrow approach sidesteps the possibility that class consciousness, race consciousness, gender consciousness, and ethnic consciousness may all be part of the same phenomenon. Moreover, an ahistorical approach based on survey items designed to measure respondents' opinions and perceptions of class and race at one point in time is not likely to unravel the complex historical interactions among various forms of consciousness and how such interacting streams of consciousness affect the overall volume and nature of collective action.

POLITICAL CONSCIOUSNESS AS AN INTERACTIONAL SYSTEM

As recent research (Klandermans 1984; Snow et al. 1986; Opp 1988; Fantasia 1988; Hirsch 1990) and this volume clearly demonstrate, cultural and social psychological factors are important in generating and sustaining collective action. Class consciousness is one of the most important cultural and ideological factors affecting the origins and outcomes of collective action. Nevertheless, class consciousness is only one important form of consciousness, and it seldom operates in isolation from other crucial forms of consciousness that affect collective action. If this is the case, class consciousness should be investigated as part of an interactive system of political consciousness that exists in all societies and lies at the core of social movement activity. The shape and nature of a specific interactional system of political consciousness will vary across societies because of varying historical, cultural, and social factors. The central argument here is that class consciousness, race consciousness, gender consciousness, and the like cannot be understood comprehensively or properly assessed as independent entities. In this view it is the interrelated system of political consciousness and the systems of human domination that gave rise to them in the first place that should become the focus of analytical inquiry. Such an inquiry would investigate the major group cleavages in any given

Must human domination be involved for something to be political?

society around which durable streams of political consciousness cluster as a result of social inequality and group struggle.

Systems of human domination give rise to political consciousness. Working-class consciousness is the workers' response to class domination; racial consciousness among African Americans is their response to racial domination; gender consciousness is a response to male domination; and so on. All fall in the same sociological family: each is a form of political consciousness oriented toward either the maintenance or the overthrow of a given system of human domination. Moreover, in any society relevant combinations of political consciousness will interact in relatively stable patterns because they flow from interlocking systems of human domination that interact in patterned ways.

This is the basic insight usually absent from studies on class consciousness. Such research tends to assume that racial, gender, and ethnic inequality stems from what Wright refers to as personal attributes. In this light, such forms of inequality are not of the same objective magnitude as class inequality, which emerges from "structural relations" that generate objective "class interest." This view is evident in Jackman and Jackman's claim that "blacks who identify with the poor make an especially instructive case, because they have two subordinate statuses, one 'cultural' and one 'structural'" (1983, 52). Of course, blacks' racial subordination is viewed as cultural, whereas their class subordination is thought to be structural. Similarly, Jackman and Jackman, when referring to the finding that working- and middle-class blacks identify strongly with their race, claim they "are increasingly likely to be emotionally preoccupied with race" (52), the obvious inference being that one's identification with class is rational and objective, but identification with race is not.

Nevertheless, racial and gender systems of domination in American society are indeed structural and objective, as is class domination. Social scientific research over many years (Du Bois 1899; Myrdal 1944; Farley and Allen 1987; Jaynes and Williams 1989) has demonstrated that black people as a group routinely experience racial discrimination and inequality in American society at the hands of the white majority. This is evident when blacks and whites are compared in terms of numerous economic, political, and social indicators. Practices of racial discrimination and domination were first institutionalized during centuries of slavery and have remained so, although in changing forms, throughout subsequent years. The complex web of institutional machinery and power relations is structural and objective, and it has given rise to a racial system of human domination. The result is that whites in every sphere of American society have reaped benefits at the expense of blacks. As a consequence, a set of identifiable and objective race interests has developed in America. Whites as a group have tended to behave historically in such a manner as to protect their racial advantage. On the other hand, African Americans have tended to behave in a manner aimed at overthrowing the system of racial domination and replacing it with racial equality. In short, there exists a history of racial struggle and racial conflict in America because there exists a system of racial domination and racial interests that have become objectified through institutions and associated power relations. These structural relations of racial inequality and the persistent racial conflict they trigger have generated white race consciousness and black race consciousness, and these two forms have profoundly affected American collective action.

Similarly, social scientific research (Cohn 1985; Milkman 1987; Hess and Ferree 1987; Epstein 1988; Reskin and Roos 1990) has demonstrated that women in America (and around the world) have routinely experienced gender discrimination and inequality at the hands of males, a fact confirmed by numerous economic, political, and social indicators. Like racial discrimination, gender discrimination in the United States has been institutionalized for centuries within a system that has given rise to identifiable and objective gender interests that translate into male interests and female interests. Consequently, there exists a history of gender struggle and conflict in America because there exists a system of gender domination and gender interests that have become objectified through institutions and associated power relations. These structural relations of gender inequality and the persistent gender conflict they have given rise to have generated male consciousness and female consciousness.

Therefore, there are systems of human domination other than class that are real and objective. These systems have generated opposing objective interests and various interrelated forms of conflicting consciousness that must be taken seriously by scholars investigating class consciousness. Hill has argued that it is a crucial mistake for labor scholars to reduce race consciousness to class consciousness. More to the point, he writes that "the tendency to deny race as a crucial factor, to permit questions of class to subsume racial issues, is based on a perspective that ignores racism as a system of domination, as it ignores the role of racist ideology in working class history" (1988, 132). Other systems of domination have been similarly ignored. Thus, an important research agenda is to explore the interlocking nature of relevant systems of domination and the varieties of consciousness that flow from them, with a view to understanding how they affect collective action.

This kind of conceptual and empirical research is currently being undertaken by scholars working in the black feminist tradition. In an insightful article that advances the understanding of black women's consciousness, King has written that "racism, sexism and classism constitute three, inter-dependent control systems." She explicitly calls for an interactive model, saying that "multiple" refers "not only to several, simultaneous oppressions but to the multiplicative relationships among them as well" (1988, 47).

Vanneman and Cannon (1987) have pointed out that a growing number of black feminist writers including Dill, Collins, and Rollins are also calling for interactive models of oppression and consciousness because existing frameworks are inadequate for explaining their empirical find-ings. Dill (1983), for example, found that black women do not rank the multiple dimensions of their oppression. This finding reveals the limita-tions of the "either/or" approach discussed earlier and calls into ques-tion the assumption that distinct boundaries exist between various forms of political consciousness. After critically examining the assumption that people rank order various oppressions that afflict them, Collins goes to the heart of the matter, pointing out that "viewing relations of domination for Black women for any given socio-historical context as being structured via a system of interlocking race, class, and gender oppression expands the focus of analysis from merely describing the similarities and differences distinguishing these systems of oppression and focuses greater attention on how they interconnect" (1990, 222). Similarly, Vanneman and Cannon maintain that "the theoretical value of focusing on women and minority workers is that it forces us to consider the interlocking connections be-tween systems of oppressions" (1987, 287). In this light, class consciousness research preoccupied only with class structure and a homogeneous work-ing class is likely to overlook the centrality of multiple consciousnesses and interlocking systems of human domination, and how they affect collective action.

DOMINATION, CONSCIOUSNESS, AND THE INTERACTIONAL APPROACH

Two crucial concepts—systems of human domination and po-litical consciousness—must be defined, for they lie at the heart of an inter-actional approach. Blauner (1972) defines a system of human domination as a constellation of institutions, ideas, and practices that successfully en-ables one group to achieve and maintain power and privilege through the control and exploitation of another group. In any given society there are usually several major systems of domination that interact in numerous ways. The nature of those interactions must be empirically determined.

Political consciousness is defined as comprising those cultural beliefs

wrong. Why is pol. defined so narrowly?

and ideological expressions that are utilized for the realization and maintenance of group interests. Political consciousness is continually shaped and influenced by concrete social and political struggles engaged in by two or more groups. This definition takes into consideration the fact that both dominant and subordinate groups develop political consciousness for the purpose of achieving their respective political and social ends. Social scientists have tended to underemphasize the political consciousness of dominant groups while focusing on the oppositional consciousness of subordinate groups such as workers, blacks, and women.

Following Gramsci (1971), we can conceptualize the political consciousness of dominant groups who maintain systems of domination from which they extract group privilege as hegemonic consciousness. And the political consciousness of subordinate groups who struggle to dismantle systems of domination that prevent them from realizing their interests can be conceptualized as oppositional consciousness. Hegemonic consciousness in classical Marxian/Gramscian terms is captured by the axiom that the ideas of the ruling class are the ruling ideas of a society. A crucial feature of hegemonic consciousness is that it always presents itself as a set of values and beliefs that serve the general welfare. In this guise, it claims to be the best societal conception for all people and the most useful and legitimate guiding ideology for the society as a whole. Hegemonic consciousness is always sustained by public institutions that are meant to attend to the general welfare: the government, schools, the media, and a host of lesser institutions presenting themselves as representative of the society as a whole and intent on benefiting the broadest range of people. In short, hegemonic consciousness is a ruling consciousness because it is rooted in and supported by the most dominant and powerful institutions of a society. Its organizational expression enables it to wrap itself in institutional garments bearing labels proclaiming its universality.

In contrast, oppositional consciousness is that set of insurgent ideas and beliefs constructed and developed by an oppressed group for the purpose of guiding its struggle to undermine, reform, or overthrow a system of domination. Oppositional consciousness is usually a reactive force, given that it is developed to battle a hegemonic consciousness utilized by ruling groups to repress potentially empowering beliefs and behaviors of an oppressed constituency. Because oppositional consciousness is often locked into a reactive stance, it usually does not reject all the viewpoints and interests embraced by a hegemonic consciousness, but only those that are repugnant to the perceived interests of a particular oppressed group. In this sense, oppositional consciousness usually does not claim to represent the general interests of a society but only those of the oppressed group seeking to overthrow the system of domination perceived to be responsible for its oppression.

There is another reason oppositional consciousness is generally narrower in scope than hegemonic consciousness. The various oppressed groups within a society are usually not equally oppressed. One system of human domination can be less exploitative and harsh than others. Moreover, those oppressed by one system of domination may in fact enjoy a position of privilege and power in another. Collins has captured this point, arguing that "depending on the context, an individual may be an oppressor, a member of an oppressed group, or simultaneously oppressor and oppressed" (1990, 225). Such is the nature of an interlocking system of human domination. Thus, oppositional consciousness is usually fashioned to confront a particular enemy and advance a limited set of interests. Rarely does a dominant group's overall ruling position come under total attack.

Given these conceptual distinctions, my approach to political consciousness can be stated succinctly. When a researcher is investigating political consciousness in any specific society, the first task is to identify, describe, and analyze the existing systems of domination and the ways in which they converge and diverge. In the American context, there are at least three major interlocking systems—class, racial, and gender domination. Thus, hegemonic consciousness in modern America is characterized by three elements: white supremacy, a procapitalist stance, and male chauvinism.

Having pinpointed the interlocking systems of human domination, one proceeds to the task of examining the various streams of hegemonic and oppositional consciousnesses connected to these systems of domination. The investigator asks, what stance do oppositional racial, gender, and class consciousnesses assume toward America's all-embracing hegemonic consciousness? How do African Americans, women, and members of the working class engage in political struggle? Do they reject the ruling hegemonic consciousness in total or only those parts that appear to block their immediate interests? If these groups vary on these dimensions, what accounts for the variation? To grapple with these issues, the analyst must employ a strategy that simultaneously investigates a variety of interacting and conflicting streams of political consciousness: white and black consciousness, male and feminist consciousness, and the class consciousness of both workers and capitalists. An investigation of how these various streams of political consciousness interact will shed light on how they affect collective actions and political options. Moreover, the unit of analysis in such an investigation must be the interactive system of political consciousness, not just one stream.

By employing an interactional approach, the analyst can investigate whether any given stream of political consciousness within a society is dominant and, if so, under which set of conditions. The person can examine whether one form of consciousness reinforces another owing to an internal logic that connects the two, or whether one group's development of oppositional consciousness and collective action against one system of domination leads another group to take similar action against another system of domination.

Focusing on the interactional system of political consciousness and domination, I now turn to several concrete historical cases. First, I address the issue of whether African Americans are race or class conscious. Next, I explore the role of race and class consciousness in the context of the United Mine Workers at the turn of the twentieth century. Finally, I examine the intersection of race and feminist consciousness during an important moment in the women's suffrage movement of the nineteenth and early twentieth centuries.

POLITICAL CONSCIOUSNESS:
AFRICAN AMERICANS, WORKERS, AND WOMEN

Numerous scholars (Leggett 1968; Geschwender 1977; Vanneman and Cannon 1987) have found that African Americans are more class conscious than whites and that they simultaneously have high levels of black race consciousness. In fact, the evidence makes it emphatically clear that even large numbers of black managers and professionals classify themselves as working class. What is more, African Americans as a group tend to identify with the poor. Writing under the influence of the "either/or" approach, Jackman and Jackman reported in a tone of surprise that "working-class blacks tend to feel just as warm toward and close to the poor as they do their own class, and middle-class blacks actually tend to express a preference for the poor and the working class over their own class" (1983, 48). The question, then, is why do African Americans exhibit such high levels of black race consciousness and working-class consciousness, regardless of their class position?

From the perspective of an interactional system of political consciousness, this is the finding one would predict. Blacks have been the victims of two vicious systems of human domination, one based on race and the other on class. They have developed a two-pronged oppositional consciousness because their very survival has depended on their understanding and combating both kinds of oppression. Historically, the attainment of high class positions by relatively small numbers of blacks has not cushioned these individuals from harsh racial oppression. And their common oppression on the basis of race and class has always linked poor and working-class blacks. The lynch rope and severe economic exploitation were different sides of the same coin.

Leggett's (1968) study was one of the first to advance the argument that class consciousness and racial consciousness may coalesce, and he provided empirical evidence showing that in the case of blacks, class consciousness correlated with racial awareness. He combined quantitative data with interview data to demonstrate that blacks, because of the exploitation and oppression they experienced simultaneously as workers and black people in the labor market and society at large, developed what he labeled class-racial awareness. What can be concluded is that for African Americans, race consciousness and class consciousness reinforce each other; each has proven necessary in the continuous social and political struggles waged by blacks to overthrow twin systems of domination. A strategy that attempts to distinguish whether class is more important than race for blacks will overlook the complex interplay between the two. Moreover, as pointed out earlier, it is becoming increasingly clear that African American women have developed a three-pronged oppositional consciousness to address their reality of simultaneous class, race, and gender oppression.

One of the central attitudes of America's hegemonic consciousness—white supremacist race consciousness—has affected collective action in both the labor movement and the women's movement. It has often been claimed that America is a "white man's country." Evidence from labor studies and studies of the women's movement suggests that this is more than just a claim insofar as white political consciousness is concerned. What has often been the case is that white supremacist interests have triumphed over worker and gender interests when whites have been called upon to elevate what they perceive as nonwhite interests over white interests. In other words, in situations where choices had to be made, white workers and white feminists usually followed the dictates of the hegemonic white consciousness rather than develop an oppositional consciousness that would simultaneously promote worker, women, and nonwhite interests. Such outcomes attest to the strength of the system of racial domination in America and to the durability of the hegemonic consciousness from which it draws support. A brief examination of the United Mine Workers of America and the reaction of white feminists during the nineteenth-century suffrage movement to the Fifteenth Amendment supports this conclusion.

Hill (1988), in a path-breaking article addressing racial attitudes in the United Mine Workers of America, laid bare the hegemonic white supremacy consciousness central to the collective action of America's white working class. Hill's investigation of the United Mine Workers (UMW) at the turn of the twentieth century was stimulated by Herbert Gutman's thesis that the UMW had shown that working-class consciousness and solidarity could prevail over white race consciousness and that the UMW had practiced racial equality so as to promote workers' interests. Gutman's analysis, says Hill, promoted the thesis that "at the turn of the century the . . . UMW was the advanced model of interracial working class solidarity, and that this pattern characterized other labor unions in varying degrees as well" (133). The task Hill set himself was to investigate race and class dynamics in the UMW in order to ascertain whether class consciousness indeed transcended race consciousness and whether the class struggle resolved the "persistent and ideologically vexing issue of race by rendering it irrelevant" (133).

Hill found that between 1900 and 1910 the UMW allowed only a small percentage of blacks to become members and that blacks were prevented from serving in leadership positions, especially at the national level. White workers insisted on racial segregation in the mines, and when they attended meetings, whites sat on one side of the hall and blacks on the other. Within the union, blacks, when they were hired at all, were forced to do the most undesirable and low-paying work. As a result, some blacks worked as strikebreakers, leading the *UMW Journal* to label them "big black buck niggers." Hill found from the evidence that "the UMW leaders were in fact openly and dogmatically racist" and that "they embraced the ideology of white supremacy, in regard to other non-white people" (173).

At the heart of this white race consciousness was the belief in white supremacy. Hill found that white workers and the leadership of the UMW also conducted an anti-Asian movement, labeling Asians "the Yellow Devil." Hill reveals the centrality of white consciousness in UMW attitudes by quoting from the *Journal*, in which its leaders wrote, "In the struggle for existence ours is the dominant race" (177). On the front page of one issue the UMW proclaimed, "Let ours be an Anglo-Saxon civilization, wrought successfully, as the world's example" (179). Hill writes that "the UMW actively joined the American Federation of Labor and the West Coast unions in arguing that they, the trade unions, above all others upheld the 'Caucasian ideals of civilization'" and that "trade unions were the white man's hope in the contest for 'domination'" (177).

Hill's conclusions are instructive: "for organized labor, [white] race consciousness and the advancement of white workers were so intertwined as to be indistinguishable" (177), and "the UMW and other labor organizations equated trade unionism with white supremacy" (183). Clearly, then,

the class consciousness of American workers cannot be adequately understood or assessed apart from the role played by a white hegemonic consciousness that dictated that the system of racial domination was to remain
intact, even at the expense of building a strong interracial labor movement
capable of toppling class domination.

Similarly, the white supremacy prong of America's hegemonic consciousness was strongly evident in the nineteenth-century women's suffrage movement. White feminists who organized the movement in the
early part of the century had close social and political ties with the aboli-
tionist movement. Indeed, this is an instance of an oppositional consciousness against one system of domination leading to the development of a
similar consciousness to confront an adjoining system of domination. In
this case, an oppositional consciousness first developed among those opposed to black slavery, and it was then appropriated and refashioned by
white women to guide their struggle against gender oppression. White
feminists of the suffrage movement and activists of the black liberation
movement were at first political allies. But the strength of this relationship
was severely tested when the Fifteenth Amendment to the Constitution
was proposed. This amendment "would permit Black men to vote but
not women of any race" (Giddings 1984, 65). The proposed amendment
pushed the hegemonic white supremacy consciousness to the forefront
among some in the white feminist movement. At issue was the possibility
that the amendment would elevate black male interests ahead of white
women's interests. They were concerned that their privileged position in
the system of racial domination might unravel if black men gained the vote
before they did.

Giddings (1984) and Davis (1983) have painted a picture of how white
supremacist consciousness prevailed among some white feminists in their
reaction to the Fifteenth Amendment controversy. One leader of the suffrage movement declared, "It would be better to be the slave of an educated white man than of an ignorant black one" (Giddings 1984, 65).
Giddings quotes an article by Susan B. Anthony, which reveals the white
race consciousness embraced by some feminists of this period: "While the
dominant party have with one hand lifted up TWO MILLION BLACK MEN and
crowned them with the honor and dignity of citizenship . . . with the other
they have dethroned FIFTEEN MILLION WHITE WOMEN—-their own mothers
and sisters, their own wives and daughters—and cast them under the heel
of the lowest orders of manhood" (66). Anthony was appealing to white
men not to forget that suffragists were white also and should share in
white privilege. In a similar vein, Elizabeth Cady Stanton wrote that it
was in the best interests of the nation that the interests of white women

outweigh those of blacks, the poor, and foreigners because white women represented refinement and civilization (Giddings 1984, 67). So powerful was the assertion of white supremacy among this group of white feminists that it drove a wedge in the women's movement from which it has yet to fully recover.

In the cases of the United Mine Workers and these nineteenth-century white feminists, we can see concrete examples of how difficult it has been for whites to break free from a hegemonic white consciousness that buttressed white interests, even when such independence could have promoted their interests by encouraging a strong alliance with nonwhites. But this is the sort of complex interactions among political consciousnesses that go unnoticed if they are not analyzed within an interactive framework.

POLITICAL CONSCIOUSNESS AND COLLECTIVE ACTION

This volume makes it clear that resource mobilization (RM) analysts and those influenced by this approach are increasingly focusing on the role that social psychological and ideational factors play in collective action. In the past, RM analysts developed a framework that brought the structural side of social movement activity into clear conceptual focus. The social psychological–cultural aspect of collective action was either underdeveloped or thought to be analytically nonproblematic. But it makes little sense to deny the importance of culture, ideology, symbols, media framing, collective identities, and meaning construction in the origins and outcomes of collective action. Indeed, the evolving consensus is that theoretical and empirical work on the cultural–social psychological aspect of collective action must lie at the center of the intellectual agenda if a comprehensive explanation of collective action is to be realized.

Nevertheless, I believe it unproductive to develop cultural–social psychological explanations of collective action outside of the structural realities that RM theory has so clearly shown profoundly affect social movement activities. Concepts such as "collective identity," "master frames," "packages," and the like should be solidly rooted within their relevant structural contexts. Otherwise the processes and mechanisms identified by these concepts will assume a reified character appearing to be central causes of collective action. What needs to be analyzed and identified are the main structural and cultural determinants of collective action and how they interact to generate or inhibit collective action.

This brings me to the relevancy of the analytical strategy advanced in this chapter for the analysis of collective action. It is possible, however, that this framework is more applicable to conflict movements than to consensus movements, although this is an empirical issue. In terms of conflict movements, my approach directs attention to structure: human systems of domination and the infrastructures of challenging groups. Central here is the determination of how such systems were structured through time and for whose benefit. Group interests become paramount because systems of domination have no meaning outside the accumulation and defense of such interests. The task of precisely identifying the groups who benefit from such a system is complex because several groups usually benefit, although unequally. An important task, therefore, is to establish the relative positions of privilege enjoyed by groups hierarchically positioned within systems of dominations and to show how such relative positions affect their political consciousness. In this approach, scholarly attention is directed squarely toward the long-standing cleavages within a society and the structural preconditions (threats of violence, polity membership, economic resources such as the control of jobs, and so on) inherent to systems of domination that enable certain groups to rule. By the same token, attention is focused on the structural preconditions (networks of communications, formal and informal social organization, availability of leadership, financial resources, and so on) central to effective and sustained protest by oppressed groups.

My approach directs attention to culture—political consciousness. Such consciousness is also analyzed within the context of major societal cleavages and systems of domination. In this view, both dominant and oppressed groups have long-standing traditions of political consciousness. Hegemonic consciousness is always present but often unrecognized because of its ability to successfully masquerade as the general outlook while simultaneously protecting the interests of dominant groups. But effective social protest informed by a mature oppositional consciousness enables challenging groups to strip away the garments of universality from hegemonic consciousness, revealing its essential characteristics. This is precisely what the modern civil rights movement accomplished in the South, forcing the nation to decide publicly on the world stage whether it would continue to be guided by a blatant white supremacy ideology.

Oppositional consciousness often lies dormant within the institutions, life-styles, and culture of oppressed groups. Members of such groups are usually not without basic collective identities, injustice frames, and the like that are conducive to individual and collective social protest. Indeed, throughout time, for significant numbers of oppressed people, the groundwork for social protest has been laid by the insurgent ideas rooted within their churches, labor unions, voluntary associations, music, informal conversations, humor, and collective memories of those elders who participated in earlier struggles. My work (1984) on the civil rights movement demonstrates how this preexisting institutional and cultural skeleton of opposition developed and matured into a full-scale protest movement in the second half of the twentieth century. Similarly, Fantasia (1988) shows how class consciousness develops out of working-class culture and concrete contemporary struggles on the shop floor. The main point is that we need research that addresses the institutional and organizational conditions under which oppositional consciousness matures and becomes combat-ready. Here is where previous resource mobilization work is useful.

But cultural phenomena are not reducible simply to organizational and structural dynamics. Indeed, varied forms of oppositional consciousness are important precisely because they are able to survive under the most adverse structural conditions. In many ways oppressed communities nurture oppositional ideas during intense periods of repression, thereby creating the social and cultural space for the emergence of more favorable structural conditions conducive to collective action. Again, more research is needed to determine the conditions under which oppositional consciousness can endure during the lean years despite the superior resources and repressive behavior of dominant groups.

Combat-ready oppositional consciousness can have an independent effect on structural determinants of collective action. Once a successful instance of protest has occurred (e.g., the Montgomery bus boycott), it affects collective action in two ways. It provides those activists who participated directly with an understanding of how it happened and why it worked, and it attracts other nonparticipants who wish to internalize these lessons so as to transplant the model to other locales, thereby increasing the volume of collective action. Thus, both sets of actors become cultural workers for the movement by further hammering out the set of viewpoints that previously lay dormant within the historic oppositional consciousness, making them relevant for the contemporary scene. In this manner, these viewpoints become the defining ideas about how to initiate and sustain social protest. The cultural workers raise the consciousness of new recruits and instruct them in organization building, fund-raising, strategy, and the like. In short, they provide the information that assists activists in building protest infrastructures.

Such actors are also critical in transplanting protest among subordinate groups in adjoining systems of domination. This is a major part of the story of how social protest spread from the civil rights movement to a plethora of movements in the late 1960s, including the student, women, gay, and environmental movements. The larger point, however, is that we need analyses of the ways in which structural and cultural determinants interact to generate or inhibit collective action and social change. This effort has been an attempt to unearth a few of the analytical stones required for the development of a comprehensive explanatory framework of collective action wherein culture meets structure.

REFERENCES

Blauner, Robert. 1972. *Racial Oppression in America*. New York: Harper and Row.
Bonnell, Victoria. 1983. *Roots of Rebellion*. Berkeley: University of California Press.
Centers, Richard. 1949. *The Psychology of Social Classes*. Princeton: Princeton University Press.
Cohn, Sam. 1985. *The Process of Occupational Sex-Typing*. Philadelphia: Temple University Press.
Collins, Patricia Hill. 1990. *Black Feminist Thought*. Boston: Unwin Hyman.
Davis, Angela. 1983. *Women, Race and Class*. New York: Vintage.
Dill, Bonnie. 1983. "Race, Class and Gender: Prospects for an All-Inclusive Sisterhood." *Feminist Studies* 9, no. 1:131–50.
Du Bois, W. E. B. 1899. *The Philadelphia Negro*. Philadelphia: University of Pennsylvania Press.
Epstein, Cynthia. 1988. *Deceptive Distinctions: Sex, Gender, and the Social Order*. New Haven: Yale University Press.
Fantasia, Rick. 1988. *Cultures of Solidarity*. Berkeley: University of California Press.
Farley, Reynolds, and Walter Allen. 1987. *The Color Line and the Quality of Life in America*. New York: Russell Sage Foundation.
Flexner, Eleanor. 1973. *Century of Struggle*. New York: Atheneum.
Geschwender, James. 1977. *Class, Race, and Worker Insurgency*. Cambridge: Cambridge University Press.
Giddings, Paula. 1984. *When and Where I Enter*. New York: William Morrow.
Gramsci, Antonio. 1971. *Selections from the Prison Notebooks of Antonio Gramsci*, ed. Q. Hoare and G. Nowell Smith. New York: International Publishers.
Hartmann, Heidi. 1976. "Capitalism, Patriarchy, and Job Segregation by Sex." *Signs* 1, no. 3, pt. 2 (Spring).
Hess, Beth, and Myra Marx Ferree. 1987. *Analyzing Gender*. Eds. Newberry Park, Calif.: Sage.
Hill, Herbert. 1988. "Myth-Making as Labor History: Herbert Gutman and the United Mine Workers of America." *International Journal of Politics, Culture and Society* 2, no. 2 (Winter):132–200.
Hirsch, Eric L. 1990. "Sacrifice for the Cause." *American Sociological Review* 55, no. 2 (April):243–54.
Jackman, Mary, and Robert Jackman. 1983. *Class Awareness in the United States*. Berkeley: University of California Press.
Jaynes, Gerald David, and Robin M. Williams, Jr., eds. 1989. *A Common Destiny: Blacks and American Society*. Washington, D.C.: National Academy Press.
Jones, Gareth. 1983. *Language of Class*. Cambridge: Cambridge University Press.
King, Deborah. 1988. "Multiple Jeopardy, Multiple Consciousness: The Context of a Black Feminist Ideology." *Signs* 14, no. 1:42–72.
Klandermans, Bert. 1984. "Mobilization and Participation: Social Psychological

Expansions of Resource Mobilization Theory." *American Sociological Review* 49, no. 5 (October):583–600.

Leggett, John. 1968. *Class, Race, and Labor: Working-Class Consciousness in Detroit.* New York: Oxford University Press.

Milkman, Ruth. 1987. *Gender at Work.* Urbana: University of Illinois Press.

Morris, Aldon D. 1984. *The Origins of the Civil Rights Movement.* New York: Free Press.

Myrdal, Gunnar. 1944. *An American Dilemma: The Negro Problem and Modern Democracy.* New York: Harper.

Opp, Karl-Dieter. 1988. "Grievances and Participation in Social Movements." *American Sociological Review* 53, no. 6 (December): 853–64.

Reskin, Barbara, and Patricia Roos. 1990. *Job Queue, Gender Queue: Explaining Women's Inroads into Male Occupations.* Philadelphia: Temple University Press.

Rollins, Judith. 1985. *Between Women: Domestics and Their Employers.* Philadelphia: Temple University Press.

Sewell, William. 1980. *Work & Revolution in France.* Cambridge: Cambridge University Press.

Snow, David A., E. Burke Rochford, Jr., Steven K. Worden, and Robert D. Benford. 1986. "Frame Alignment and Mobilization." *American Sociological Review* 51, no. 4 (August):464–81.

Thompson, E. P. 1966. *The Making of the English Working Class.* New York: Vintage.

Touraine, Alain. 1983. *Solidarity.* Cambridge: Cambridge University Press.

Vanneman, Reeve, and Lynn Cannon. 1987. *The American Perception of Class.* Philadelphia: Temple University Press.

Wright, Erik Olin. 1985. *Classes.* London: Verso.

Index

Abortion, movement against. *See* Right-to-life movement
ACORN group, 239
Action mobilization, 35
Action-oriented frames, 68
Action technologies, 255
Actor in social movements, 6–9, 40–43
Affinity groups, 62–63, 64
AFL-CIO, 207, 216
African Americans: role of black church, 313; feminist theory and, 361–62; political consciousness of, 362, 365–66; black women's consciousness, 362. *See also* Civil rights movement; Race consciousness
Agency problem, 181
Alliance and conflict systems, 95–96, 98
Almond, Gabriel, 181–83
Articulation modes, 138, 139–40
Associative movements, 239–40
Attention-calling acts, 73
Attribution modes, 137, 138–39

Benefits and costs. *See* Costs and benefits
Benford, Robert, 69–70, 80
Bernstein, Basil, 139
Birmingham riots, 322
Bonnell, Victoria, 354–55
Boundaries, 111–14
Breakdown theory. *See* Malintegration theory
Britain, class consciousness in, 352–54
Buechler, Steven, 106–7

Cannon, Lynn, 356, 357
Canvassing door-to-door for fundraising, 261–62
Capacity-to-contribute criterion, 215

Capitalism, petty, 243–44
Catholic church. *See* Roman Catholic church
Catnets, 94, 308
Causal attributions, 138–39
Challengers, communities of. *See* Communities of challengers
Chernobyl, accident at, 70
Chicago school, 327–28
Churches. *See* Religion
CISPES. *See* Committee in Solidarity with the People of El Salvador
City twinning movement, 208–9, 216, 220
Civic infrastructures, cooptation of. *See* Cooptation
Civil rights movement: collective action frames, 189–90, 190–92; collective identity in, 163; master frames, 145, 146, 148; role of mentalities, 190–92; Mississippi Freedom Summer project (*1964*), 61; role of oppositional political culture, 190–92; political influence of, 321–22; resources of, 234, 318n9
Clamshell Alliance, 46, 64
Class analysis, 329
Class consciousness: ahistorical approach to, 356–57; critique of treatment in American sociology, 356–59; in American tradition, 355–56; in Britain, 352–54; conceptual narrowness of research on, 356–57; either/or dichotomous thinking in research on, 358–59; in European tradition, 351–55; in France, 354; as perceptions and images, 355–56; in Poland, 355; race consciousness and, 358–59, 365–68; in Russia, 354–55; as social process, 351–55; of working class, 352–55

375